28-01

GAME
CHANGER

HOW THE ENGLISH PREMIER LEAGUE
CAME TO DOMINATE THE WORLD

MIHIR BOSE

Marshall Cavendish
Business

Cover design: Cover Kitchen

Copyright © 2012 Marshall Cavendish International (Asia) Pte Ltd
Published in 2012 by Marshall Cavendish Editions

An imprint of Marshall Cavendish International
1 New Industrial Road, Singapore 536196
genrefsales@sg.marshallcavendish.com
www.marshallcavendish.com/genref

Other Marshall Cavendish offices: Marshall Cavendish Corporation. 99 White Plains
Road, Tarrytown NY 10591-9001, USA • Marshall Cavendish International (Thailand) Co
Ltd. 253 Asoke, 12th Flr, Sukhumvit 21 Road, Klongtoey Nua, Wattana, Bangkok 10110,
Thailand • Marshall Cavendish (Malaysia) Sdn Bhd. Times Subang, Lot 46, Subang Hi-
Tech Industrial Park, Batu Tiga, 40000 Shah Alam, Selangor Darul Ehsan, Malaysia

Marshall Cavendish is a trademark of Times Publishing Limited.

A CIP record for this book is available from the British Library.

ISBN 978 981 4328 18 0

Printed and bound in Great Britain by
TJ International Limited, Padstow, Cornwall

CONTENTS

OTHER BOOKS BY MIHIR BOSE

Football

The World Cup: All You Need to Know

Manchester DisUnited: Trouble and Takeover at the World's Richest
Football Club

Manchester Unlimited: The Money, Egos and Infighting Behind the
World's Richest Soccer Club

Manchester Unlimited: The Rise and Rise of the World's Premier
Football Club

Behind Closed Doors: Dreams and Nightmares at Spurs

Cricket

The Magic of Indian Cricket

A Maidan View — The Magic of Indian Cricket

A History of Indian Cricket

Cricket Voices

All in a Day: Great Moments in Cup Cricket

Keith Miller: A Cricketing Biography

General Sports

The Spirit of the Game

Sports Babylon

Sporting Colours: Sport and Politics in South Africa

The Sporting Alien

History and Biography

Bollywood — A History
Raj, Secrets, Revolution: A Life of Subhas Chandra Bose
The Memons
False Messiah: The Life and Times of Terry Venables
The Aga Khans
Michael Grade: Screening the Image
The Lost Hero

Business

How to Invest in a Bear Market
Fraud — the Growth Industry of the 1980s
The Crash: the 1987–88 World Market Slump
Crash! A New Money Crisis: a Children's Guide to Money
Insurance: Are You Covered?

To Igal Yawetz and Keith Perry
for many wonderful football moments
and for being such true friends.

Introduction
THE ENGLISH ARE BACK

It is the summer of 2009. A sweltering day in Singapore. Crowds have gathered in the city state to welcome a football team. But this is not a local team. This is Liverpool — a team from Singapore's former colonial masters.

The 2009–10 Premier League season is about to start. Liverpool are on their pre-season tour and the crowds thronging the Padang, a former cricket ground, and other venues in the city look as if they are welcoming a team of conquering heroes. At one stage during the ceremonial parade the players take a ride on a boat. Crowds lean over bridges and walls on either side of Marina Bay, Boat Quay and Clarke Quay to shout out the names of their favourite players. Very few of the squad are from Liverpool, indeed few are even qualified to play for England, representing as they do many other nations from around the world. As these players are mobbed by a largely Asian crowd of Chinese origin, they demonstrate the appeal of modern international sport and its ability to bring people together.

What makes the delirium of this welcome extraordinary is that Liverpool have not come to Singapore as champions of England, let alone Europe. Their past glories are receding into history as they are going through a barren spell, having won no trophies the previous season. Many of the people gathered on every available balcony and vantage point have never been to England, let alone Liverpool. But they know everything about the team, the songs, the chants of their supporters, their history. And like all true Liverpool fans they hate Manchester United with a passion, they even sing anti-United songs, although that is another city that perhaps remains forever foreign to them.

The crowd here includes Muslim women. As I mingle among them they tell me of their love for Liverpool and how they identify with the players. But once they notice I have a cameraman in tow they suddenly become reluctant to talk, lest their parents find out. Off camera, however, they are more than happy to reveal their intimate knowledge of the club from Anfield.

As I walk around Singapore, it is soon evident that for the people of this island this love extends beyond Liverpool to all of English football. Almost all the major clubs have their followers. Indeed there is almost an obsession with the Premier League. Some have even changed their sleeping habits on match days just to be able to watch the games live on television. Singapore is eight hours ahead of the UK, so on Premier League match days people go to bed around 7pm and get up around 4am to follow the evening match being broadcast live from England.

Mayur Bhanji, football producer for World Sports Group, who grew up in Leicester and now lives in Singapore, reflects:

> Liverpool has one of the biggest fan bases with two clubs. It is a very tribal following. The Singapore fans of Liverpool passionately hate Manchester United and vice versa. For big matches like Carling Cup finals a thousand of them will gather and watch it on giant screens. For big tournaments people will even change their working habits to take in the coverage from Europe. So for Euro 2012 people started working at five in the evening, finishing well past midnight so that they could take in the 7.45pm kick-off at the Euros. All the major English clubs have targeted these fans and Chelsea have been particularly active trying to target disillusioned fans of other clubs who are not doing so well. These fans follow success and do switch loyalties.

Now take a three-hour flight west to Kolkata and come into the city centre by metro.

Kolkata, if not quite Kipling's "packed and pestilential town", is as dirty, smog-ridden and clogged with traffic as ever. Although built by the British Raj, and once the capital of British India and the second city of the Empire, those imperial days have long gone. The city venerates those who fought the Raj for India's freedom. Opposite the memorial left behind by the British to honour the dead of two world wars is a statue of a man who in his desire to see a free India allied himself with the Germans and Japanese during the Second World War.

The city is part of a state that for more than 30 years from 1977 to 2012 was ruled by hardline Indian communists. It is a city where strikes can shut the whole city down for days, an activity the locals call *bandh*. It means "stop" and it literally stops everything in the city. Every political demonstration involves liberal displays of the red flag.

But the metro station is an oasis in this city of decay, filth and turbulence. For a start it is spotlessly clean. What is more, it also advertises England's Premier League. The video screens on the platforms are showing the matches played the previous night. As the crowds gather to wait for the next train they look up at the screens and exchange knowledgeable gossip about the two English teams locked in passionate combat. Some of them are supporters of the teams, and a few even wear T-shirts of Premier League teams. As passengers leave the metro, vendors with merchandise of various English clubs approach them hoping to strike a deal.

The Premier League is well aware of its global reach. At grounds like Stamford Bridge or the Emirates advertisements, signs and messages from Korea, Japan and Singapore are common. Towards the end of the 2011–12 season as Arsenal and Manchester City warmed up on the Emirates pitch, both sets of players wore T-shirts advertising a match between the two teams in Beijing's 'Bird's Nest' National Stadium on the opening day of the Olympics Games in London. It was meant to demonstrate that while the Olympics was coming to the British capital for a record third time, English football was going global.

The Indian Premier League, the richest tournament in cricket, was modelled on the English Premier League. And in the summer of 2011, flat horseracing, keen to arrest its decline, concluded after extensive research that it needed to model its season on the Premier League, including a Champions racing day like the final day of the Premier League season. Nic Coward, then chief executive of the British Horseracing Authority, now back with the Premier League, explained to me why it wanted to adopt the winning Premier League formula:

> What the Premier League did was to focus on quality, promote the game very hard and lift the whole profile of football. The new racing championship will mean taking the crown jewels of our season across the key distances and saying to consumers: these are the races you really need to care about.

Even Peter Cruddas, the disgraced former Conservative Party treasurer, in soliciting funds for his party, offered dinner with Prime Minister David Cameron as an opportunity for "premier league donors".

Politicians have learnt to recognise the appeal of the Premier League and are keen to use it for their own political ends. This became evident when, soon after becoming Prime Minister, David Cameron decided to visit India. Cameron was keen to forge a new relationship with Britain's old colony. He led one of the largest such delegations to accompany a British leader abroad, including Chancellor George Osborne and almost a third of the cabinet. The team was carefully selected to develop the right business relationship with Asia's emerging power. It included several businessmen, and among the 60-strong delegation on the plane with Cameron was Richard Scudamore, chief executive of the Premier League.

A few months later, Jo Johnson, a Conservative MP, and Rajiv Kumar, secretary general of the Federation of Indian Chambers of Commerce and Industry, edited a book called *Reconnecting Britain and India*. They included a chapter by Scudamore. It was entitled "Can 1.3 billion Indians learn to love football? The opportunities for expanding the Premier League in India".

Scudamore wrote:

> We now count India as one of the Premier League's key overseas markets. Our relationship with the broadcaster ESPN Star Sports means Indians have had the opportunity to watch Barclays Premier League matches for over a decade, with five matches shown live every weekend. Viewing figures are difficult to break down by territory, but suffice it to say that there are record numbers watching in India, and this has been reflected in the growing value of broadcast rights in the region... ESPN Star started broadcasting live Premier League football in the late 1990s. It has now been six years since it began providing a specific Hindi commentary feed for all Barclays Premier League games.
>
> [In November 2010] we saw the first Indian-owned company, Venky's, take a controlling stake in one of our clubs, Blackburn Rovers. This season, we have had Absolute Radio, the station owned by the Times of India Group, become one of our radio rights holders in the UK. Late in 2011, we plan on India being one of the destinations for the Barclays Premier League Trophy tour, an exciting new development which will give the Indian public the opportunity to visit, for free, a state-of-the-art, fully interactive visitor centre, showcasing the league, its clubs and players, as it tours the globe over the coming three years.
>
> Our clubs have also sought to enhance their links with India in a number of ways. Some have specific commercial partnerships with Indian companies, others have opened up popular bars and cafes, and many are running regular football training camps across the country... For the past four years, India has been one of the countries we have focused on in our lead international development project, Premier Skills. Premier Skills is a collaboration between the Premier League and the British Council: it sees coaches from Premier League clubs, with real expertise in using football to tackle wider social issues, help to develop community football coaches all over the world. We have run Premier Skills in four Indian locations: New Delhi, Kolkata, Goa and Kerala, training close to 200 new male and

female coaches. These coaches may be school PE teachers, run amateur football sides, or work with local charities.

After listing all the other things that were happening, Scudamore concluded: "Our links with India are growing fast: this is just the start of a beautiful friendship."

As with Singapore, this love for Premier League football did not suggest that India itself was a football giant. Far from it. The country has only once qualified for a World Cup finals, back in 1950, and then failed to make it to Brazil because FIFA, the world body, would not allow their players to play in bare feet — that being the custom in Indian football. Since then India's decline in the international game has been such that they have struggled to compete even in Asia, a continent they once dominated. There could be no better proof of the appeal of the Premier League.

The same goes for the purchase of Blackburn by Venky's in November 2010. Blackburn Rovers was one of the founding clubs of the old Football League in 1888, when the town was at the heart of the Lancashire cotton kingdom that ruled the world. Those days of glory have long gone. Ironically, it was another, rather more famous Indian, Mahatma Gandhi, who played a part in King Cotton's demise and ensured Blackburn's decline. The British conquest of India had ended India's pre-industrial dominance and made of it a supplier of cheap goods, such as cotton, to British manufacturers. These finished goods were then exported back to India, further enriching Britain. Gandhi, in his drive to free India from British rule, tried to convince Indians that they should not use cloth made in Lancashire towns such as Blackburn, but use home-spun cotton instead. That would both hurt Britain and demonstrate to his fellow Indians they had something of their own to cherish rather than always worshipping everything their English masters produced.

Back in the 1930s, on a visit to England, Gandhi had even visited Lancashire towns explaining why his campaign against Lancashire cotton was necessary to free India. If Gandhi were still alive he would have been astounded that nearly a century later a modern generation of Indians had returned to the same part of the world to buy a football club.

It was clear that Blackburn had been presented to the Rao family, who own Venky's, as an English brand they could rescue and develop for profit. Blackburn would have been sold to them as the club that won the Premier League in 1995, one of only five clubs to win it since its inception. What made the sale even more attractive was that the club was seen as tremendously undervalued. Its total enterprise value was £45 million, including around £20 million of debt, approximately half of what Real Madrid paid Manchester United for Cristiano Ronaldo and not much more than a few years' earnings for Wayne Rooney. Nothing attracts a businessman to a deal more than the feeling he is getting a jewel rather cheap. And a club that shares glory that only Manchester United, Arsenal, Chelsea and Manchester City have managed in 20 years is surely a jewel? The fact that there is a large Asian population in Blackburn which could be tapped into was also an attraction.

Venky's subsequent handling of Blackburn has not won them much credit; indeed they were the butt of jokes at the first Asian Football Dinner at Wembley early in 2012, and the club is a long way from the giddy heights it reached in 1995. After the 2011–12 season saw the club relegated, fans expressed intense angers towards Venky's management or lack of it. The Premier League's defence was that they could hardly be expected to account for individual management styles. As Scudamore put it:

> We don't sit here regretting that the owners have actually bought the club. What you do regret — for the sake of Blackburn and their fans — is that the performances of the team have led to them being relegated.

The Premier League chief admitted that he sympathises with supporters' discontent but does not think that the rules should have blocked the takeover. Scudamore added: "I can understand why they will feel aggrieved because they've got a situation where other people owning that club, and managing that club, weren't making the decisions that the fans themselves would have made."

Their acquisition of the Lancashire club did make the Raos famous in India. It was clear they saw their purchase as promoting them into the premier league of India's rich. Apart from Venky's poultry business, they also have extensive property holdings, but they are far from the top 10 richest Indian families. This made their purchase of Blackburn all the more interesting. Before the Raos bought Blackburn, other super-rich Indian families were linked with Premier League clubs, particularly the Ambanis, who are at the very top of the rich list. But while the Ambanis looked at several clubs, including Liverpool, they did not open their cheque book. The Raos clearly viewed the purchase of a Premier League club as a great status symbol. They would only have to turn on their television sets in India to discover the Premier League's status as football's greatest brand. The 24-hour news ticker at the bottom of their screens would include scores of Premier League matches. Indians probably watch more live Premier League matches, including the 3pm Saturday kick-offs, than most do in Britain.

However, English football's appeal is no recent phenomenon. Tony Fernandes, who bought QPR during the 2011–12 season, has a vivid memory of how he fell in love with West Ham:

> Growing up in Malaysia we used to get these matches, after about three months. The programme was called Star Soccer, a Central TV production. Generally they showed matches between Stoke, Wolverhampton Wanderers and Birmingham; it was awful football. The pitches were really muddy and it was all long ball. And one day I saw this team playing Wolves, West Ham. They played from the back, and they played really attractive football and I was like "Wow!", and that was it. I said "I'm going to support West Ham." I started listening to Paddy Feeney on the BBC World Service.

But in those days news of English football was limited to the written media, the broadcasts of the BBC World Service and the odd televised game. The Premier League's rise is in a different dimension. Television and the internet make its impact instant. It demonstrates that in many parts of the world where the Union Flag was long ago lowered, where British troops and administrators have long since departed, the power of England still shines. This is a power not of the gun or even of British commerce, but of modern English football. The political empire has gone, the football empire lives on.

You could say it illustrates what Sir Richard Turnbull, the penultimate Governor of Aden, told the former Labour Defence Secretary Denis Healey: "When the British Empire finally sank beneath the waves of history, it left behind it only two monuments — one was the game of Association Football, the other was the expression 'Fuck off'."

Turnbull said this in the 1960s when nobody had even conceived of the idea of the Premier League. Now, as the Labour MP Tristram Hunt has put it, the Premier League is one of the best British exports. Few could have anticipated its impact when the Premier League was launched. At one level its rise can be seen as a continuation of the familiar story of the British inventing most of the sports the world plays, or at least codifying their rules and regulations. It once again illustrates the ability of the British to invent products and brands whose appeal extends far beyond their borders.

When the Premier League was founded in 1992, La Liga in Spain and Serie A in Italy were the dominant European leagues, secure in their own homelands and in the wider world. Italian football had even invaded England's football scene, being broadcast every Sunday afternoon on Channel 4. But in the last 20 years all that has changed. Premier League teams may not always match the skills of the top teams in La Liga or Serie A but its dominance as a global force cannot be denied. It is the league that millions around the world want to watch every week.

Its rise has been helped by wider forces in football and society. The Premier League benefited from the fact that the British government has always given football clubs a great deal of freedom to operate as they please. This lack of regulation would be anathema to the Americans, for all their proclaimed love of the free market, and is considered unacceptable in most other European countries. But it was also helped by the changes to the European club competitions, which coincided with its launch. A further spur was the decision by the European Court of Justice in 1995 to back an obscure Belgian player, Jean-Marc Bosman, in his fight for freedom of movement. This revolutionised the European transfer market and came at a crucial stage in the development of the Premier League.

But the real fascination of the Premier League is that it emerged at a time when the English game was at a very low ebb. Indeed, only a few years before its foundation it had seemed that the game might not even survive in its own homeland. For two desperate decades in the 1970s and 1980s English football was racked by hooliganism, racism and a feeling in the English establishment, as one influential newspaper put it, that this was a slum game which had long outlived its usefulness. English football was also physically dangerous and had witnessed many deaths at football matches. It was against this dismal background that the Premier League was launched in a very British, indeed English, way where the idea of global reach was not a factor or even much discussed. The initial idea was driven by a few clubs trying to make a bit more money from television. But, just as the old East India Company — given the exclusive license to trade in India by Elizabeth I in the hope it would make money for her beleaguered kingdom — went on to secure a great empire, so the Premier League, almost despite its antecedents, was to become the most powerful league in the world.

The Premier League has completed 20 years, and this is an opportune moment to look back at its remarkable rise. The league has been celebrating its 20th birthday with a plethora of special awards and its website has highlighted the journey from childhood to an all-powerful adult. As you would expect from any such official celebration, there is careful editing. So it makes much of Eric Cantona the match-winner, but no mention of his infamous kung-fu kick. While a photo gallery of 20 years shows many dramatic moments, including former Liverpool goalkeeper Bruce Grobbelaar in action, there is no mention of the match-fixing scandals and controversies resulting in high-profile court cases that have also marked the last 20 years. But in fairness the league can point to the fact that for all the dark moments there has been much to celebrate.

The inaugural season in 1992–93, with 22 teams in the Premier League, later reduced to 20, did not always play to full houses. That season the Premier League grounds were only 69.6 per cent full, the season's aggregate attendance was 9.75 million and the Premier League's total income was £46 million. The 20th season saw 13.4 million fans attend the matches with average stadium occupancy in excess of 92 per cent for the third season in a row. For 15 years Premier League stadiums have been more than 90 per cent full.

During the 2010–11 season Premier League clubs' combined revenue rose by 12 per cent to £2.3 billion, dwarfing their European rivals. As they made money the clubs invested, spending £99 million on stadiums and facilities during 2010–11, which took total investment in facilities over the last 20 seasons to more than £2 billion. The tax man was also kept happy. Of the British government's tax intake from the 92 professional clubs of £1.2 billion, the Premier League contributed approximately £1 billion. And this was a socially aware league, with 4.5 million beneficiaries from the Premier League's Creating Chances programmes in 2011. This, boasted the league, reached out to "the heart of the communities in which the clubs operate, working across the areas of community cohesion, education, health, sports participation and international". The league also worked with local police forces and encouraged participation in eight Olympic sports. Indeed, at the of the 2011/12 season, the League could proudly boast that it distributed £189.4 million, 15% of its season's turnover for what it calls 'good cause projects' such as youth development and parachute payments to relegated clubs. This figure is nearly four times the earnings of the League back in 1992/93 and such largesse enables the League to boast that it is unique in Europe; "no other European foorball league invests in six divisions below it".

The Premier League bosses must have felt they were in dreamland as the 20th season ended. No Hollywood or even Bollywood scriptwriter could have invented a better finish. Not only did the drama last almost to the last kick of the season — with two teams finally separated by goal difference, no title race could have been closer — but it produced new winners of the Premier League. To put the icing on the cake, the winners were a club who had not won it for 44 years and whose rise meant that the dominance of Manchester United was threatened by a neighbour from across the city rather than from other cities.

The finale was comparable to that in 1989. Arsenal, required to win 2–0 at Liverpool, scored their second goal with almost the last kick of the match to win the title. But that was just one match. The rest of the league season was long over. It was also an evening match, which was televised only in Britain. In those days matches were broadcast live to a few Scandinavian countries, but only on Saturday afternoons. In 2012 the Manchester City vs. QPR match was part of a final day when all 10 fixtures kicked off at 3pm. Such a traditional start never happens during the rest of the season but this was a finely choreographed television event, with the coverage extended to 212 territories, reaching 650 million households with an estimated cumulative global audience of 4.7 billion. That final day made history with all the matches broadcast live in the US, Fox showing nine of the games and ESPN US one — Manchester City vs. QPR.

In the lead-up to the Sunday climax, City's Ivory Coast midfielder Yaya Toure, whose two goals at Newcastle in the penultimate match meant victory in the final match at home to QPR would secure them the title, had stoked up the fires by declaring: "I wanted to come to the club to make a story and my decision was to come to City. Of course, some people make some speculation about other things, but, for me, when you are a football player, you always want to go where you can be loved and be the best player. At Barcelona, I was a good player [where he won the 2009 Champions League] but at City I am an important player for the team."

Toure also revealed some dressing-room secrets. After City's defeat at Arsenal on April 8, which had left United eight points clear at the top, their manager Roberto Mancini had publicly conceded the title. But privately, behind closed doors, he told the players they could still emerge triumphant. According to Toure, Mancini said: "Guys, we don't have to give up, you know, because the Premier League is like that and maybe United can drop some points and we can come back. We have to believe to the end because we're in the most competitive competition in the world and, most importantly, we have to keep going, keep winning and maybe we'll be close to them."

This suggested that Mancini was not quite the simpleton many of his critics had made him out to be when City had wobbled during the run-in. The day after City's dramatic come-from-behind victory at the Etihad Stadium, 100,000 people crammed the streets of Manchester in celebration. With Abu Dhabi's oil wealth backing their club, they were confident that while Manchester United had seen off other rivals over the years, including Chelsea backed by Russian billionaire Roman Abramovich, City could now go on to forge a dynasty as long and as enduring as the one Sir Alex Ferguson had created at Old Trafford.

This success story led Sir Dave Richards, the chairman of the Premier League, to boast:

I always had a vision of the Premier League from being there right from the word go in 1989. When we talked about the Premier League we wanted a super, super league. I wanted to make our football the best in the world. It is what drives you. The best clubs, the best players, I wanted the best league. I wanted the best people playing in the league and working in the league.

However, like the editing out of Cantona's kung-fu incident, this is a bit like the man who, having reached the top of Everest, decides to ignore the many problems he encountered on his way to the summit. Back in 1989, not many people were expounding the vision that Richards claims he had then. If they did entertain such hopes, they kept very quiet about them, and with good reason. When those responsible for the formation of the league began their planning, English football was a wreck that looked incapable of renewal, let alone world dominance. Many had written it off as a lost cause. Let us now revisit that bleak landscape to appreciate the long trek the Premier League had to undertake to get to its current place in the sun.

PART 1

PHOENIX FROM THE ASHES

Chapter 1
THE VANISHING CROWDS

During the 1980s English football was battered by multiple crises involving public safety and public order. The interlinked problems of making football grounds a safe and pleasant environment for spectators and combating a surge in hooliganism, racism and violence descended on a sport whose finances, governance and leadership were completely unable to cope with them.

From 1975 to 1986 attendances at English Football League matches fell by a third. For some years, snooker became more popular on television than soccer. Very few league clubs were solvent, and almost all of them were private fiefdoms of the businessmen (or sometimes entertainers) who kept them afloat. Protected by obsolete and arcane Football League rules governing share ownership and transfers, football club directors were virtually unaccountable to their shareholders, let alone to their fans or the wider community. Not surprisingly, most club directors were a deeply conservative force in the game, and opposed to changes which, though they might be profitable, threatened the stability and, above all, the hierarchy of English football. Significantly, it was a non-League club, Kettering Town, who were the first to adopt shirt sponsorship, rather than a League club.

The governance of English football, which had always suffered from the long-standing division between the Football Association and the Football League, was weakened still further by personal rivalries between the leaders of League clubs. These rivalries intensified in the 1980s, for two main reasons. First, a number of clubs were taken over by individuals with very personal agendas: Irving Scholar at Tottenham Hotspur and David Dein at Arsenal had a new business model and social vision for their clubs; David Evans at Luton had political ambitions and became a vocal Conservative MP; Robert Maxwell took over a succession of clubs to satisfy his compulsive needs for commercial, political and personal recognition. Second, there was a growing perception by the five or six biggest clubs in the First Division that they were entitled to a higher share of the revenues from English football, which inevitably produced a counter-reaction from smaller clubs, who acquired prominent champions through the 'axis' of Ken Bates at Chelsea and Ron Noades at Crystal Palace.

Poorly financed and poorly governed, English football faced further problems in the 1980s from Margaret Thatcher's government. It was led by a Prime Minister with no interest in football and no sympathy or identification with its supporters. When eventually forced to take notice of football by the disasters of 1985 — the Bradford fire, the Birmingham riot and, above all, Heysel — she saw all of its problems through the prism of law and order. Soccer hooligans became another "enemy within" — people to be contained and controlled to protect mainstream society — although the measures she chose for this purpose, in particular segregation and ID cards, penalised mainstream, law-abiding fans just as much as hooligans. Thatcher expected the football authorities to offer total co-operation with her control agenda. Large transfer fees convinced her that football could afford the necessary changes with no extra financial support from government. She appointed a series of loyal lightweights as sports ministers to impose that agenda on football and sacked them when they did not prove tough enough.

Thatcher's approach inevitably influenced the police, who increasingly saw football crowds in terms of control rather than public safety. When allied to poor leadership and technical incompetence, this mindset had a lethal impact at Hillsborough.

In coping inadequately with all of these problems, English football had little or no help from the media, particularly the tabloid press, whose football coverage was widely blamed for encouraging abuse of unpopular players or managers, for fostering racism and xenophobia among fans, and for covering hooligans in ways which boosted their self-esteem and made ordinary fans more fearful. Football reporting reached its nadir at Hillsborough with the *Daily Mirror*'s publication of intrusive pictures of private horror and grief and *The Sun*'s invented accounts of drunken and vicious behaviour by Liverpool fans.

Broadsheet newspapers, particularly *The Times* and *The Sunday Times*, did not help the cause of football by portraying it as a pastime for a dying underclass, which (like its supporters) faced extinction for failing to adapt to economic change. In one notorious leader, after the Bradford fire and the Birmingham riot, *The Sunday Times* described English football as a "slum game watched in slum stadiums by slum people". (The Murdoch papers took this line in the mid-1980s, before their proprietor had decided to use football to sell satellite dishes.)

But the broadsheets were right about one thing. By the end of the

1980s it had become a deeply depressing experience to attend an English football match.

False nostalgia has created the illusion of a golden age of spectatorship before the advent of all-seat stadiums and the commercialisation of English football in the 1990s. In this imagined era, stadiums may have been rough and ready but they were also welcoming and intimate, where good-humoured fans bantered with the players and with each other, where families could enjoy an afternoon out but which children could safely attend on their own and where grown-ups would stand aside for them to get a better view.

Going to a football match in the golden age had a ritual quality. Men knocked off work on a Saturday, went home only to collect any children attending the match, and met friends in a pub near the ground. The children would be parked outside the pub and issued with crisps and soft drinks, while fathers and uncles had a couple of pints inside. For many boys, it was a coming-of-age moment to be invited inside the pub for their first pint (tacitly ignoring all their illicit teenage experiments).

The group would walk together to the match; there might be some singing and chanting, and someone might make a racket with a rattle, but nothing was allowed to get out of hand. They would buy a cheaply produced programme with basic information about both teams and possibly some intimate but unrevealing details about one of the home players ("favourite post-match meal: steak"). The group would go to their chosen end of the ground, without tickets, a short time before kick-off, and would be admitted without inspection. They would go to stand in a familiar spot, where they could expect to meet other fans whom they knew or had at least met before. But if the home team were playing towards the opposite goal, they were free to change ends to cheer on their forwards, or dispatch the children to do so. They could also elect to do this at half-time.

They were free to drink alcohol while watching the match, either queuing to buy it from the club or having a nip of their own from a private flask. The food on sale at clubs was traditionally awful, especially the pies, but the group would tell familiar jokes about it and speculate which animal had supplied the contents of the pie.

The return journey would be interrupted to listen to the full results from the BBC at 5pm on a transistor radio. If the group did not have one of their own, they could listen freely to someone else's, even an away fan's. The group would walk back from the ground, analysing the match with each other and neighbours, including away fans. The pink'un or green'un Saturday football results paper would be purchased, children would be parked at home, high tea or supper briefly consumed and further analysis might then be conducted over further pints at the pub.

In all phases of this day, football spectators could expect the minimum interference from the police or other agencies. They largely policed themselves. If people got out of hand, they were quietly called to order by other fans who were accepted as authority figures. A strong line would be taken against any language or conduct which might distress children or the somewhat rarer women spectators.

This era of football spectatorship was already under threat in the 1970s and was over in the 1980s, although for a long time the football authorities, individual clubs and even the police continued to assume that it was still happening.

In a Sky Television documentary in June 2007, *How TV Changed Football For Ever*, a number of celebrity football fans shared more accurate memories of football matches in the 1980s. Former *Daily Mirror* editor and Arsenal supporter Piers Morgan declared: "The experience was disgusting. You went to revolting stadiums, ate horrible pies, drank disgusting beer and had a fight." He was echoed by James King: "I just have memories of concrete, just like concrete corridors, cold, grey, damp concrete as you go up on to the terraces. And you would go down every Saturday and you would stand up and it would be raining. It always seems to be raining when I think of those football matches of the 1980s. And it would be cold and it would be tough."

During the 1980s it came home to football fans that nearly all grounds were inconveniently located, with nowhere to park. Unlike continental Europe, England saw almost no new purpose-built stadiums in the post-war era. The major club grounds remained in densely built inner-city locations, which their traditional working-class fans had often abandoned for the suburbs during the affluent 1950s and 1960s. If these fans retained their loyalties to their old club they were forced to travel by car or public transport to watch home matches — an elementary fact to which few clubs, if any, made any practical response.

In effect the English professional football experience was now the opposite of "bussing" as practised in America. There, after the Supreme Court had outlawed segregation in schools, it had become common for black kids to be bussed to white neighbourhoods to take advantage of the better schools there. Now, on match days, white fans, many of whose parents had migrated out of the inner cities, voluntarily returned there to watch football. While they did so the migrants who now lived there usually ignored the football taking place on their doorstep.

In another curious reversal of the American experience, football embraced segregation in order to cope with fan violence. The Americans spent much of the 1950s and 1960s trying to eliminate segregation based on colour from their society. English football in the 1970s decreed that fans could only watch if there was strict segregation between fans of rival teams. For all the changes that have since occurred in football, this separation of home and away fans still exists, with grounds having large signs directing them away from each other. And even in new stadiums such as the Emirates, Arsenal's ground, it is made clear even in the executive box areas that fans should not be wearing the colours of the visiting teams.

It did not help that the clubs made no effort to win over the new occupants of the housing which their fans had vacated, particularly if they came from minority ethnic groups. They gained a degree of local support from middle-class families, who had 'gentrified' their neighbourhoods in a search for reasonably priced family houses within easy reach of their places of work. But the clubs did not gentrify themselves. They made little or no effort to meet middle-class tastes and standards in their facilities. As football spectating become more and more uncomfortable and dangerous, middle-class families found different ways to spend their Saturdays.

By the 1980s, the neighbourhoods of most major grounds, particularly in London, were socially and communally mixed, combining pockets of affluence with densely packed and poorly maintained housing estates in which poor people and recent immigrants were dumped by the authorities. (At the troubled Broadwater Farm estate in Tottenham, scene of one of the riots in 1985, no fewer than 80 per cent of residents had asked their local council to move them elsewhere.)

As drunkenness and violence increased in the 1980s, the journey to a major football match was at best arduous and at worst dangerous. At motorway service areas, railway stations and other major hubs, law-abiding fans were at risk of running into organised gangs of young people who attached themselves to one of the contending football clubs. These gangs' purpose was to establish territorial rights by violence or simply to enjoy an outbreak of unrestrained fighting. At any point of the journey, peaceable fans were likely to hear provocative, threatening or obscene language and racist abuse. The respected people who once kept order in the crowd stopped going to matches or kept their heads down. The banter and camaraderie between fans disappeared and rival supporters were segregated and shepherded towards their destinations by sullen police.

The neighbourhoods of grounds on big match days were frequently abandoned by their inhabitants. Pubs and cafes would be closed and local shops boarded up. Householders would barricade their property, attempt to remove their cars and resign themselves to fans using their streets or even front gardens to throw litter, smash bottles, vomit and urinate. The last may have reflected the primitive sanitation on offer at even the biggest grounds. Tim Lovejoy recalls: "Urinals were just massive great rooms where people were just weeing up against a wall. It would be four or five feet deep, it wasn't the most attractive thing to do." As an 18-year-old on Arsenal's North Bank in 1983, Piers Morgan remembers being struck by a large container of yellow liquid. "Further enquiries revealed it was a pint of urine. Somebody had pissed in a pint glass and lobbed it on my head, and I was one of their own. God knows what they did to the opposition fans."

During the 1980s very few families would allow their children to go to a football match alone, or to wander off alone in a football ground, even assuming it was possible. This privilege was progressively lost as fans were confined or even caged in designated areas.

By the end of the decade, peaceable fans, already enduring multiple dangers and discomfort, were confronted by a government determined to treat them as potential enemies of society. Upwards of 15 million English football fans were faced with the prospect of carrying an identity card, showing it to a police officer on demand at any time and in any public place on match day, and submitting themselves to searches on demand.

This was the state of English football spectatorship when the Premier League came into being. In later chapters, I shall examine how the Premier League, and new revenues from television, created a different form of spectatorship and fundamentally new relationships between fans, clubs, administrators, government and wider society. But first I want to look in more depth at the events which led English football into a permanent spectator crisis and brought it close to extinction.

In January 1971, 66 spectators were crushed to death on a staircase trying to leave Ibrox Park in the closing minutes of a Rangers-Celtic match. The youngest was nine, more than a third were teenage boys, and all but one of the dead were male. A further 145 were injured. This disaster was instrumental in forcing government to get involved in football.

The response also displayed certain features which became commonplace in later disasters. There were persistent rumours that it had been caused by crowd behaviour — not violent behaviour but the attempted return of a mass of fans when they heard the cheers for a last-gasp equaliser for Rangers. These rumours persist to this day, although they have long been shown to be untrue.

There was widespread incredulity that it occurred in a stadium which was thought to be a showpiece. This was summed up by the Rangers right-back, Sandy Jardine:

> You could not comprehend it. Even then, Ibrox was one of the most modern and safe grounds in Europe, by the standards of the day. I remember being on the ground staff as a 15-year-old and part of my duties were to sweep the terraces. I remember sweeping the stairs and the barriers were so solid you could not imagine them being twisted like that.

In fact, the disaster had occurred on the very same staircase where a fatal accident had occurred 10 years previously. Although the Fatal Accident Inquiry cited improvements since then and exonerated Rangers Football Club, Sheriff J. Irvine Smith took a very different view when he awarded damages to the widow of one of the victims. He found that little had been done to improve safety and expressed the view that Rangers had decided that "if the problem was ignored long enough it would eventually disappear".

At the official level, the Conservative government under Ted Heath set up an inquiry into the safety of all British football grounds under a senior Scottish judge, Lord Wheatley. He recommended the licensing of football grounds by local authorities, based on expert advice from fire and building inspectors. The government did not tell Lord Wheatley that only six months before Ibrox the Scottish Office had specifically rejected this policy: "The Secretary of State [for Scotland] considers that the improvements which might follow the introduction of a licensing system would at best be marginal... and he therefore feels no step should be taken to introduce legislation to this end at the present time." This was revealed only by the release of official papers 30 years after the event. Suspicions of a cover-up have featured regularly in the response to later British football disasters.

The Labour government of Harold Wilson followed up the Wheatley inquiry with a working party on crowd control under the Scottish junior minister Frank McElhone, a Glasgow MP. The context for McElhone was set largely by media responses to one of the first hooligan incidents to grab national attention, the so-called "Battle of Barcelona" in 1972 when rampaging Rangers fans clashed with Spanish police (still under the Franco dictatorship) in celebrating their team's European Cup Winners' Cup final victory over Moscow Dynamo. Rangers became the first of many British clubs to be banned from European competition.

McElhone's report made several recommendations which were to become commonplace in responses to the football troubles of the period: perimeter fences, segregation of fans, restrictions on alcohol, more seating and the use of attendance centres for convicted hooligans on match days. Labour's Minister for Sport, Denis Howell, set up his own working party on crowd troubles.

Based on Wheatley's recommendations, Howell introduced the Safety of Sports Grounds Act in 1975, which for the first time set standards, mainly on fire safety and infrastructure, for all major British football grounds and a time limit for their implementation. Of all British sports ministers, Howell was far and away the most sympathetic to football and the best informed. He had been a top-flight referee and had a good working relationship with leading club chairmen and football administrators.

Aware of the financial implications of his legislation for clubs and equally aware that he could get no public money from his hard-pressed Chancellor Denis Healey, Howell found an ingenious new source of income for football. He induced the pools promoters to set aside some of the profits they made from Spot-the-Ball competitions — which were technically an unlawful lottery — to finance a new grant-making Football Grounds Improvement Trust. By the end of that Labour government in 1979 this had been joined by the Football Trust, which had the wider objective of helping football clubs to help their local communities, although this attracted far fewer applications from clubs. From 1975 to 1987, English clubs took £20 million for safety improvements from the first trust and only £3 million for community involvement from the second.

Under Howell's influence the Labour government stayed focused on safety issues in football rather than a public order agenda. He considered making some big matches all-ticket but resisted the idea of identity cards for supporters. He gave no support to the FA's demand for the restoration of corporal punishment (abolished as a judicial punishment by the Attlee Labour government of 1948).

Characteristically, English football was slow to acknowledge the existence of football-related violence. Although it had been present since the beginnings of organised football in the 19th century, and although incidents began to rise sharply and attract media attention in the 1960s, the football authorities did not identify violence as a British problem. In the early 1960s the Football League had in fact wanted English clubs to withdraw from European competition because of the threat of violence from foreign supporters.

By 1979, it had become clear that football-related violence was not only increasing but changing its character. What might be called the traditional pattern of spontaneous clashes between rival fans had been joined by a new wave of organised destruction by gangs or 'firms' of young men who had adopted violence as a lifestyle choice and a means of self-expression.

The 'firms' emerged in the mid-1970s as an evolution of the earlier skinhead culture. As Margaret Thatcher shrewdly spotted in 1985, many were affluent, a theme which was regularly emphasised in the media. In August 1985 Frank Keating of *The Guardian* identified some key characteristics of the new breed of football hooligan. "They are not necessarily unemployed and some may even have professional jobs or be university students... they may well be married and be family men with mortgages... they may well exhibit good, even innovative, skills in the organisation and planning of hooligan activities." Terry Last, convicted leader of the Chelsea Headhunters, was a solicitor's clerk at a leading London firm, respected there as a hard worker who was affable to colleagues.

Confirming Keating's comment on organisational skills, West Ham's Inter City Firm funded their travel with a series of underground warehouse 'rave' parties. (Independently of soccer hooliganism, these were a regular source of media scare stories of drug-taking and violence in the 1980s.) When ICF members went to Bologna for the 1990 World Cup, they stayed at the five-star Carlton Hotel. Making money in the black economy or from the support of families and comrades enabled unemployed hooligans or those in low-paid work to meet the high costs of the hooligan lifestyle.

Whether affluent or not, the organised hooligans favoured smart labels in casual clothing (so much so that Burberry tried to keep their products out of their hands). They enjoyed stealing such items, from stores or, better still, from rival firm members. They could afford to travel overseas, where their general hatred of all foreigners provoked authority almost as much as their fighting and stealing.

The best-known firms attached themselves to leading inner-city clubs: Manchester United's Red Army and the rival City Guvnors, Chelsea's Headhunters, West Ham's Inter City Firm, while even lowly Grimsby had its Cleethorpes Beach Patrol. Unlike traditional football hooligans, the firms were not terribly interested in football. They adopted particular clubs largely to give themselves a sense of identity and to have a pretext for despising other firms. When the police started to crack down on hooligans, the firms abandoned scarves and other club paraphernalia to escape detection. For the same reason, they stopped using special trains and coaches. Their top priority was to claim territory as their own, not just within football stadiums but more importantly at transport hubs and major public places within cities (which made their conflicts more visible and frightening to ordinary people and more accessible to the media). The proudest boast of firms was to "stand their ground", and to be "first in" to a fight, even when outnumbered.

When interviewed (as they were with increasing frequency in the 1970s), firm members regularly referred to violence as better than drugs and sex. (During the 1970s, when homosexuality was legal but still generally ostracised, membership of a firm gave many covert gays an outlet for intense romantic longing for other men. Women were merely trophies for firm members and all the important activities of a firm — fighting, stealing, confronting authority, travelling, intense drinking and drug-taking — were male rituals.)

The firms horrified respectable people and the media because they actually enjoyed being identified with violence and mayhem. West Ham's Inter City Firm pioneered the use of "calling cards", left beside their battered victims with the words: "Congratulations, you've just met the ICF".

The firms were a factor in several celebrated football incidents in the 1970s, including Manchester United at Ostend in 1974, Tottenham Hotspur in Rotterdam in the same year, Leeds in Paris in 1975. They also attached themselves to the national team, and were blamed when England fans damaged the national stadium in Luxembourg in 1977 after a dreary victory over one of football's minnows. More importantly, the firms attracted media coverage which was widely blamed for exaggerating their importance, flattering their members and deterring ordinary fans from going to matches. The most notorious example was the *Daily Mirror*, which in 1974 began to publish "league tables" of football hooliganism — an obvious incentive for lower-placed firms to escalate violence to move up the table.

The outspoken racism and xenophobia of many firms made them a natural target for British far right movements. In 1977 the National Front brought out a youth newspaper, *Bulldog*, to appeal to them. The following year the NF began to leaflet crowds at Chelsea, Millwall, Arsenal and West Ham, which it identified as its likeliest sources of recruits. *Bulldog* soon felt confident enough to invite fans to "join the fight for race and nation" and at West Ham the NF even had a successful souvenir stand. NF organisers began to target fans of the England national team in the early 1980s, and made themselves known at all of England's matches in the 1982 World Cup finals.

When England toured South America in 1984, John Barnes scored a wonderful solo goal in a friendly against Brazil in the Maracana stadium in Rio as England won 2–0, their only victory on Brazilian soil. Yet a group of NF-supporting England "fans", Terry Last among them, on the flight from Montevideo to Santiago told journalists England had won only 1–0 in their book: they didn't recognise goals scored by black players. They even tried to mount an assault on Barnes in Chile, until a group of English football writers intervened.

Neither the football authorities nor the government distinguished themselves in their response to the far right's attempted infiltration of English football.

The football authorities essentially ignored it, leaving some fans to organise counter-action. The left-wing Anti-Nazi League formed several football networks in the late 1970s, particularly among Spurs and Leyton Orient fans. The clubs concerned frowned on these efforts. Spurs directors threatened legal action against "Spurs against the Nazis" and the Orient chairman responded to local clashes between anti-Nazi and British Movement fans by threatening to ban the anti-Nazis.

The government did not react at all until 1984, when presented with video evidence of National Front supporters among misbehaving and violent England supporters in Paris and South America. The then Minister for Sport, the anonymous Neil Macfarlane, promised an investigation but nothing happened. Nor did the government react to the evidence presented to the Popplewell Inquiry into Crowd Safety at Sports Grounds of racist literature being distributed to Liverpool fans at Heysel.

In a way, the National Front and other extreme right groups were an asset to the football authorities. They provided a pretext to blame racism in English football on a minority of outside agitators and ignore the fact that racist attitudes were deeply entrenched in the game itself. For years, racism was a taboo subject in English football. It does not figure in Graham Kelly's otherwise candid autobiography *Sweet FA* among the problems that faced him over 20 years as a senior football administrator.

Racism and xenophobia have been present in English football since its inception. They have been reflected in the FA's in-and-out relationship with FIFA and its delayed entrance into the World Cup, and still more in the stereotyping of non-white and foreign players and spectators in the media. For example, in the 1950s no one thought it comic or abnormal when a newsreel commentary described the Italian football team as "tricky little ball players from Spaghetti Land".

Non-white or mixed-race players in British football always faced a high hurdle to overcome the received impression that they were lazy or irresolute or volatile or simply incapable of performing in the cold, and the handful that broke through into League football could expect abuse not only from opponents and opposing fans but from their team-mates and their own club's supporters.

Ricky Heppolette provides a typical example. He was an Anglo-Indian player regularly tipped as a future England prospect at the start of his career.

After success with Preston North End, he was signed for a sizeable fee by Orient in 1971. He and his non-white colleagues Laurie Cunningham and Bobby Fisher endured constant abuse from fans, culminating in an away match against Nottingham Forest. There he snapped after what his manager George Petchey described as "the most appalling provocation", and had a punch-up with Forest's Northern Ireland international Tommy Jackson. In 1973 Heppolette signed for Terry Venables at Crystal Palace, lured in part by the promise of joining a go-ahead club with modern attitudes. Instead he endured constant racial abuse from a team-mate. It was unchecked and Heppolette left after a few months for Chesterfield.

When Viv Anderson, from a black West Indian family, made his debut as an 18-year-old for Nottingham Forest against Newcastle in 1975 he was met with a volley of racial abuse. At Carlisle, he was pelted with fruit — a commonplace insult by fans, accompanied usually by monkey gestures. When he reported this to his manager, Brian Clough, he was famously instructed to get back to his place and fetch Clough "two pears and a banana".

Around this period black players like Anderson began to break into the England team and were actually hailed as its saviours from mediocrity and failure. But even then the black players had to endure stereotyping. Don Howe of Arsenal described them as "the hungry ones", and other managers and commentators regularly praised the flair or technique which was thought to reside in all black players. After the England team failed to qualify for the 1978 World Cup, *The Sun* created an all-black Dream Team under the heading "England's Black Magic Soccer Eleven. Presenting the Key Men in our football future". Putting black players firmly in the box labelled Entertainment, Ron Atkinson introduced his three signings for West Bromwich Albion, Cyrille Regis, Laurie Cunningham and Brendan Batson as football's answer to the black pop group, the Three Degrees. As Atkinson saw it, he was actually promoting his players as the Three Degrees were about to perform in Birmingham. The fact that they were female black singers did not seem to register with him. (More than 20 years later, Atkinson had to resign as an ITV football pundit after making a racist comment into a live microphone about Chelsea's Marcel Desailly.)

By January 1981 the problem of racist abuse and chanting at English football grounds led David Lane, as chairman of the Commission for Racial Equality, to call a meeting with the chairman and secretary of the FA, Sir Harold Thompson and Ted Croker. Lane commented that the problem had grown even though black players had become accepted and applauded. He was especially concerned with the open activities of far Right groups selling newspapers and recruiting outside football grounds and leading racial abuse of players and other fans inside them. He invited a response from the FA, but nothing happened. Instead Paul Canoville was abused by home fans on his debut for Chelsea, Garth Crooks faced racist chants and banners at Spurs, Cyrille Regis faced regular monkey chants and received a bullet in the post when he was called up for England. In 1987 John Barnes of Liverpool was photographed back-heeling a banana thrown by an Everton fan amid chants of "Everton are white".

Underneath the media radar screen, racism against non-white players and teams was commonplace in English amateur football in the 1970s and 1980s. In an incident reminiscent of apartheid South Africa, the Union Jack club in Bradford refused to serve drinks to the Afro-West Indian club team and supporters. Several Afro-Caribbean or Asian-based clubs were refused admission without good reason to local leagues.

As a reporter for *The Sunday Times* I myself had experienced racism. Once, covering a Norwich vs. Arsenal match in the 1980–81 season, I had seen National Front members sell their literature outside Carrow Road with the vendor shouting: "Get your copy of the *Bulldog*, get your colour supplement." And on the train journey back as I went past one large, fat Arsenal supporter he looked at me and cried out: "Coon, coon, hit the coon over the head with a baseball bat." He then got up and started following me. It was my extreme good fortune that by the time he did I had gained some distance on him and by the time he caught up a policeman was present. As it happened he was a black policeman. Whatever the Arsenal supporter may have felt about the policeman's colour, this was one "coon" he could not trifle with. A few weeks later, returning from a Nottingham Forest vs. Leeds match, I was worried I would not escape a beating. I was first taunted by boys about my colour and then surrounded by some Chelsea fans. They turned the lights of the compartment off and had begun to rough me up prior to a beating when, fortunately, the train arrived in London and fear of the police made the thugs flee.

Of course my experiences paled in comparison with what black players had to face in the 1970s and 1980s. Brian Stein, who had left apartheid South Africa as a child because his father was politically active, was part of a fine Luton team built by David Pleat:

> My heroes were Pele, George Best. In England we lived in Willesden and the first thing that struck me was that there were no black footballers. When I started playing I heard this myth about black players not having stamina. They couldn't run for 90 minutes. Even Pleat said this to me.

Players lack stamina, when it is snowing they can't get it going. This was in 1977. I was only 19 then.

Pleat took over as first-team manager in 1979 and soon realised that Stein was different. The driver of the Luton coach could not have been more right wing. His support for apartheid was vigorous and he often voiced his dismay over the ban imposed on white South African sports teams. Pleat, aware that Stein might get into a row with him, said: "Whatever you do, do not argue with the coach driver. It is a waste of time." Stein avoided any major rows but there was always the crowd:

> You would get mostly supporters shouting uggh-uggh-uggh-uggh-uggh, monkey noises whenever you had the ball, or throwing bananas. Cup game against a team from the Third Division. Wigan or Hartlepool. Got a lot of stick. We played a game in the '80s. Cup match. One of the players called me black something. I did not let that go. I gave him a bit of stick. In the early '80s Chelsea crowds gave a lot of stick to Paul Canoville, terrible abuse, much more than either Ricky Hill or I received. They destroyed him. Millwall was particularly nasty — Phil Walker had a terrible time.

But there are two abiding, horrific memories for Stein, both from the supposedly friendly, warm North of England — Blackburn and Burnley:

> Early in my career, the North was much worse. Past Birmingham the black explosion of players did not develop. Blackburn was one of the worst. Burnley, they spat at me. At Blackburn I was a sub and I was walking through the tunnel. It was just before the match and the crowd were throwing things. Coins, bananas. By the tunnel at Blackburn the crowd were close. I was spat at. I was very upset, like. I nearly spat back. I felt like Cantona did when he was abused but I did not react like him, although then and later I had lot more abuse.

Then there was the night before a game at Burnley when he and Ricky Hill decided to go for a walk round the town:

> It was a Friday night. This was about six in the evening. Not very dark. Just went for a walk to stretch our legs before dinner. Ricky and I, we were sharing a room as well. As we walked we became aware of a couple

of kids with their parents. The kids pointed at us and said, "Look, there is a darkie", and they were laughing as if they had never seen people like us. It was like the Dark Ages.

Stein was intensely aware that he played in a Luton team with brilliant black players watched by all-white crowds: "At most we would have 50 black supporters, mostly friends of players. A lot of my friends used to come to watch. A lot of my friends would end up in fights." In 1988 Stein left England to play football on the continent, with Caen in France, for whom he played for three years from 1988 to 1991:

> The crowds watching us were predominantly white, but it was different. To be honest, more African players were involved. Different sort of atmosphere. I was more easily accepted. Uggh-uggh-uggh-uggh-uggh monkey chants? None of that in France. True, France being a big country, you do not get a lot of away support but whatever opposition supporters were there they did not get at me. The teams had a lot of black players and a lot of them were French black players. The French crowds did not exhibit the racism English crowds can.

His experiences abroad were similar to those of Luther Blissett, born in Jamaica and a hero at Watford. Blissett had evolved a code when it came to coping with racism:

> If people spat at me, I ignored it. Players did spit on me, in isolated instances in the league, or supporters when I was going for a corner. As long as it was not against me in the face. But if anybody spat at me and it hit me in the face I would have turned on them. Then the gloves came off.

It took Italy, where Blissett went to play for AC Milan in 1983, for him to realise that the game can generate passionate support while avoiding the hatred then endemic to English sport.

> Italy was fanatical support but I was very well treated. In Italy it is a national pastime. Everybody will have an opinion but there is no name-calling, no spitting. In Italy fanaticism is about football, it is not about hating the other team or their supporters. I think there is hate in English football, a lot of hate. I don't know the real reason for it. But something has changed. It has become far more organised. (He was speaking to me in 1995.)

Garth Crooks, perhaps the most articulate footballer of his generation, was a working-class boy for whom football provided a route to fame but who disdained the gold bracelets and the fancy trappings thought mandatory: "I had to be 15 per cent better than the white player to get the same chance." And he is quick to stand up to anyone who seeks to categorise him. "Whenever I go to one of the football dos, I gravitate towards the black players. Once Ray Wilkins said to me, 'What is it with you guys, always with the brothers?' I said, 'Ray, when you come you always congregate with Bryan Robson, should I read anything into that?' Ray went quiet after that."

But Crooks can never forget the terrible day when he made his debut for Stoke at St James' Park. It was a November night in 1978:

> I was the only black player on the park. Terry Hibbitt, Jimmy Greenhoff, Alan Hudson, Peter Shilton, Denis Smith, John Mahoney, Terry Conroy were playing. I was 18 years old, and I was the butt of the most cruel racism — jokes, chanting, the whole Gallowgate Kop in unison singing racist songs and shouts. Every time I touched the ball there would be deafening monkey noises — uggh-uggh-uggh-uggh-uggh-uggh — and just abuse. I have never felt so alone, so vulnerable, so stripped of my being. Denis Smith, John Mahoney and Terry Conroy wanted to protect me. They tried to protect me. They couldn't, the whole crowd was on me all the time. At half-time Tony Waddington, the Stoke manager, took me off. I did not want to come off. Never mind, you are coming off, he said. My purpose was to perform to the best of my ability, to show them on my debut. I couldn't. I was in tears as he took me off.

His move to Spurs, which made his career, brought another dimension. Here was a fashionable, rich north London club whose predominant support was Jewish but whose boardroom at that time had no Jews.

> In racial terms my presence was very important. Chris Hughton was already there, very quiet, very unassuming. At Spurs I had to put up with the images of the stereotypical black. Certain people at Tottenham saw me as a bit of a rogue, not really capable of mixing with the middle classes very well, unable to conduct myself very well.

Against this background, it is hardly surprising that English football failed to attract non-white fans. This failure persisted even throughout the 1990s when English football made strenuous efforts to oppose racism. The most prominent initiative, Let's Kick Racism Out of Football, was launched jointly by the PFA, the Commission for Racial Equality and the Football Trust, and within a year all but one of the professional league clubs in England and Wales had signed up to its 10-point plan. This effort was supplemented by multiple individual initiatives from clubs, fanzines and community groups.

However, in 2001 the FA Premier League's national fan survey found that only 0.8 per cent of "active top-level fans" were Black British or British Asian. This represented a rise of only 0.1 per cent since the previous survey in 1997, and compared to a total minority ethnic representation of 13 per cent in the UK population. The same survey found that 7 per cent of all Premier League fans had reported witnessing racism against other fans and no fewer than 27 per cent had reported racism displayed against players at matches.

As the Premier League celebrated its 20th birthday, confident it had laid to rest the ghost of racism, fears that it might resurface led to high-profile cases and prompted Paul Elliott, the first black captain of Chelsea, to revise his views of how the Premier League had coped with racism.

Elliott has a chilling story of how he was regarded by his own white team-mates when he made his debut for Charlton against Crystal Palace back in the 1980s.

"We were at the team hotel," recalled Elliott, "The waiter was taking our orders. A player ordered scrambled eggs and beans. When the waiter came to me, the gentleman said to the waiter, 'Get Paul some coon flakes.'" At the start of the Premier League's 20th season, Elliott would have dismissed this as a story from the dark ages of football. Now, the former central defender reflected sadly: "The most disappointing thing for me is that we thought the problem was licked. We in England have been the leading light in world football in the fight against racism but it has come back to our own playground. We have to ask: did racism really go away? The answer is racism was managed, not eradicated."

The admission had added poignancy, for the 48-year-old spoke to me just after he had been awarded a CBE in the Queen's Birthday Honours for services to equality and diversity, the highest honour given to a player in the Premier League era. It indicated that English football had come a long way but perhaps the journey had not quite reached the happy conclusion many had assumed.

Chapter 2
THE IRON LADY'S TERRIFYING GAME

Two days after Chelsea beat Bayern Munich to win the 2012 UEFA Champions League the *Daily Telegraph* led its front page with a picture showing the British Prime Minister celebrating the win. That in itself was no surprise. Cameron is an Aston Villa supporter and has made much of his football connections and his love for the game. But what made the picture interesting was that Cameron was standing next to President Barack Obama and only a few feet away from German Chancellor Angela Merkel.

Two years earlier Cameron had sat next to Merkel as England were thrashed 4–1 by Germany in the 2010 World Cup. Now an English team had beaten a German side and that via a penalty shootout, hitherto considered a German speciality. The report noted how, as Didier Drogba scored the clinching penalty kick, Cameron threw his hands in the air in a double fist pump while Merkel looked glum. Barack Obama was described as standing diplomatically between the two, paying rapt attention to the game but with his hands firmly clasped behind his back.

What Cameron told the press was described as "playful trash talk" directed at Merkel.

> It's not often you get to watch an England-Germany game with the Chancellor, it goes to penalties, and England win. So this was a historic moment. There was no bet. There was a lot of cheering, and then there was a make-up hug.

The fact that the leaders of the G8 nations, who had convened to discuss the crisis in the Euro zone and a possible default by Greece, took time off to watch a football match showed the power of the Champions League, particularly as they were meeting in Chicago. But this also demonstrated how far the British political establishment had travelled during the Premier League years. Political leaders were now eager to be associated with the game. Cameron's Chancellor of the Exchequer George Osborne, a Chelsea supporter, was even happier than his boss and wrote an article expressing his joy. Both Cameron and Osborne see themselves as disciples of Mrs Thatcher but the Iron Lady had no truck with sport and would have found such a celebration totally incomprehensible. Indeed, had Mrs Thatcher had her way, it is possible that the scenes witnessed in Chicago might never have occurred as the world of football would have been entirely different.

In his memoirs the former FA chief executive Graham Kelly described Margaret Thatcher as "a bully who despised football". He thought that few of her ministers cared about the game and those that did were afraid to speak out in its interest. His view was shared by Michael Foot, the former Labour leader and passionate Plymouth Argyle supporter. In 1986 he spoke in the House of Commons on the Second Reading of the Public Order Bill which brought in new measures aimed at hooligans. Foot said plaintively: "I do not understand why the government have such a hatred of football — perhaps it is because no one in the Cabinet understands what football is about or what happens at the weekends." He added: "The government seem to feel that if the clubs go bankrupt, so much the better, because that is how the market system works."

There was much truth in Kelly's and Foot's analyses. Margaret Thatcher had no personal interest in sport of any kind, and no one in her close circle afforded her any insights into football. Her husband Denis was a golfer and a former rugby referee, her son Mark played cricket for Harrow's first XI, her daughter Carol enjoyed skiing. Her favourite minister, Cecil Parkinson, had been an athlete. Football's strongest supporter in her Cabinet, Nottingham Forest fan Kenneth Clarke, was certainly not "one of us". Thatcher appointed a series of anonymous sports ministers with little or no knowledge of football, and ignored them. The Home Secretaries who introduced her football legislation, Leon Brittan and Douglas Hurd, had no knowledge of the game. Her main advisor on football was the idiosyncratic right-wing MP for Luton South, David Evans, who as owner of Luton Town promoted a controversial ban on away supporters.

Accounts of English football in the 1980s present a picture of desperate resistance to a Thatcherite agenda of control and free-market ideology.

However, it is important to realise that Thatcher left football alone for the first six years of the Premier League. Her only intervention in that period was to apologise to the Italian government for the misbehaviour of English fans in Turin at the 1980 European Championship. Hooligans had led a mass charge against Italian fans who had taunted them when Belgium took a shock lead against England. In a slow and inept response, the Turin police had used baton charges and then CS gas to disperse the troublemakers. Further violence followed in away games against Switzerland and Denmark and the FA pleaded for government action against hooligans but there was no response. However, Thatcher's early years did impact strongly on English football, but rather as fallout from her free-market policies than as a result of deliberate action.

First, her economic strategy in the early 1980s threw thousands of working-class football fans out of work in traditional industries, especially manufacturing, and led to major shifts in the nature of work in the economy. In 1979 unemployment peaked at 1.464 million, but by 1985 it had reached 3.284 million. In the West Midlands the unemployment rate reached 13 per cent in 1985, while in the North West it was 14.1 and in the North 15.7.

From 1980 to 1985 the number of jobs in coal, oil and gas extraction fell from 361,000 to 309,000, in construction from 1,206,000 to 994,000, in transport, post and telecommunications from 1,464,000 to 1,308,000, and in metals and mechanical engineering from 3,867,000 to 2,840,000. Only three sectors (out of 16) showed any gain. Health jobs rose from 1,214,000 in 1980 to 1,489,000 in 1985, banking, insurance and finance from 1,669,000 to 2,039,000 and wholesale/retail, hotels and catering from 4,204,000 to 4,213,000. In London in 1985 unemployment rose above 7 per cent, a figure which would have been considered shocking before the 1980s, and much of it was concentrated in inner-city pockets close to major football grounds. In Tottenham some estimates put it as high as 50 per cent in 1985. The service sector accounted for 75 per cent of all jobs available in London and the South East.

These developments meant that many traditional supporters, especially in football's heartlands, simply could no longer afford to go to football matches, even when basic admission prices for a First Division match were as low as £3.50. Average First Division gates fell from 30,000 to 20,000 over five years. Moreover, the traditional jobs which vanished in the early Thatcher years were those which engendered a strong sense of community and hierarchy and where seniority commanded respect. Their disappearance robbed football of some of its authority figures who helped to keep crowds in order, and therefore left football more vulnerable to the affluent or would-be affluent young hooligans mentioned in the last chapter.

Second, the Thatcher government's response to the miners' strike and to the riots of 1981 ensured that public order and the policing of threatening or violent mass behaviour became a subject of intense debate between the political parties. This ensured that when football forced itself into Mrs Thatcher's attention in 1985 she viewed its problems as another challenge to public order, to be met by the identification, isolation and punishment of "troublemakers". Towards the end of 1985 a fresh set of inner-city riots reinforced this effect, so that football-related measures recommended by the Popplewell Inquiry, which was set up in response to the Bradford fire on May 11, 1985, were tacked on to a general Public Order Bill and debated in that context.

Third, the successful Falklands War reinforced the nationalism and xenophobia of English fans overseas. During the war itself, English football fans in Spain for the World Cup carried banners calling themselves "Soccer's Task Force". Inspired by the success of *The Sun's* "Gotcha" headline after the sinking of the Argentine cruiser, the Belgrano, popular newspapers started to adopt the language of warfare for football matches. Before England's match with Germany at Euro 96, *The Sun* declared "Let's Blitz Fritz" but the *Daily Mirror* outdid them with its "Achtung! Surrender" front page. By the mid-1980s English hooligan firms regularly negotiated mutual truces overseas to form a "coalition force" to take on foreign fans and police.

Early in 1985 a series of disasters led Margaret Thatcher for the first time to intervene actively in English football.

The first, in March, was a massed battle between Luton fans and visiting Millwall fans, in which heavily outnumbered police had been forced to retreat. It resulted in 47 injuries, a new record for English hooligan violence. Mrs Thatcher, like much of the nation, saw the images on television, including that of a Millwall skinhead kicking a policeman attempting to give the kiss of life to a colleague. She summoned senior figures from the FA and the Football League to Downing Street and demanded that the FA should change its rules to make all clubs responsible for all incidents at grounds. She also wanted clubs to accelerate the introduction of CCTV, to bring in stronger perimeter fences and called for tougher sanctions on misbehaving players. Already focused on means of identifying football fans, she also demanded a report from the FA within six weeks on the use of membership schemes.

Thatcher expected the football authorities to take full responsibility for dealing with crowd problems and was surprised when the FA's Ted Croker responded by blaming the government for foisting society's hooligans on football. The government set its·face against any extra financial help for football and rejected the FA's plea for a part of pools betting duty to be spent on ground improvements.

Worse followed in May with the Bradford fire. A stand in the Valley Parade stadium, dilapidated and shockingly maintained, caught fire, killing 56 fans and injuring more than 260. On the very same day a brawl between Birmingham City and Leeds United fans led to the collapse of a wall which killed a teenage fan attending his first football match. The government set up an inquiry into both events, chaired by Sir Oliver Popplewell, a decision criticised by the opposition for lumping together two unrelated incidents and for weakening the focus on safety issues. Some critics at the time wondered how well Popplewell understood football: he was a distinguished amateur cricketer who had played in the same public school side as England's former cricket captain Peter May, the "wet" Tory Cabinet minister Jim Prior and the louche novelist Simon Raven. He was later to become president of the Marylebone Cricket Club.

Then on May 29, 1985 came the decisive event which shaped Thatcher's attitude to football: the Heysel disaster in Brussels. A massed charge by Liverpool fans at rival Juventus supporters at the European Cup final led to 39 deaths, all but one of them Italian. Again, she had seen the event on television. There were other important contributory factors to the disaster, especially the dismal state of the ground, thoroughly inept planning by UEFA and the Belgian authorities, and the inexperience of the Belgian police on the spot. These were generally ignored, not only in Mrs Thatcher's response but also that of other politicians and most media commentary. The focus was on the behaviour of the Liverpool fans.

Without waiting for a government response or an edict from UEFA, the FA withdrew all English clubs from European competition.

Mrs Thatcher apologised to the Italian government (again assuming personal responsibility for fans' misconduct) and released an immediate statement which established the theme of control and punishment of troublemakers. "Football used to be our national game. It was renowned for its sportsmanship. There are some people who are upsetting the whole thing. Everyone wants to get those before the courts... Now that is why it is so important to get good television cameras. I'm not only talking about television for transmission, I'm talking about *total observation of football crowds*" [my italics].

In a Commons statement on June 3, 1985, Mrs Thatcher said that Popplewell's remit would now include issues arising from Heysel, which would reinforce its emphasis on public order rather than safety and maintenance issues. She rejected Labour opposition calls for a wider inquiry into the origins of football-related violence, telling former Home Secretary Merlyn Rees: "I do not believe that it would help to have an extended, indefinite inquiry into the causes of crime which has been with us as long as man has existed." She added: "Violence is caused partly because there is now more money and far more mobility than there was in the past, and that enables people to move from one soccer club to another much more quickly."

After Heysel there was a four-year standoff between Mrs Thatcher and the football authorities over her demand that all football fans should carry some form of identity card. Other parts of the government's programme, prompted by Popplewell, were less contentious, although the imposition of an alcohol ban was modified after desperate lobbying from clubs.

Before dealing with these events, I want to comment briefly on the response of some of the media to the football disasters of 1985. Essentially they demanded a new model of English football, far more akin to leading American sports, in which clubs would be run as modern entertainment businesses, treating fans as customers, giving them a safe and welcoming environment, and competing for their loyalty against alternative weekend leisure pursuits. Some commentators demanded that football clubs should more or less abandon their working-class fan base. It was 10 days before Heysel that *The Sunday Times* produced its leader denouncing English football as a slum game for slum people.

These commentators echoed prevailing Thatcherite orthodoxy by demanding the extinction of clubs which were unable to remodel themselves in the face of market conditions. *The Sunday Times* "slum" leader continued: "If people do not want to watch a match there is no reason in the world why 22 men should be paid to play it. Football, like any other professional entertainment, is nothing if it does not draw crowds on its own merits. Subsidising entertainment is a contradiction in terms." A few days earlier, *The Daily Telegraph* had suggested that "the time is approaching when only a handful of big clubs, such as Tottenham, Liverpool, Everton and Manchester United, will earn sufficient money to cope with renovation and replacement". In the wake of Heysel, *The Sunday Times* followed up its attack on the "slum" game by calling for a new breed of entrepreneurial owner: "As long as local worthies in sheepskin coats can sip their gin and tonic in the directors' box at half-time and gain a bit of status and profit in the process, what does it matter what is happening among the masses on the terraces?"

In fact, several clubs were already experimenting with new models of football enterprise. The most advanced was Tottenham Hotspur, who played a key role in resisting government policies which threatened to strangle this enterprise at birth.

Shortly after her Commons statement on Heysel, Mrs Thatcher called another football summit at Downing Street. She promised that the government would be actively involved in seeking solutions to football's problems, took note of the FA's pleas for tougher sentences for convicted hooligans but again rejected their call for a reduction in pool betting duty to help finance ground improvements. Nothing resulted from the summit except another working party under MP Neil Macfarlane, the second of her low-profile sports ministers. Continuing her pursuit of controls on fans, she asked the FA to impose compulsory membership schemes on clubs under their disciplinary rules.

Then, without waiting for an expected interim report from Popplewell, the government rushed through an act to ban all sales of alcohol at football grounds, and on coaches and trains carrying fans, in time for the start of the 1985–86 football season, then only six weeks away. (In fact, alcohol had not been available in the grounds at Bradford, Birmingham or Heysel.) The ban on alcohol sales at grounds threatened a major loss in revenue for clubs, especially those who had built executive boxes or had plans to install them. Several critics also pointed out that the ban would only encourage fans to drink more outside grounds and arrive later and drunker for the match, creating extra hazards before kick-off.

At this point I am able to draw on an interesting unpublished source, the diaries of Richard Heller, who was working in 1985 for Labour's Shadow Home Secretary, Gerald Kaufman. These diaries often have a Pooterish quality as Heller gleefully records the small triumphs of a political researcher's life (such as Neil Kinnock using one of his lines) or, more often, laments its small disasters. However, on this subject it is a more than useful source in giving an insider's account of the evolution of Labour policy and the skilled Parliamentary tactics by Gerald Kaufman which brought some elements of it into law.

Although a long-serving Manchester MP, Kaufman had little interest in football or sport of any kind. However, he was acutely sensitive to the views of Labour MPs on any issue. Although Labour had been annihilated in the General Election of 1983, the majority of League clubs were still represented by Labour MPs, who took a close interest in their welfare. More importantly, Kaufman wanted to win back support that the Labour party had forfeited on law and order issues. Although determined to resist Mrs Thatcher's authoritarian agenda, he was equally determined to identify the Labour party with popular policies on crime and policing. Heller's diaries show many approaches to Kaufman from within football, including a grandiose but wholly unoriginal plan for football safety from Robert Maxwell, for which Heller composed a suitably grateful reply. However, he reveals that the best organised and most effective representations came from Tottenham Hotspur.

This was hardly surprising, as the club was undergoing a revolution in football administration. Two property developers, Irving Scholar and Paul Bobroff, had acquired Tottenham at the end of 1982 in a brilliantly organised secret coup which had managed to turn the League's arcane ownership rules against the previous chairman, Arthur Richardson, who had thought they protected him. They had then reorganised the club's affairs with the aim of creating an integrated football, leisure, printing and sportswear business, under the umbrella of a holding company. Daringly, they had floated the holding company on the Stock Exchange. For two years they grappled with a legacy of debt, lax financial and administrative controls and a stadium which combined an over-priced new stand with obsolete and dangerous older parts.

Their ambitions were seriously threatened by the poor image of football after the Heysel disaster and, more immediately and directly, by the blanket alcohol ban. On the day before the alcohol bill was presented to the House of Commons, they invited Kaufman and Heller to White Hart Lane to lobby them. Heller's diaries reveal that he and Kaufman were extremely impressed: "They know what they are doing. GK agrees with me that they are real estate niks." Although Scholar and Bobroff were already beginning to disagree over the future of their new business they presented a united front that day. Scholar was candid about the need for renewal of the older parts of the ground, at one point gesturing and saying he felt ashamed of asking people to pay to watch football there. When the tour of the ground was over, Bobroff did most of the talking, emphasising the importance of executive boxes. Heller was impressed by both men's homework: "They've read GK's speeches."

They stressed that the new boxes were not only important as a revenue raiser but for attracting a better class of football fan into the ground. Realising that this argument might not appeal to a Labour politician, Scholar and Bobroff were astute enough to wrap it up with promises that the new revenues from wealthier fans would fund ground improvements for the poorer ones and a range of community projects (this at a time when football in the community was a rare concept within football clubs).

Their lobbying had no immediate effect, since the Labour party came out the next day in support of the total ban on alcohol sales, for political reasons. But they had established an argument in Kaufman's mind which was powerfully supported by Denis Howell and by the Labour MP Tom Pendry, who chaired the All Party Football Group in Parliament.

Bobroff established a dialogue with Heller (who was a genuine football fan) over the next 18 months as the government's policies on football evolved and with them Labour's response. Heller bagged several sets of tickets to Spurs matches (undeclared in those more relaxed days).

Bobroff and Scholar maintained three clear priorities in all their representations: relaxing the alcohol ban, resisting David Evans' attempt to ban all away fans and, most of all, resisting ID cards.

Of course, they talked to many other people apart from the Shadow Home Secretary (who was out of power and unlikely to return to it in the near future) and his obscure assistant. Scholar lobbied the Metropolitan Police and civil servants and had constant direct battles with ministers. In the book I wrote for him, he said: "It took almost the rest of the 1980s to get it right [football hooliganism] and in the process we had to struggle through stupid government panaceas, temporarily encouraged by an extremely short-sighted away-fan ban by

Luton. Mrs Thatcher threatened to be one of the most destructive influences on football, and David Evans was not far behind. I'm not sure who was the worst."

But in all their efforts they showed a special awareness of Kaufman's perspective — and even Heller's. At one point, Heller mentioned to Bobroff a fan's letter proposing the licensing of football directors; Bobroff sent him a summary of all the responsibilities which he and Scholar had discovered at Tottenham (this fascinating document is unfortunately missing from Heller's archive). The two were discussing the possibility of a special membership scheme for young people aged 16 to 24, the peak ages for hooligan offences, when Heller was sacked for dissent against Labour's defence policy.

Popplewell produced his interim report in July 1985. In a short time, he concluded that the Bradford fire had been caused by accident rather than hooliganism, and would not have happened if the club had complied with the existing guidance on safety at sports grounds. He made recommendations to amend this guidance and to improve safety generally, particularly on evacuation procedures. But more attention was focused on his dramatic comments on hooliganism. Rather wildly, he likened the Birmingham vs. Leeds riot to the battle of Agincourt, and suggested that if the hooligan problem was not overcome, "football may not be able to continue in its present form much longer". He urged all clubs to consider a membership scheme to allow the exclusion of visiting fans, without offering any detailed suggestions for how it might work.

Popplewell also suggested that the police should have new stop-and-search powers to prevent fans carrying missiles or smoke bombs. He asked the government to consider creating a new offence of chanting obscene or racist comments at football matches. The government's immediate response was to bring the grounds of clubs in Divisions Three and Four into the scope of the safety designation regime, from which they had previously been exempt, but they also seized on his comments on membership schemes to advance their agenda of identifying and controlling football fans.

Popplewell maintained his general support for membership schemes in his final report in January 1986. After successful lobbying from football interests, he recommended a relaxation of the alcohol ban at grounds, to allow drink to be served in executive boxes out of sight of the match, and more importantly out of sight of the ordinary fans who would still be denied it. The Labour party, also influenced by worrying figures of lost revenue to football clubs, supported this shift in policy. (Richard Heller wrote in his diary: "It's goodbye to equity and rich fans can get drunk to save football.") Popplewell rejected the idea of all-seat stadiums because he thought that hooligans would rip up seats to use as weapons. Most significantly, Popplewell sought a new general offence of disorderly conduct at football matches and renewed his call for new police powers to stop and search football fans. These were not supported by the Labour opposition and were a key battleground when the government introduced them in a new Public Order Bill.

As already mentioned, that bill was presented against the backdrop of a new series of inner-city riots in the autumn of 1985, which had received continuous dramatic coverage in the media and caused real public fears of a breakdown in law and order. This was especially true of the riots at the troubled Broadwater Farm estate, in Tottenham, in which PC Keith Blakelock was murdered. None of the riots, which had also broken out in Brixton and the Handsworth district of Birmingham, had anything to do with football, but they reinforced the government's determination to treat all of football's problems in the context of law and order.

The bill received its second reading on January 13, 1986. Its main purpose was to redefine the ancient offence of riot and create new criminal offences to deal with mass disorder. Among them was a general offence of "disorderly conduct" which the government also hoped to apply to low-level offences at football matches. The bill also provided new powers to control organised marches and assemblies, which the Labour party disliked, and introduced new offences related to racial hatred and its incitement.

The government used the bill to ratify the relaxation on alcohol sales in executive boxes, but it also proposed a new regime of exclusion orders to ban convicted hooligans from football grounds. The new Home Secretary, the patrician Douglas Hurd, acknowledged that this regime would require membership cards and he expected the clubs to move swiftly to introduce them. He announced that convicted football hooligans would have their photographs taken, a provision caustically mocked by Gerald Kaufman: he and senior police officers "mused upon the possibility that the photographs could be pasted into albums and that police officers could while away long winter nights turning the pages and admiring these mug shots. We were sure that it would be impossible for such photographs to festoon the turnstiles of football grounds with stewards comparing, one by one, the faces of customers in the queue with these pin-up pictures. It would be impossible to imagine any situation more likely to provoke a riot rather than keep out a rioter."

The bill moved into detailed scrutiny in standing committee, where the Labour party, led by Gerald Kaufman, put up a barrage of amendments. Heller's diaries on this are not only a useful source on the history of English football and public order but also give an insight into how opposition parties, even when heavily outnumbered, were once able to influence the content of parliamentary legislation. Essentially, Labour's tactics relied on bottling up the bill in the standing committee (with a few dozen members) before it could be taken back to the full House of Commons to complete its stages there and move on to the House of Lords.

These tactics were well-suited to Gerald Kaufman, a fanatic for detail. (Heller wrote: "GK can spot a misplaced comma in a bill at a range of 200 yards.") Kaufman marshalled Labour's small team of MPs to produce 365 amendments for the standing committee — all carefully drafted to stay within the rules of order so that the committee would have to debate them. These tactics threatened the government's entire parliamentary timetable (not to mention the summer holiday plans of MPs and peers) — and made the government ready to consider concessions to the Labour party in exchange for releasing the bill from standing committee. (Today the government has much greater control over the entire legislative process and these tactics rarely work so effectively.)

It was fortunate that Hurd elected not to serve on the standing committee, because Kaufman could not stand him. Heller's diaries record: "GK furious again with Hurd; he just skims along the surface of everything and gives off this phoncy liberal image." Instead the Public Order Bill was piloted by a genial and hardworking minister of state, Giles Shaw, unusual among Tory MPs in representing a Northern constituency. He understood Labour's tactics and the bill slowly and formally worked its way through the standing committee until the key private meeting when Kaufman presented his terms for releasing the bill. The most important areas of contention were in the non-football parts of the bill, although they would have a bearing on the control of crowds and hooligans. Kaufman secured a much tighter definition of the all-purpose offence of "disorderly conduct", which among other effects denied the police indefinite powers to stop and search football fans. By contrast he secured a power of immediate arrest for racial hatred offences.

In the football section, Heller's diary entry for April 6, 1986 records a concession which gave him special satisfaction. "Today the government did something that makes my job worthwhile: they accepted one of 'my' amendments to the Public Order Bill. This was the Labour amendment to allow the courts to order the exclusion from football matches of people convicted of racial hatred offences. I persuaded the Labour front bench to have it tabled and then include it in our 'shopping list' of desired concessions from the government." He added, accurately: "In fact, exclusion orders will be useless at keeping any class of troublemaker out of football matches," but concluded, justifiably: "Nonetheless, this will be the first attempt in British law to be directed specifically at racists who prey on football. Once in the law, it will be very hard to remove."

In spite of Labour's amendments, the Public Order Act 1986 advanced the government's agenda of controlling football fans through identity cards. Mrs Thatcher had latched on to this as her personal remedy for football's problems and a series of ministers followed her bidding. For three years they tried to foist them on English football. Before examining their efforts I am going to cite one more passage from Heller's diaries, in April 1986, which sets out Labour's alternative policies on football-related hooliganism. These are interesting because they were deliberately intended to be popular: they reveal what many English voters wanted for football in the 1980s. Heller's list comes in the draft of a Labour law-and-order document to be called *Protecting Our People*. "A Labour government will:

Extend measures against hooligans at football grounds to cricket, rugby and other sports, as soon as incidents show this to be necessary. Already, cricket matches are being spoilt by drunkenness and other spectator abuse.

Try to ensure that convicted hooligans at sporting events report to attendance centres or perform community service during the times of all important matches.

Make ticket touting a criminal offence. Ticket touts outside major sporting events are a source of exploitation and fraud, and their presence makes it difficult or impossible for the police to separate rival groups of fans.

Try to ensure that convicted hooligans at sporting events are prevented from travelling abroad — if necessary by confiscating their passports. [This was a regular demand from MPs of all parties and the media in the 1980s: curiously the Thatcher government resisted it on civil liberties grounds. The Blair government introduced it in the Football Disorder Act 2000.]

Ban alcohol on ferries and planes carrying fans to important matches overseas.

Improve police detection and intelligence against hooligan gangs and 'firms' at sporting events, especially those linked to political extremist groups.

Give financial support from central government to football and other sports to improve clubs' links with their local communities and their efforts to deter hooligans and make grounds safer.

Almost all of these measures were eventually introduced, but under the Thatcher government they mattered far less than the drive for identity cards.

In July 1986 Mrs Thatcher told the football authorities that she was pleased with clubs' progress in installing CCTV, and with a 46 per cent fall in football-related arrests since the beginning of the year. Her new mood was only temporary and was altered by reports of football fans misbehaving on trains and ferries. She appointed a new Minister for Sport, Richard Tracey, who demanded a new report within six weeks from the football authorities on their plans for membership schemes. The Football League then annoyed her, and the media, by throwing Luton out of the League Cup because of their unilateral ban on away fans. *The Sun* denounced the "spineless men" of the Football League and in the football comic strip, *Roy of the Rovers*, player-manager Roy Race followed Luton's example and banned away fans from Melchester Rovers.

Two new membership schemes emerged and vanished and then in February 1987 Tracey and his Home Office colleague Douglas Hogg produced an eight-point plan for English football. All clubs were to produce schemes to reserve a minimum of 50 per cent of space at grounds for members with cards. Legislation was threatened to secure this. The response from clubs did not satisfy Mrs Thatcher and she appointed yet another Minister for Sports to crack the whip on English football.

The new appointee, Colin Moynihan, not only knew quite a lot about sports but had represented his country at the Moscow Olympics, returning with a silver medal in the rowing eights. In the process he had defied Mrs Thatcher, who had wanted the British team to boycott the Games as a protest against the Soviet invasion of Afghanistan. So when after, the 1987 election, he was summoned to Downing Street he was not confident of getting the job of sport that he really wanted but expected to be sent to Northern Ireland. He was also well aware of the Iron Lady's complete lack of interest in sport:

> When to my delight she told me I had got sport, she also said that I should make sure that I was up at six o'clock to listen to the *Today* programme. If there was ever anything that was wrong on the *Today* programme, I should ring immediately and demand an opportunity to go in and correct it. Then she said, "For some extraordinary reason the press are fascinated by sport and it's likely this will lead on the *Six O'Clock News* and could you please keep it quiet until then." Of course as a very young man — I was 31 — I was rather surprised I got the job. But the moment I walked out of Number 10, all the press were in their usual position on the other side of Downing Street, saying, "Well, Colin, congratulations, you got sport then?" I just smiled, didn't say anything, went back to my very small flat, didn't call a soul and, sure enough, it led the *Six O'Clock News*.

Moynihan, who also had good contacts among international sports administrators, pushed hard for the government's target of 50 per cent reserved membership space, despite very lukewarm support from the police. Only 41 League clubs (fewer than half) had achieved this by the summer and many clubs claimed that their ground configuration simply did not allow it. Moynihan announced his intention to shake up the laggards, especially the top six League clubs. He also proposed the use of breathalysers at club gates.

In summer 1988 Mrs Thatcher saw more unpleasant football scenes on television. This time it was English fans at the European Championship in Dusseldorf. She demanded that England withdraw from all international competition. Moynihan supported her and upped the government's demand for identity cards. He now wanted them for *all* admissions to football grounds, and threatened to enlist UEFA to impose them right across Europe. This demand was unrealistic but it signalled a new government strategy of denying support for English clubs' return to Europe unless they fell into line on identity cards.

At the end of 1988 the government introduced the Football Spectators Bill. It was an enabling bill: if passed it would allow the government to impose a compulsory national membership scheme by order without having to debate any of the details. The football bodies were ordered to nominate members to a new Football Membership Authority or face government nominees. Irving Scholar played a leading role in resisting compulsory ID cards, and at one meeting with Moynihan he made the minister admit his real motivation. "Finally, prodded beyond endurance, he cracked. Suddenly he said, 'You've got to understand, Irving! I see your points but my career is on the line here!'... It was probably the most honest answer I have ever got from a politician, and it made me realise that the real driving force behind the ID scheme was Mrs Thatcher."

Under the radar of Mrs Thatcher's government, important changes were happening in football spectatorship, particularly in terms of fashion and style. The proliferation of fanzines gave a voice to intelligent, self-mocking football fans. The most successful, *Foul* and *When Saturday Comes*, acquired a national following. In international competitions, Scottish and Scandinavian fans created a new and also self-mocking image for themselves, wearing extravagant national costumes and make-up and displaying exaggerated stereotypical behaviour. In contrast with the English fans who had called themselves Soccer's Task Force in 1982, Scottish fans attending a match against Russia held up banners reading "Alcoholism vs. Communism".

Changes in fan culture had no influence on the government. In April 1989 it was still determined to impose a huge apparatus of control on English football supporters. They would have become the first people since the war to be obliged to identify themselves on demand to the police. On match days they would have been subjected to stop-and-search powers if a police officer thought that they might be journeying to a football match. They could have been banned from public places and public transport and denied the right to buy alcohol. They would have had to undergo this regime for the dubious pleasure of watching a football match in dismal, disgusting and dangerous conditions, crammed into pens and ordered about by police and stewards. Such conditions could well have finished English football as a spectator sport. But then came Hillsborough.

The worst disaster in English football killed 96 Liverpool fans at the FA Cup semi-final against Nottingham Forest on April 15, 1989. The survivors then had to endure the *Daily Mirror*'s intrusive photographs of the horrors they had undergone and *The Sun*'s dishonest reports of their misconduct. But the reality was incontrovertibly established by the inquiry under Lord Justice Taylor. The disaster had nothing to do with crowd misbehaviour. It was brought about by unsafe conditions at the ground and bad decisions by the police. All the government's apparatus of public order and crowd control measures were shown to be either irrelevant to the disaster or actual contributors. By trying to prevent what they thought was an attempted pitch invasion, and a public order offence, the police had actually prevented fans from saving the most vulnerable people from being crushed to death.

It is no consolation to the victims or the survivors to say that Hillsborough set English football on a new course. The immediate result of the Taylor inquiry was the suspension of plans for ID cards. The subsequent report blew them out of the water. Taylor said bluntly: "I therefore have grave doubts whether the scheme will achieve its object of eliminating hooligans from inside the ground. I have even stronger doubts as to whether it will achieve its further object of ending football hooliganism outside grounds. Indeed I do not think it will. I fear that, in the short term at least, it may actually increase trouble outside grounds."

In place of the Thatcher government's obsession with football as a public order problem, Taylor's prime recommendation addressed the conditions of English football spectatorship. He demanded all-seat stadiums. It represented a huge demand on clubs, even with the support from public funds which Taylor recommended, but on the eve of the Premier League it set a new agenda for English football, along the lines which some of the broadsheet newspapers had demanded after Heysel. Fans would have to be treated as customers and offered an entertaining experience in a modern, safe, welcoming environment.

To fulfil that agenda it would not be enough for the top clubs to cream off the traditional revenues of English football. They needed a totally new stream of income. Providentially, new forms of television arrived to deliver this to them.

Chapter 3
MONEY FOR CARLOS KICKABALL

On May 18, 1992, the newly established English Premier League did a deal which changed the future of English football, British sport and British media, and even had an impact on global politics.

This was the sale of television rights to Premier League football matches to a consortium dominated by BSkyB, the satellite broadcasting company owned by Rupert Murdoch. The value of the deal was generally reported at the time as £304 million over five years. This figure was misleading: it suited both sides to exaggerate it. But, however expressed, it represented a totally new scale of revenue for the leading clubs, which transformed football spectatorship and football finance.

The additional revenues made it possible for clubs to implement the recommendations of the Taylor report for all-seat stadiums and to create a far safer and more pleasant experience for spectators than had been the case for most of the previous 20 years. BSkyB's coverage of Premier League football fulfilled its promise to take the game beyond its traditional support and make it more attractive to women, families and the more affluent. The deal allowed the clubs to meet the expectations of this new audience.

But just when football was attracting spectators willing to pay far higher admission prices and to spend more money at grounds, the deal also ensured that live spectators ceased to be the main concern of the clubs. It meant that gate receipts were dwarfed by the revenue derived from television, both directly and indirectly through the enhanced value of sponsorship and advertising.

The deal also magnified the income disparity between Premier League clubs and the rest, and within the Premier League, between the leading clubs competing for European honours and the chasing pack. This had an enduring perverse effect: the more valuable it became for clubs to be in the Premier League at all, and to become one of its top clubs, the more money they had to spend on players to maintain that status. The deal thus brought English football into the modern era of hugely inflated wages and fees for players and managers and commissions, legal and otherwise, for their agents. The sums required to maintain or improve Premier League status proved increasingly beyond the means of the traditional owners of football clubs — hence the influx of foreign capital and ownership.

The same model of spectatorship and finance was gradually adopted by other British sports, particularly cricket and both forms of rugby, although a far less developed transfer market allowed traditional forms of ownership and control to survive longer. Put simply, there are no regularly televised British sports which have not become dependent on the revenues they earn through television. The interests of their regular spectators and participants have become secondary. If television requires a change in a sport's rules or its format or the season in which it is played, the fans and the players simply have to put up with it.

As far as media history is concerned, the deal was crucial for Rupert Murdoch. He understood this — as did his defeated rival, Greg Dyke of ITV. The deal transformed his struggling British satellite operation. Instead of haemorrhaging money, it became a cash cow, enhanced his power in British media and British politics and helped finance new operations across the globe. His satellite operation not only became a permanent part of British broadcasting but relegated terrestrial broadcasters to also-rans in the transmission of sport.

The story of the historic deal is a story of two broadcasters who knew what they wanted. The victor, Rupert Murdoch, had more money to promise and better tactics than the loser, Greg Dyke. Even so, Murdoch's victory, in football terms, came from a last-gasp winner in extra time.

The leaders of the Premier League clubs had no such clarity of vision. They were united only by the common belief that they deserved more money at the expense of lesser clubs — the belief which had brought the Premier League into being. They were divided by long-running factional rivalries and personal vendettas. Many of their decisions, including the crucial final decision in favour of BSkyB, were made for negative and reactive reasons, and to avenge and correct decisions made before.

Again in football terms, the television saga was a cup-tie over two legs. The first leg was won in 1988 by ITV against a satellite broadcaster, British Satellite Broadcasting (BSB), in alliance with the BBC, because ITV's 'manager', Greg Dyke, picked off the top five clubs. He stuck to these tactics in the second leg, in 1992, but the result was reversed. A new satellite-BBC alliance defeated ITV by cultivating the smaller top-flight clubs against the top five (although one of the top five, Tottenham Hotspur, had already changed allegiance).

The Premier League clubs were lucky to have a competent negotiator, their newly appointed chief executive, Rick Parry — although this too was the result of a negative decision. The club chairmen gave the job to Parry largely because they could not agree which of them should conduct the negotiations.

In the following account of the story, I have been fortunate enough to draw on a collection of Parry's working papers and contemporary notes of the negotiations and their aftermath. They form a major part of an archive of material supplied to me by Chris Akers, a key player in the proposal by the Swiss Banking Corporation for a dedicated Premier League television channel (see below). The Parry papers are revealing both on the big issues at stake and the personalities (especially his notes and marginalia, which are often rather rude).

Parry saw deeper than many of the chairmen he served. Like them, he realised that the advent of a satellite broadcaster with deep pockets, such as Murdoch, dramatically improved the bargaining power of the new Premier League. But he also saw that satellite television could actually allow the Premier League to take control of all the revenue streams from televising its matches and of the coverage and marketing of its 'product', Premier League football — if the Premier League ran its own satellite service. Parry was tantalised by this vision. He was offered two schemes to achieve it. One never gained traction but the other — a proposal worked up by the Swiss Banking Corporation — was under active consideration until a late stage in the negotiations between the Premier League and Murdoch and Dyke. Parry's papers throw new light on one of the great might-have-beens of modern English football.

But this is getting far ahead of the story. We need to start with the first leg, won by ITV in 1988 — what could be called Dyke's winner, with assistance from the leading clubs known as the Big Five (Manchester United, Liverpool, Everton, Arsenal and Tottenham).

One factor united the fractious world of English football in the 1980s: loathing of the perceived cartel between BBC and ITV. All clubs, especially the leading ones, believed that the cartel had denied them the rightful value of sales of televised matches. In 1985 the two broadcasters had faced down football's negotiators, including a blustering Robert Maxwell. The BBC's dour Jonathan Martin told them bluntly: "Football rates itself far too highly. It has no God-given right to be on television. It's not our job to underwrite and subsidise the game." He and his genial colleague, John Bromley of ITV, refused to raise their then offer of £4.5 million for the following season, and when Maxwell and the rest persisted with their demands, BBC and ITV simply withdrew Football League coverage from British television. It was replaced by the new and far more manageable television favourite — snooker — and by films with mass appeal.

The broadcasters' lockout had an immediate impact on clubs great and

small. The lesser clubs lost their share of television revenues -
a season — which often meant the difference between ruir
bigger clubs, those most often televised, discovered for t
television promoted attendances rather than reduced ther
dramatically. By September 1985, the Big Five were ready to sue for peace
and accept the existing offer of £4.5 million, as long as they could keep it
for themselves. They revived plans for a breakaway Super League, which were
almost instantly leaked to the *Daily Mail*. The leak produced a mixture of bluster
and offers of compromise from the League and the threat of a players' strike,
which were resolved by the Heathrow Agreement (which we will look at later).
Heathrow and the subsequent ejection of all the existing League management
committee significantly altered the balance of power in favour of the Big Five,
but its new negotiator, Philip Carter of Everton, was no more successful in
forcing the broadcasters' hands. He was compelled to accept a take-it-or-leave-
it offer of £1.5 million for the remainder of the 1985–86 season. In July 1986,
the broadcasters forced him into a two-year extension worth £3.1 million
per season with no guarantee of any income from recorded football.

These events left nobody satisfied in English football. The Big Five were
blamed by smaller clubs for being greedy and destructive but secured no extra
financial reward from all their manoeuvres: their revenue per televised match
actually fell.

The advent of pay-TV brought new opportunities for English football
clubs but also new tensions between the Big Five and the rest.

By 1988, two companies were fighting for the infant British pay-TV market.
Rupert Murdoch's British Sky Broadcasting was already up and running,
although largely dependent on films and repeats of British comedy shows. Its
competitor BSB had yet to transmit. BSB resolved on a bold move to leapfrog
its rival: a generous bid for the right to transmit live First Division matches.

The Big Five first learnt of BSB's move from Trevor Phillips, the Football
League's commercial director, in a confidential note in January 1988. Irving
Scholar of Tottenham Hotspur, who was better informed about media issues
than his colleagues, led the response. He welcomed the arrival of serious
competition for the BBC-ITV cartel, but he could not contemplate a deal for
a satellite broadcaster which had not even put its satellite into orbit. Football
needed exposure: it could not become a fringe activity, watched on television
"by the sort of audiences that watched the Epilogue on BBC". He favoured
another short-term deal with the terrestrial broadcasters until both cable and
satellite had got underway and offered new possibilities.

Scholar recognised that a generous cash offer would appeal to smaller clubs who were rarely shown on television. He was right, especially when BSB's offer was unveiled in June 1988. The initial offer of £11 million was over three times the value of the current television contract — and BSB promised to raise it to £25 million a year if live football delivered their targets for subscription income. Significantly, BSB offered the League a share of subscription income and advertising revenue: they even threw in part of the revenues from boxing and other sports. This gave their offer a strong appeal to Phillips and to Graham Kelly, then the League secretary. Like Parry four years later, they saw a partnership with pay-TV as a means to control the coverage of football on television.

One man took this offer very seriously indeed: Greg Dyke, the new head of ITV Sport. Unlike most other leaders of British terrestrial broadcasting, Dyke was alarmed by pay-TV, especially in sport, where it might rob ITV of the high-spending young male audience beloved of advertisers. He wrote later: "I decided that my job was to try to derail the process and pinch these live football rights from BSB." Dyke was unable to persuade the BBC to join him in an alliance to kill satellite broadcasting at birth: Paul Fox, BBC's managing director, was nervous that this would be poorly received by Margaret Thatcher's government at a time when the Corporation was fighting to preserve the licence fee. Worse still for Dyke, BBC actually teamed up with BSB by offering new terms for *Match Of The Day*. The cartel had been broken. ITV was on its own.

Dyke's problem was that he could never persuade the ITV companies to outbid the total cash on offer from BSB. They did not share his view of the threat from pay-TV and after their experience in 1985 they did not regard football as essential for building an audience. Dyke turned for advice to a football expert, Trevor East, the deputy head of sport at Thames Television, who set up a meeting with Arsenal's vice-chairman David Dein at London's then fashionable Japanese restaurant, Suntory. Dyke and Dein quickly discovered a personal rapport and a common interest. Dein wanted more money from television for the big clubs and Dyke had no interest in spending money to show the lesser clubs on television. Together they worked out a plan to approach the Big Five.

Dyke entertained their representatives on June 16, 1988 at another fashionable London restaurant, the Belfry. At a personal level he made a breakthrough when he admitted (in Dyke's words "semi-confirmed") that the BBC and ITV had operated a cartel. He made it clear that he wanted an exclusive deal with the top clubs. It would be worth less money in total than the BSB offer — but of course they would not be sharing it with all the other 87 Football League clubs.

On June 23, Dyke made a formal offer to the Big Five. I am indebted to Ron Noades, the former chairman of Crystal Palace, for showing me a copy of

Dyke's letter to Martin Edwards of Manchester United, which he has kept in his briefcase for the last 15 years.

> I'm writing in my role as Chairman of the ITV Sports Committee to invite you formally to put to your board our offer to buy the exclusive rights to televise from your grounds all matches in any domestic football competition, with the possible exception of the FA Cup. The terms we are offering are the following:
>
> A four-year agreement starting 88–89. All sums will be increased by RPI each year. In the first year we will pay you £1 million for the exclusive rights to televise from your ground.

A key provision was Clause 3:

> We guarantee to broadcast a minimum of one live game from your ground each season. We would have the right to broadcast a maximum of three. No more than one of these live games will be broadcast in midweek. ITV will pay you a total of £50,000 for each live game transmitted as compensation for loss of income. As part of this contract ITV would buy all British broadcasting rights of the match covered. Overseas rights would remain with the club. Should your club appear in any European tournament ITV would have the first option to negotiate television rights.
>
> This offer is based on a number of conditions which would apply to five clubs — Tottenham Hotspur, Arsenal, Everton, Liverpool and yourselves collectively. These are: the offer is withdrawn unless all five clubs accept the terms offered. ITV agrees to broadcast no more than 20 live games in a season, covering all domestic football. A maximum of six of these would be played and broadcast each week. Finally, in the contract ITV would have first option to negotiate for the four years beyond 91–92 and a right to match the best bid. All five clubs [would] have used their best endeavours to assist ITV to participate in the non-exclusive right to cover the FA Cup.

In a subheading Dyke set out "Bases of Proposal for ITV's Future Coverage of Football", written in a more personal style.

> Our understanding is that BSB's offer will be worth about £150,000 a year to each of your clubs. Compared with the existing £70,000 you received, that is an attractive offer. Gentlemen, ITV is prepared to pay £1 million a year to each of you, the five top clubs — Liverpool, Everton,

Arsenal, Tottenham and Manchester United — to buy the exclusive rights insofar as they are available to televise from your grounds in any domestic competition. The agreement would start 88–89 and cover four years. RPI increase. Five-yearly contract with a first option to negotiate.

Significantly, he added:

ITV would be prepared to pay an additional sum of £2 million to buy the exclusive television rights for a further number of First Division clubs, between five and ten. We would like to discuss with the original five the number and identity of the clubs to be included. ITV wishes to play a total of 20 live games in a season, maximum six played midweek. We would broadcast live matches from the grounds of the first five clubs on a minimum one occasion and a maximum of three.

These terms are incorporated into a legal agreement which all parties are free to enter into. In the event of any parties [being] unable to deliver what is agreed as a result of their legal obligations the agreement is clearly null and void. I hope these terms are acceptable to your board and we can have a long and fruitful relationship.

At the League's AGM on June 24, Kelly learnt for the first time that ITV were talking to Dyke about a possible Super League. Significantly, his informant was Jonathan Martin of the BBC, confirming that the old cartel had been broken. The news provoked a backlash against Dein and Philip Carter, of Everton, who were accused of having a conflict of interest and faced demands that they should stand down from the League's negotiating team. Dein was also accused of leaking details of negotiations.

A brief war of words, administrative manoeuvres and legal threats ensued between the League and ITV and its supporters among the Big Five. Dyke escalated the pressure. At a second meeting, he and the Big Five agreed to cut a "second tier" of five clubs into the exclusive deal: West Ham, Newcastle, Aston Villa, Nottingham Forest and Sheffield Wednesday. They would play as the ITV Ten. The Football League took out an injunction against a breakaway by the 10, but this was countered at an emergency meeting of all 22 current First Division clubs, attended by Dyke. He was gratified when they all threatened to join the split.

The Football League capitulated to their demands. The Heathrow Agreement was rewritten to give the First Division 75 per cent of television income instead of 50 per cent. For the Professional Footballers' Association, Gordon Taylor conceded half of its entitlement to 10 per cent of television income, an issue which re-emerged four years later. By now, Dyke and his ITV offer were the only game in town for the League, since BSB had withdrawn its bid. The ITV deal matched BSB's first-year offer of £11 million, with a total value rising to £53 million over four years. ITV would show 21 live matches, mostly late on Sunday afternoons. It also bought the recorded rights to League matches but decided not to use them, thus killing off *Match Of The Day*. The League clubs approved the ITV deal at an EGM on the auspicious date of 8/8/88, although such was the ill-feeling that it was never formalised or signed.

Unknown to the clubs, Dyke had agreed to a secret protocol with the Big Five to allocate them a guaranteed number of televised matches. The effect was to boost their share of both the direct television income and the value of sponsorship and advertising hoardings.

Football pulled in excellent audiences for the ITV companies, helped by their concentration on matches between clubs in their region. They were especially lucky in their first season, when 11 million watched the final thrilling match in which Arsenal snatched the First Division title from Liverpool with Michael Thomas' last-minute goal. ITV's coverage was highly attractive to advertisers, especially brewers, some of whom gave it a fifth of their total advertising budget.

The match was to go down as a game-changing moment and two prominent Arsenal fans used the match as a peg to produce books on football. The first of these helped shape the perception of many towards the game. Back in 1973 Hunter Davies had been given unprecedented access by Tottenham Hotspur to write his classic *The Glory Game,* which provided an intimate look inside a football club. This Arsenal victory produced very different books.

Three years after manager George Graham had engineered the victory at Anfield, Nick Hornby, an Arsenal supporter, wrote *Fever Pitch*. This genre of writing may have been common in the United States but was then unknown in England: an educated sensitive fan articulating how his love for his favourite team affected his life. And 20 years after the match, Jason Cowley, another Arsenal supporter and by then editor of the New Statesman, used it as the centrepiece of *The Last Game: Love, Death and Football at the End of the Eighties*. The blurb described it as "a compelling memoir of how one astonishing game of football came to symbolise the end of an era in the nation's history".

Dyke could bask in the glory of a great victory but the costs were more than financial. He antagonised all the clubs by insisting on Sunday matches with 5pm kick-offs. Dyke was very much in line with thinking in television. Bryan Cowgill, widely seen as an innovator of sport on television, had long held the idea that the ideal time for live football on television would be on a Sunday evening at about six in the evening. And Sky would eventually settle on 4pm on Sunday for its main match.

Faced with Dyke's 5pm kick-offs, clubs protested that this was an inconvenient time for fans, especially away supporters forced to rely on Sunday public transport. One of his main allies, Martin Edwards of Manchester United, complained that their fans often arrived home after midnight on Sundays and then had to work the next day. Dyke ignored the protests. It was the first demonstration that the interests of TV scheduling would outweigh those of paying spectators. There would be many more. More importantly, he had made lasting enemies among the smaller clubs, especially Chelsea's Ken Bates. Although they did not know about the secret protocol, they could count their appearances on *The Big Match* and confirm their view that the ITV deal had been a stitch-up by the Big Five. Bates memorably complained that Arsenal and Liverpool were shown "more often than f***ing *Coronation Street*".

The smaller clubs took their revenge in September 1989 by removing Carter and Dein from the League management committee. Worse still, in the following year Bates and his ally Ron Noades of Crystal Palace induced the League to withdraw its plan to reduce the First Division from 22 to 20 (with a promise of ultimate reduction to 18), which had helped to avert the top clubs' breakaway in 1988.

The retention of a 22-club First Division meant less money and less power for the Big Five — and more votes against them and Dyke when the deal came up for renewal in four years' time.

There was one other cloud on the horizon for Dyke and ITV. The BBC-BSB alliance remained intact and it acquired a package of football broadcast rights including the FA Cup, the Charity Shield and England internationals, and some lesser competitions such as the Simod Trophy (later re-sponsored by Zenith Data Systems) and the Autoglass Trophy for teams in Divisions Three and Four. Perhaps because not many people watched them, these proved an important training ground for young television producers and allowed them to pioneer techniques for more exciting coverage.

These football assets, especially the production talent, were a valuable inheritance for Rupert Murdoch when BSB merged with his Sky operation in 1990. As we shall see, they also played a crucial role in the way an evening newspaperman from Aberdeen, lured to BSB, changed the face of televised sport. But to do that he needed the creation of a league not tied to the old Football League. The television rows had now made this all the more possible.

ITV's victory, the manner in which it was won and the response of the Football League clubs deepened the fault lines in English football. The major clubs, especially the Big Five, were more determined than ever to extinguish their obligations to support the lesser clubs. For the third time in a decade they planned secession from the Football League. This time they hit on the idea of using the FA as a vehicle rather than going it alone. That decision was inspired. It was legally more sound and freed the top clubs from the fear of FA sanctions, especially disqualification from Europe. It exploited over a century of antipathy between the two organisations and it gave the secession legitimacy. Instead of looking greedy and selfish, the big clubs could claim to be aligning their money and power with the body which represented the summit of English football — the England team — and its grassroots, the dedicated volunteers who ran school and youth football and the amateurs who turned out on village and park pitches on freezing Sundays. Irving Scholar summed up the key advantage of using the FA: "Past attempts at breakaways had resulted in the big clubs being portrayed as villains. This time we were part of the process of making the national team better." In a short time, the Premier League became an autonomous organisation, dedicated to its own interests, with its own rules, officials and above all, money. But at its inception it was possible to believe that English football would re-integrate and renew itself under a revived FA.

There had never been any shortage of plans to reform English football, but they had regularly foundered either on the inertia of its institutions or on the personal and sectional interests of its leading personalities. Two of the most radical plans, by the distinguished academic Sir Norman Chester, were extinguished for those reasons. In 1968 he had tried to give the FA a modern management structure with an executive committee: the members of existing committees refused to give up any power and turned the new committee into a dustbin.

In 1983, as English football was tottering under multiple crises, a second Chester report came up with more radical proposals: a First Division reduced to 20, the entire Football League reduced to 64, regionalisation of the lower reaches, much tighter financial targets and reporting for all clubs, and, above all, a long-term strategy for change in English football. All of these were rejected outright by the football authorities and club chairmen. Rather than give him a hearing, the Football League management committee gave Chester a tea service, which he did not want. He commented publicly that the League had "no PM, no Cabinet and no policy".

After Chester's second failure, new ideas for reform began to emerge based on the thinking of Alex Fynn, a sports marketing expert with Saatchi & Saatchi. Fynn suggested that the commercial value of matches in any sport depended on their uniqueness as an 'event'. A world heavyweight boxing contest or the final of a major football competition were compelling 'events' which would always attract a huge following of live and television spectators. Routine contests between middle-ranked performers had no such following and attracted only a core of loyal support. This analysis suggested that in order to maximise its revenues, English football needed to increase its scarcity value, with more matches between top clubs and fewer matches between lesser ones (except between local rivals). Fynn believed that international matches were bigger events than domestic ones and that successful international performance enhanced the value of domestic contests.

During the 1980s, Fynn's theories, backed by detailed commercial analysis of the advertising revenues gained from football, won support from the two most go-ahead football club directors, Irving Scholar and David Dein. His thinking underpinned the commercial logic of a reduced First Division, whether or not independent of the Football League, but it also held out the promise of a higher priority for the interests of the national team, which made it attractive to the FA as well as the big clubs. At Dein's suggestion, Fynn made an important presentation to the FA Council in January 1991. Overcoming his initial embarrassment at wearing a scruffy pair of driving shoes, Fynn presented a plan for a new pyramid structure of English football. At the apex would be the England team, immediately below it a reduced First Division, below that two lesser divisions, and below them a network of regional divisions. With this new structure, he predicted that English football could generate a vast increase in television revenues if it could agree to 34 live televised games.

At this point the FA's director of coaching, Charles Hughes, told Fynn, to his astonishment, that the FA had abandoned all hope of agreement with the Football League. It was encouraging the top clubs to break away into a new, 18-member Premier Division — under the FA.

A key member of Fynn's audience was Graham Kelly, chief executive of the FA for nine months. Kelly's was an astonishing appointment — recruited from the Football League. His inside knowledge of the FA's arch rival, from nearly 10 years as its secretary and then chief executive, were invaluable to his new employer and the breakaway clubs in the final power struggle. Kelly had formed a dim view of the Football League's leadership and was convinced that only the FA could make the overdue changes needed to save English football.

Kelly had hardly taken office when he witnessed the Hillsborough disaster and had to provide the FA's instant and longer-term response. His memoirs indicate the scale of the demands on him in the crisis, especially the abuse and hostility he faced from Liverpool supporters, including one outright assault. They give an unfortunate impression of a man pre-occupied with immediate administrative issues, particularly whether and when the game should be replayed. His flat narrative seems inadequate to the horror of its subject. It makes no mention of *The Sun*'s dishonest reporting of vicious behaviour by Liverpool fans which did so much to stoke up emotion and misdirect attention from the real issues of public safety and misguided methods of crowd control. But in fairness to Kelly, Hillsborough strengthened his personal commitment to reform English football.

After coping with the immediate crisis of Hillsborough and giving evidence to the Taylor inquiry, Kelly became embroiled in the everyday politics of English football. In summer 1990, the Football League and the FA had an often farcical dispute over the punishment of Swindon Town, who had confessed to multiple secret illegal payments to their players. Then, much more seriously, Kelly failed to prevent the League from restoring the First Division to 22 clubs. As mentioned above, at an EGM in August 1990, the League capitulated to insistent pressure from Ken Bates and Ron Noades. This fateful decision had very different implications for Kelly and the Big Five, but it brought them closer together. For Kelly, this was a reactionary move which threatened the England team. With reduced pressure and fatigue in the smaller First Division, the England players had put in a much improved performance in the World Cup in Italy. For the Big Five, the restored 22-club First Division would dilute the revenues they needed to improve their grounds in the aftermath of Hillsborough. But the decision helped both Kelly and the Big Five to wash their hands of the Football League.

Notwithstanding this retrograde decision, the League's chief executive, Kelly's replacement Arthur Sandford, and its commercial director Trevor Phillips were both all too aware that English football needed root-and-branch reform. They wanted the League to take charge of this, and, displaying rare agility, they were the first to produce a master-plan. Issued in October 1990 under the title "One Game, One Team, One Voice", this was a forward-looking document, with ideas for stadium standards, coaching, youth football, health, television income and sponsorship: its authors later claimed bitterly that Kelly stole them all. The League document also wanted England to bid for the 1996 European Championship or the 1998 World Cup.

Crucially, it suggested a joint board to run the whole of English football, with 50–50 representation between the FA and the Football League. This would extinguish the power of the FA Council and give the League a totally new influence on key issues such as the England team, the whole of amateur football and the laws of the game. It was therefore anathema to the FA and Kelly was determined to kill it for his new masters. As for the Big Five, by now they had no desire to increase the power of a Football League which they did not control and which ignored their interests.

The League made serious mistakes in trying to sell their plan. One was comic. Doug Ellis of Aston Villa absent-mindedly left an envelope behind at FA headquarters: it revealed a secret plan by the League to replace the FA Cup. Another was to rely too heavily on the sympathy of the Minister for Sport under the new government of John Major. Unlike his predecessor, Major enjoyed football. One of his last acts as Chancellor of the Exchequer was to meet a long-standing request from the FA: he released funds from a cut in pool betting duty to help clubs pay for the renewed stadiums demanded by Taylor. (In its first year this generated £80 million for the Football Trust: the biggest grants went to Chelsea, Sheffield Wednesday and Manchester United.) But Major followed Thatcher in appointing another Minister for Sport, Robert Atkins, who was a political lightweight with no knowledge of football. His influence in the struggle between the League and the FA became more and more peripheral. Eventually, under the wise guidance of Kenneth Clarke, he abdicated from football politics.

When the League's representatives on the FA tried to secure discussion of "One Game, One Team, One Voice", Kelly gave it a massive kick into touch. He told the FA that he and senior staff were preparing their own "blueprint for English football" and he had little difficulty in persuading them to wait for that.

Independently of the struggle between the League and the FA, another significant event occurred in the second half of 1990. By then Irving Scholar's commercial and football dreams at Tottenham Hotspur had turned to dust. The club had won nothing for years. He had fallen out with Paul Bobroff, his partner, and was reviled by angry fans. The ancillary businesses in clothing and ticketing had foundered and the club were drowning in debt. To purchase Gary Lineker, they had been forced to rely on a secret loan from Robert Maxwell. A press leak of that loan in September forced Maxwell to make a formal bid for the club. With the vocal support of fans, the club's manager, Terry Venables, scrabbled to put together a counter-bid. Ironically, the two contestants for the stricken club were both "larger than life" self-promoting characters without any real money of their own. Tottenham Hotspur's uncertain future hung over the formation of the Premier League and removed the influence of a pioneer in English football. The outcome at Spurs had a major influence on the television battle, but that is a later story.

In December 1990, the FA, the League and the Big Five moved further apart. On December 6, David Dein of Arsenal and Noel White of Liverpool met Bert Millichip, the long-serving FA chairman. They told him that they did not want to see more power given to the League and that they saw no hope within the present Football League of major clubs raising enough money to implement the Taylor recommendations on ground safety. White was a crucial figure. Representing England's most successful club of recent times, he was a "voice of football" which Millichip could not ignore. Liverpool had a reputation for letting other clubs initiate contentious proposals. Dein took care to cultivate White and ensure that this time he and his club would be in the lead. Millichip called in Kelly. Dein and White were surprised to discover how much he agreed with them. A week later, on December 13, Kelly revealed key features of his forthcoming blueprint, including a national plan to implement the Taylor report for stadiums, a Junior England club, an ambitious and improved development programme for young players and more football in the community schemes. Crucially, he also proposed a separate limited company to exploit all the commercial properties of the FA to help the grassroots.

By now, Kelly had reason to believe that these properties might include a new league of the top clubs. He persuaded White and Dein to endorse the recruitment of an outside consultant to assist in its creation. His choice was Rick Parry, an accountant who had worked successfully in 1987 on reforms to the Football League. Parry's early life had echoes of Kelly's: both had been fine schoolboy goalkeepers in the North West but missed out on professional careers. But Parry had wider experience than Kelly of sports administration and politics at the top level, having worked for the Los Angeles Olympic Committee in 1984 and on Manchester's failed Olympic bid in 1985. He combined inside knowledge of football with independent expertise. These made him an important capture for Kelly. So too, in the acrimonious year ahead, did his sense of humour.

Parry quickly mastered the legal and technical issues involved in detaching the top clubs from the Football League, including pension schemes, players' contracts and agreements with the Professional Footballers' Association (PFA). An especially awkward issue was the League's three-year notice rule. While Parry and Kelly grappled with these problems, Fynn worked on marketing and commercial prospects for a new league. He persuaded Kelly to commission opinion research on fans of all the current 20 First Division clubs. It found equal support, 41 per cent, for an 18-club or a 22-club top division. The biggest argument for the 18-club supporters was to help the England team. Unfortunately, the FA did not release these results until after the Football League had published their own survey (from all four divisions), with the headline result that seven out of 10 fans opposed a breakaway Premier League.

By March 1991 Kelly and Parry had won over all the Big Five to the cause of an independent Premier League, although at this stage it remained a secret. Kelly and Parry based their case on the promise of fewer games for the top clubs and players and better preparation for the England team. Both of these arguments relied on a clear commitment to reduce the new league to 18 clubs.

They also cited stronger commercial prospects, improved development of young players, recognised qualifications for managers and, above all, an end to turf wars between the new league and the FA. The Big Five representatives formally committed themselves to a breakaway from the Football League at a meeting in the Everton boardroom. They were quickly joined by Norwich City, Aston Villa and Manchester City. The Premier League plan was made public in a press release on April 5. It caused a media storm, but three days later, with minimum fuss, the FA Council threw out the Football League master-plan and endorsed Kelly's outline blueprint, including the Premier League. However, it left two key issues open: the number of clubs in the new league and the number of seats they would hold on the FA Council. The meeting set aside the Football League regulation requiring three years' notice to quit.

On April 30, the FA's executive committee heard Fynn give an upbeat assessment of the new league's commercial prospects. Based on analysis by Saatchi & Saatchi's research company, Zenith Media, Fynn suggested that total income could rise to £112 million in their first season — assuming a single television deal for all the key football properties, the new league, the FA Cup and England internationals. Fynn received no gratitude and his estimate, particularly on merchandising, was attacked by several present, largely for personal reasons. He received no support from Kelly. Notwithstanding the attacks, Fynn's figure of £112 million became established and was used regularly thereafter in the media to attack the new league.

The Football League continued to bluster against the Premier League and to threaten legal action to frustrate its formation, but more and more First Division clubs signed up for it. In May, Bert Millichip met all the First Division clubs and made a fatal concession — they could determine the eventual size of the Premier League. This undermined a fundamental premise of the new league — the reduction to 18 clubs. Many years later Parry would recount the crucial meeting to me:

> The Premier League was the idea of the then Big Five. But if the Big Five had launched the new league, none of the other clubs would have trusted them. It was agreed that the FA would take the lead and incorporate it into its new blueprint for the English game. At that first meeting, the FA plan was unveiled: 18 clubs in the top division instead of 22, blank Saturdays before an international to help England. One of the club chairmen, Ron Noades or Ken Bates, said, "OK, we can understand the rationale for 18 clubs but is there any scope for compromise?" Sir Bert just said, "Oh, it's your league. You decide." He said this within the first five minutes of the

very first meeting at Lancaster Gate held to discuss the formation of the Premier League. If Sir Bert had said, "No, this is non-negotiable. It's 18 or nothing and you have got to do this and that for the sake of the England team," would the clubs have agreed? Probably. Without the FA's approval, the Premier League could not have been formed.

Bert had lived up to his nickname of "Bert the Inert" and undermined a fundamental premise of the league — the reduction to 18 clubs. Rick Parry was quick to realise the implications: the smaller clubs, not the bigger ones, still less the FA, would become the dominant force in the new league. Kelly did not fight for 18 clubs. Although he still had no formal status beyond being a hired consultant, Parry was becoming more influential than Kelly, his patron.

Long before the Premier League had come into being, or given Parry any kind of post, he was actively exploring new television opportunities. On May 14, 1991, with Kelly, he met Sam Chisholm and his deputies, David Hill and Roger Moody. A note by him records Chisholm saying: "BBC/ITV should be very worried about us — and are!" Parry himself was looking for a £25 million deal (there was no mention of Kelly's ambitions). Parry saw no merit in the terms of the 1988 BSB deal — "put together by amateurs". Two days later he sent a memo to Kelly on the current state of television negotiations. The BBC wanted no more than a highlights package, Dyke wanted an exclusive deal worth £19 million for 25 live matches (including a pledge of £1 million for a pay-TV venture), and BSkyB had held out a range of figures, starting at a basic £25 million non-exclusive deal for 25 live matches. Parry's memo urged Kelly to "look creatively at timing of matches. Follow NFL example." He imagined a share-out among terrestrial broadcasters: BBC highlights on Saturday, ITV a live match on Sunday and BSkyB 25 live matches on Monday evening. He concluded with a warning: "Dyke may play dirty!"

On June 20, the FA published the final version of Kelly's blueprint. It was a comprehensive document with 84 proposals (some virtually identical to the Football League's discarded master-plan), mostly covering worthy matters such as better coaching structures for young players, research directed at improving standards of refereeing, a new international sports institute, and implementation of the National Plan for Stadia. The blueprint annoyed the PFA and the newly formed Football Supporters' Association, who claimed that they had been ignored. All of these issues were completely eclipsed in media coverage and public reaction by the formation of the Premier League and Fynn's estimates of its commercial value.

The new league would start in season 1992–93 with 22 clubs and be reduced to 18 by 1996–97. The second and third divisions would have 24 each, with promotion and relegation at each level, including promotion from the Conference. The blueprint suggested that the lower reaches and the Conference might be regionalised. All Premier League clubs would have to meet certain financial and accounting standards, and to provide seating for at least 20,000 spectators.

One of the many might-have-beens of English football was a plan for a second division of the breakaway Premier League. Ron Noades of Crystal Palace was its main advocate. He told me:

> The Premier League didn't think that the Football League clubs would be that interested, but I had said that I could get a Second Division of 18 clubs for Division Two of the Premier League, so that we would end up with two divisions breaking off. They really didn't believe that I could do that and I said, "Give me seven days to get all of the clubs in Division Two (as it was at that time)." I think I got 17 clubs to say that they would resign from the Football League and join a Second Division of the Premier League. The ones I couldn't get were the likes of Port Vale and Grimsby. In other words, the very minor ones that would see themselves not in the 18. I had 24 to contact, or 22 — I can't quite remember — and I was about five short and they were all the ones that knew they wouldn't be in the 18 that were selected.

Noades believed that two divisions would have given the Premier League far more bargaining power against television:

> The clubs always felt that the four divisions held us back and we all shared TV revenue. So we thought that two divisions breaking away could schedule soccer on television completely. We wouldn't be in danger of Rochdale vs. Aldershot being shown against one of our matches and reducing viewing figures, or anything like that.

Had such a change taken place then, the financial problems that have plagued the old Football League could have been considerably reduced. But this illustrated how little faith the rest of football had in the Premier League. Nobody in the wider football world could see it succeeding or even desired such an outcome.

By the time that the FA blueprint appeared, all the First Division clubs were onside and the Football League's resistance crumbled. On July 31, it lost its legal challenge in the High Court. The PFA grudgingly withdrew its threats to strike (although they were to revive later in a dispute over television receipts). The Football League capitulated, in exchange for compensation worth £3 million, half of what it had initially demanded.

The Premier League came into formal existence by stages: a founder members' agreement on July 17, 1991, notice of withdrawal from the Football League, a tripartite agreement on September 23, 1991, between the FA, Division One and the Football League, and finally, on February 23, 1992, acceptance of the blueprint. The founder members were Arsenal; Aston Villa; Chelsea; Coventry City; Crystal Palace; Everton; Leeds United; Luton Town; Liverpool; Manchester City; Manchester United; Norwich City; Nottingham Forest; Notts County; Oldham Athletic; Queen's Park Rangers; Sheffield United; Sheffield Wednesday; Southampton; Tottenham Hotspur; West Ham United; Wimbledon. (West Ham, Notts County and Luton were relegated in the last season of the First Division, to be replaced in the first season of the Premier League by promoted Blackburn, Middlesbrough and Ipswich Town.)

At each stage the clubs and the FA had to resolve disputes over the governance of the new league. The result, in every case, was to establish the autonomy of the league and its members at the expense of the FA and its objectives.

The commitment to 18 clubs was abandoned. Instead the league gave itself a target of 1997 to reduce itself from 22 to 20.

The league would have no FA directors. It would have only a two-man board: Parry, the acting chief executive, and the part-time chairman Sir John Quinton. He was chairman of Barclays Bank, which had sponsored English football during its dark days in the 1980s. In an astute manoeuvre, Ken Bates ensured that it would have no permanent committees (which might be dominated by the Big Five). Instead all decisions were to be taken by the full membership, one club-one vote, with a two-thirds majority.

Finally, the Premier League rejected Fynn's proposal for joint negotiation of TV rights. After years of developing the commercial case for the league in embryo, he was frozen out when it was finally born. The Premier League would sell its own rights when the ITV deal expired in 1992 — and the task was entrusted to Parry and Quinton.

On August 9, 2011, Sky Television screened a documentary to celebrate its capture of the televised rights to matches in the newly established English Premier League. It drew together memories from winners and losers. Here is Vic Wakeling, Sky's innovative sports producer: "Just before the Premier League breakaway, Sky had covered, live for the very first time, England's cricket team in the West Indies. It convinced Rupert Murdoch and Sam Chisholm that live was going to be very, very important... And the Premier League was a marvellous opportunity. Sport was, as Rupert has often been quoted as saying, the battering ram."

David Dein of Arsenal said: "ITV thought they should win it because they were the incumbent and, at the last minute, BSkyB trumped them, they just hit the table with more money." Vic Wakeling confirmed this: "Sam Chisholm virtually said, how much do you need and you've got it."

Rick Parry, the Premier League's chief executive, and negotiator of the epochal deal, declared: "I never tried to envisage what this might become or what it might look like. I was always absolutely convinced this was unlocking potential which would enable English football to be at the very pinnacle of club football."

Former FA executive Lee Walker believed that the deal "was a 100 per cent good thing. I don't think we could have done that with 92 clubs. We couldn't have moved on into the global capacity that Premier League clubs have now got."

Martin Edwards, the former Manchester United chairman, said: "I cast my vote, which was obviously for ITV, and we lost that. But who could say it was a bad thing now? It's been a phenomenal ride with Sky." He added: "Barely anyone could have seen how successful the Premier League was going to be." His judgment was echoed by Greg Dyke: "No one could have known that this would become the pre-eminent league in the world. No one could have known that the television rights would have become worth a fortune everywhere. I mean, you've only got to go on holiday anywhere in the world and you can watch more Premier League football than you can in this country. You can watch virtually every game."

Parry, Edwards and Dyke may have been genuinely surprised at the scale of the Premier League's success. But they, and all the other protagonists caught up in the drama of the deal, knew that television was going to shape its character and its destiny. Naturally, for the competing broadcasters this aspect of the deal was less important than its implications for the British broadcast landscape. But both Dyke and his successful rival Chisholm genuinely thought that each of their networks had something distinctive to offer English football.

For the football clubs, the main priority in making a deal was to exploit the rare opportunity of a competitive seller's market for their product and generate the massive revenues they needed for survival after Hillsborough. But the more far-seeing club chairmen — and their negotiator Rick Parry — saw possibilities in satellite television to own and exploit new sources of revenue, create new relationships with customers, and control the coverage and presentation of football. As Parry wrestled with the conflicting interests and egos of club chairmen, he realised that a dedicated satellite channel would give the new league and its administrators control over the clubs. Like American football teams, they would become part of a single commercial franchise — and unable to survive independently.

In the run-up to the deal, the football interests were offered two proposals to create their own Premier League channel. One, from a production company called Full Time Communications, never advanced very far, largely because it was based on coverage of all English football matches, including the FA Cup, England internationals, the residual Football League and other assorted cup competitions. Parry and his new employers were never prepared to bundle up their new and hard-won rights in this way. The other proposal, from the Swiss Banking Corporation, was a serious contender until a very late stage. Parry's archive shows the strength of his attraction to a dedicated Premier League channel and its promise of new riches through pay-per-view. One can view the story of the deal as the story of a mirage — Parry driving his caravan of football clubs towards an oasis of a pay-per-view channel that was never there.

In the end, Parry settled for a conventional sale of television rights. The proceeds were incomparably higher than any previous sales, but Parry obtained no share of BSkyB's subscription income — made possible only by the inclusion of Premier League football — and he made no headway on pay-per-view. Nor did he fulfil his objective of controlling the coverage and presentation of English football. As it happened, BSkyB did an excellent job for him in showcasing English football and winning it new spectators on the screen and at grounds, but this was all achieved on the broadcaster's terms and in pursuit of its own interests.

After the deal, English football became much richer, much more fashionable, much more sought after by commercial and media interests, and far more self-confident. The clubs spent a great deal more money on must-have items (especially footballers and managers) to achieve success among their peer group. But all this was achieved in a state of dependency on revenues from television coverage in the control of others. English football after the BSkyB deal behaved like a teenager with an indulgent parent.

And what a parent.

In November 1990, Britain's competing satellite services merged into one: BSkyB. Merger was a polite term: it was effectively a hostile takeover by Rupert Murdoch. It gave him a monopoly operation with nearly two million cable and satellite subscribers, and, as already noted, a package of rights in English football (in alliance with the BBC).

But Murdoch also inherited enormous problems. The merged entity was losing £14 million a week: one board member, Frank Barlow, representing

Pearson, a major shareholder, was seriously concerned that it was trading while insolvent, an imprisonable offence. In January 1991, Murdoch agreed with his bankers a restructuring of $8.2 billion of debt, in which he promised not to prop up BSkyB with funds from his major companies, News Corp and News International. The new chief executive, Sam Chisholm, launched a cost-cutting exercise, which shocked victims and observers with its abrasive speed, scale and style . In April BSkyB made a new call on its shareholders. All through the first half of 1991, Chisholm and Murdoch worked furiously to resolve two urgent problems arising from the merger. One was a series of cripplingly expensive movie deals, a legacy of the competitive war between Sky and BSB. The other was the threat of legal action from manufacturers and retailers stuck with unsellable BSB "squarials". Both problems were addressed, and Hollywood insiders were amazed at Chisholm's ability to beat down the major studios.

By June 1991, BSkyB was already contemplating greater involvement in football. It took an essential preparatory step when Murdoch rang Alan Sugar, the chairman of Amstrad, supplier of BSkyB satellite dishes. He urged Sugar to back Terry Venables' bid for Tottenham Hotspur against "that fat c**t Maxwell". Sugar had never been interested in running a football club but his interests were aligned with Murdoch's. Through Sugar, Murdoch could see off Maxwell, whom he still regarded as a major competitor and a permanent barrier to his expansion into football (Maxwell's dramatic death and exposure were only weeks away). Murdoch did not want to acquire Tottenham Hotspur himself, which would give rise to a conflict of interest when and if BSkyB bid for television rights to the Premier League. Sugar at Tottenham Hotspur would be an ally, if not a proxy. Sugar agreed to support Venables and on the night of the takeover to complete the deal, even lent him the £3 million Venables needed as the Tottenham manager did not have the money. It was another 10 days before Venables repaid Sugar. The Venables-Sugar "partnership of equals" managed to acquire Tottenham Hotspur on June 22.

By the end of 1991, BSkyB was far more stable. It had over 1.8 million subscribers via satellite and another 430,000 on cable, principally taking the movie services. But it was still losing £1.5 million a week on revenues of £330 million, and accumulated debt was still nearly £2 billion with rising interest charges. Murdoch and Chisholm badly needed new subscribers (three million represented breakeven) and new income. They considered buying the programmes of Thames Television, a company due to leave the ITV system by the end of 1992. That would have given BSkyB established favourites such as *The Bill* and *This Is Your Life*. Murdoch thought the price too high. That left Chisholm with three familiar options.

It was established in the television industry that viewers were prepared to pay extra for only three types of programme: pornography, major movies and sport. The first raised too many problems. Having just extricated itself from high-priced movie deals, BSkyB was in no position to go back to the movie companies. Sport offered much better prospects. BSkyB had done well from cricket and rugby league and had already groomed new talent on its football coverage. The new Premier League was an obvious target. The clubs concerned might be losing spectators on the pitch but they still had a huge loyal following of families viewing at home — highly attractive to advertisers. Chisholm could also sense a vulnerable competitor. He knew that ITV was unpopular with the smaller clubs who made up the majority of the new league and that all clubs were unhappy at being forced to play matches at 5pm on Sunday. He also thought that ITV's coverage had become dreary and complacent. He had an existing alliance with the BBC and he knew that the BBC had long given up on the idea of mounting an independent bid for live coverage of big league matches. It was simply unaffordable, and the BBC's ambitions were limited to the restoration of *Match Of The Day* on Saturday evenings, which Dyke had casually extinguished in 1988.

Above all, Chisholm knew that the Premier League's new management team, Parry and Quinton, wanted a serious competitor to ITV in the negotiations for a new contract. Having just done battle with top movie bosses, he probably felt confident Parry and Quinton had no experience of television.

Parry's ability to negotiate with the television companies worried David Dein. Dein persuaded the Premier League clubs to set up a television working party consisting of himself, Ron Noades and Bill Fotherby of Leeds United. It met on October 10, 1991, and recommended the sale of a shared package almost identical to the one proposed by the discarded Alex Fynn: one live game on terrestrial television, one on satellite, one highlights programme and one weekly promotional magazine-type programme on terrestrial. Parry's growing self-confidence is indicated by his note on a working dinner: "Lots of dirt on Dein... Alex Fynn is complete disaster... Rubbish proposal by Dein (kids put it together) on satellite channel."

Antipathy to Dein allowed the working party to die of inertia and the Premier League clubs decided to leave Parry and Quinton in sole charge of the negotiations, with the right to appoint their own specialist advisers. That did not prevent rival club chairmen from meeting competing broadcasters on their own.

Dein held informal talks with his personal friend Greg Dyke, which he felt entitled to do as a courtesy to the incumbent contract holder. Over dinner at London Weekend Television's headquarters, Dyke offered bait to the Big Five clubs. They would each get £1 million per year for four seasons in exchange for exclusive live rights to their home matches. On their acceptance, the same offer would be made to the next five, and then to the five below that. There would be a live match on ITV every Sunday at 4pm.

Meanwhile, Dein's rivals, Ron Noades and Ken Bates, flew to Manchester to talk to BSkyB. This was followed by a meeting at Murdoch's apartment in London's exclusive St James district, a deliberately flattering location normally reserved for elite visitors. However, contrary to some published accounts, Murdoch was not there himself and there was no serving of champagne and smoked salmon. I have an account of the meeting from Ron Noades. He and Bates were joined by another director of Crystal Palace, Bernie Coleman. He had become an expert in selling sports rights to television as chairman of the English Test and County Cricket Board's marketing committee, and had negotiated the latest television contract for domestic cricket. Noades remembers a meeting of 10 people — he and Coleman and Bates representing football and a BSkyB team headed by "the little guy — Sam Chisholm".

At that stage, BSkyB were bidding only for one competition — the Football League Cup. "We thought about that and said, 'Why buy a competition, why not buy the whole of football?' So they set up a meeting in Chesterfield Street to discuss what we were talking about. Ken and I went in and Ken may have said he wanted £50 million but we wanted £25 million for the whole of football. They were a bit knocked back. I'm pretty sure we started at 50 but we wanted 25. Ken and I knew what we were going to do. We were like two fingers wrapped round each other. We trusted one another."

Whatever figure Bates mentioned, the Chesterfield Street meeting brought no immediate result. A Parry note of a meeting with BSkyB on November 27 records: "Shambles. Noades/Bates at cross purposes — ludicrous ideas from Hill!" Bates simply aimed to break ITV's monopoly, but Noades thought that the real end game was pay-per-view. For BSkyB, David Hill thought there was far too much football: the season should be greatly truncated like the American NFL (evidently, these were his "ludicrous ideas"). Parry noted: "The long-term strategy MUST be to retain MUCH greater control of OUR product, instead of maximising short-term cash. As short-term objectives, the next deal should aim for consistent coverage each week, spread between channels and mixing live matches with deferred coverage." He would insist on the inclusion of a magazine programme.

Besides seeing Dyke, Dein pursued a revolutionary proposal from Chris Akers at the Swiss Banking Corporation (he would later run Caspian, the owners of Leeds United). Akers offered the Premier League a channel of its own, beamed from the same Astra satellite used by BSkyB. Assuming broadcasts of at least one live Premier League match every day of the week except Thursday, and a total of 32 each month, Akers envisaged profits of up to £50 million for the Premier League in its first season. Dein was impressed and passed the proposal to Parry. He too was impressed and went on talking to the SBC team until April the following year, only weeks before the final deal. Parry even hoped that ITV and BSkyB would support the concept of a Premier League satellite channel, although this would mean that each of them would abandon control of the most valuable broadcasting property in English television. The problem for Parry in the SBC proposal was the need for the Premier League to guarantee £20 million each year. The cost and risk were too high for the infant league and its members and Parry reluctantly abandoned the SBC proposal.

Apart from SBC, Parry had a more daring proposal for a Premier League channel from an obscure (to him) outfit called Full Time Communications (FTC). It had been worked up by Gerald O'Connell, who had pioneered the Clubcall telephone service (which offered fans a dedicated number for information about their clubs) and the Sportscast broadcast service, available in pubs and betting shops. Alex Fynn's associate Lynton Guest (who had once played keyboards for the manufactured boy band Love Affair) discovered Sportscast by accident in a pub, and it led him to seek out O'Connell and advise his company. FTC proposed a subscription channel at £10 a month, which would allow fans to see every single Premier League and Football League game — recorded in full. It would therefore not compete with live football. FTC estimated a take-up of one million homes, generating revenues of up to £100 million in its first year. It ought to have been a tempting offer — non-exclusive and making no demand for live games. But it never gained momentum. Parry was uncertain about FTC's funding (which was his pretext for not pursuing it) but the biggest obstacle was sharing coverage with the Football League. Guest set up a Christmas meeting (over mince pies) between FTC and Graham Kelly, but by now Kelly had no influence on the television negotiations and he could only refer FTC to Parry.

On December 30, 1991, Parry wrote himself a preparatory note for a meeting with Paul Doherty of ITV. "Arguments should be: they get first choice (if we give it), willing to take less money per game." But 32 matches might be too many, and there should be no saturation coverage which would depress viewing figures. "Dyke may walk away and come back. DON'T be confrontational — dangle BSkyB but don't hit them over the head with it." He thought that a Premier League pay-TV station could be a good rival for BSkyB but worried about its expense. He concluded: "Best solution is an all-sports channel."

Immediately on returning to work in the new year, Parry sent a briefing note to Quinton for their forthcoming meeting with Jonathan Martin of the BBC and Brian Barwick, editor of *Sportsnight* and *Match Of The Day*. Accurately he said that BBC's top priority was the restoration of *Match Of The Day* to its traditional Saturday evening slot and that it might negotiate separately with the FA. Parry said that he had no fear of a return of the ITV/BBC cartel, although he suggested (inaccurately) that the BBC was unhappy with its current alliance with BSkyB. He himself favoured the restoration of *Match Of The Day* and thought that the BBC might bid £5 million for the relevant rights.

The next day he sent Quinton a note which reveals another might-have-been in English football. "Met Venables — very keen on own TV station. Been talking to Bernie Coleman!!!! Can be up and running in three years."

On January 6, Parry briefed Quinton for a crucial meeting the next day with Greg Dyke and Trevor East of ITV.

He emphasised that he and Quinton were to take sole charge of all Premier League negotiations with ITV. The FA would negotiate separately but in tandem. They should resist exclusivity. He described Dyke (whom Quinton had never met) as "an aggressive wheeler-dealer, not a programme maker". His brief was to fight off satellite television, and if given the opportunity he would be ruthless in picking off selected clubs.

Parry gave Quinton a new breakdown of the current ITV bid: £16.5 million a season for 25 Premier League matches, a pledge of £1 million for a joint venture on pay-TV, £4 million from a joint sponsorship deal and a £2.5 million guarantee against overseas sales. ITV were looking for a real partnership with the Premier League, but through an exclusive deal, or certainly one shutting out BSkyB. Parry himself favoured a deal with ITV because BBC was too poor to buy live football and BSkyB had too small an audience for sponsors. But he thought ITV should be ready to pay £25 million to £30 million for live football rights (which compared very favourably to Continental European rates) and he wanted better match selection.

At the meeting the next day, Dyke emphasised his hostility to BSkyB, who would use football to drive dish sales. If the Premier League wanted ITV to partner BSkyB it would affect the ITV offer, but not if the BBC were a chosen partner. He said that ITV was already paying too much for football: ITV would bid what it could afford in a new deal and would not be talked above it.

At the meeting, Dyke and East suggested that since Barclays were already carrying billions of BSkyB global debt, Quinton should be reluctant to award the satellite broadcaster a contract which would force them to increase their borrowing. This was a curious and dangerous argument: as BSkyB's banker he would know that broadcasting Premier League football was their best, if not only, chance of repaying their debts. (No one in the whole bidding drama seems to have called upon Quinton to recuse himself as an interested party — another apparent oversight from the ITV team.)

Far from dissuading Murdoch, Quinton gave him lunch and urged him to bid. Murdoch himself recalled: "He said that we should bid, because they wanted to make sure there was competition for the rights. But the real work was being done by Sam [Chisholm], who was talking the money, and David Hill [Chisholm's deputy, who had worked, like him, for Kerry Packer], who was telling them all the great things we would do with the broadcasts."

Chisholm saw Quinton and heard a vital message about the rules for the bidding. there were none. Quinton told him. "There is a knock 'em down, drag 'em out negotiation, and the last man standing is the one who wins." It was a formula ideally suited to Chisholm's negotiating style. It also concentrated power in Parry's hands. With no rules of procedure, he was free to negotiate as he saw fit and present the bids to the clubs as he saw fit. Above all, he could arrange for a vote on his own motion. He had the future of English football in his hands — but he had no formal status until December when the new league got around to appointing him its acting chief executive.

Unlike ITV, BSkyB realised the pivotal role of Parry. In retrospect, Chisholm said simply: "We dealt with Parry. Parry was the guy we put our money on." With a loser's bitterness, Dyke later wrote: "Parry had fallen in love with Murdoch. He was a little man from Manchester who got wooed by Murdoch. It was not the first time that had happened." He claimed that Parry told him later that Murdoch was "the most impressive man he had ever met".

In spite of their helpful conversations with Quinton, it was by no means certain, in January 1992, that Murdoch and Chisholm would bid. The major shareholders, especially Barlow of Pearson, urged Chisholm to do so. He recalls: "All of Sky was basically Australian, and I'm not sure they realised the importance of soccer in the UK [at the time]. I remember Sam saying, 'We may not be able to afford the Premier League.' I said, 'If you are going to have a sports channel in the UK, you have got to have the Premier League.' I think if we hadn't got it, the chances are [BSkyB] would have failed again."

Before committing himself to an independent bid, Murdoch asked Chisholm to sound out Dyke about making a joint offer with ITV. The two men met at the then fashionable Langan's Brasserie in London. Dyke still thought ITV was certain to win and had little time for Chisholm or his offer. Later he wrote: "Chisholm was an overweight, mouthy Australian who had been brought up as one of Kerry Packer's henchmen and styled himself on Packer. He had been brought in by Murdoch to save the company. Over lunch he was pretty blunt. He told me that Rupert Murdoch had approved what he was about to say. 'Mr Dyke, why don't we get together to fuck these football clubs?'" There is also a politer version. Dyke was dismissive. He agreed only to think about the idea and agreed to get back to Chisholm in a few days. When Chisholm called him a few days later, Dyke was still thinking. Chisholm decided to wait no longer.

It was another of English football's great might-have-beens. Dyke passed up the chance to re-impose the television cartel against football. The rebuff induced Chisholm to invite the BBC to join the BSkyB bid, exploiting the Corporation's limited resources and its dream of reviving *Match Of The Day*. Its director-general John Birt expressed its position with uncharacteristic clarity: "The technology allows, for the first time, rights holders — soccer, movies, whatever, to extract more of the value of their product from the consumer. And the simple strategic analysis showed that it was impossible for the BBC to follow that. Our alternative strategy was to recognise that some of those sports would inevitably go to sports subscription services, and that's the process which will continue in the future. We needed a strategy to protect the licence payer's interests. What was it? It was to see high-quality recorded sport, in the case of soccer. So we thought we served the licence fee payer's interest by negotiating to maintain *Match Of The Day*."

Throughout the bidding war, there was an extraordinary reverence for *Match Of The Day*, which helped BSkyB. In an interview with me, Parry himself said: "I'd grown up with *The Duchess of Duke Street, Kojak, Match Of The Day*. That was Saturday night entertainment. *Match Of The Day* for me was always an institution. For me, you could not have contemplated going over to satellite-only coverage. That would have been untenable, but the balance of live on satellite with a comprehensive highlights package on terrestrial was an excellent mix. We were negotiating anyway with the BBC, kind of unilaterally right from the start."

Meanwhile, on January 10 the Swiss Banking Corporation put their proposal to Quinton by letter. They suggested that ITV's current television coverage of English football was inadequate. The present system of auctioning rights every four years left England's football authorities powerless when the auction was over. SBC therefore proposed the formation of a new company, including the Premier League, to acquire all broadcasting rights and exploit them. It would be adequately capitalised to guarantee the Premier League an improved annual return, with the expectation of further profits through its residual rights in the company.

An internal SBC memorandum dated January 13, which appears in Parry's papers, fleshes out the SBC proposals and suggests the arguments it put to the

Premier League. SBC was assembling a consortium to establish a dedicated football channel. It would broadcast throughout the year for a minimum of six hours on weekdays and a maximum of 12 hours on Saturday and Sunday. There would be at least three live matches each week of the football season, to be scrambled (therefore for subscribers only). The company intended to raise £50 million in equity and debt, and expected an appetising annual IRR (internal rate of return) above 30 per cent. This was based on a Henley Centre forecast that 10 per cent of all households would be able to receive the new Soccer Channel in August 1992, rising to 25 per cent by 1996. Among these households, the centre forecast a 44 per cent subscription rate in August 1992, rising to 56 per cent in 1996. It would use an established distribution system (established at BSkyB's expense) and generate revenue from a mix of subscription and pay per view, together with on-screen advertising, sponsorship, sale of rights, licensing and merchandising — and that took no account of likely broadcast sales overseas.

On January 28, a "state of play" memo from Parry to Quinton gave his response to the SBC proposal. By his calculations it offered the Premier League £35 million a year over four years, plus a 20 per cent equity stake. He suggested that the Premier League could get as much from established broadcasters with less risk, and recommended holding off on the dedicated channel concept for three years, when it would be just as attractive. However, 10 days later he urged Quinton to keep options open for the SBC proposals.

The January 28 memo had a more urgent issue to consider — the renewed threat of a players' strike.

The PFA leader, Gordon Taylor, who had reluctantly acquiesced to the breakaway of the Premier League, could see the prospect of a massive increase in income from television. He resolved to reassert his union's dormant claim to 10 per cent of television revenue. Parry resisted the claim. He was determined not to allow the PFA to become a party to the television negotiations. A PFA share of 10 per cent would give them more than the Football League and they would probably divert the revenues intended for players' insurance and education towards paying players' wages in cash-strapped lower division clubs. Quinton tried to confront Taylor, but he misjudged the public mood. People were much more sympathetic to professional footballers (in an era before wages went insane) than they were to other groups of strikers — and they certainly preferred the players to the "greedy" Premier League chairmen. In February 1992, Taylor won a strike ballot of his union members by the overwhelming margin of 548 to 37. Parry and Quinton, supported by the always vocal Ken Bates, wanted to maintain a hard line, but Martin Edwards, Doug Ellis and other club chairmen knew that a strike could wreck the new league before it had started. They worked out a compromise which gave Taylor almost everything he wanted: 10 per cent of the first £10 million of television revenue, 5 per cent of the next £10 million, 2.5 per cent of the next slice and 5 per cent of all revenue above £30 million, and a minimum guarantee of £1.5 million.

Despite the strike threat, negotiations gathered momentum.

On February 11, Quinton had another lunch with Murdoch. He spelt out the Premier League's expectations from a new deal, and asked BSkyB to respond to all the possibilities — including a Premier League dedicated channel. This idea simply would not go away.

The following day, Dyke tried to pressure Parry and Quinton through a press leak that ITV were ready to offer the Premier League £20 million a year for a four-year exclusive deal. But Dyke's ambition to kill off BSkyB was fatally weakened by the attitude of the BBC. Although very much the minor partner, the BBC offered BSkyB status as a broadcaster and, more importantly, a far bigger audience for its share of any football package. These were vital assets for BSkyB with the club chairmen they had to win over.

On February 14, Parry briefed the club chairmen on the progress of negotiations. He expected the first round of formal bids in the coming week. He would judge them by their long-term benefits for English football, particularly the quality of television coverage and the creation of a football archive, as well as short-term cash, and the bids would take time to evaluate. He told the clubs that there were four would-be players in the television market. They could identify ITV, BBC and BSkyB but he did not tell them about SBC.

By March, Parry and Quinton had an idea of the bids they were likely to receive. However, they would be complex and not like-for-like in their elements. They decided to seek independent help in evaluating them. To Fynn's indignation, they ignored both his and Saatchi's expertise. Instead they called on the market research firm Academy (owned by Saatchi's rival Lowe Howard Spink) for advice on sponsorship potential and asked David Plowright, former chairman of Granada Television, to advise on the broadcasting issues. Fynn thought Plowright a bad choice, since he had had an acrimonious departure from an ITV company.

The so-far-spurned FTC then followed Dyke in leaking their proposal to the media. The reporters placed its lifetime value at £500 million, an eye-watering figure when set against ITV's £20 million a year. But they now discovered Parry's doubts about their funding. (In fact it was guaranteed by members of the Saudi royal family, but FTC could not make this public in time to influence Parry and Quinton.) They also discovered that Parry would not be party to a deal with the Football League. Although the FTC bid foundered, it made Parry aware that he could get better offers from the competing broadcasters.

On March 12, SBC wrote to Parry, warning him against a short-term sale of rights to BSkyB before setting up a dedicated football channel. "In a deal with BSkyB, Football (*sic*) — SBC regularly used this term to mean any football authority — will inevitably cede some, or indeed all, control over distribution, and in this context merely controlling production would not be beneficial." SBC had taken note of Parry's view that the time was not right to broadcast football exclusively by satellite. They were therefore modifying their original proposal for a company to acquire all Premier League rights. Instead, they were working towards a dedicated Astra-transmitted subscription football channel, jointly owned by Football and a consortium of investors. For three years, ITV, BSkyB and the BBC would broadcast roughly the same amount of football as currently. Then the new football channel would become the exclusive broadcaster of live football, to the maximum allowed by UK or EU competition law. Football would own 50 per cent of the channel at its inception, rising to 75 per cent after five years. They cited new Henley Centre forecasts of two million subscribers by 1995–96, generating income of £100 million by 1997–98.

On the same day Parry briefly noted an unsatisfactory meeting with Sam Chisholm: "Enthusiastic but indecisive. No figures mentioned!... Does NOT like football channel. Sees football on sub channel with other sports. On Swiss Bank proposals, 'people will NOT [pay] £10 per month for wall-to-wall football!' Will match ITV + pay-per-view possibilities. Wants RP to go to LA to meet Rupert! Formal bid within 14 days."

Sam Chisholm made his new offer with the BBC in tow: for the first time it promised the restoration of *Match Of The Day* on Saturday nights. Chisholm also held out the temptation of pay-per-view to Parry. As a first step, he suggested that if BSkyB got the Premier League contract it would shift its sports coverage to subscription. (Until then its revenues had derived entirely from conventional sales of advertising.)

Throughout March and April, BSkyB used a programme inherited from BSB to win influence and gather intelligence. *Footballer's Football* offered viewers gossip and insights from insiders in the game. In the critical weeks, BSkyB made a point of inviting club chairmen in both camps as contributors, including Bates, Noades, Dein and Edwards. The producer Vic Wakeling recalled: "Of course they were led away and had a couple of drinks and they would tell us what they thought was going on." Trevor East warned Dyke that this was giving ITV a problem. ITV prepared to make a fall-back bid for the residual Football League, offering Trevor Phillips an exclusive deal worth £6 million a year. Meanwhile, Trevor East continued to talk to Parry. Later he claimed that on April 13, 1992, Parry promised him his support for the ITV bid. Parry was still tempted by the SBC bid and invited ITV to be part of its proposal, but Dyke was hostile to all satellite ventures, not only Murdoch's. He offered only to send an ITV representative to a working party.

In April, East had two crucial meetings with Parry whose content would be greatly disputed. On April 13, he offered Parry a new increased ITV bid. At £30 million a year, it would top the current joint offer from BSkyB and the BBC. By then, East was confident that ITV enjoyed the support of 11 club chairmen. To them and Parry he attacked BSkyB for its limited audience. Parry made no substantive response. He did not want to commit himself and he had not yet given up on the SBC proposal. Twelve days of silence ensued, and then the two met again in a bar in Manchester before a Chris Eubank boxing bout. That meeting left East highly encouraged, at least on his own account. Parry told East that his rivals would have to come up with £100 million a year to beat his new offer. East had been worried that ITV's bid was underpriced in its early years, but Parry said this was not a problem and that he would support the ITV bid. According to East, he and Parry shook hands on it. He certainly felt confident enough to disappear on a two-week family holiday.

Parry's true state of mind was revealed in a memo to Quinton on April 23, entitled "What Has Happened?"

He laid the current ITV and BSkyB/BBC bids side by side and pronounced: "While both are interesting, neither is satisfactory and we are not yet in a position to simply choose one or the other." He rated ITV's combined offer at £32 million a year: £18 million from ITV for 30 live matches, £4 million from European satellite rights with Screensport and ESPN (most under existing contracts) and a perimeter advertising deal with Dorna worth £10 million. He assessed the rival bid at £39.5 million a year: £25 million from BSkyB for 60 live matches, £4.5 million from the BBC for *Match Of The Day*, and £10 million from sponsorship through IMG. He was especially disappointed that BSkyB had shown no interest in a joint venture on subscription TV, and proposed to keep all subscription income generated by Premier League football to themselves (this was prophetic). The clubs would not like 60 live matches and the smaller BSkyB audience would hit sponsorship income.

He was still attracted by the idea of a football channel, especially since SBC had modified their approach and suggested that it could sit alongside terrestrial football for three years. He warned Quinton that ITV was lobbying individual clubs and that others had responded positively to SBC's approach. He now favoured making a non-exclusive deal with ITV if they would end resistance to subscription television. That would allow the Premier League to set up a consortium to develop the subscription-based football channel, with the ultimate possibility of buying up the full rights to Premier League matches.

In fact, Parry was hoping that BSkyB would raise their offer. They did so, although their new figure of £200 million over four years included hypothetical income from sponsorship and overseas sales, and some even more speculative income from pay-per-view. BSkyB's direct commitment was lifted to £30 million a year.

Parry fixed May 18 for the club chairmen to meet and vote on the bids. The vote would be taken on his recommendation rather than on each bid side by side. At this point, Parry ruled out the SBC and FTC bids: he did not tell them about the May 18 meeting and that their proposals would not be put to the club chairmen.

BSkyB intensified their lobbying of Parry. They took him to see their state-of-the-art subscription management facilities at Livingston (a go-ahead new town in Scotland), which impressed him. He then had a personal meeting with Rupert Murdoch, who guaranteed the full backing of his newspapers to promote the Premier League if BSkyB won the deal. Parry warned Dyke that he was ready to switch his support to BSkyB, especially since it was now allied to the BBC. Dyke angered Parry by threatening to repeat his tactics of 1988 and doing a deal directly with the clubs.

On May 14, the two sides made a formal presentation to club chairmen at White's Hotel in London. Chisholm showed them an enticing video of Sky's pay-TV deal with rugby league in Australia. It had made the sport so rich that it could afford to invite Tina Turner to sing in a stadium. He also hinted that BSkyB might increase its current bid.

Dyke was now seriously alarmed. In the weekend before the vote by the club chairmen on May 18, Dyke hauled East away from his family holiday. They spent Sunday May 17 on the telephone at Dyke's home in Twickenham, inducing ITV companies to increase the value of the ITV bid. By the small hours, they had managed to raise it to £155 million over five years, based on showing 30 live games a season. Dyke added in income from overseas sales and sponsorship to raise the estimated total lifetime value of the bid to £262 million. East was to present this directly to each club chairman, and Parry, in the lobby of the Royal Lancaster hotel, before they met in the conference room.

At daybreak on May 18, Chisholm was nervous. He rang Parry and asked if he had heard anything. Nothing, said Parry, but he would stay in touch. When he received his copy of the new ITV bid he read it quickly, realised that it would just top BSkyB's offer, and rang Chisholm to warn him and urge him to bid higher. He agreed to delay the clubs' meeting and the vote. Chisholm held an emergency meeting with the company's advisers, Arthur Andersen, who advised him not to match ITV. He ignored them. Chisholm woke Rupert Murdoch in New York in the small hours and secured authority to raise BSkyB's offer. It would now be worth £35 million in the first year, for 60 live games, rising to nearly £40 million in the fifth year. Throwing in the revenues from the BBC, projected overseas sales and anticipated sponsorship generated a headline figure of £304 million, which was never actually reached. He pulled Parry out of the meeting and gave him the new offer over the telephone and by fax.

Waiting in the hotel lobby, East had a series of unnerving experiences. He was surprised to see Alan Sugar dart out of the meeting and head for a hotel telephone. He heard Sugar talking to someone about the ITV bid and urging the other party to "blow them out of the water". (Sugar claimed he was talking to his girlfriend, but latter admitted it was Chisholm.) Worse still was encountering the Nottingham Forest representative. Instead of sending their chairman, Fred Reach, regarded as an ITV loyalist, they sent their commercial director, Paul White, who had been given no briefing from the club. East gave him a frantic 30-second briefing (wasting some precious moments on expletives) on the content of ITV's new bid. Then Terry Venables walked into the lobby, late for the meeting, and East complained to him about Sugar's behaviour: Venables shrugged.

Parry returned with the new BSkyB offer and recommended accepting it. He began by listing the three satellite options: SBC's original go-it-alone dedicated football channel; SBC's modified proposal, with a football channel owned by a consortium; or falling in with BSkyB. He said that it would be too risky to challenge BSkyB since it had such a huge lead in encryption and subscription management systems (all those tours of Livingston had paid off). Moreover, BSkyB was offering the Premier League a partnership to exploit pay-TV, and would split future net pay-per-view revenues 50–50.

He explained the headline figure of £304 million over five years. BSkyB would pay £191.5 million in that period for 60 live matches a year, initially £35 million, rising to £39.5 million in the final year. The BBC would pay £22.5 million over five years for *Match Of The Day*, overseas sales would total £40 million and there was a guarantee of £50 million from sponsorship through IMG. Over the five years, it was worth £41 million more than the latest total bid from ITV, who had offered nothing on subscription services and revived a threat to pick off the big clubs. Among other reasons for favouring BSkyB, Parry listed "the personal commitment of Rupert Murdoch, backed by the credibility of News International". Neither the Liverpool representative nor anyone else mentioned *The Sun's* Hillsborough coverage.

In the lengthy debate that followed, Parry and Quinton both knocked down arguments against BSkyB, mostly from Manchester United, Everton, Arsenal and Liverpool. The threat to sponsorship income from reduced television audiences was not an issue, they suggested, because many clubs were locked into existing contracts. They cited research to disprove the claim that 60 live televised matches would be saturation and promised there would not be too many unpopular Monday matches.

From Parry's notes, and other accounts, no one in the room suggested that it was unfair to low-income fans to make them pay more to watch football on television — an argument which has convulsed cricket ever since major match coverage moved to satellite.

The club chairmen split three ways. Dein, Edwards, Ellis and Peter Robinson (replacing Noel White as Liverpool's representative) were still in the ITV camp. Sam Hammam of Wimbledon favoured instant acceptance of the new BSkyB bid but other small clubs wanted more time to examine the two bids in detail. Dein put this argument forcefully, complaining that the new BSkyB bid had appeared on a scrap of paper and was backed only by Parry's word. Sugar made a key intervention: only BSkyB could deliver pay-per-view.

Dein tried to get Sugar disqualified from the vote as an interested party, since his company supplied BSkyB dishes. He was alone: the meeting voted against him by 20 to 1. The writing was on the wall for ITV. Sugar's role generates controversy to this day, but Ron Noades told me: "I don't think Sugar bought Tottenham to help Sky. The only thing is we're sitting in the room and we're all very conscious of the fact that Alan Sugar is making dishes for Sky. We all knew that. He didn't have to declare it." He added, candidly, that Sugar's participation "had to be all right because we knew that we couldn't win the vote without Tottenham Hotspur".

Parry's recommendation for BSkyB won the vote by 14 to 6. ITV's supporters were Arsenal, Manchester United, Liverpool, Everton, Leeds and Aston Villa. It was a revenge of the smaller clubs for 1988. There were two abstentions — still unrevealed. Alan Sugar cast Tottenham's vote in BSkyB's favour. Spurs had supported ITV in 1988. Their switch was decisive. Had they stayed with ITV, a 13–7 vote would have denied Parry's recommendation the two-thirds majority it needed under the rules which he himself had drafted.

After the vote, Parry asked all the disappointed parties to accept the verdict and allow him and the clubs to concentrate on the task of creating a successful Premier League. This pious hope was not fulfilled.

Greg Dyke went to court to frustrate the deal, claiming that Parry had acted unfairly by disclosing the terms of ITV's ultimate bid to BSkyB and not giving him a further chance to top Chisholm's winning offer. The entire procedure was irregular and arbitrary and each bid should have been presented and analysed in the same manner. He was unsuccessful: the court upheld the conduct of the bid. Dyke also campaigned against the BBC's conduct: by favouring and facilitating Murdoch's bid they had made an improper use of licence payers' money. (Dyke repeated this charge in his memoirs with a personal attack on the BBC chairman, Duke Hussey, as a friend of Murdoch.) Dyke took a more practical revenge on the BBC by programming aggressively against the restored *Match Of The Day*. Faced with Clint Eastwood and Arnold Schwarzenegger movies, the BBC's flagship programme lost most of its young male viewers. Saturday evening viewing was in general decline, as people found other forms of entertainment. The relaunched programme captured around four million viewers, compared to 12 million in its heyday.

ITV did pick up the rights to broadcast Football League matches — a consolation prize that meant so little to Dyke that it is not even mentioned in his memoirs. ITV also got a toehold in the Premier League by securing the rights to clubs' League Cup matches and the European matches of Leeds, Manchester United and Sheffield Wednesday. The FA, on the sidelines throughout the Premier League negotiations, fell in with the BSkyB-BBC alliance, selling England home internationals and the FA Cup in a four-year deal worth £75 million. Parry sold the radio rights to Premier League matches to BBC Radio 5 for just £65,000 a year.

SBC also threatened litigation, claiming that they were due a "success fee" from the Premier League for their work in devising proposals for the Football Channel, finding potential investors, and, not least, being used as a stalking horse to secure a better deal from BSKyB. This claim was settled out of court.

The disappointment of FTC in the failure of its proposals for a dedicated channel was to produce a more creative result. Its partner production company, Chrysalis Television, picked up the rights to show Italian Serie A matches on British television. On the terrestrial Channel Four, it acquired over two million viewers, comfortably beating BSkyB's first season Premier League audience.

As the new league prepared to kick off there was tremendous hostility between the small and big clubs and on September 13, 1992, with the league only weeks old I reported in *The Sunday Times* why at its birth the Premier League was split asunder:

> Born in acrimony and intrigue, the fledging Premier League remains hopelessly split. The latest example of the division between the clubs came last Monday when the league met to consider a sponsor. Eight clubs

— Arsenal, Manchester United, Liverpool, Everton, Aston Villa, Leeds, Nottingham Forest and Queen's Park Rangers — blocked a proposed £3 million deal with Bass put forward by Rick Parry, the Premier League's chief executive. Although the other 14 clubs voted for the deal, they could not get the two-thirds majority they needed. Amid acrimonious scenes, Ron Noades, the chairman of Crystal Palace and a leading proponent of the Bass deal, stormed out of the meeting.

I quoted one insider as telling me: "Monday's vote was a question of the biter getting bitten. This all dates back to May 18 when the smaller clubs voted for the BSkyB deal. The bigger ones did not like it then, they do not like it now and their vote against Bass was their way of getting their own back."

At one of the meetings of the clubs Parry had presented three possible sponsors — Lucozade, Bass, and Ford. Lucozade was ruled out because rival drinks manufacturers already sponsored clubs. Ford did not attract a single vote and Bass got nine. With many of the clubs having sponsored links to drinks and car companies, they favoured a neutral sponsor, a financial institution such as Barclays Bank or Cornhill Insurance. A proposal to that effect had attracted 11 votes. The eight opposed to Parry's proposal for Bass believed he had not tried hard enough to find a neutral sponsor. I went on to say:

> Their resentment against Parry has grown because they believe he has allowed BSkyB to have live television games on Sunday and Monday sponsored by Ford and Foster's for a combined fee of £3 million, none of which will go to the clubs.

So great was the bitterness with the 14 clubs due to meet at Tottenham a few days later, that Sam Hammam of Wimbledon even called on the FA to debar the eight from the Premier League, alleging that they were acting as a cartel, an allegation denied by the eight.

Feelings against the eight were so high that the previous day the Chelsea match programme carried a vituperative attack on the eight and on David Dein in particular by Ken Bates:

> The original concept was that an elite of English soccer would emerge following the line of the National Football League in the USA. There individual commercial negotiations are subservient to central commercial contracts which give a central negotiating arm far more strength and power to get the right terms for the individual members, the proceeds

of which are shared equally. It would appear that a small number of club chairmen, or in the case of Arsenal their vice-chairman, believe they have some God-given right to an advantage — an unfair advantage — over their fellow members.

Bates then made some further remarks which *The Sunday Times*' lawyers felt could not be repeated for legal reasons.

Amid this row, one proposal was made to return to the idea of an all-in-one sponsorship of the Premier League, the FA Cup and the England team. But that was never on. And although over the years the Premier League was often involved in strife, and the Bates-Dein battle continued for many years both at the Premier League and the FA, the league not only survived but prospered.

It had emerged at just the right time when the world of football and the world at large beyond football was changing. Nobody could have anticipated these changes but they helped this breakaway English football league, which had started very much as a child of the FA, become richer, more fashionable, much more sought after by commercial and media interests, and far more self-confident than its parent. Sir Dave Richards, the current chairman of the Premier League, believes that it is the original founders' agreement to share 50 per cent of television revenue equally between the clubs, and 50 per cent according to clubs' final league positions and number of television appearances, that has been the bedrock of the league's strength.

However, the clubs that were overjoyed to receive this television money proved to be far from wise spenders. Having started in 1992 with television revenue of £52 million a season and moved in 2012 to £1.2 billion, much of this went on players' wages. As the Premier League got ready to start its 20th season its accountants knew this spending on players was setting new, unwelcome records. Total wages across the Premier League that season rose by £201 million, 14 per cent, to almost £1.6 billion. This meant it consumed over 80 per cent of its £241 million increase in income. And what was more worrying, for the first time in the history of the league the crucial ratio of income to wages exceeded 70 per cent. Before the Premier League had started, clubs like Manchester United kept that ratio down to 50 per cent. United still managed that but many of their rivals chasing success did not and did not even want to. Just two years after the new league was formed, the man who had helped secure Sky the deal was sounding the alarm. As we have seen, Alan Sugar's call to Chisholm during the chairmen's meeting was crucial in getting Sky the deal. As I reminded him of that, he said:

Yeah, yeah, yeah, there wouldn't have been a Sky deal without that phone call. What I am saying now to the Premier League and to the FA is, drag as much money as you can out of the television people because they are commercial animals. The fatal error has been in distributing all that money to the clubs.

He then revealed that back in the 1993–94 season he proposed that only half the television money should be paid to the clubs:

I said to the league chairmen, do not give all of it to us. Please give us half. All it has meant is that the money has gone to Carlos Kickaball and slippery Giovanni, his agent. Clubs got £40 million a year and they spent every single penny on Carlos Kickaball Mk I. When that got increased to £150 million a year, what did we do? We spent every single penny on Carlos Kickaball Mk II. Did any one of those clubs keep any of that money? No. Did they even put themselves into more debt? Yes. We set the market pace here. We attracted the Carloses of the world to this country because we pay players £100,000 per week. Other countries don't do it, with the exception of a couple of anomalies in Barcelona and Real Madrid. So if you only released half of the money to the clubs then we would have had to set the limits at maybe £40,000 a week.

As for the argument that this would have prevented the Premier League becoming the world stage for football, Sugar responds: "Would we not have seen Drogba, or Cristiano Ronaldo or Michael Ballack here? I still say even releasing half the money, they would still be here."

The Sugar plan was for half the television money to go to a fighting fund managed by a Premier League Trust:

Let us say one season the clubs were being offered £150 million a year, and then £75 million goes into the Premier League Trust. The 20 clubs all get a point for that year. £75 million divided by 20, each club's point is worth £3.7 million. Every year you build up points like you build up air miles. Even if a club are relegated the points belong to them and can be used. But not for bloody players' wages. They are to be used for new pitches, new roofs, new stands, or to hire new physiotherapists.

And this money Sugar proposed would not have been paid directly to the clubs:

You want to build a new roof. The Premier League Trust say just tell the builders to send us the bill. We are not letting you get your dirty mitts on the money, because we're worried that you are going to spend it on players.

But, as Sugar sadly confesses, his plans met with derision:

It got laughed at. Terry Brown of West Ham said, "Oh don't be stupid Alan, it's our bloody money." Ken Bates of Chelsea said to me, "Don't be daft, don't tell me what to do with my bloody money." I said to Ken, "Ken, it's not your bloody money, don't you understand? Ken, if at the end of the season, you were able to say to me, my share of the fighting fund is £7 million, I would say you're a clever man and shake your hand. But what you're doing is, you're arguing with me at Tottenham Hotspur because you want to sign Carlos Kickaball, and so do I. So I'm in an auction with you and in the end I have pissed all my money up the wall and so have you.

Not surprisingly, players' union chief Gordon Taylor, whose members have benefited so much from playing in the Premier League, disagrees:

People say we must try and make sure too much money does not go out of the game to players; excuse me, maybe they go in fees to agents. If you weighed up Portsmouth's agent fees, they could pay the revenue of the club but players are the game. That's who people pay to watch. I'm not saying they could do it exclusively, I am not saying the players were the most important thing in a game but people pay to watch the players. We won't have professional football unless somebody is prepared to pay to watch them live ideally. Because television wants packed crowds. But you don't hear a film director saying, "We must make sure in the film industry that money doesn't go out of the industry to actors." You don't hear somebody say to a concert promoter, "We must make sure that money doesn't go out of our industry to the Elton Johns." But that's what people say sometimes at football. They think, never mind the players, let's get on with the game, and I'm saying, they don't pay to watch the directors, the agents, the bank managers.

But if the money was often wasted there can be little doubt that BSkyB fulfilled its promises to promote English football and present it in a new way, although Chisholm's initial efforts, featuring fireworks and dancing girls, attracted widespread derision. So did his efforts to change the rules, when he pleaded for bigger goals and lobbied FIFA to end the possibility of goalless draws. (He was especially worried that American viewers would not tolerate them in the 1994 World Cup in the USA.) But BSkyB quickly found their touch. As we shall see, its success was largely the work of one talented producer who had never wanted to work in television and had a burning desire to bring to English viewers the kind of coverage long enjoyed by American football fans, with many more cameras, greater use of slow-motion replays and articulate former players reborn as analysts.

In the run-up to the Premier League's first season, BSkyB staged a £5 million advertising campaign, centred on the promise "It's A Whole New Ball Game" and targeted especially at women and families. As I mentioned earlier, it also secured English football's biggest sponsorship package to date, worth £4.5 million over three years, from Ford Motors and Foster's lager (no one suggested that might be a dangerous combination).

Most dramatically of all, BSkyB put its Premier League coverage on to subscription and merged it with its other sports coverage. Viewers were given until the end of August to sign up to BSkyB's package at a discounted rate of £2.99 a month, after which the cost rose to £5.99 a month. Labour politicians and the Football Supporters' Association were outraged, but BSkyB quickly met its target of one million subscribers. Chisholm later remembered seeing sacks of mail filled with cheques at his company's headquarters: "It was absolutely unbelievable. It was like Christmas every day." Within a year, the company's losses had been transformed into an operating profit of £62 million. Subscription income made football profitable television on far smaller audiences than terrestrial broadcasters had achieved. It did not matter to Chisholm that only half a million watched his company's first televised live game between Nottingham Forest and Liverpool.

None of this income flowed into the Premier League and the eventual agreement between it and BSkyB, in August 1992, contained the stark clause 9.1: "For the avoidance of doubt, there shall be no obligation on BSkyB to introduce pay-per-view." So much for Parry's dream of a new stream of income for English football: the agreement left this dependent on the goodwill of BSkyB.

The new Premier League had put its fate in the hands of Rupert Murdoch's enterprise. BSkyB's money and talent gave it a dominant voice in English football issues great and small. So great was this control that Sky could also signal when matches should kick off. The Premier League agreement had a technical but highly symbolic clause 14 (b): "The kick-off for each half [of a broadcast match] shall be on a signal given by BSkyB."

PART 2

CHANGE FROM NEAR AND FAR

Chapter 4
THE OTHER SCOTSMAN

The story of the Premier League on the field is fundamentally the story of a Scotsman, the son of a Glasgow shipyard worker. Yet that man, Alex Ferguson, also played a key role in the rise of another Scot who led a revolution in the coverage of football on television. Unlike Ferguson who, as this book is being written, has no immediate intention to retire, Andy Melvin is just about ready to spend more time with his grandchildren. Yet but for Ferguson he might never have got involved with television in the first place.

The year is 1980 and Melvin has every reason to be happy in his life. He is working in his home town of Aberdeen for the local evening newspaper, the *Evening Express*, covering Aberdeen FC. His duties include working on the *Green Final* football paper, published every Saturday afternoon just after the final whistle. Ferguson, the Aberdeen manager, has smashed the age-old monopoly of Celtic and Rangers and is taking Aberdeen to new heights, including into Europe, and Melvin loves his work. As Melvin recalled to me:

> Alex and I butted heads until we developed a kind of mutual respect. We were both Scots, and feisty, but eventually we had a fantastic relationship. So much so, and it just shows how different things are then from now, I used to travel on the team bus. Can you imagine that in the 21st century? So, I would sit on the team bus from away games back to Aberdeen. Willie Miller and Alex McLeish would get sent into the chip shop and return to the bus with chips and fish and stuff, which we would eat on the way home. Dick Donald, the chairman, would have his trilby on the back of his head. It was lovely. He was a plain man but not an ordinary man and Aberdeen have never done anything since he died. Alex was a pall-bearer at his funeral. Those were fantastic days.

Then suddenly in 1980, Bob Patience, the sports editor at Scottish Television, rang and offered Melvin a job. "I thought to myself, why on earth do I want to go and work in television in Glasgow? Glasgow was a horrible place. Ibrox, Parkhead and Hampden Park — that was all Glasgow was to me. Little did I know, it's my favourite city in the world now. I told Bob, 'I ain't going to Glasgow. I'm not going to work in television. I've got the best job in the world, I follow Aberdeen Football Club, they are successful, and I am following them round Europe.'"

Not long after Melvin had turned down STV, his phone rang. It was Alex Ferguson and without any preliminaries Ferguson thundered:

"What the fuck are you doing?"
"What are you talking about?"
"You've been offered a job in telly, and why are you not going?"
"Well, I've got a great job, I love it here, you know."
"You're only 28. You're young. You've got to be ambitious."
"Hang on, you were offered the Wolves job last year, you didn't take that."
"That's not being fucking ambitious, forget about that. You've got to take this job, you're young, you've got to be ambitious."

Reflecting on that call that changed his life, Melvin says: "You get an idea how he can win players over. He shouts and bullies you into things. So I went home and said to my missus, 'I tell you what, I think he's right, I think we should go.'"

But even as he made the decision to leave the world of print for television, Melvin was worried. "I changed my mind 10 times. Not about television, about leaving Aberdeen. For me it was no different to New York, or London — just smaller in a way. And I was worried about leaving a fantastic job."

Melvin was not to know it but he was leaving a medium that would soon be struggling for survival. The Saturday green'un, like the traditional pink'uns all over Britain, were dying off and although his old Aberdeen evening paper still exists we have reached the twilight of the written word for sports journalism. Television and the internet can bring the latest news to people so much faster. "All those Saturday papers have gone," reflects Melvin, "it's very sad, the whole world has changed. Why would you get a Saturday pink'un, or a green'un, or whatever, when you can sit and watch Jeff Stelling on Sky on a Saturday afternoon?"

Melvin soon realised that he did not want to be front of camera: "That's not the place to be in television. The real fun was behind the camera. So I became a producer/director and learned the TV business — but with journalism as my background, which is sadly lacking these days."

Roll on nine years and Melvin took a call that was to mark another huge change in his life. It was 1989 and the call came from Bryan Cowgill. "Ginger Cowgill was a guy who had invented stuff like *Grandstand,* the BBC's Saturday afternoon sports show. He was a god." An innovator of sport on television, he had also long held the idea that the ideal time for live football on TV would be on a Sunday at about 6pm. Cowgill's first question to Melvin was:

> "Have you heard about what's going on in satellite television?" I said, "Yeah, kind of." He said, "Will you come down to London for a chat?" I said, "With respect, Mr Cowgill, you don't know anything about me." He said, "I know everything about you." I thought, "Oh shit." I flew down to London on a hot day, and met Bryan Cowgill at the offices of the sports and media group IMG in Kew.

Cowgill told Melvin he was setting up a dedicated sports channel that IMG had been commissioned to run for the newly established satellite broadcaster, British Satellite Broadcasting. But when Cowgill offered Melvin the chance to be "part of a satellite revolution in sport", the Scot's initial thought was, "A sports channel? That's not going to work. I was 39 and had a young family, two young boys. I was happy in Glasgow — loved it."

As they were talking Cowgill opened a drawer and took out a contract which he put in front of Melvin. For all his misgivings Melvin agreed to sign but could not help thinking: "Fuck, this is a leap of faith."

His STV colleagues, including his best friend Dermot McQuarrie, thought he had lost his marbles. "They told me, 'You're mad, you're walking out on a job for life.'" But Melvin felt he had a chance to be in at the start of something and a gut feeling that this was right. Within a year, McQuarrie and many others were to be sacked by STV in a cost-cutting exercise. McQuarrie would eventually find a home with Fox Television in Los Angeles but as Melvin points out: "As I went to work for BSB, they were no longer on air at STV."

Cowgill had recruited a man with a passionate desire to rescue televised sport from what he saw as the ghetto where it had long been confined:

> I was always aware that televised sport was a poor relation in television terms. It was seen as unimportant by the loveys who ran television at the time. We had to duck and dive around *News at Ten, Wogan* and *Coronation Street,* and all that sort of stuff. We knew our place. People

were fed rubbish in sport. I remember one year watching the Ryder Cup and being told we have to interrupt the golf coverage to go to the 2.30 at Kempton Park. A live football match, and there weren't many, used to go on air and go straight to the kick-off, get to the final whistle and then off air. We were always aware that the public were being short-changed.

What made this impossible to bear was that, "Living in Glasgow for 10 years I knew football is the opiate and sport was too important to be treated in this way."

At STV, Melvin had introduced some technical changes to the traditional BBC way of covering football and he is most proud of having got permission for seven cameras to show the Scottish Cup final. "I was dancing round my office, thinking I'd really got a result. But while I directed the Scottish Cup final I knew it was shit. We needed more cameras, better camera positions, better video recording, and replays, and commentary. But there was no budget."

Now sitting in Cowgill's office, having accepted the job of launching a dedicated sports channel, Melvin made another key decision:

As I sat in his office Bryan said to me, "Now we need a top analyst, who's going to move football forward. Do you think we should get Ian St John?" I said, "No, because for a start, Ian St John is synonymous with ITV. We need someone who's played the game recently, who can talk about players that he's actually played against. We should get Andy Gray." Bryan asked, "Do you think we can get him?" And I said, "Hang on a sec." I sat in front of Bryan Cowgill, got my book out and rang Andy Gray.

Gray, a tough centre forward with 22 Scotland caps, was at home. Having won two English First Division titles with Everton, he had fulfilled his boyhood dream of playing for Rangers and his 10 goals had helped the club, managed by Graeme Souness, win yet another Scottish title. But satisfied as Gray felt about this, the club had released him and he was wondering what to do next. At 33 he was aware his knees weren't going to hold out much longer.

Melvin asked him: "What are you doing?" When Gray replied: "Nothing," Melvin said: "Just answer yes or no — do you fancy a career in television?" Gray paused for five seconds before saying "Yes". Soon afterwards, the two met in the bar of a hotel near Heathrow.

I don't know what Andy was earning in football when he quit. But we offered him £50,000 a year, which was a lot of money then and Andy Gray was skint. He leapt at the chance and became our football analyst.

But there were huge problems in building the new sports channel. BSB had had technical difficulties just getting on air. There was so little for Gray to do that when he rang to say he had been offered a chance to play for non-League Cheltenham Town as a centre half by a friend who was managing the club, Melvin let him go back to football. And even when BSB went on air they could show very few live games. BSB had failed to get the rights to the old Football League and as Melvin recalls: "We had a bit of Scottish football, a bit of rugby league — I mean, literally, bits and pieces — a bit of the Zenith Data Systems windscreen-wiper shield, whatever." So when Ron Atkinson wanted Gray to become his assistant at Aston Villa, Melvin said: "Yeah, as long as you can still do bits for us, go and do it. He did a year with Villa and then realised he couldn't combine both. He had to choose and he said, 'I want to do TV — I don't want to go into football management'. And we said, great."

BSB, run by Anthony Simonds-Gooding, appeared at first to have all the right ideas and state-of-the-art technology. The problem, as Melvin soon realised, was that "it was run by a load of foppish people in pinstripe suits and BMWs who liked having long lunches". And they fatally underestimated a rival satellite broadcaster. This was Rupert Murdoch's Sky which, like BSB, also boasted a dedicated sports channel called Eurosport. "Rupert's men were street fighters and they got on air first."

However, with both channels losing money the logical solution was a merger which, as Melvin admits, "was a takeover but called a merger. Rupert had realised that the two of us couldn't survive. Sky got rid of Eurosport and the only thing from BSB that Sky took was our sports channel. So we all moved from Chiswick out to Isleworth, which was then a building site. BSkyB was born, but we were losing £14 million a week."

As we have seen, in May 1992 BSkyB won the rights to cover the new Premier League, or as Melvin puts it, "Rupert and Sam [Chisholm] took all the chips, put them all on black, and said, right, spin the wheel — and bought the Premier League." A few days after the dramatic bidding process at the Royal Lancaster Hotel, Melvin, then still based in Scotland, got a call from BSkyB's director of sport David Hill, who now runs Fox Sports in Los Angeles. "All he said was, 'We've got it, you better get down here.' And I went, 'Phew, shit — we're on air in August.' I had a house in a lovely part of Glasgow, kids at school and all that. But he insisted, 'You've got to come down here.'"

Hill had summoned Melvin to a production meeting and as Melvin flew into Heathrow from Glasgow he was ready for a fight. "I went into his office thinking to myself, 'Hang on, I've got this fucking Australian who's going to tell me about how to make football programmes. Right — I'll tell him about production, he's not going to tell me.'"

Melvin was all too aware of Hill's reputation. He had worked for Kerry Packer in Australia and been responsible for many of the television innovations that had marked Packer's World Series Cricket. Some were very welcome, such as having cameras at both ends of the ground so that the viewer always saw the game from behind the bowler's arm. But others were controversial. Players abandoned their traditional whites for coloured clothing. And when a batsman was out for a duck, a cartoon duck was super-imposed on the screen to accompany him on his slow trudge back to the pavilion.

As Melvin walked into Hill's office in Isleworth, the Australian shut the door, reached into his drawer and took out a sheet of paper. "Hilly's very much one for the theatricals, he loves an audience and he loves a stage. And he said to me, 'There you are.' I took this bit of paper and I said, 'David, this is a blank sheet of paper.' He said, 'Exactly, just make it fucking good.' I said, 'Great.' And I thought, 'Wow, first of all, that is man-management — that is how to motivate people — and second what an opportunity to re-invent the wheel.' Think about it. This is in May. And we are on air in August. I decided, right, first of all, we've got to continue the work we started two years ago with BSB."

For Melvin this meant getting the best out of Gray, whom he calls "one of the most intelligent guys that I've known." Given what has happened to Gray since, with his ousting from Sky in 2011 for sexist comments, this may seem highly questionable. We shall look at the events that led to Gray's dramatic fall later but Melvin insists he has no reason to alter his opinion of his fellow Scot, who in the last 20 years was to become his closest friend and whose sacking by Sky he has found very difficult to accept:

When David Hill told me to re-invent the wheel after BySkyB got the Premier League, of all the people who were an inspiration, Andy Gray was the greatest. I can't think of any one person who made a greater contribution to the success of Sky. Not Sky Sports, the whole of Sky. People forget, 20 years ago, when we'd nothing, we were scrambling around trying to make a name for ourselves, what he contributed was far more than anyone else. Andy Gray has made more of an impact on televised sport in ways that people will never understand. When people hear what I am saying they will go, "Ah, don't be silly, you're just another Scot who doesn't understand." But Andy gave us so much. You learned more about football sitting down with him over a few beers than most journalists and TV people who think they know football will ever know.

And he inspired everyone around him, as he did when he was a player. Andy Gray and I worked so closely together, hand-in-glove. In talking with him, which I did all the time, by squeezing him and draining him dry of all his knowledge, I realised how we should mould this new football coverage for the Premier League.

This would lead to one of the major innovations in the televised coverage of football:

Andy Gray and I were drinking beer in a bar in Heathrow, which is something we continued to do for the next 20-odd years. He'd be drinking Rolling Rock, and I was drinking Sandy ale. There I am asking him questions about football endlessly and he just wants to talk about football or women. The empty bottles are lined up on the table in front of us and Andy moves them round to illustrate moves in football as we're talking about the sweeper system, or a flat back four, or whatever. I'm aware that we're getting loud and there are people watching and listening. Next day he called me or I called him, and we said, this is what needs to happen in football coverage. We need to give the public some depth, and substance. So I started a programme called *The Boot Room* in the very first year of the Premier League.

The programme, which had conscious echoes of the Anfield Boot Room, was very simple in concept.

We had a couple of flats with boots hanging up — there was a hamper with a Subbuteo table, and Subbuteo men. Each week we would get a guest, an ex-player, or a current player, or a current manager, to sit next to Andy. They would just move the Subbuteo men around and talk about football. And everyone's going, "Fucking hell."

The original programme ran at 7pm on a Thursday evening:

The week's matches had been played, we were analysing them and looking forward to the next set of matches. We had Andy Gray and Bobby Moore discussing how England won the World Cup in '66. Now for a football fan that is like feeling, "I have died and gone to heaven". Never been done. Why had it never been done? Because football and sport weren't given enough time on television — weren't given what they deserved.

Eventually we had Eric Cantona discussing French football, international football and by then we knew we had a very special talent in Andy Gray.

Now it looks very clunky but we used to get bits of videotape of matches and Andy would put the tape in a big video-machine, press play, and stop and start the video. It sounds so obvious now. But at the time it wasn't being done anywhere in the world.

The whole world got the idea from us. I remember Andy Gray and I went to Amsterdam for this exhibition of TV technology to see if there was any new technology out there that we could use for football analysis. Taking Andy there was like taking coals to Newcastle. As we walked through this exhibition of different TV companies from around the world they were all showing clips of... Andy Gray. Some of them were offering improved technology but they were all using him as their example. Does it sound pompous to say that football analysis around the world developed from us moving bottles around in a pub one night? But I think it did. When we moved those bottles that night both of us got the idea. We knew it was new. The public had been starved of this. I tried to give the public, sports fans, football fans, what they wanted, not what people thought they should have. When David Hill said, "Make it fucking good," I thought, "What we've got to do is make programmes that we want to make." Necessity is the mother of invention.

Gray himself recalls that Melvin had got the idea of a tactical analysis show from America but felt *The Boot Room* would only have a limited shelf life: "It was only meant to run for a year but it actually ran for about three years, and after that Andy [Melvin] thought it would be a great idea to bring that into the studio on a Monday night and make Monday a totally different show. Monday night football was born."

By the time the Thursday *Boot Room* show had become *Monday Night Football*, Melvin knew that his pairing of Gray with Martin Tyler — poached from ITV — had also forged a new style of commentary:

In the days of Kenneth Wolstenholme, Brian Moore and David Coleman, the commentator would simply talk and talk and talk. When he'd run out of the things to say, the colour man would come in and say something. We sat them together and I told them, "That's got to stop. You've got Andy Gray here: let's re-invent commentary. It's got to be a co-commentary. It's a conversation between two friends who are excited about football. Martin Tyler takes the play-by-play; Andy, you come and tell us things that we don't know. Don't tell me things I can see. I can see it was a shot that went three feet over the bar. Tell me why, how." Andy got that immediately. Each one knew his role and that's how it went.

Gray, who describes Melvin as his "great mentor", says Melvin allowed him to paint on a blank screen:

I had a fabulous board that was white, it was absolutely clean when I started and they went, "Go on, that's yours. Go and play with that." I was given things to do, machines to enjoy. Andy Melvin never gave me any training. I would go in on a Monday morning and he would say, "See this piece of machinery here?" I'd go, "Yeah, yeah." He says, "Well, you're using it tonight. Good luck." Andy thought I'd be a natural for some reason. If you've got time on television to develop ideas then it's fabulous. I never studied anywhere. From day one at Sky I was on open talkback with Richard [Keys, the presenter]. It means whatever's going on in the gallery I could hear. There wasn't silence in my ears. It was not keyed. A lot of people aren't on open talkback because it's difficult to take in. But I wanted to take it in because I wanted to learn. I never realised I was creating anything different.

The only instruction he received from Melvin before he and Tyler, with Keys in the studio, called the first live Premier League game, Nottingham Forest vs. Liverpool on August 16 1992, was:

He wanted Martin and me to be more American in our commentary style and not to wait to be invited in, as my old dad used to say. His only remit to me was, "Tell me something I don't know, tell me something I haven't seen." We could spend hours previewing the game, building it up and then spend another hour at the end analysing it all, which terrestrial stations couldn't. For the Nottingham Forest game our show lasted five hours.

At first Sky tried to get Gray and Keys to wear the sort of clothes they felt would work on television. "They used to give Richard these very bright jackets," recalls Gray, "but we soon got rid of them and started wearing our own clothes."

Sky has since been criticised for over-hyping matches. Melvin says: "We always try to accentuate the positive, of course, but I'd say our editorial integrity is sound. I remember watching a European Cup final — Red Star

Belgrade versus Olympique Marseille in the '80s — and the commentator kept telling me why this was a crap game: "Oh, this is terrible, Red Star Belgrade are playing for a draw, this is awful." He was virtually telling me to switch off. And I thought that's wrong. How to turn that round and accentuate the positive? We're not saying it's a good game but give the viewers something to hang on to here — why is it a bad game? What needs to change? What does the opposition have to do to break down this Red Star Belgrade team? So be positive, give the viewer something."

Melvin's desire to connect with the fans always made him wonder "how we could move it on". This led to bringing fans into the studio, which Melvin sees "as probably the first kind of social networking. We wanted to give fans a voice. Even back in 1992, we used to do vox-pops". He admits it also helped "fill the two hours of pre-game show". Fans in the studio lasted a few seasons before the 2011–12 season saw a new innovation. *Monday Night Football* was extended to 11pm and in the final hour Gary Neville, who has taken over Andy Gray's role, got involved in Twitter, which for Melvin is "a brave call, if you imagine some of the tweets".

It is also part of making a distinction between televised football on Sunday and that on Monday:

On *Monday Night Football* we try to make an analysis programme out of it and change it completely. A different kind of programme altogether. On a Sunday afternoon we still feel the best thing to do is go to the game. Make it an event, make it we're going to the game, that kind of feeling. We always say, you can't beat going to the game. If you can't go to the game, watch it on TV — but going to the game's important.

This creates something of a contradiction for television. They want huge numbers to watch their televised matches yet be able to report from matches with packed stadiums. So from the beginning, admits Melvin, "I gave instructions to cameras not to focus on empty stands. Absolutely right. I've often chastised directors for taking shots of empty stands."

Melvin feels wholly justified in this, arguing:

There aren't many empty stands in the Premier League. People said that live television will keep crowds down. That doesn't seem to be the case. The Premier League's able to attract the best players, thanks to money from TV all round the world, not just Sky money. And it seems to be working. I think football's in a better place now.

Along with this change in commentary tone came the decision to put in more cameras. Melvin, who thought Christmas had arrived early when he got seven cameras for a Scottish Cup final, had experimented with camera positions even before the start of the Premier League. The Zenith Data Systems had seen new camera positions behind the goal. Now the Premier League saw mini-cams:

> Nobody had heard of mini-cams — steady-cams, super-slow-mo and all these things. Suddenly the technological innovations were coming out of the woodwork, they were coming at us all the time, because we were now a vehicle for innovation.

Although Sky was losing money, BSkyB chief executive Sam Chisholm was willing to fund innovations. "Sam Chisholm," says Melvin, "had a rule that bills must not be paid unless there was red around it and the bailiffs at the door. Because there was no money. Fifty years earlier the mantra of people like Sam Goldwyn and Louis B. Mayer was, 'Save it everywhere else but put money on the screen.' And that's what Chisholm believed. He said save money everywhere — to increase the production budget."

Sky knew it had to make money from the Premier League and had set about it from the start. I had been a Sky subscriber before the advent of the Premier League and all I had to pay was just over £400 to get the Amstrad dish installed to watch Sky programmes. Within weeks of Sky securing the Premier League rights, I was told that to watch Sky Sports I would now have to pay £2 a month. Twenty years later the monthly subscription had risen to £70 and, as Murdoch foresaw, football has rescued his business and made his satellite station profitable. But from the start Chisholm allowed Melvin to have more cameras and bring in better technology and better screen graphics.

> I cannot remember how many cameras we had in the first match. In those days the stadiums were old and run-down, they were only just being redeveloped. So we put cameras where we could. We're thinking, you must never ever have a situation where you cannot tell if it was offside or not. You must have a camera on the 18-yard line. You must have a camera on the goal-line — was the ball over the line? You cannot leave the viewer wondering, "Oh, well, we'll never know."

When the Premier League started, Serie A in Italy was considered the most prestigious football league in the world and in Britain Channel 4 screened its matches on Sunday afternoons. Melvin studied their coverage and instinctively recoiled from it:

> They always put art before answers. If there was a great goal, or a controversial incident, they would rather show a replay of a player or manager's reaction than answer the question: was it offside? Was it a handball? We always put answers before art. There's always time for art later — answers come first. My mantra was always: what is the guy in the Horseshoe Bar in Glasgow saying about this game? The Horseshoe Bar is, probably, the best bar in the world. It's got loads of tellies and real football fans. I always think, we mustn't leave the guys in the Horseshoe Bar in Glasgow thinking, "Was that over the line? Was that a handball? Was he offside?" We've got to answer the questions.

But there was another decision which not everyone feels has benefited the game. From Sky's first televised match, Melvin decided there would be cameras concentrating on the dug-out and the managers:

> We always focused on the managers when the dug-out was facing our main cameras. Never before had television concentrated so much on managers and managers' reactions. Before Sky there were so few cameras, they had to stay focused on the pitch. Sometimes we've got cameras trained only on the managers because managers are part of it. You can say the game is an occasion, but there's more to the occasion than just the football.

This new focus soon caused trouble with Melvin's old friend, Alex Ferguson: "In that first year of the Premier League we had a camera on Ferguson at a Manchester United game. At that time this was very unusual. But it's part of the drama and the theatre of football."

The problem was with the drama that Ferguson was putting on that day:

> Fergie was rampaging up and down the touchline. He was making a fool of himself. He had his mad head on. He phoned me next day and said, "Right, you stitched me up last night." I said, "Hang on Alex, you were the one who was going mental up and down the touchline." "Oh no, you stitched me up — you're barred." That's something we've heard many times over the 20 years — Fergie saying you're barred. For him this was the ultimate sanction, he won't talk to you and he didn't talk to us. I said, "OK, fine, we're barred." So Fergie didn't speak to us for six months of the

first season. Imagine — the Manchester United team that was to win the title for the first time in 27 years.

Relations were restored the night Manchester United beat Blackburn Rovers and at the presentation of the trophy Melvin decided he would stay with the celebrations.

We were due off air at 10 o'clock or 10.30 and I said to our transmission: "Whatever's following us, drop it — we're staying on air." Because there was a party going on, and everyone was singing, we had shots of some including Matt Busby, singing *Always Look on the Bright Side of Life* — fantastic. The next day, I got another call saying, "Aye, I've just seen it. Yeah. This is Fergie. It was good. All right. All right. OK." So that was peace. You know what he's like.

Over the next 20 years Ferguson would regularly ban other media. His most famous was the ban on the BBC in response to a BBC documentary about his son's activities as an agent. The ban lasted several years and only ended in the 2011–12 season after a personal intervention by Mark Thompson, the BBC director-general. But despite this Ferguson and all the other managers have relished the focus on them as it has helped to create the cult of the manager. Sky's coverage has helped turn the manager into a celebrity, whose every action is judged to be as important and worthy of attention, if not more so than the players under their control.

When Pele described football as the beautiful game he meant the show put on inside the white lines. Over the years the coverage pioneered by Melvin at Sky has created a spectacle of not one football event but two, with the off-field action around managers, be it Jose Mourinho or Arsene Wenger, attracting as much attention if not more than the performances of Didier Drogba or Cristiano Ronaldo. The manager has become the message.

Not all managers are comfortable with this and one man who feels particularly vexed by it is England manager Roy Hodgson, formerly of West Bromwich Albion. When Arsenal played Udinese at home in the 2011–12 season, Hodgson was one of Sky's pundits. Wenger was serving a touchline ban and had to sit in the stand. For Sky the big question was, what was Wenger doing? Was he communicating with his players? Throughout the match Sky could not keep its cameras off Wenger and as Hodgson recalls:

Sky was more interested in Wenger than the field of play. I don't want to be seen as a dinosaur who says it was better in the old days. But the fact is football has changed, it has made celebrities and stars out of managers and coaches. Fifty years ago you did not see Spurs' manager Bill Nicholson very often unless you were a Tottenham supporter living in the Tottenham area. Otherwise you would have to wait for Charlie Buchan's Football Annual to come out at the end of the year to see what he looked like. I am sure in those days if a football manager moved out of his town he could walk down the street without being recognised. That would be impossible now. Television and the cult of celebrity has increased our role.

Hodgson is an atypical English manager, having enjoyed more success abroad than at home, a man who reads novelists such as Philip Roth and John Updike, goes to the opera and on Monday nights at 10 switches over to Sky Movies Indie to watch foreign films. However, when it comes to the game he is a strong traditionalist:

> The people who pay to watch football don't pay to watch coaches. More and more we are becoming celebrities and the camera is on us and our actions but really and truly that is not how it should be. When you go to a football match you should watch the performers. When I go to the opera I do not spend a lot of time looking at the orchestra conductor, I watch the singers on the stage.

The result of Sky's desire to turn a football match into an event is that even when the cameras are absent, you will see managers on the touchline performing as if they warranted as much attention as the players.

I became aware of this towards the end of the 2011 season during a match between Preston and Ipswich in the Championship. The most fascinating performer on show was the Preston manager Phil Brown, once of Hull. With an earpiece in his right ear he kept making what seemed like barking noises throughout the match. His barking had little effect on the players, they lost — indeed, they had already been relegated — but Brown was clearly putting on a display as if it was his show as much as his players'.

Hodgson confesses that he finds this focus on managers uncomfortable: "I am never happy when the television cameras are on me. When the game starts I am still naive enough, old-fashioned enough, to concentrate on every ball kicked. Some managers are more camera-conscious, but I am less camera-conscious."

He also shrewdly observes that some managers, such as Wenger, are not only more conscious of the cameras but they also prepare for the post-match press conferences:

Arsene says that sound bites after the game are very, very important. I am aware of that but I am more of a chancer. I do not prepare for interviews as well as I should. I let the questions come. If I were clever I would think more before I gave post-match interviews. That sound bite gets thrown out to the public and it also gets thrown out to your players. The sound bite is important to get your message across to the fans and also to your players.

Hodgson's Liverpool experience illustrates the trouble unguarded sound bites can cause. Some on the Kop will never forgive Hodgson for expressing his admiration for Sir Alex Ferguson, the *bete noire* of Liverpool fans.

But if the rise of the manager as celebrity is here to stay it imposes an obligation on managers. As Hodgson puts it, they must realise that they are not mere coaches of players but also leaders:

In my early years as a coach, I never gave leadership a thought. I only started giving some thought to the leadership side when I went to Malmö in 1985. I started being very successful and I got invitations from companies to give talks on how to create a winning team. Business wanted to use sporting models. It opened my eyes. It forced me to analyse what is important, what I believe in.

However, many managers seem to believe in nothing. They love the limelight but are not prepared to even consider that management also means accepting the responsibilities of leadership. Jose Mourinho does not willingly accept the obligations of leadership and the tragedy for modern football is that it is Mourinho and his ilk who set the standard for managers, not the likes of Roy Hodgson.

These changes in our perception of the game have occurred as Sky has fashioned its coverage of the Premier League. In that time the idea of going to a pub to watch football or any other sporting event also developed as a result of Sky's coverage. Sky made sure it was available in pubs from the moment the Premier League was launched. Melvin recalls:

Viewing of televised sport was common in American bars but unknown in this country. That is why we called it *Monday Night Football*, as they did in America. In the early days, if pubs had a Sky subscription, they could put it on. It was later when they realised there was a business here. But I remember having the debate, should we black it out in the pubs because here we are asking people to subscribe and then by having it in the pubs we're giving it away.

Over time the broadcasting chiefs realised the money to be made and introduced a special subscription for pubs, further boosting Sky's revenue streams.

By then innovations such as the post-match presentation of a bottle of champagne to the man of the match was seen as a key part of the game:

> We worked with our first sponsors, Carling, and came up with the idea. We never had much time to think about it, we just kind of worked on the hoof — we would move from stadium to stadium, and think on the road, sit in cars, in hotel bars and discuss it. It consumed us all. But it's wonderful when you start something from scratch. If you've got an open mind and you're a genuine fan — and most people at Sky are genuine fans — right from day one we wanted to make programmes that people would want to watch, that we would want to watch. In the television business nowadays, if people can't decide whether to have tea or coffee, they'll set up a focus group and then they'll send people out to do research. In the early days, Sam Chisholm used to say, "Go by your gut. If your gut isn't good enough, I'll find somebody whose gut is good enough." That concentrates your mind.

Sky's innovations have also involved taking ideas from radio and making them work on television. Back in the 1970s, LBC, a new commercial radio channel, had to devise a football programme while lacking the live commentary rights held by BBC Radio. LBC's solution was to have reporters phoning in from various grounds with updates on matches and have guests in the studio talking about football. In 1997 Sky launched an updated television version of that idea, presented by a man who had worked at LBC, Jeff Stelling:

> In those days BBC Radio broadcast a second-half commentary on a match. If you had no interest in the two teams involved, you switched off. Ever since then I have always thought that, for a Saturday afternoon programme to work, you must make it varied and interesting. People are always dipping in and out, they have different interests and you must make sure you have something interesting for everybody.

The programme was born out of necessity — a Saturday afternoon football show which cannot show any live action.

> At that time on a Saturday we cannot even show a blade of grass, let alone any live shots from the matches. People often say that it would be nice to

see the goals as they go in. But we cannot. Indeed we have to make sure
that, when we go to our reporters at the ground, we so position them in
front of the cameras that no part of the pitch can be seen.

The show features Stelling surrounded by ex-players such as Phil Thompson,
Charlie Nicholas, Matt Le Tissier and Paul Merson. Stelling's job is "to get the
footballers to air the sort of views that the punters want. If I criticised Steven
Gerrard, what weight can it carry? But if Phil Thompson, who like Gerrard has
lifted the European Cup, and is Liverpool through and through, does then that
makes it different."

Former players are often reluctant to be too critical of fellow professionals
but Stelling has never had any problems getting Thompson to express an
opinion. "Phil is the most opinionated man on football I have ever met. That
man could start a fight in a phone box. He is passionate and not afraid to
express an opinion." However, his allegiance to the Liverpool cause is such
that Stelling's producers have decided that Thompson had better not be asked
to comment on Liverpool matches: "If Liverpool are losing 4–0 to Fulham,
Thompson could still be expected to see some good in Liverpool. So now we
do not ask our four experts to comment on matches which involve their former
teams, making them act more as neutral observers."

Stelling's fellow journalists have long accepted that the programme's
penchant for show business is combined with a shrewd news sense, a
recognition reflected in the fact that, for five successive years, he has been voted
Sports Broadcaster of the Year, the sort of winning run any Premier League
club would covet.

Not that Sky has found it easy to get all its innovations accepted. *Monday
Night Football*, presented as an extension of the weekend, was poorly received
at first. And many clubs resented having to play on Monday nights. Liverpool
were one of the clubs who received an exemption, although Melvin denies any
deal was made not to show them. "Liverpool let it be known they would not
appreciate being on *Monday Night Football*. Because they had fans coming
from Ireland."

Sky's first Monday night match, Manchester City vs. QPR on August 17,
1992, replete with dancing girls, jugglers and fire-eaters, provoked much media
derision. Melvin notes:

That was an idea of David Hill's. Clever, actually, because even the cynics
were at least talking about us, even if only to say how stupid this is. And
we let fireworks off at the end. But that stopped, because one time at The

Dell in Southampton, fireworks were landing on a petrol station nearby. I was not worried about tradition-breaking. It was exciting. As David Hill said, people want more. People accused us of using gimmicks but there were gimmicks for a reason. I've never accepted the fact that what we put onscreen have been gimmicks, because everything we do, and everything we offered are analysis tools. I always say, is this a gimmick that contributes nothing, apart from, look how clever we are. Or is this something that can really contribute to the experience and enjoyment of the viewer? If it's the latter, then we explore it, see if it works. That's the difference between gimmick and something that works. I think that's important.

However the introduction of the Sky Striker pom-pom girls, a blatant imitation of American cheerleaders, proved one gimmick too many and lasted only one season.

Another of Hill's innovations came close to being scrapped only a few weeks after it was introduced:

One day David Hill came to me and Vic Wakeling [then head of Sky Sports] and said, "I've got to tell you, I've got this great idea." And we both went, "Fuck." David Hill was the kind of guy who got 100 ideas an hour — the most fertile brain in television, without a doubt. Still is. He's a genius. And I don't use that term lightly. Hilly's great idea was to take the score and the time and put it on the screen. I remember thinking, "Oh fuck — why have we not thought of that before?" It had never been done. Anywhere in the world. Can you believe it, only 20 years ago when you were watching football, you'd switch on and you didn't know who was playing, you didn't know the time, and you didn't know the score.

This was introduced for the Charity Shield, the traditional season opener. For this inaugural Premier League season it was between Leeds, the winner of the last First Division title, and Liverpool, the FA Cup winners. But for some fans used to the old ways the new information Sky provided was too much.

Within a few weeks, David Hill came and said, "I've got a problem. We're getting letters. People are complaining it's interfering with my enjoyment. Chisholm's told me to take it off the air. You have got to take that off the screen." I can't imagine who was complaining, no-one was watching, a few pubs and stuff like that. I remember saying to Hilly, "Please David — don't do it. Leave it." He said, "I'll give it another month." But game after game after game it stayed and, of course, once it's established, it's established. Other people started doing it and then that was it.

Some of the changes Sky introduced were down to the fact that they had, as Melvin admits, no alternative. Sky's live Sky afternoon match kicked off at 4pm but the programme started two hours beforehand:

> We had a pre-game show of two hours every Sunday. We came to the two-hour mark because we had got nothing else to fill it with and decided let's fill it with pre-game show. I was charged with the responsibility of filling this two hours and making it entertaining and it gave us an opportunity to create stars, create personalities of players who weren't household names.

With the Premier League having just been launched, players were not then the superstars that they have since become:

> Access was a lot easier then than it is now. It has become more difficult because they see us as part of the establishment now. But then players were interested in what we were doing. They saw something new. The huge explosion in their wage packets had not occurred. Now the modern players have never known anything else, so they take us for granted. It would be wonderful to have the sort of access that American reporters have, going into the dressing rooms. We've never asked to have it written in the contract because I don't think we should ever start waving contracts at each other. We should have a mutual understanding that it's in everyone's interest to promote the game of football. I'm not sure football has grasped that and we're not going to push it, we'd rather work on relationships.

In those early days, Sky also had developed a relationship with match officials and wanted to take it further:

> Twenty years ago we met with the two Premier League representatives who were running the referees and we said: "Look, we can do this for you. We could really make the Premier League so far ahead of everybody else, because of the advance in [stump] cameras [which were everywhere in cricket at the time]. We can put [stump] cameras in the goals — you'll never see them, you'll never feel them, but they're there and they will tell you if the ball's across the line or not."

Melvin recalls that Ken Ridden, the FA's director of referees, reacted as if he had been assaulted:

> He said, "Och, no." And then we said, "Right, OK, you don't want that, but we can do this: why don't you do what rugby does, and mike your referees? We understand why you wouldn't want to mike them straight on air, because you'll pick up too much bad language. Why don't you let the commentators get a feel of what they're saying, so that at least the commentator can explain to the viewer why you've made that decision?" And once again, absolutely flatly, "No. We're not ready for that." And they have not moved on.

If anything, as far as referees are concerned, the Premier League over the years have moved back.

> At the start of the Premier League, we could go into the referee's room and talk to the referee. We can't now. Some referees were becoming a bit too high-profile — I think it was Graham Poll who was becoming very high-profile. It was, funnily enough, the season that he quit that the Premier League said, "Right, that's it. No more talking to referees." Which is a pity.

Football's Luddite reaction to television has meant of all the major sports, football is the only one that does not use technology to help its officials on the field of play. Yet Sky uses technology relentlessly in its coverage, with the result that viewers see more of the game than the officials. This was to be vividly illustrated in the 2011–12 season when in Sky's main Sunday match Manchester City, then leading the Premier League, faced Tottenham at home. Tottenham at that stage had an outside chance of the title but their hopes of winning the league for the first time since 1961 were effectively ended when they lost 3–2.

The match, while not quite an English classic, had all the combination of skill and passion and the never-say-die attitude that makes English football so appealing. Tottenham, having gone 2–0 down, fought back to make it 2–2, and were within a toe-poke of scoring a third in injury time before a last-minute penalty won it for City. The Premier League could rightly have advertised the match as the sort of spectacle that few leagues in the world could produce.

Yet the major talking point was the incident the referee did not see and which proved a game-changer. The man who scored City's penalty, Mario Balotelli, had deliberately stamped his studs on Tottenham's Scott Parker. He should have been sent off long before he got the chance to score the winning goal. Millions watching round the world saw it. The one man who mattered did not: the referee. After the match, the referee, Howard Webb, admitted that had he seen the stamping he would have sent Balotelli off.

But while the referee did not have access to the video evidence the FA's disciplinary unit had and the Italian was banned for four matches. What is more, City accepted the verdict without protest. Immediately after the match City had gone into the classic three wise monkeys' act, which coaches and managers adopt when their players are accused of wrongdoing: "See no evil, hear no evil, speak no evil". But once the FA had acted, City fell quiet as if they accepted the justice of what had been done. The problem here was not only that justice had not been done, as the original mistake could not be corrected, but that television viewers saw and knew more about the game than the match officials. And this is now a regular occurrence in the game.

As Melvin puts it: "The Balotelli stamping incident was shown in a second. It would be very easy for a [fourth] official to tell the referee, 'This has happened'. What's the problem?"

Football's refusal to embrace technology means it is effectively forcing its own officials to admit they have not seen incidents which the world at large has seen. In other words they are being shown up as inadequate. If the resultant loss of respect for officials is not bad enough, this situation also causes spectators to focus not on the football but rather on the incidents that were missed and might have changed the game had they not been missed. The result is that players whose misdeeds have been missed make the headlines rather than those who sparkled on the field of play.

Melvin can argue with vehemence that Sky gave "gave football the opportunity to embrace the public. We helped the Premier League, we put it on the map. It is the most watched league in the world, and it is Sky's pictures that go all over the world."

But in so changing the landscape Melvin is also aware that many football fans have forgotten what the past was like. Until well into the 1980s, the only domestic game that was televised live was the FA Cup final. Live televised league football did emerge in that decade but only a small percentage of the games were covered and this remained the case in the early years of Sky's coverage. Today nearly a third of the Premier League schedule, 138 out of 380 games, are televised live on Sky and other channels and a perception has grown that it was ever thus. And this is upsetting for Melvin:

> Some representative from Hibs in the SPL, which is in a terrible state, wrote an article in the *Daily Record* saying the trouble is that television's

ruining the game up here because we're moving games around, and our attendances are down. And you go, hang on a second — first, your attendance is down because you're second bottom of the league — and when are you going to embrace the fact that football is no longer three o'clock on a Saturday afternoon. Children don't go up chimneys any more, and men don't go to football wearing flat caps, and have to stand there getting rained on. Times have changed. And it will never go back to the way it was. It's a team game, and the media is part of the team. What is professional sport? It doesn't cure cancer. It doesn't help the homeless. It doesn't solve hunger in Third World countries. Why should we take it so seriously? But sure, it binds people together socially, and it's fun. It's an entertainment. It fulfils no other function. These guys are song-and-dance men, they're entertainers. We should all just say, come on, let's stop getting too serious about it, shall we?

However, Sky could not ignore a serious issue which arose in January 2011 and which led to the departure of Gray and Keys. In creating this new world of televised football, had Sky failed to ensure it did not encourage the sort of behaviour that would be considered totally unacceptable in a modern workplace? Melvin is justified when he says: "We at Sky changed televised sport: the way people watch it, the analysis, the stats, the style of commentary, the style of presentation." Yet the series of incidents involving Gray and Keys suggested to many that certain attitudes may not have changed.

Before a Wolves-Liverpool match at Molineux, Gray was caught on camera making sexist remarks about the presence at the game of a female assistant referee, Sian Massey. He and Keys were also heard suggesting that Massey and other female assistant referees "didn't know the offside rule".

"It happened," Gray told me, "on a Saturday morning. I got a call on Monday from Andy just telling us, 'Don't come in today for *Monday Night Football.*'" Gray and Keys were also sent final warning letters but the feeling was that they would keep their jobs.

"The reason," says Melvin, "I said, 'Don't come in' was, let's see if we can just put a lid on this. Just don't give it any more fuel, let's just hope it goes away."

But it would not go away. More footage emerged of Gray making sexist remarks about Massey and also of an incident recorded a month earlier showing him making a suggestive comment to his colleague Charlotte Jackson followed by laughter from him and Keys. "It escalated," says Gray, "from there for some reason, I've no idea why."

The escalation meant Gray had to be sacked. Melvin recalls his crucial meeting with Barney Francis, who had taken over from Vic Wakeling as head of Sky Sports:

> Barney's a good guy, a caring guy, a young man with a future in Sky and just about one of the first things he had to do was when he was told he's got to sack Andy Gray. He came into my office, shut the door and he looked like a ghost. He says, "I've got to sack Andy." I said, "Barney, he's my mate, I'll do it. I'll call." He said, "No, as you often say to me, you reap what you sow. I wanted this job, I will accept the responsibility." So he went through to his office, he picked up the phone to Andy, and he told Andy I'm sorry, I've been told you've got to be sacked. The conversation lasted 20 seconds. I then picked up the phone to Andy and I heard his voice. And all he said to me is, "Wee man, don't worry about it, I've had 20 great years." And I couldn't talk. I was crying. It was horrible. It was three o'clock in the afternoon, I packed my bag, I left the office, I drove down to Chiswick, where I was living at the time, and I just went into the local pub and I ordered a glass of wine. I just sat there, absolutely dazed. My mind just went through all we'd achieved, all we'd done. I couldn't believe it would end like this. It was then I said to myself, it's time I was out of here. I was 58, and I thought, when I get to 60, I'm out and I'm 60 now and I'm going to retire next year. I am wrung out.

As deputy managing director and head of production, his time was spent in meetings and he had decided it was time to call it a day.

Sky announced that Gray had been sacked for "unacceptable and offensive behaviour".

The next day Keys met Francis and resigned.

Melvin accepts that his closest friend did not realise what was acceptable and what crossed the line:

> You know what's funny, Mihir? He's so intelligent. And he's no more a sexist than you and me, or a racist, or an anything-ist. But the amount of times I've sat him down in front of me and said, "It's got to stop." "What, what, what?" "You having jokes with the black guy, whatever. You can't do that." "Ah, we're just having fun. He gives as good as he gets." "That's not the point. You can't do that any more. Or the make-up girl — you can't keep talking to her like that." "Ah, but it's only fun." He never understood. For such a clever guy, he never understood the difference between fun and where it crosses the line.

Gray's defence of what he said about Massey is:

> This was a private bit of banter released to the social media and for some reason the press tore us apart. I have no problems with a woman referee. It wasn't a criticism, it was a light-hearted quip. I wish I'd never said it and, if I caused Sian any problems, then of course I'm terribly disappointed. Richard phoned her, apologised on our behalf and she said, "Don't be so stupid, guys."

As for Charlotte Jackson, Gray says:

> Again, it's probably an old man trying to be funny. It was no more than that. Charlotte knows us very well.
>
> For 17 years, my life was a dressing room and everyone who's been in a dressing room knows what kind of banter goes on. It's a place where you can get ripped apart at times by your fellow players. We had a dressing room at Sky where we wanted people to feel comfortable and we had conversations about many things. In 20 years in studios up and down the country I've heard people saying things off camera that would make your hair curl. I do not see myself as sexist. Not in a million years.

As proof he reveals that the rector of the church in Lower Slaughter in Gloucestershire for his third marriage recently was female. "Veronica [James] was fantastic and we had a lovely Church of England wedding. There you are."

What Gray is implying here is if he can accept female priests, which have caused such division in the church, how can he be sexist? His critics may argue that this is on a par with those who make racist remarks, and then add that some of their best friends are black.

For Gray the sacking meant the loss of a job, said to be worth £1.7 million a year. "My job affected so many other people. I've got lots of family and friends that I looked after financially because of what I earned. Overnight I couldn't look after them any more."

Until then Gray had always felt sure that he was in control of his life. "I'd always thought nothing would faze me." Now he was overwhelmed with doubt, "I was on the floor. I've never been like that in my life." When I asked him if he thought that was the end of his life, he says, "Yes."

So did he think of killing himself? The 56-year-old looked up and said: "I would be lying if I said I didn't." When I asked again, his blue eyes were crystal clear as he looked at me and said in a steady voice: "Yes."

Three weeks after he was sacked, Gray and Keys were hired by talkSPORT for a daily show. While this was for Gray "a lifeline", he added: "I had never felt like I have felt from January 25 onwards. I watch Sky every day so it's there in my face, in my home. I'm not one of those who take anything for granted. I used to wake up every day and say, 'Thank you Lord for this.' A bit of the joy has gone." The heaviness is all the more difficult to shift because Gray cannot accept that he is remotely sexist, despite what the camera showed.

With Sky's internal footage released to the world, the speculation was that Gray's dismissal might have been related to the phone-hacking scandal. Gray, whose phone was hacked, was then suing the *News of the World*, ironically on the advice of Francis and Melvin. Having settled with Sky — and also separately settled his phone-hacking case, all Gray can say is: "I'm not at liberty to criticise anybody or anything about Sky." What he is sure of is he could have done nothing to rescue his 20-year Sky career. "I think minds were made up."

When I put it to Melvin that, with internal Sky material being released, was there some sort of plot, he replied:

> Yes, there was. Richard Keys called it "dark forces". I can't argue with that. What upsets me is when it's your own people, people in your own company, doing these things. At the time of the Gray-Keys business, some of our own Sky staff were tweeting things that were just unbelievable. People whose jobs were there because of the talent of Andy Gray. It lets people be disloyal which I think is the worst thing. It was hard. What happened over Andy Gray and Richard Keys just shook me — that something so small can be blown up into something so big, with such great relish and enthusiasm. Therefore you should never underestimate the power of media.

Gray, who does not expect to get back into television, remains proud of the fact that he helped Sky create a new profession:

> Sky created a new profession of a sporting broadcaster when a footballer finishes. You look now at how many people are finishing playing football and either going into radio, television, to broadcast full time. They are not going into management because it's more fun doing the other one. That's what Sky has created, a new industry. I remember going in to see Hilly about a new contract. I'd had a good couple of years but I was still wet behind the ears so I went in very sheepishly to see David. He was in his office, door was always wide open, screaming "Aaarrrggghhh" in his Aussie brogue. I said, "Well, what about a little rise, David?" He went,

"Listen Andy, this is how it goes: right now there's not an industry. We don't have an industry. Where would you go if I said we don't want you? Nowhere because there's nowhere out there for you. One day we will be in an industry and you will hold the aces and if I'm here you can walk into my office and I'll give you whatever you want." That was just before the Premier League. And he was right and that's exactly what's happened. We've created an industry where ex-footballers now can go and earn huge amounts of money.

Gray himself was to benefit and when in the 1995–96 season he very nearly became manager of Everton, Sam Chisholm made him change his mind with "a fantastic offer — one that I couldn't turn down".

After Gray's dismissal by Sky, he was almost instantly replaced by Gary Neville, although Melvin denies this was a forced choice after Gray was sacked:

We pushed him very quickly into the role vacated by Andy Gray, but Gary Neville we had targeted. Gary Neville was selected before Andy Gray and Richard Keys were sacked. We recognised that he was intelligent, he was articulate, he has got all the medals and he's opinionated. We thought that's a good start — I wonder if he can be a broadcaster. So we threw him on air, as we do. We don't do pilots and stuff like that, we just say, "You're in it — if it works, it works." And he's been tremendously successful. He's a very smart guy, very self-deprecating. I think the first day he came into the office, he offered to go and get the teas for the lads. They went to the canteen, and he says, "Can I just have a chip butty?" and he just wanted to be one of the lads. Why wouldn't he be?

Roy Hodgson's arrival as England manager led to Neville's recruitment to his staff as a coach. But he made it clear he wanted to carry on as broadcaster, in effect sharing jobs as Andy Gray had done in the early days of televised football. But although many in the media, particularly ex-players, advised him he could not fulfil two roles, both Sky and Neville seemed certain this could be managed. It showed how far televised football, the England coaching set-up and the world of media had come in the 20 years since Melvin started planning his changes.

Chapter 5
THE UNEXPECTED EUROPEAN TWIST

On April 25, 2012, Real Madrid played Bayern Munich in the second semi-final of the season's Champions League. Chelsea, having beaten Barcelona, awaited the winners, but what made the match remarkable was that it was not only shown live on terrestrial television in Britain but the main evening news, *News at Ten*, was delayed for half an hour to accommodate the penalty shootout that decided the match. What is more, British viewers complained that for a brief moment ITV had switched away from the Bernabeu, home of Real Madrid, to highlight Mark Austin, the presenter of the news, only to find him adjusting the buttons of his jacket. To an extent it was a commentary on the nature and power of modern sport, its ability to go where politicians could not. The televising of the match and the interest in the Champions League occurred against a backdrop of serious questions being raised as to whether the Euro zone could survive and with elections in both France and Greece indicating the rise of xenophobic parties that wanted nothing to do with Europe.

But the focus on the match by the English media showed how far European football had come for the English audience. Even a decade ago, let alone in 1992 when the Premier League was created, it would have been unthinkable for terrestrial television in Britain to focus in this fashion on a match involving a German and a Spanish team with no direct British interest. It marked the culmination of two decades when the English national game, and the growth of the Premier League, had been hugely influenced by developments in Europe. A year before the Premier League was launched, radical changes took place in European football that would shape the thinking and profoundly influence the growth of the league. A year before that a little known Belgian player would start on a legal journey which would end in the European court, whose judgement would dictate both who played for Premier League clubs and ultimately how much they were paid. Just as political Britain grew more sceptical about the euro, footballing Britain embraced Europe and drew strength from it.

English football's love affair with Europe had taken time and indeed started with rejection. Back in the 1950s, when the French launched the European Cup, seizing on an idea popularised by a couple of French journalists, English football had shunned the upstart competition, seeing it as one of those continental ideas that had no place in the English game. Chelsea, champions in 1955, were not allowed to participate and it required the vision of Matt Busby for Manchester United to defy the Football League and enter their team in 1957.

By the time the Premier League was created European football was hugely important to the leading English clubs. And as the league prepared to celebrate its 20th anniversary, top English clubs made it clear that for many of them qualification for the Champions League meant more than winning the FA Cup, which would have been heresy back in 1992. Given that the league was created ostensibly to strengthen the FA, it would have made no sense had it been suggested that as a result of the growth of the league, the FA Cup, the FA's flagship tournament, would become a second-class competition. And this European journey to a new football world began at exactly the same time as the Premier League itself, with one key decision even taken at a meeting in London.

In 1991, just as Rick Parry was planning the Premier League from a small office at the FA's London headquarters — so small it was tucked away below the stairs at Lancaster Gate — in Switzerland UEFA had concluded that the European Cup had to be scrapped. Lennart Johansson, then UEFA president, recalls: "The European Cup was dying. There was no money to be made from football."

Over the years the bigger clubs had always felt the knockout format of the European Cup should change. It meant they were always at risk of early elimination and they wanted more security. As Gerhard Aigner, then chief executive, put it to me:

> About that time [in 1991] we had more approaches, especially from Spanish clubs, but also other clubs were speaking to us. Real Madrid submitted some projects of how one could change the competition and how could they have more matches. The idea was to take away the risk for investments. They said, "We invest in players and so on and we need to have more matches instead of having knockouts". The English clubs did not get involved, not in writing. But they all wanted, of course, more matches.

Owners of high-profile clubs in Europe would discuss the drawbacks of the European Cup when they were drawn against each other. They talked of how much better a European "Super League" would be. Clubs would no longer be under the control of UEFA and there would be regular match-ups such as Barcelona vs. Bayern Munich or Real Madrid vs. Manchester United. These and other guaranteed matches involving the continent's most exotic names were all the more appealing as they held out the prospect of being huge money-spinners for the clubs. Aware of such talk, UEFA was keen to bring forward its own version of a Super League tournament.

Just as UEFA were formulating their plans, they were contacted by two marketing men they knew well. Events moved in a way that almost exactly paralleled the moves that led to the formation of the Premier League. The only difference was that while the Premier League was hatched over dinners in London between a select group of clubs and Greg Dyke, plans for the UEFA Champions League first emerged at a dinner in Zurich followed by one in Munich.

The two men who contacted UEFA were Klaus Hempel and Jurgen Lenz. They had worked for Adi Dassler, the founder of Adidas and the man credited with bringing big money into sport. But Dassler was now dead, his marketing company ISL — which handled UEFA and FIFA business — was changing and these two men did not much care for the changes. Aigner says:

> They left because the Adidas family wanted to take more of an operational role. The son-in-law was all of a sudden to be the big guy. They didn't agree with the new philosophy and they left. We were called by them as to whether we would meet them for dinner. They said they wanted to say goodbye, because they were leaving.

Johansson recalls their meeting like this:

> They said the European Cup is a dead duck. They brought the idea of the Champions League to be promoted with the help of television and sponsorship. Even then, ticket sales for the European Cup were not bringing in much money. Much of the income came from marketing and sponsorship. We were both taken by the idea.

Aigner insists that at the first dinner some time in 1990 Hempel and Lenz did not suggest the idea of the Champions League but they helped flesh out plans UEFA had already been working on:

We had made our plans of a change and it just happened that two people from TEAM [Television Event and Media Marketing, the company they set up in Lucerne in Switzerland] had left ISL. They did not come to us with a proposal. It just happened by coincidence. We had been talking about what changes can be made. At the first dinner all they told us was that they were leaving. We asked them whether they had a project and they said, "Yeah, well, we're trying to set up our own business." Then we said, "Well, look, you know we are actually making plans," and we discussed these plans with them. We had already thought of how things can be organised for this new competition. But we didn't know the commercial background. We knew that television was upcoming and keen to have more football. We did not have a precise idea of what our chances would be to set it up and make it commercially viable. We knew that we had a good project. But to evaluate exactly how much the concept is worth, how many sponsors it can attract and so on, that was what we discussed with them. They then formally worked on the proposal and provided an estimate of how much money could be made from these matches.

For both Johansson and Aigner these were men they could trust. This was very important as they were about to enter unchartered waters. And as Johansson points out:

Football is very conservative. The UEFA executive was opposed, the national associations were opposed and even the players did not like the idea. We spoke to the Barcelona players, including the Bulgarian Hristo Stoichkov, and they all said no, do not change the European Cup. I also met Silvio Berlusconi. He came for a meeting and I could see he was very tired. He had had a few. He was not interested in the project. I was keen to know why he was opposed to the idea. I told him, "From a political point of view it will bring you support. The Italian people will like it. And it will be good for your club, AC Milan". In the end he came round and thanked me for it.

The man who was to become Italy's Prime Minister indicated his change of heart when he told *World Soccer* magazine in 1991: "A European championship for clubs is inevitable. The new format is a step in the right direction, but only a step. The European cups, as they have been organised, have become a historical anachronism. It's economic nonsense that a club such as Milan might be eliminated in the first round. A European Cup that lasts the whole season is what Europe wants."

But while Berlusconi could be persuaded, it was not so easy for Johansson and Aigner to convince their own executive. Aigner recalls they were hesitant,

> ... because this was a completely new venture now. We had to give them a complete idea and examples so they could get a clear picture of what was happening in club football in Europe. The danger for a Champions League was the UEFA Cup [for high-placed teams who had failed to win their leagues]. Television showed all the UEFA Cup matches live on Wednesdays from midday until late in the evening and the big television markets like England, Germany, Spain, France had three or four teams in that competition. But in the Champions Cup there was only one team from the big market and sometimes they were eliminated by another team. So there was little attractiveness from a commercial point of view in the Champions Cup.

In March 1991, Johansson and Aigner got the idea approved by the UEFA clubs competition committee at a meeting at UEFA's Swiss headquarters. The following month they headed for London for a UEFA executive meeting. And in a central London hotel on April 17, just 12 days after the Premier League plan was made public — and a short tube ride from where Greg Dyke and the Big Five had first plotted an English breakaway — the UEFA executive debated Johansson and Aigner's new league. It was very late that evening before they agreed that, starting in the 1991–92 season, the European Champions Cup would no longer be a knockout cup as it had been ever since the inaugural event in 1955–56.

"The proposal," says Johansson "was only accepted by the UEFA executive a few days before the deadline, at about 12 o'clock at night, during the meeting in London. There were a number of other conflicting issues they were considering and by then the members were probably too tired, so they voted for it. We came down to the lobby of the hotel and told TEAM."

UEFA then summoned an extraordinary congress to get the consent of the national associations.

Bert Millichip, then FA chairman, under whose auspices the executive had met, welcomed the move, arguing that this would prevent Europe's leading clubs "from making an early exit and devaluing the final".

However, the soul of football conservatism was well represented by Bayern Munich manager Uli Hoeness. The former German international vigorously denounced the plan. The new league format would ruin Europe's most prestigious competition because the excitement of the knockout system would be lost. "You lose a home game, then an away match and then nobody bothers to come and watch because you can no longer win the group. It will kill the attractiveness of the European Cup."

Within a decade, Hoeness and Bayern vice-president Karl-Heinz Rummenigge would be actively involved in a plan for a 16-club Super League involving mid-week matches and no promotion and relegation. The man who could see no value in any change to the old European Cup now saw great merit in a competition where the greats of Europe always played each other and their matches were televised round the world. But by then the cautious changes UEFA had approved in London had become much more radical.

The present format of the UEFA Champions League took almost a decade to develop, during which UEFA came close to losing out to a group from Milan with their own plan for a breakaway of Europe's elite. But bumpy as the road was, Europe finally arrived at what is effectively a mid-week European League. To appreciate how cautiously UEFA had to move to ensure it did not antagonise the game's conservative wing, consider that for the 1991–92 tournament matches were still played on a knockout basis in the early rounds. It became a league only when the eight quarter-finalists were drawn in two round-robin groups, playing each other home and away, with the two group winners qualifying for a one-match final played at a neutral venue. To add to the complications, Red Star Belgrade, who had won the Cup the previous year — making them the last winners of the old competition — had to play all their matches outside Yugoslavia because of the conflict at home. In May 1992, Sampdoria, winners of Group A, met Barcelona, who had topped Group B, at Wembley and Ronald Koeman's winning free-kick in extra time ensured that the Catalans took the Cup for the first time. Just as the Premier League years have been dominated by Manchester United, so Barcelona from the beginning exercised tremendous influence on the Champions League. They may not have won it as many times as United have won the English title but they have been the trend-setters of the competition, the team to beat.

It was not until the 1994–95 season that the Champions League finally began to resemble the "Super League" vision of many. On December 2, 1993, UEFA announced that the successor to the European Cup, once the dream of every club who won their domestic league, would effectively be closed to half of UEFA's membership of 48. Only the top 24 ranked champions would be allowed in, with the rest consigned to the UEFA Cup. The defending champions and the seven other clubs with the best European records over the previous five years would go straight into the league phase of the competition, which would be expanded to four groups of four instead of two groups of four. The remaining eight teams in the groups would be the winners of first round home-and-away ties held in the month of August. The top two teams in each group would then qualify for the quarter-finals in the spring of 1995. The competition would then continue along traditional lines until the final in May, which that year was staged in Vienna.

Competing clubs would thus be guaranteed the income from three home matches on top of set appearance money and bonuses per point. UEFA cleared Wednesday nights for the Champions League, Tuesday nights for the UEFA Cup and Thursdays for the European Cup-Winners' Cup.

By this time an equally radical change had taken place in how the competition was marketed and sold to television and sponsors. Aigner recalls:

> The first year the clubs continued to market their rights for their matches themselves and they had to bring their accounts to us. The commercial result based on the accounts that these clubs delivered to UEFA was very poor. Of course they were not very honest. And they showed that all together they made 15 million Swiss francs for all the matches. We had offered 65 million for the year after [1992–93 season]. So the clubs were in a difficulty. They couldn't say no to a UEFA project which would give them five times more than they had been paid the year before.

After Klaus Hempel and Jurgen Lenz established TEAM in February 1992, UEFA signed up with them to establish the new centralised marketing project. Unlike the arrangements ISL had with football and many other sports, TEAM operated on a commission basis, with all contracts to be signed by UEFA. Centralised marketing meant UEFA asking each club to "turn over" commercial and marketing rights for the Champions League to UEFA in return for fixed payments for qualification to the final eight, a fee for every match won in the league, and additional fees for reaching the final.

But in taking this bold step UEFA was also taking a risk. It was guaranteeing the clubs a certain sum of money. Before this UEFA was merely the regulator of matches, so what a club made from the European Cup depended on their ability to sell their rights. Now UEFA was becoming the financier. It had some 15 million Swiss francs in the bank but this would not be enough to cover payments to clubs if the project failed. This greatly worried the UEFA treasurer and he wanted bank guarantees from TEAM. Aigner narrates how difficult this was:

Our treasurer wanted to have a bank guarantee. Lennart and I didn't think it was needed. We knew that we had a good project. Hempel and Lenz said it would make money and our treasurer wanted them to provide bank guarantees that the money would be there. Hempel and Lenz had to bring in some German industrialists who had enough power to get the bank guarantees for 65 million Swiss francs.

One can understand the treasurer's concern, but as Johansson points out: "They had to work hard to get backers. However, while we were taking a chance with the Champions League, the bigger chance would have been carrying on with the old European Cup. It was dying. We could not save it."

But while TEAM found the backers, UEFA still had to get out of its contracts with ISL. "We had a contract with ISL," recalls Aigner, "and we had big problems with them because ISL wanted to have the Champions League themselves. We came out of that contract and said we want to have an agency for the Champions League which had a single focus. That means we can't have an agency that also does business for other competitions."

It was only in 1995 that UEFA secured the final rights and TEAM could now fully implement its concept of bringing the language of marketing and sponsorship so common in American sport to Europe for the first time. As Craig Thompson and Ems Magnus of TEAM Marketing AG put it:

The unique vision of the UEFA Champions League was the centralised marketing concept with its key partners: the clubs, television, and sponsors and suppliers cooperating closely with UEFA, and its marketing agent TEAM. The operational agenda was that each of the three partners should contribute to the concept while at the same time receiving direct benefits. The first priority for the new marketing concept was to have a strongly branded product that would clearly stand out and be unique in the busy sports world.

First, a name for the competition had to be found. It was decided to use "UEFA Champions League" as it was a league composed of champion clubs. A logo was created that was composed of eight stars formed in a sphere like a football. The stars represented the "star" football clubs of Europe. A choral-classical musical anthem was also developed from a theme of Handel's. This simple yet striking new logo, combined with the classical music theme, gave the new competition an elevated image and prestigious feel. The Champions League was born!

The new marketing concept was both innovative and commercially adapted to the changing market conditions. Each sponsor would receive exclusivity in its product area, not only in the stadium as was previously done, but also on TV, with commercial airtime spots and programme sponsorship. By linking stadium advertising together with on-air sponsorship, it became almost impossible for non-sponsors to associate with the competition.

The three pillars of stadium advertising, commercial airtime, and programme sponsorship generated a "multiplying media effect" that offered new levels of recognition to the sponsors. A "less is more" approach was taken and a maximum of eight international sponsors was decided upon. The sponsor package included four stadium advertising boards, ticket allocations, and identification on TV interview backdrops and in the VIP and press areas. Each of the sponsor ticket holders was also invited to specially arranged hospitality suites before and after the matches.

By the time this vision was written in 2003, the Champions League had finally settled into its present format and could boast worldwide success. However, five years earlier, in the summer of 1998, a sudden tempest had blown up and for a time it seemed UEFA's house of football might be blown away. The attempted ambush also demonstrated how the leading Premier League clubs had come to see the benefits to be derived from a European league tailored to their needs. But while the breakaway ultimately failed to take off, it would never have even reached the runway without the support of leading English clubs such as Manchester United and Arsenal, with Liverpool a more reluctant participant. And the episode showed that, less than a decade after they were barred from European competition, English clubs were now considered crucial partners by European marketers keen to make money out of a new continent-wide tournament.

Bizarrely, the breakaway plan was first revealed in a bar in Brazil. In May 1998, in a low-ceilinged bar of the InterContinental Hotel in São Paulo, three representatives of Manchester United were settling in for early evening drinks. The trio — Peter Kenyon, Maurice Watkins and Glenn Cooper — were attending a sports conference organised by Pele, then Brazil's sports minister, to help local football clubs restructure themselves and learn from English models like Manchester United. Suddenly they are approached by a Swede and two Italians, who wanted them to look at a presentation called Project Parsifal, named after Wagner's last opera. It was a code name for a European mid-week Super League of 24 or 32 teams. Peter Ecelund, Andrea Locatelli and Paolo Taveggia were representatives of a company called Media Partners — or "the unknown boys from the Milan tennis club" as they were later derisively described by some at UEFA.

Not all were from Milan but seven of the top management were Italians, the president Rodolfo Hecht Lucari was an AC Milan supporter and Locatelli had played for AC Milan. It was this Milan connection, and the fact that Hecht and Taveggia had worked for Berlusconi, that led to intense speculation that they were really front men for the Italian media magnate. Media Partners denied this, saying that while many of the partners had worked for Berlusconi, they were the sole owners of their company. They boasted a good track record in sports rights, having put together football's first pay-per-view television contract in Italy. What they shared with Berlusconi was the belief that one day a European Super League would attract the best clubs in Europe and make the sort of money not available in the existing UEFA competitions. The Berlusconi view was: "There will be a league formed outside UEFA with a team from each country sponsored by that country's biggest company... a league like American football's NFL, which will attract millions of viewers."

The Italians were already known to Kenyon and he was impressed with what he saw:

> It was a new concept for a European football competition and it would derive significant revenues and give ownership back to the clubs. They'd done an awful lot of work on it. It was intriguing from two points of view. First and foremost, the quality of the advisers that had been involved with the project. It was obvious from the outset that this wasn't something that had been put together the week before. There'd been significant research done on competition formats, TV revenues, club ownership and rights.

UEFA made much of the fact that Real Madrid, who had won the Champions League for the first time since 1966, would now bank some £8.5 million, while Manchester United as beaten quarter-finalists had received £5.37 million. Media Partners suggested each club would earn four times as much money under its plan and that UEFA had consistently given the clubs a raw deal. Only 55 per cent of UEFA's total income of £155 million came back to the clubs, UEFA itself kept nearly £30 million and TEAM, the company that did the deals for UEFA, got nearly 12.5 per cent of the gross take. Media Partners promised that its European Super League meant that the top clubs themselves, and not UEFA, would own the league. This was immensely attractive.

Membership of the new league was to be determined by merit and also by status, such as previous record in Europe, size of the club, etc. The most radical proposal was that there would be a group of founder members who would enjoy permanent membership of the league because of their size and wealth.

For the 1998–99 season Inter Milan, four-time winners of the Champions League, had failed to qualify for Europe. This was the second year Milan were out of Europe and as Hecht had said: "It's a tragedy. The question is how do you deal with that? I think sport in Europe is ready to be privatised."

Inter had proposed to UEFA that in such situations clubs like themselves with an established pedigree in Europe should be given a wildcard, in much the same way tennis players who do not qualify on their form for tournaments can get in on their past record. The UEFA executive decided that football was not tennis. All this led the top clubs in Europe to look hard at Media Partners' proposals and on July 2, the first of many meetings was held at the London offices of Slaughter & May. In attendance were the two Milan clubs, AC and Inter, Juventus, Ajax from Holland, Marseille and Paris Saint-Germain from France, Borussia Dortmund from Germany, United and Arsenal from England but nobody from Spain.

The proposal had split Arsenal with David Dein, the vice-chairman, opposed to it and the rest of the board in favour. Dein was a member of UEFA's competitions committee, which ran all the European competitions including the Champions League. However, the Arsenal board, led by chairman Peter Hill-Wood and supported by the rich businessman Danny Fiszman, were keen, so keen that they had already been given a Media Partners presentation at Highbury. It was decided that while Dein could not go, Fiszman and Ken Friar, the managing director, would represent the English champions.

Other meetings were held, with Franz Beckenbauer and Karl-Heinz Rummenigge representing Bayern Munich, Rick Parry representing Liverpool and also a representative from Turkish side Galatasaray. United saw Liverpool's fleeting visit as the sign of the eternal fence-sitter or, as the saying in football goes, "letting others do the dirty work, arriving late and then drinking all the champagne".

The American bankers JP Morgan were willing to finance the project for the first three seasons to the tune of £2 billion, a sum they planned to recover through the sale of television rights. The plan had flaws and it raised the question of where UEFA stood in all this. Interestingly, during the turmoil Formula One boss Bernie Ecclestone rang Aigner, who recalls: "I know that Ecclestone was approached by Media Partners, because he called me twice. He wanted to know whether UEFA had more or less agreed to the project of Media Partners. He was surprised when he learned that UEFA was opposing their plans."

Aigner insists he never believed that Media Partners would rock UEFA:

"Because I knew that their project was not viable. It was bad and then I spoke to the clubs. They immediately agreed with me that it was not a good idea to have a closed league."

However, the fact that UEFA lobbied the clubs showed how much Media Partners had rattled the organisation. In the past UEFA had shunned direct contact with the clubs, insisting that UEFA only spoke to national associations. If clubs wanted anything they should go through their respective FAs. But now Aigner himself approached the clubs and, in order to stop Media Partners, agreed to radical surgery on UEFA's European competitions. The big casualty was the Cup-Winners' Cup. This was the competition where English clubs had always done well. It was the first European club competition to be won by a British club, by Tottenham Hotspur in 1963. It was also the first European trophy Alex Ferguson brought to Old Trafford. As we shall see, this had a huge impact that extended to the boardroom at Old Trafford and formed the backdrop to United's decision to float on the stock market.

But now this link between countries' domestic cup competitions and Europe was gone. All that mattered was how clubs performed in their domestic league. This proved a boon for the Football League which was allowed to maintain a link with Europe as the winners of the League Cup were given entry to the UEFA Cup. This was rich in irony, given that the League Cup had originally been founded as a carrot to dissuade English clubs from taking part in the old European Cup. And it marked the start of the decline of the oldest cup competition in football: the FA Cup. At the end of the 20th season of the Premier League, when Tottenham met Chelsea in the FA Cup semi-final, both managers made it clear that qualifying for the Champions League took precedence over winning the FA Cup. Even a decade earlier such an idea would have been unimaginable.

There were also major changes to the Champions League. A qualifying round was introduced for those countries whose champions did not automatically qualify for the league. This qualifying round also featured the fourth-placed teams from England, Italy and Spain. The qualifying round meant that some past winners of the European Cup, such as Celtic, now had to negotiate an additional hurdle to reach the main competition, whereas some teams who had not even finished as winners of their own league qualified automatically, as did the teams who finished in the top three of the English, Spanish and Italian leagues. After the qualifying round, the Champions League became a league of 32 clubs, with two separate mini-league qualifying stages before a final knockout phase. Aigner accepts that the second group phase was a bad idea. But, as he explains, UEFA had no choice at the time:

We had to agree to it to get things going again. There was the pressure of the clubs. They wanted to have more matches and we had to agree to a system where they had these extra matches. But we knew that these matches were not very valuable. In the end, after two years we abolished the second group phase. There was proof that this phase was a disaster.

Michel D'Hooghe, UEFA and FIFA executive member and a qualified Belgian doctor, has since told me that it was pressure from the medical people at UEFA which forced the change. The doctors pointed out that the extra matches were creating too much work for the players and would be bad for their health.

It was only in 2003 that the current set-up was finally set in stone. The big television markets were rewarded with places in the Champions League, four teams each from England, Germany, Spain and Italy. There is also a sporting classification which kept France down to three. Once the Cup-Winners' Cup was disbanded for the 1999–2000 season, the UEFA Cup switched to Thursdays and the Champions League expanded to Tuesdays. It also enabled UEFA to sell rights not only to terrestrial television but also have Champions League matches on pay-TV.

Aigner admits that the new arrangements mean that "only clubs who have the money can win European Cups". Money comes through television and marketing and this favours the big markets. "The big markets are England, Germany, Spain Italy and France. We took the money from the big markets and you can only take it from the big markets."

For almost three decades after England had accepted the value of European competition, the big ambition for English club managers was a top-six finish, since this secured a place in one of the European competitions. Now managers of ambitious clubs set their sights on a top-four finish. Only then could they be sure of Champions League football, bringing with it both the excitement of top-class football for their fans and, crucially, the money that can buy and keep the best players. Back in 1998 the clubs, encouraged by fans, had rejected Media Partners' idea of a closed league. But the effect of the Media Partners ambush was that the Premier League had, in effect, a closed entry to the Champions League. Until Tottenham and then Manchester City broke through in the second decade of the 21st century the same four English clubs — Manchester United, Chelsea, Arsenal and Liverpool — qualified for the Champions League almost every year.

This meant, of course, that the original concept of the tournament, matching the league champions of every country from the previous season with the purpose of crowning the true champions of Europe, had now ceased to exist. Indeed, in the 1998–99 Champions League, while UEFA were wrestling with Media Partners, Manchester United and Bayern Munich reached the final. Neither side had won their domestic league the previous season. Kaiserslautern had won the Bundesliga in 1998, while Arsenal were English Double winners. By the time the 20th Premier League season came around, the fact that Champions League finals often involved teams who were not champions was almost taken for granted. Neither Bayern nor Chelsea had won their respective leagues in 2011. Indeed, Chelsea went into the final having finished sixth in the 2012 season and well aware they would only take part in the following season's Champions League if they won the trophy. Their victory on penalties in Munich meant that Tottenham, who had finished fourth in the league, were bumped down to the Europa League in 2012–13.

UEFA took even longer to fashion the Europa League from the UEFA Cup and make it a viable second European competition. Its status as the also-rans' competition was emphasised by the fact that teams who finished third in the group stages of the Champions League then had a second chance in the Europa League. This link was derided by many, as were the efforts of UEFA to develop a centralised marketing similar to the Champions League. The moans and groans were loudest in England where commentators, fans and even managers loved to pour scorn on the competition. But UEFA could point to the fact that, apart from England, the rest of Europe had embraced it with enthusiasm, and it now draws a global audience of 634 million viewers. This compares very well with viewing figures for the Premier League.

In 2010–11, 25 per cent of UK individuals watched the Europa League on UK television. In 2009–10, the tournament's biggest audience on Channel 5, a terrestrial channel, was for the final between Fulham and Atletico Madrid, with 4.7 million viewers (20 per cent audience share). In 2010–11 it was for Liverpool vs. Braga, with 3.5 million (14 per cent share), and in 2011–12 it was for Tottenham vs. PAOK Salonika, with 2.3 million (9 per cent share).

In the Premier League the biggest TV audience on Sky in 2011–12 was 2.4 million for the Chelsea vs. Manchester United match, with a 14 per cent audience share. And in 2010–11 the biggest was 2.7 million for Chelsea and Liverpool, again with a 14 per cent share.

And the money, if not quite in the Champions League class, was still substantial. So Porto, the winners in 2010–11, received €7,837,046 while Braga, the side Porto beat 1–0 thanks to Falcao's goal in the all-Portuguese final, earned €4,528,191. But all this was dwarfed by Villarreal, the Spanish team whom Porto defeated in the semi-finals — they collected a combined €9 million.

The changes to the Champions League and Europa League were incremental and took many years, but the other impact of Europe on the Premier League came like a thunderbolt on a single day in December 1995. And all because a Belgian footballer could not move to a French club. Nothing like this had been seen in the game before. The Premier League, along with all other European leagues, had to cope with the effect of this case brought by a little-known midfielder from Belgium. But like the creation of the Premier League, this story too began in 1990, just as the Premier League plans were taking shape.

In the summer of that year Jean-Marc Bosman, a Belgian youth, wanted to move from Club de Liege in Belgium to French second division side Dunkerque. Bosman was out of contract and had he been English nobody could have prevented him moving. Following the abolition of the maximum wage, English football had developed a transfer system whereby a player at the end of his contract was free to move elsewhere. If his club did not want to release him because they felt the money they were getting was not enough, the transfer had to be settled by a football tribunal. It was a case of deciding how much money the selling club could claim.

However, Belgium still had the old system. Liege refused to ratify his transfer as Dunkerque could not meet the fee the Belgians demanded. Instead Liege offered Bosman a new contract with a 60 per cent wage cut. It was this that made Bosman take to the law and he had a ready weapon: the free movement of labour. A local court ruled that he was indeed free to join Dunkerque but the Belgian football federation, fearful of the wider consequences of losing their authority, appealed against the decision.

By May 1991, the Court of Appeal in Liege confirmed the verdict of the lower court that Bosman could move freely to his new club. The appeals court later asked the European Court to analyse the transfer system under competition articles 85 and 86 of the EC Treaty. But in addition they also asked the court to rule on the "three-plus-two" rule and whether this violated the free movement of workers across the EU under article 48 of the treaty. This was to prove crucial. The UEFA rule had been introduced to make sure clubs did not stuff their teams with overseas players. It specified that a club playing in a UEFA competition could field three foreign players plus two "assimilated" players who had progressed through their youth set-up. The classic illustration of the "assimilated" player was Ryan Giggs, who qualified to play for Wales but was brought up by Manchester United and therefore considered "English" in club football terms.

At the time this test case was referred to the European Court few in football paid much attention to it. But more than five years after the original hearing, there was a devastating verdict. Not only did Bosman win his case, but the European Court of Justice in Luxembourg struck down the three-plus-two rule and in the process completely reshaped football. At the time, the Dutch Euro MP Jim Janssen van Raaij pronounced it "the end of modern slavery" while Lennart Johansson called it "an attack on football". The gulf in attitudes reflected how differently those who ran football viewed this compared to the wider world, but everyone instantly recognised that this was a game-changing verdict.

But before we examine the implications, spare a thought for poor Bosman. He had engineered all this but benefited least from it. Having been in limbo for five years, by the time the decision was made it was too late to revive his career. The legal battle forced Bosman to live in his parents' garage for almost two years and wrecked his first marriage. In later years a bloated, balding Bosman confessed that when he lived alone in Liege, he was dealing with depression and alcoholism and survived on £625 a month in benefits, including £180 paid by the state for his heating. FIFPro, the international players' union, contributed £200,000 for him to fight his case — yet that money went to lawyers and court costs. The cash compensation awarded to him by the court, around £312,000, went to settling tax bills. And plans for a grand testimonial match, which FIFPro had promised to organise, never materialised. Instead he had to contend with a match in Lille in front of just 2,000 fans. Bosman became a pariah within his homeland and was effectively blacklisted throughout European football.

As he told *The Sun* in 2011: "I have my place in history and I had a long fight to achieve what I did. I don't want everything I did in my life to be for nothing. I'm happy for footballers earning a lot of money. I'm not jealous. I gave my career so European players wouldn't work like slaves. I just want to be recognised. People know there's a 'Bosman ruling' but they don't realise there's a guy who has given everything, who became an alcoholic." His fellow players, following in the wake of his victory, could take to drink in celebration, not misery. And his victory over Liege, a small Belgian club, meant that clubs all over Europe now enjoyed the sort of freedom they had always wanted but never dared to imagine they would achieve.

The European Court had ruled that all regulations restricting the employment of EU citizen footballers within other member states were illegal. There could be no restrictions on clubs regarding the number of players they signed from other EU countries. Clubs could now field in Europe the same team they fielded in their domestic competitions. Manchester United benefited the most. In the early years of the Champions League they had struggled with the three-plus-two rule and had had to change their teams for European matches. Now Sir Alex Ferguson was able to field his first-choice XI in Europe and it was hardly a surprise that, two years after the Bosman ruling, United reached the semi-finals of Europe's premier club competition for the first time since 1969. Two years later came their *annus mirabilis* of 1999 and in that Champions League final at the Nou Camp only five Englishmen were involved.

The word English needs stressing. Since then much has been written about how Bosman and the rise of the Premier League meant that English clubs no longer fielded British players. But in football the word British means nothing as there is no British team. The more relevant question is, who is qualified to play for England? English clubs have always had non-English players in their teams. But before the Bosman ruling they were generally from the other Home Nations of Scotland, Wales and Northern Ireland. The Bosman ruling meant all of Europe and beyond now became an open house to English clubs. The effect of this can best be judged if we examine three seasons in the Premier League, the year the league started, the season following the Bosman ruling and the 20th season just concluded.

In the first Premier League season in 1992–93 all the clubs had an abundance of English-qualified players, 15 each at Manchester United and Manchester City, 20 at Tottenham and 24 at Arsenal (see Appendix pg 354, fig.1). The non-qualified were essentially British with a scattering of foreign nationals. By 1996–97 these numbers had changed but every team in the Premier League could still field an XI qualified to play for England (Appendix pg 356 fig.2). At the beginning of the 2011–12 season, more than 15 years after the Bosman ruling, six teams could not, Wigan had five English qualified and Arsenal and Fulham six each (Appendix pg 358, fig.3). Eight other teams had between 11 and 14 players. Only Norwich, who had just been promoted, had 18. And just as significantly, the non-English players were not from Britain but from around the world. All this had been highlighted on Boxing Day 1999, when Chelsea, then managed by the Italian Gianluca Vialli, became the first English club to field an all-foreign starting XI. This would not have been possible without Bosman going to court. He may not have been much of a player but he had changed and reshaped the world of English football for ever.

In the years since 1995 the Bosman ruling has led to other changes in the transfer regulations. It led to transfer windows allowing player transfers only twice in a season, once at the start and once in the middle. But most significantly, it greatly increased player power. The court ruling meant that footballers were now free to move when their contracts expired. And this in turn paved the way for footballers to earn multi-million-pound salaries. Sport could no longer be exempt from EU competition rules and had to be treated like any other business. The net effect was that unless a club arranged a transfer before the player entered the last year of his contract he was free to move at the end of it. This tilted power decisively in favour of players and away from clubs.

Now players, particularly high-profile stars, were masters of their own destinies. And as free-agent players they could suddenly demand huge signing-on fees and salaries on the basis that the club they were joining did not have to pay anything in transfer fees. Football clubs were powerless to prevent their best players from leaving at the end of their current deals. Conversely, players under contract could demand bigger, better and longer deals — because the threat of being able to leave for free, especially if they would otherwise command high transfer fees, was something clubs could not ignore.

This led to many high-profile cases when footballers used the Bosman ruling to their benefit, moving to a club in the last year of their contract: Ruud Gullit (Sampdoria to Chelsea 1995); Patrick Kluivert (Ajax to AC Milan 1997); Brian Laudrup (Rangers to Chelsea 1998); Steve McManaman (Liverpool to Real Madrid 1999, where he earned about £14 million over five years in La Liga). In the Premier League the most significant was, arguably, that of Sol Campbell, Tottenham to Arsenal in 2001, the last year of his contract. Campbell was the first high-profile player to cross the north London divide since goalkeeper Pat Jennings in 1977 but it represented a new world. Technically, Campbell was a free transfer but for Arsenal the cost was huge. He joined on a £20 million four-year deal, the sort of money that before Bosman might have been paid in transfer fees.

The growth of high-profile player power has also led to the rise of the international football agent. At the start of the Premier League football refused to recognise agents. While they worked as agents they publicly operated as if they were not agents. As we shall see in the bungs story, they often lied about what work they actually performed for clubs. But now they were in the open and following the Bosman ruling, as players became more powerful, so did their agents. Not only do agents receive fees from a club for bringing an out-of-contract star player to them in the first place, but they also negotiate a cut of any signing-on fees or loyalty bonuses demanded by their clients. The power possessed by the most prominent of agents, specifically those who have been smart enough to act internationally, increased so exponentially in such a short space of time that the phrase "super-agent" was created. Individuals such as the Israeli Pini Zahavi, the Iranian-born, British-educated businessman Kia Joorabchian and the Portuguese football agent Jorge Mendes — arguably the most influential football agent in the world at present — have become almost as famous as their playing clients.

And where previously lower-league clubs could develop home-grown talent through academies, safe in the knowledge that when the appropriate time came they could sell those players for financially lucrative transfers, their star attractions could now leave for free at the end of their deals. To prevent their best players leaving on a Bosman transfer, clubs began signing their star names on long-term deals; a scenario that was fine until an unexpected relegation or an unseen misfortune, like the collapse of ITV Digital, for example. At this point expensive weekly deals for non-performing players became more of a burden to the club's finances, as the likes of Bradford City, Derby County, Leeds United and Sheffield Wednesday have all found to their cost in recent years.

But here again British immigration rules and English football's acceptance of these rules have made things difficult for this country and indeed led to an inflationary spiral of transfer fees. Two years after the Bosman ruling, in March 1997, FIFA, which governs international transfers, announced it would change its transfer rules "to ensure equal treatment for all players moving between clubs within the European Union". Basically this meant that players from non-EU countries who played for clubs within the EU would also be able to move to other clubs within the EU on free transfers once their contracts expired. But while other European countries eagerly went down the cosmopolitan route, allowing young players from non-EU countries to play for their clubs without any restrictions, English football retained a crucial restriction.

It could do nothing about EU players moving to an English club, or a non-EU player from an EU club going to an English one. But when it came to non-EU players who did not have an EU club, the British Home Office, with the active help of football, insisted that the players should meet certain very specific criteria. They should be established players in their home countries, having played in 75 per cent of representative matches for their country in the previous two years. Also the country concerned had to be in the top 75 of the FIFA world rankings. The Home Office, advised by the professional game, which includes representatives of the Professional Footballers' Association, vets who can get a work permit. The net effect is that young talent from non-EU countries cannot come to England.

Peter Ridsdale, now director of football at Preston North End, describes the effect this had when he found two talented young players from a non-EU country:

> When I was at Leeds I had two 16-year-olds from Australia, Brett Emerton and Harry Kewell. Harry qualified for a British passport through his father and was no problem. But Brett did not and we could not sign him. He left to go to Holland to play for Feyenoord. In Europe they do not

have the restrictions we have and in 2003 he came to Blackburn. Now he was coming from an EU club and allowed in but it meant Blackburn paid a transfer fee. This is money going out of the game in this country because we have rules which no other EU country has.

The Blackburn fee was not disclosed but was believed to be £7 million. Feyenoord had signed him for £415,000. It was a classic illustration of English football embracing European change but doing so in a manner which did not always benefit English clubs.

The impact on all this on English football cannot be overestimated. Had this rule for non-EU players not existed young players from non-EU countries could come to England quite cheap as they do elsewhere in Europe. Instead non-EU players come at a high price from EU clubs in Europe. And where once money from the top clubs in England went down the divisions providing a trickle down equality of sorts, it now flows out of the country doing nothing for English football. In the 2010–11 season a net £364 million was received by overseas clubs from the English game. This was a whopping 219 per cent increase on the £114 million of 2009–10. As the authors of the Deloitte report put it this record level showed "the drive by English clubs to source the world's best talent, irrespective of origin".

Like many in football, Aigner agrees that Bosman produced "the biggest impact on European football, there is no question of that. The decision of the European Court is a catastrophe and continues to be a catastrophe. Clubs cannot keep their players. The three-plus-two rule was a good rule and the European Court on its own initiative included that aspect in the Bosman decision. That was going beyond Bosman, Bosman was not asking for that. What the European Court wanted to show was basically they had a say in this matter. They wanted to, in a way, punish UEFA."

Aigner is convinced the punishment could have been avoided had FIFA followed UEFA's transfer rules:

We had in UEFA a transfer system, which with the permission of FIFA, was used in the EU area. This would not allow a club to say no to a transfer for a player who was at the end of his contract. It was a system wherein the new club and the old club had to agree on compensation. If they couldn't agree there was a panel of experts from which the clubs could choose a chairman for arbitration. Each club had a representative and those two representatives agreed on the chairman. The panel then worked out a deal.

The problem was that FIFA had refused to withdraw their rules and allow us to uniquely operate the new system. So we had two transfer regulations, parallel rules. Belgium had agreed to the UEFA transfer system but the club didn't sign the certificate of transfer for the player, which was possible according to the FIFA rules. FIFA later blamed UEFA but it was the FIFA rules that were a problem. We had a better system, we had been using it for quite a number of years already because we knew the risk that existed in the EU. Had the FIFA rules been withdrawn, UEFA would have granted players permission to play for the new club and Bosman would have been transferred without any problem.

To make matters worse, many of the clubs did not appreciate the new world that was being created. Aigner recalls:

The decision having come in on December 15, the clubs agreed to continue to play that season with the old rules, even if the European Union said from now on, immediately, this three-plus-two rule doesn't apply any more. Then at the end of the season UEFA wrote to its members and said, "Look, how do you feel about continuing with these old rules and agreeing on them." We immediately got a letter from Glasgow Rangers threatening to take us to court if we wanted to insist on the three-plus-two rule. They didn't realise the consequences of the decision. As it has turned out they were one of the victims of the decision. What happened with the European Court decision was that clubs needed extra money and clubs like Rangers did not have the money to compete with the big ones.

Scottish managers like Alex McLeish understand what the effect of Bosman has been on the smaller countries. As he put it to me: "Scotland has been devastated by the Bosman ruling." The final word should go to Bosman's lawyer, Luc Misson, who said in 2005, marking the 10th anniversary of the judgement: "He gave his career to a court case to serve a cause, but he sees that the transfer fees are still there, quotas on home-grown players are making a comeback and the rich clubs are richer and the poor ones are poorer."

The Premier League had been created so that a few of the bigger clubs in England could get what they thought was their fair share of money. Now from Europe had come a double whammy which completely changed the world they lived in and further increased inequality in the English game. Europe in that sense had proved both a friend and foe.

PART 3

THREE MEN AND THEIR BALL GAMES

Chapter 6
THE ULTIMATE MODERN MANAGER

The story of the Premier League and the three managers who shaped it could be the start of a joke: there was a Scotsman, a Frenchman and a Portuguese... Except that the Premier League is far from a joke and these three men, Sir Alex Ferguson, Arsene Wenger and Jose Mourinho, have stamped themselves on it in the 20 years since it was launched in a manner unique to English football and, arguably, the world. In the process they have changed the way the manager's role is perceived and created a very different kind of manager from those who used to manage in the old Football League.

It is very much a reflection of the Premier League story that none of them are English and that when the League kicked off in 1992 two of them, Wenger and Mourinho, were totally unknown in England. Mourinho had just begun working as a translator for Sir Bobby Robson, who had taken over as manager of Sporting Lisbon. The former England manager was looking for a local coach with a good command of English to work as his interpreter and Mourinho was happy to do just that.

Sir Alex Ferguson was, of course, already well known but few would have predicted that long before the Premier League had celebrated its 20th birthday he would be hailed as the most successful manager in British football history. The prophecy seemed especially unlikely on the opening day of the new league, August 15, 1992, when Manchester United were beaten 2–1 by Sheffield United, with Brian Deane scoring the first Premier League goal.

Ferguson, then plain Mr, had enjoyed success but only in Scotland where, during his eight triumphant years with Aberdeen, he had made his name by breaking the dominance of the Glasgow Old Firm of Celtic and Rangers, bringing three league titles, four Scottish Cups, one Scottish League Cup, one European Cup-Winners Cup and one UEFA Super Cup to Pittodrie.

Yet despite this winning record, Manchester United's directors were not totally sure he was the right man when they looked to replace Ron Atkinson in November 1986. Atkinson, in charge at Old Trafford since 1981, was the first manager Martin Edwards, the then United chairman, had appointed after sacking Dave Sexton, whom he had inherited. Under Atkinson, United had won the occasional cup, but the league seemed unattainable. This feeling was heightened during the 1985–86 season when United started with 10 wins in a row and looked as if they might overhaul Tottenham's record of 11 in a row set at the start of the 1960–61 season. But then United stumbled so badly that, long before the end, their title chances were gone and they finished fourth.

Atkinson's departure became inevitable after a humiliating League Cup defeat at Southampton. On the flight back north that November evening the talk turned to replacing him. One director, Mike Edelson, recalls:

> For away matches four or five friends would join us and we would fly there. But there were only two of us on the flight to the Southampton game, Martin [Edwards] and me. There was a discussion with Martin about what we should do about Atkinson. The next day Martin rang and said the other two directors — Maurice [Watkins] and Bobby [Charlton] — were at Old Trafford and they were talking about what we'd been discussing last night. Could I come down? My office is only about 10 minutes away, so I went. We narrowed it down to two options: Terry Venables and Alex Ferguson. Terry Venables wasn't really available because he was at Barcelona. They were still in the European Cup and they wouldn't release him, we thought. We decided it wouldn't be worth considering Terry. So Alex was obviously the first option, considering the relative merits of the two. The only thing against Alex was that no Scottish manager had ever successfully come from Scotland to England. Matt Busby was Scottish but he had never managed in Scotland.

Bill Shankly had managed Scotland during the war, but his league clubs were all English.

Earlier that year, during the World Cup in Mexico, Charlton had spoken to Ferguson when he was managing Scotland and said if he wanted to move to England he should think about getting in touch. Two years earlier, in 1984, Ferguson had very nearly moved south and according to Spurs chairman Irving Scholar had shaken hands on a deal to come to Tottenham. The pair had met twice in Paris and everything seemed agreed, only for Scholar to learn that Ferguson's wife Cathy did not fancy moving to London. Curiously, Ferguson makes no mention of this episode in his autobiography. In June 1999, a week after Manchester United completed the treble by winning the Champions

League, Scholar, waiting by the carousel at Nice airport, ran into Ferguson. As they chatted the Scot introduced Scholar to Cathy and Scholar said: "Ah, you are the woman who stopped him coming to Tottenham." Cathy Ferguson just looked at Scholar and said nothing. This is, of course, Scholar's version. An alternative view is that Ferguson might have moved had Tottenham offered him a five-year deal but having started with two, they offered three and would not budge further.

So, in November 1986, the four United directors in the Old Trafford boardroom discussed how they could approach Ferguson. Watkins had got to know him when Gordon Strachan had joined Manchester United from Aberdeen, but it was Edelson who volunteered to make the call:

> We were all in the room having the conversation and somebody said, "How can we get in touch with him?" I said, "I'll phone the club." I did not know him. I just rang him. I spoke to the girl on the switchboard at Aberdeen and asked for Alex Ferguson and she put me through [according to Ferguson, Edelson told the switchboard operator he was Alan Gordon, Strachan's accountant, and faked a Scottish accent]. When Alex came on the phone I told him I was a director of Manchester United and asked him if he'd like to speak to Martin Edwards. Martin said, "Would it be possible to have a chat?" and Alex said he'd clear it with his chairman. He had an option in his contract that if a really big club — Rangers, Tottenham, Manchester United — were interested, he was allowed to speak to them. It was all done within hours. We rang him on the Wednesday, Maurice and Martin went up on the Thursday and spoke to him, and Ferguson came down on the Friday. By this time Martin had spoken to Atkinson.

It was not so much the money but the lure of managing Manchester United that brought Ferguson to Old Trafford and as he took over on November 6, 1986 he was in no doubt about the size of the task he faced. Ferguson inherited from Atkinson a team languishing fourth from bottom of the First Division. It was a dispirited, underachieving squad that, much to the supporters' annoyance, had been unable to match or even challenge Liverpool, then the dominant force in English football.

Ferguson could not have had a worse start, losing his opening match 2–0 at Oxford United. United finished 11th in the 1986–87 season. Although they were runners-up behind Liverpool in 1987–88, it proved a false dawn — the following season they finished back in 11th place, two points behind Millwall and QPR. Ferguson ended 1989 as the bookies' favourite for the first managerial sacking in the 1990s. At Christmas he was 4–7 to be sacked before the beginning of the 1990–91 season but that soon became 2–5 with William Hill. Had chairman Edwards got rid of Ferguson that season, not only would nobody have blamed him but he might have won over some of the fans who by then had turned against him over his stewardship of the club.

One of the most dramatic nights of that season came on October 25, 1989, when Tottenham beat Manchester United 3–0 at Old Trafford in the third round of the League Cup. There was an attempt to storm the directors' box to assault Edwards. He recalls:

> I was taking a bit of abuse in the box from some supporters. Someone in front of the box did actually try to get into the box and I think a steward or somebody intervened to stop them. I've had abuse before and I'm used to it, really. I mean, there are not many people who actually like abuse and I certainly don't like it. But to my mind it goes with the territory, doesn't it?

The abuse had reached such a point that Edwards would often vacate the directors' box and watch much of the match from high up in the main stand. Edelson says:

> There was a little box that the announcers used just at the back of the stand, just near the door to the directors' box. There was a bit of glass, about the size of a standard desk, that looked out on the pitch and Martin used to go there.

For Ferguson the lowest point was the 5–1 defeat by Manchester City. Yet Edwards would not hear of sacking the manager, even though by doing so he might have got the fans off his own back:

> It was a tough time for us and there was a lot of pressure for us to do something. A lot of supporters and fans don't always realise what's going on in the background at a football club and we knew how hard Alex was working behind the scenes.
>
> Don't forget, that year we spent an absolute fortune on players. We brought in Mike Phelan, Paul Ince, Gary Pallister, Danny Wallace and Neil Webb — and all those players at considerable cost in support of Alex. [United spent around £13 million in the transfer market.] The last thing we were going to do was suddenly pull the rug from underneath him, because we knew how hard he was working.

Ferguson would later reflect that when he came to United he saw it as more than a job: "I am not kidding. This isn't just a job to me. It's a mission. I am deadly serious about it — some people would reckon too serious. We will get there. Believe me. And when it happens, life will change for Liverpool and everybody else, dramatically."

Maybe Edwards sensed some of this determination and was also impressed that Ferguson had revived the youth policy first launched by James Gibson and Walter Crickmer back in 1938 and developed so brilliantly by Busby. He had also started to tackle the drinking culture centred around players such as Paul McGrath, seeking to make the club more professional and the players fitter and more capable of coping with a hard league season. Webb, never the most successful signing at Old Trafford, found himself a victim of this tougher approach when he sought to join the England squad for what Ferguson regarded as a meaningless friendly. United claimed Webb was unavailable through injury, but when Webb later told the England manager Graham Taylor he was perfectly fit, a furious Ferguson had his revenge by omitting him for United games. Webb was eventually sold back to Nottingham Forest for £800,000, barely half what United had paid for him in 1989.

"We knew," says Edwards, "it was going to take time for [Alex] to learn the English game, because when he came down from Scotland he didn't know perhaps as much as he thought he did about English players. As we knew how hard he was working, we never lost faith in him. What we were trying to do was to resist all the pressure."

Edwards denies there was ever any pressure from the rest of the board although one story, which quickly did the rounds at Old Trafford, was that as Edwards opened one board meeting, he said: "If anyone wants to talk about Alex Ferguson leaving they must leave the meeting now."

But it is indicative of the deep distrust that developed between some fans and Edwards that even when his faith in Ferguson had been completely justified, fans still found it difficult to accept that he had not considered sacking the Scot. And over the next 20 years Ferguson did come close to leaving United, even declaring he was going before changing his mind.

The decision not to sack him, therefore, tends to be seen as one of those chance events that happened almost despite Edwards. Jim White, a journalist and United fan, takes this view:

> Edwards did stick by Ferguson but I believe there has been post-event rationalisation. I know Bobby Charlton says they did not think of sacking him but I am sure the axe was poised and had Ferguson failed to beat

Nottingham Forest in the third round of the FA Cup in 1990 he would have been sacked.

This match, widely seen as marking the turning point for Ferguson's fortunes, came midway through the 1989–90 season. Brian Glanville, writing in *The Sunday Times* on the day of the match, said that Ferguson's "transfer policy has been a disaster, his team selection has often made little sense and results, given the greatness of the club, have been abysmal. Today his job literally hangs in the balance. Comparisons with what Ferguson achieved at Aberdeen have little relevance. There, king of the castle, he was unquestionably a most successful manager. This, however, was rather as though one might flourish off Broadway, but fail on Broadway itself. The stakes at Old Trafford are vastly bigger, the expectations far larger, the competition so much more intense."

Ferguson certainly had need for prayer. As he put it later: "For that last 15 minutes it was eyes shut and praying. That's when you need the luck." This came in the shape of Mark Robins, a 20-year-old striker, the son of a policeman, who scored the only goal in a 1–0 win.

Ferguson went on to win the FA Cup after a replay victory over Crystal Palace at Wembley, securing what would prove to be the first of the 37 items of silverware he has so far brought to the club. That FA Cup triumph was followed by success in the European Cup-Winners Cup, which they won in 1991 together with the League Cup, yet the Holy Grail of a first league title since 1968 continued to elude him.

Ferguson had prepared meticulously for the Cup-Winners' Cup final against Barcelona on May 15, 1991. He consulted Steve Archibald, who had played for Barcelona, and also relied on a Dutch friend, Tom van Dalen, to make the right arrangements at Rotterdam, where the final was staged. Before the match he presented Johan Cruyff, the Barcelona manager, with a bottle of single malt whisky, just as he had eight years earlier to Alfredo Di Stefano, the Real Madrid manager, when Aberdeen knocked Real out in the same competition. Ferguson wanted history to repeat itself and United won 2–1, although the second goal by Mark Hughes was probably offside.

The victory proved a launch pad for United's flotation on the stock market a month later. The advisers had delayed flotation, hoping for a win. On June 10, 1991, the first dealings in Manchester United shares took place on the stock market. Ferguson never much cared for the stock market and could have walked out of Old Trafford soon after the Cup-Winners' Cup victory. He was sounded out by an intermediary on whether he would be interested in becoming manager of Real Madrid but rejected the approach, keen as he was to bring the league title back to Old Trafford. This seemed unwise when the last season of the old Football League saw United installed as odds-on favourites, only to lose out to Howard Wilkinson's Leeds. It seemed that Ferguson, while not quite the no-hoper of 1989–90, would, like many a United manager before him, be a winner of cups but not the championship that all United supporters craved. The launch of the Premier League would confound this judgment, proving that Ferguson not only had luck but uncanny timing too.

The recruitment of Eric Cantona in November 1992 was a wonderful illustration of this, coming as it did with the new league barely four months old. The story is now part of Old Trafford folklore. On a drizzly November afternoon, Ferguson is telling Edwards that he needs a new, world-class striker. His initial target had been David Hirst, a physical, powerful striker at Sheffield Wednesday. However, in what proved a game changer for United and the Premier League, Sheffield Wednesday had rejected United's £3.5 million offer. In the event, Hirst's career was to peter out amid a succession of injuries. Ferguson had always felt that United had missed out on Cantona, who had joined Leeds earlier that year and had been a crucial figure in taking the league title back to West Yorkshire for the first time since 1974. Just as Ferguson mentioned Cantona, Bill Fotherby, Leeds' managing director, came on the phone to ask Edwards if United would be willing to sell their Ireland full-back, Denis Irwin. Edwards countered by asking Fotherby about players Leeds might want to sell. Ferguson scribbled Cantona's name on a piece of paper and passed it to his chairman, saying: "Ask him about Cantona."

Edwards said to Fotherby: "Any chance of you selling him and we'd be interested. Need to be pretty quick, mind you, because we have the money for a striker and want to do some business now."

Cantona had shown both his good and bad side at Leeds: 14 goals in 35 games, including two hat-tricks, but his indiscipline had led to tensions with Wilkinson. Fotherby, having consulted Wilkinson, told Edwards that United could have Cantona for a mere £1 million. "That's an absolute steal," Ferguson cried, when Edwards broke the news.

The day the deal was done Edwards had lunch with Edward Freedman, the marketing man he had recruited from Tottenham to make sure United matched the north London club in the money-making business. Over lunch, Edwards was keen to talk about what he had done, so he asked Freedman:

"If there were any player you could pick in this country at the moment, who would it be?"

"You couldn't buy him."

"Why, who is it then?"

"Eric Cantona."

"How much would you pay?"

"He must be worth at least £4–5 million."

"I can get him for £1.2 million."

"It can't be true," said Freedman, blissfully unaware of what Edwards had already done.

Emlyn Hughes, the former Liverpool and England captain, predicted that Cantona would be a disaster for United and that was the conventional wisdom. The term *enfant terrible* could have been invented for the Frenchman. In December 1991, he had responded to being sent off while playing for Nimes by throwing the ball at the referee. At his hearing he was banned for one month, and Cantona's response was to walk up to each member of the disciplinary committee in turn and shout "Idiot!" into his face. His ban was increased to two months, and Cantona promptly announced his international retirement at the age of 25.

Cantona had always stood out both with his ability on the field and his antics off it. Fairly early in his career Cantona was nicknamed Le Brat. This came after he had punched Bruno Martini, the then French goalkeeper, who was also Cantona's team-mate at Auxerre, the club he had signed for when he was 15. Then, soon after joining Olympique Marseille, he threw his shirt at the referee and called their manager Henri Michel "*un sac de merde*", a shitbag. The club suggested he seek psychiatric help and banned him for a year. He was then loaned to Montpellier but had another fight with another team-mate.

A few weeks later he was in Sheffield for a trial with Wednesday, and actually played in an American six-a-side tournament for them. The ground in Yorkshire was covered with snow, however, so Wednesday could not see Cantona play on grass. While they dithered, Howard Wilkinson snapped him up for Leeds. Cantona may have only scored nine goals during his time in Leeds but his unshakeable self-belief had an instant effect on the club. But then Wilkinson had found him an impossible character to manage and at that stage there was no reason to believe that Ferguson would find managing Cantona any easier.

But the Frenchman developed a remarkable understanding with Ferguson, fell in love with the club, instilled belief and confidence in his fellow players, and a superstar, "King Eric", was born. Freedman could not get enough of Cantona to sell the United brand. As he told me: "Eric was on T-shirts, sweat shirts, whatever I could do with him. We did books, calendars and magazines. I sent someone over to spend a whole weekend with him in France taking photos. With Cantona I made every possible product."

In retrospect United's first title win in 26 years might have seemed predestined, particularly after Cantona's arrival. But although United recovered from their opening-day defeat by Sheffield United, the lead in the Premier League changed hands 15 times before the middle of February 1993. Norwich City were surprise contenders and were top of the table at Christmas. Their manager Mike Walker saw his club achieve similar success to that of their neighbours Ipswich in the 1960s and 1970s, qualifying for Europe for the first time and beating Bayern Munich in the process. Walker was so highly valued he was controversially poached by Everton but proved a failure in the North West, being sacked a season later as the club who had promoted the concept of the Premier League as one of the "Big Five" came perilously close to relegation.

The top half of the Premier League contained only three clubs who had won the title in the previous 24 seasons — Aston Villa, Liverpool and Arsenal. The old order, it was assumed, had changed thanks to the redistribution of television wealth. For many years, this sort of congested league race had been the norm in the old First Division. It was only in the late '60s that the competition became increasingly restricted to just a few prominent clubs.

For United the belief that they could finally do it came with a 2–1 win over Sheffield Wednesday on April 10, 1993, clinched by a Steve Bruce header seven minutes into stoppage time. Ferguson and his assistant Brian Kidd both celebrated wildly on the edge of the pitch when Bruce scored. And so on Sunday, May 2, United clinched their first English league championship since 1967 when Aston Villa were beaten 1–0 at home by Oldham. Ferguson, then 51, had opted to play golf instead of watching the match on Sky and did not realise that United had taken the title until he returned to the clubhouse to be informed of Nick Henry's winner for Oldham. His joy could not be contained. "This is the greatest achievement, the greatest moment of my football career. I couldn't have asked for anything else," he said.

The triumph meant that Ferguson had laid the ghost of Scottish managers failing when they came to manage south of the border. He had now completed the domestic treble of trophies — the league championship, FA Cup and League Cup, just as he had done with Aberdeen. But in this inaugural season, the Premier League had not quite engineered a dramatic finale. The competition dribbled on, and United only got their hands on the trophy on May 3, when they beat Blackburn Rovers 3–1 at Old Trafford. Premier League chief executive Rick Parry presented the trophy to Bryan Robson and Steve Bruce with Sir Matt Busby looking on from the stands.

The final weekend programme saw Queens Park Rangers play twice within three days at Loftus Road — the west London club beating Aston Villa 2–1 on Sunday May 9 and then Sheffield Wednesday 3–1 on Tuesday, May 11. That

Tuesday also saw Arsenal lose their last game 3–1 to Tottenham at Highbury. While the match had little riding on it, there had been a Tottenham board meeting at the Arsenal ground beforehand when the first rounds in Alan Sugar's war of words with his manager Terry Venables were fired. By the end of the month the whole world knew what a "bung" was.

United's triumph was to be a taster for Ferguson's all-conquering class of '94, when United did the Double. Manchester United became only the fourth team in the 20th century to complete the League and FA Cup Double (Tottenham 1960–61, Arsenal 1970–71 and Liverpool 1985–86 being the others). Any chance of a domestic treble was thwarted by Aston Villa, who beat United 3–1 in the League Cup final at Wembley.

The club's first-choice XI (signed over the course of six seasons) boasted a 100 per cent record in the games they played together in that Double season. Peter Schmeichel, Steve Bruce, Gary Pallister and Denis Irwin were the defensive bedrocks (alongside Paul Parker at right-back). Roy Keane and Paul Ince provided bite and creativity alongside Bryan Robson in midfield. Ryan Giggs and Mark Hughes were home-grown forwards, with Cantona the catalyst who turned a very good team into one of the greats.

Reflecting in 1997 on his first title success four years earlier, Ferguson would say: "The 1994 team had mental toughness — so many of them. Real tough bastards."

But if Ferguson believed Cantona had been tamed he was in for a rude shock when on January 25, 1995, he took his team for a mid-week league match at Selhurst Park. Cantona's volcanic temperament boiled over in spectacular style. The Frenchman was sent off four minutes after half-time after kicking at Crystal Palace's Richard Shaw.

On his way to the dressing room, which at Selhurst Park involves walking round the touchline quite close to the home fans, the Frenchman was subjected to a stream of abuse from Crystal Palace fans. One fan, Matthew Simmons, a 20-year-old glazier, had run to the front of the stand from his seat 11 rows back to abuse and taunt the United player. He not only called into question his parentage but his origins in racial terms. Cantona, unable to contain his anger, jumped across the advertising barriers that divided him from the fans to launch an infamous kung-fu style kick and then a punch on Simmons. The two then exchanged punches before police and stewards broke up the fight. All of which was witnessed by millions watching on television.

Graham Kelly, the chief executive of the Football Association, announced that Cantona would be charged with "misconduct that has brought the game into disrepute". He went on:

What happened last night was a stain on our game. If any offence is proved, the player concerned is bound to face a severe punishment. The Football Association believes last night's incident was unprecedented in our game. It brought shame on those involved and worst of all on the game itself. We especially deplore the appalling example set to young supporters who are the game's future. It is our intention to do everything in our power to prevent such a disgraceful event happening again.

Maurice Watkins, who was to play a central role in this drama — the voice of reason for United, as the *Manchester Evening News* called him during this affair — had not seen the incident. But the moment it happened he went to the dressing room to find Cantona sitting very quietly there. United, realising the seriousness of the incident, was torn about retaining Cantona.

After the game, Ferguson had said:

In charting Eric's career everyone agrees he reacts when he feels an injustice. It wasn't really a kick at the guy [Richard Shaw]. It was just a wee flick. We've seen guys do that before. It wasn't really a sending-off offence, but because he was Cantona he was sent off. There were two bad tackles on him in the first half and the referee didn't even speak to the opponents. Some referees would have clamped down immediately in that game at Crystal Palace. Others, as you saw, didn't. All we ask is that he gets the same fair treatment as anyone else.

But despite this defence of his man, for some time after the Selhurst kung-fu kick, it seemed that even Ferguson thought that it would mean the end of Cantona in England, or for that matter, any football. This was certainly the opinion of many in the game. Even the United hierarchy were undecided. The following night, Watkins met Edwards, Roland Smith and Ferguson at the Edge Hotel in Alderley and there was no consensus as to what should be done about Cantona. If Inter Milan had offered more money, Cantona might have gone. A few days before, their general manager Paolo Taveggia had rung Edwards inquiring about Cantona, but his approach had been rebuffed. He was at Crystal Palace that night watching Cantona but while Inter came back later it was to buy Paul Ince.

It was decided that Cantona would be suspended until the end of the season — a classic lawyer's decision driven by Watkins. United were seen to be taking action and by pre-empting any FA punishment, United felt this might discourage the FA from doing worse. Watkins was bent on damage limitation, both on behalf of Cantona, who was being represented by his firm, and United.

It produced some high drama including this moment at the FA hearing when, from his seat next to Cantona, Watkins heard the Frenchman, after apologising to the FA, the fans, his team-mates and the club, say: "And I want to apologise to the prostitute who shared my bed last evening." Kelly recalls: "Maurice turned, his mouth dropped open and he almost fell off his chair." Gordon McKeag, one of the three-man FA tribunal hearing the Cantona case, misheard and turned to Geoff Thompson, the chairman, and said: "What did he say? 'He prostrates himself before the FA?'"

"Yes," said Thompson, eager to get away from the subject.

Cantona was such a star that Ian Stott, the third member of the disciplinary committee, actually wanted his autograph. Thompson told him he could not ask for it, as this would demean the hearing. However, throughout the hearing Cantona was doodling on a sheet of paper. It turned out to be a sketch of Thompson, which Cantona presented to Thompson at the end. Thompson on his own initiative passed it on to Stott.

Later that day, the FA decided that United's suspension was insufficient and Cantona would be banned until September 30. Two members of the FA commission, Thompson and McKeag, wanted a longer ban but Stott, perhaps star-struck, persuaded them to limit it to September 30. Watkins could not contain his anger as he felt that the press release the FA were issuing would seriously prejudice the criminal trial Cantona was to face.

Cantona was originally sentenced to serve a prison sentence; Watkins got him out on bail which on appeal was reduced to 120 hours of community service. At the end of it, Watkins decided that there had to be a press conference. Cantona agreed but only if he was allowed to speak. Just before the press conference began, Cantona came to Watkins' hotel room and, taking a piece of paper, started to write.

He asked Watkins: "What is the name of the big boat when they catch fish?" Watkins told him it was called a trawler. Then Cantona asked: "What is the name of the big seabird?" Watkins replied: "A seagull."

Having had a Watkins tutorial, Cantona went to the press conference and uttered his by now immortal lines: "When seagulls follow the trawler it is because they think sardines will be thrown into the sea." Watkins, not sure he should have allowed Cantona to speak, pretended he did not know what Cantona was on about. The Frenchman had once again proved how clever he was. The exact meaning of Cantona's words would be debated for weeks and in that time his unique offense, assaulting a spectator, was completely overshadowed.

By then details had also begun to emerge of the fan he had assaulted and the tide had turned in Cantona's favour. Matthew Simmons' past was revealed to be that of an undesirable petty criminal. In 1992 he had been convicted of attacking a petrol station attendant with a spanner. He pleaded guilty to assault with intention to rob and was sentenced to two years' probation. During the court hearing witnesses at the match described how Simmons had shouted at Cantona: "Fuck off, you French bastard" and "Fuck off back to France, you mother-fucker." Simmons admitted shouting at Cantona while pointing to the dressing room but maintained he had said: "It's an early bath for you, Mr Cantona."

After the Cantona incident was long over Simmons, who had been charged with threatening behaviour with the intent to cause a person to believe that immediate unlawful violence would be used against him, was brought to court for his hearing.

On May 2, 1996 the London *Evening Standard* reported how at the hearing in Croydon, Simmons kicked the back of the head of the prosecuting lawyer and grabbed his throat. This took place just as the chairman of the bench at Croydon, Mrs Mary Richards, found Simmons guilty. Simmons threw himself over a table and lunged at Mr Jeffrey McCann, the prosecuting lawyer's back. He ripped off the lawyer's tie and grabbed him by the throat. It took six prison officers and policemen to pull Simmons off as he kept yelling: "I'm innocent. I promise. I swear on the Bible." Police struggled to handcuff him and drag him from the court.

During his exile Cantona had talked of quitting and Ferguson had to fly to Paris to talk him out of it. This happened when the FA sent a warning letter to United after Cantona played in a practice match against Rochdale behind closed doors. Ferguson, who called it a "silly" letter and one probably written by an FA official with "a bee in his bonnet", went on to say: "I mean, we've had games many times against teams like Stoke, Rochdale, Bury and Oldham, you know, closed-door games were you've got suspended players or one coming back after injury. That goes on throughout the country, so to say all of a sudden you can't play in one because you are still suspended was a bit much. I think maybe Eric felt he couldn't win. They weren't going to allow him to win."

But in the end, persuaded by Ferguson, Cantona did return and what is more his return was heralded by his marketing sponsors Nike. The company had run advertisements which suggested Cantona was saying sorry but on careful reading it turned out he was joking. So in one entitled Apology, Cantona said sorry for scoring twice against Chelsea in the 1994 Cup final and missing a late chance against Newcastle. He also said: "I apologise for only scoring once against Manchester City", in the 5–0 drubbing by United. After City complained, the reference to the club was removed. There was also a Nike advert which had Cantona standing in the doorway of what looked like prison gates along Sir

Matt Busby Way, Cantona wearing his No. 7 shirt with words that read: "He's been punished for his mistakes. Now it's someone else's turn." Two United fans paid £1,200 out of their own pockets for a poster which showed Cantona's face under the headline: "We'll never forget that night at Selhurst Park (when you buried that amazing volley against Wimbledon)."

Not everyone wanted Cantona back or appreciated the humour that preceded his return. Certainly not Brian Clough. Writing in the *News of the World* on the Sunday that Cantona was to play his comeback match, he thundered:

"I don't give a damn if I never see him again. I have been known to clip a few people but what he did at Crystal Palace last season was completely over the top. If I had been his manager I would have done what Howard Wikinson did at Leeds. sold him without hesitation." And after putting Cantona on the same level as the supporters Clough had clipped round the head for invading the Forest ground, he went on:

"It's my view that Cantona did exactly what they did. He went somewhere he shouldn't have been — flying into the crowd feet first. He had been sent off and should have walked round the track, gone into the dressing room, had a shower, put on his smart French designer clothes and waited to get on the coach." Cantona may have sublime ability, conceded Clough, but "on occasions I don't think he is in his right mind. There's something wrong with the man."

Ferguson and United clearly did not see it that way. Their faith in the Frenchman was justified and his return, against Liverpool in October 1995 at Old Trafford, was typical of the man. Not only did he create the goal that put United into the lead barely a minute into the match — but he scored an equalising penalty with 20 minutes remaining after Ryan Giggs had been fouled. Cantona went on from there and his 14 league goals contributed directly to 18 points won during the season — he scored the winner in five 1–0 games and struck crucial goals for United in three draws as they marched to another title.

Confirmation of Cantona's rehabilitation came when on the eve of the Cup final, on May 9, 1996, he was voted the Football Writers' Footballer of the Year. But at the award ceremony he showed he had not lost his ability for verbal mystification by declaring: "Some criticisms mean nothing so I compare them to toilets and think, 'Screw them'. It has been a long year but what a beautiful one."

However, his banishment from the game also seemed to have matured him and taught him to control his passions. The next day a Cantona goal helped United to their second Double, as they beat Liverpool. In a poor final his goal five minutes before the end was the one memorable moment and Cantona became the first foreign player to captain an FA Cup-winning team. To add to the misery on Merseyside, Liverpool had worn cream Armani suits for their pre-match Wembley walkabout — a fashion faux pas that has haunted them ever since.

However, as Cantona led his United side up the steps to collect their winners' medals, three supporters insulted him and spat at him. For good measure a Liverpool fan in a red wig swung a punch at Ferguson as he followed his team up to the Royal Box. Cantona wiped the spit away with his hand and, unlike his reaction at Selhurst Park, said: "The Liverpool fans were just very disappointed. But it did not spoil the team's victory."

On May 18, 1997, six days before his 31st birthday, Cantona stunned football by announcing his retirement. The enigmatic Frenchman said: "I have always planned to retire when I was at the top, and at Manchester United I have reached the pinnacle of my career. I have had a marvellous relationship with everyone at the club, not least the fans, and I wish Manchester United even more success in future." For Ferguson it was "a sad day... he is one of the most gifted and dedicated players I have had the pleasure of working with. Whenever fans discuss United's greatest side, you can be sure that for many Eric's name will be high up on the list."

His absence during part of the 1994–95 season showed just how important he was. Had he been present it is possible that Blackburn, who had re-emerged as a power in the last years of the old First Division, bankrolled by steel magnate Jack Walker's millions, might not have stolen United's thunder. For Ferguson this was doubly galling as the club were managed by Kenny Dalglish and their title challenge had been spearheaded by 34 goals from Alan Shearer, a player he had wanted to sign.

Ferguson's rivalry with Dalglish, a fellow Glaswegian, went back years: the pair had played against each other for Rangers and Celtic reserves (though Dalglish is nine years younger and, unlike Ferguson, enjoyed a spectacularly successful playing career). Ferguson was well aware of the burden Dalglish imposed on him. Months before Ferguson took over at Old Trafford in November 1986, Dalglish had burnished his reputation by winning the League and FA Cup Double in 1985–86, his first year as player-manager.

The pair brought their Scottish quarrels south, having initially clashed in the build-up to the 1986 World Cup finals. Ferguson had been appointed Scotland manager — Jock Stein died the previous year — and he decided to leave Liverpool defender Alan Hansen out of his squad for Mexico. Dalglish then pulled out just before the finals, claiming his injured knee was not up to another summer of football — a decision many felt was an act of solidarity with his Anfield team-mate.

The pair's most famous feud was sparked following a 3–3 draw at Anfield in April 1988, when Ferguson complained to a radio reporter about Liverpool's intimidation of referees. He said that it was no surprise managers "have to leave here choking on their own vomit, biting their tongue, afraid to tell the truth".

Dalglish, holding his new-born baby daughter Lauren, heard this as he passed by. He interrupted the interview to say: "You'd be better off talking to my baby. She's only six weeks old but you'd get more sense from her than him."

There seemed little danger of the two extending their feud when Dalglish resigned through ill-health in February 1991. But, lured back by Walker, he led Blackburn to promotion in 1992 and then persuaded Alan Shearer to reject United and join Rovers. After finishing fourth and second in consecutive seasons, Dalglish was ready to lock horns with his fellow Scotsman again.

As the two sides took the title race to the last day of the 1995 season, Ferguson commented that "we're hoping for a Devon Loch situation", a reference to the racehorse that failed to win the 1956 Grand National despite being lengths clear of the field. Blackburn did lose three of their last five games but managed to do enough to claim their first championship for 81 years. They clinched the title despite losing to Liverpool since United could only draw at West Ham. Because Dalglish had responded to Ferguson's jibe by asking, "Who's Devon Loch?", the United manager's letter of congratulations contained a PS: "Surely your dad must have told you about Devon Loch!"

Years later Ferguson would suggest his falling out with Dalglish was not permanent and that he admired Blackburn for their resilience and spirit good Scottish characteristics. Indeed, their relationship changed in the wake of the Hillsborough tragedy. Ferguson ordered United fans to head for Anfield in a display of sympathy — a move that his rival did not forget. Dalglish wrote in his autobiography: "As long as I live I will never forget that exceptional gesture from Fergie."

Later Ferguson agreed to write a foreword to Dalglish's autobiography, although it could be argued that his phrase "You only need six people to carry your coffin" suggests that he didn't necessarily regard Dalglish as the most clubbable of men.

But Ferguson's clash with Dalglish was in the long run not his most significant rivalry. Dalglish's title triumph with Blackburn proved something of a swansong and two other managers were to mount much greater challenges. But before they emerged an Englishman briefly tried to get the better of Ferguson, only to find he had bitten off more than he could chew.

The 1995–96 season had seen a major structural change, with four teams relegated as the Premier League contracted to 20 teams. However, it will be always be remembered as the season when, with a few well-placed comments, Ferguson paved the way for one of the Premier League's most iconic images and created the legend of his prowess in psychological warfare. Popularly dubbed "mind games", they demonstrated how he could use the global or domestic spotlight to gain a psychological edge and plant seeds of doubt into the minds of an opposing manager.

Kevin Keegan was to prove the most spectacular victim of this. Newcastle, having been promoted only two years previously, looked as if they might satisfy Tyneside's hunger for the championship for the first time since the 1926–27 season. Manchester United had begun the season badly, losing 3–1 to Aston Villa — their worst league defeat for three years. Ian Taylor, Mark Draper and Dwight Yorke, from the penalty spot, scored in the first half; David Beckham pulled one back with eight minutes remaining. In the summer Alex Ferguson had sold key players such as Mark Hughes and Paul Ince. Steve Bruce was suspended, while Ryan Giggs and Andy Cole were ruled out through injury. United's line-up at Villa Park that day was: Peter Schmeichel in goal, a back four of Paul Parker, Denis Irwin, Gary Neville and Gary Pallister (who was replaced by John O'Kane after 59 minutes); the midfield was Lee Sharpe, Nicky Butt, Roy Keane and Phil Neville (who was replaced by Beckham at half-time); and Brian McClair and Paul Scholes in attack.

That evening, Alan Hansen uttered the immortal words on *Match of the Day*:

> I think they [United] have got problems. I wouldn't say they have got major problems. Obviously three players have departed. The trick is, always buy when you are strong. So he [Ferguson] needs to buy players. You can't win anything with kids. You look at that line-up for Manchester United today and Aston Villa, at quarter past two when they get the team sheet, it's just going to give them a lift — and that will happen every time he plays the kids. He's got to buy players. It's as simple as that. The trick of winning the championship is having strength in depth. They just haven't got it.

On January 21, Newcastle had opened up a 12-point lead over both Liverpool and Manchester United, which, with 15 matches remaining, appeared to be insurmountable.

January 21, 1996	P	W	D	L	F	A	GD	PTS
1 Newcastle United	23	17	3	3	45	19	26	54
2 Liverpool	23	12	6	5	46	21	25	42
3 Manchester United	23	12	6	5	41	27	14	42
4 Tottenham	24	11	8	5	33	24	9	41

But United, traditionally strong in the second half of the season, began to claw back the deficit and Newcastle faltered. Monday, April 3, 1996 witnessed one of the most exciting matches in Premier League history, when Liverpool beat Newcastle United 4–3. Stan Collymore, Liverpool's £8.4 million signing (then a British transfer record), scored the winner in the final seconds to condemn Newcastle to their fourth defeat in six matches. That goal produced the indelible image of Newcastle United manager Kevin Keegan with his head in his hands in the Anfield dug-out.

In one comment, Ferguson suggested that other teams tried harder against United than against Newcastle and in particular that Leeds and Nottingham Forest might not try their best against Newcastle in their forthcoming matches. This lit the fuse for Keegan. On April 30, he made an extraordinary outburst live on Sky TV. Speaking to presenters Richard Keys and Andy Gray, shortly after Newcastle had lost 1–0 to Leeds United, Keegan rose passionately to Ferguson's bait:

Keegan: We just want to keep our hopes alive. A lot of things have been said over the last few days. Some of it almost slanderous. We have never commented. We have just got on working, trying to pass the ball like we do in training…

No, no. Things have been said about… I think you've got to send Alex Ferguson a tape of this game, haven't ya? Isn't that what he asked for?

Gray: Well I'm sure if he was watching it tonight he could… tonight Kevin, he could have no arguments about the way Leeds went about their job, they really, really tested your team.

Keegan: And we're playing Nottingham Forest on Thursday and he objected to that? Now, that was fixed up months ago, we were supposed to play Nottingham Forest. I mean, that sort of stuff, we're… it's… it's been… we're bigger than that.

Keys: But that's part and parcel of the psychological battle, Kevin.

Keegan: No! That's when you do that with footballers like he said about Leeds… and when you do things like that about a man like Stuart Pearce… I'm… I… I've kept really quiet but I'll tell you something, he went down in my estimation when he said that. We have not resorted to that, but I'll tell ya, you can tell him now, he'll be watching it, we're still fighting for this title and he's got to go to Middlesbrough and get something and I'll tell ya, honestly, I'll love it if we beat them! Love it!... It has really got to me. I have voiced it live. Not in front of the press or anywhere. I am... even going to the press conference. But the battle's still on and Manchester United have not won this yet.

This was possibly the first time that Ferguson had psychologically crushed an opponent in such a humiliating manner in public. But it was not to be the last.

In the end Newcastle finished second — which remains to this day the highest league position achieved by an English manager in the Premier League (along with Ron Atkinson of Aston Villa in 1992–93). Some believe that the £6.75 million spent on bringing Colombian striker Faustino Asprilla from Parma was the catalyst for Newcastle's downfall. While Newcastle could only draw their last two games United's charge yielded seven wins in their final eight games and a four-point winning margin. Within a year, Keegan had left Newcastle, claiming he had taken the team as far as he could but not before his favourite St James' Park memory: Philippe Albert's sumptuous chip over Peter Schmeichel to seal an extraordinary 5–0 win over Manchester United in October 1996.

The pair renewed their rivalry when Keegan took over at Manchester City and during his second spell at Newcastle. Reflecting on his clash with Ferguson, Keegan later said:

> For a day or two I really disliked him. I wouldn't say we're close now, but we have talked a lot. I've sold players to him, he's sold players to me, I've done charity things for him, he's done them for me. But if you're asking me do I love him (laughs)... I totally respect him.
>
> He's managed a huge club for 20 years. I've got a terrific record against Alex Ferguson compared with most people, too. It probably isn't level, but I've managed teams that have beaten his teams 5–0, 4–1, 3–1. Two Manchester derbies. So I would say I've come out relatively well against him.

By this time, in the late 1990s, Ferguson's relationship with his chairman Martin Edwards had begun to change, with Ferguson revealing how different he was to the manager who had preceded him, Sir Matt Busby, and one who had been a rival, Terry Venables.

Busby had been seen as a potential owner of United and the thwarting of his ambition by the Edwards family was seen by many United supporters as the man of football losing out to the man of money. Ferguson, in contrast, has never shown the slightest interest in owning the club. And unlike Venables, Ferguson was not interested in forming companies and never expressed the view that he could manage clubs better than their existing owners. His problem with Edwards was that he was not properly rewarded for his work. As Ferguson put it very candidly in his autobiography, *Managing My Life:* "Conversations with Martin Edwards are usually straightforward and pleasant until you ask him for more money. Then you have a problem." It is unusual for a manager to be quite so blunt about his employer but by this time Ferguson's status as the untouchable of Old Trafford meant that he had nothing to fear.

Their relationship had steadily worsened after a cosy start in the late 1980s. Back in the winter of 1988, they were so close they had driven to Nottingham Forest's City Ground together hoping to persuade Brian Clough to sell Stuart Pearce to United. It proved a wasted trip as Clough, not keen to see them, pretended he was not in his office. But it showed how Edwards and Ferguson worked well together.

Edwards and Ferguson were drawn together by their common predicament. Both were somewhat beleaguered, Ferguson seeking success, Edwards money. In debt and unable to raise the money to rebuild the Stretford End, and troubled by abuse from the fans, Edwards had told Ferguson in the summer of 1989 that he had had enough and was planning to sell. Not long afterwards, he had his famous lunch with Michael Knighton at Old Trafford and agreed to sell the club. A decade later, with Edwards rich and Ferguson hailed as one of the greatest managers of all time, success had dissolved the common need that once had kept them together.

Ferguson is always referred to as the "boss" of Manchester United but for Edwards he was an employee — the most important employee, but by no means the only figure. While Ferguson rules supreme over his domain, the field of play, this is quite separate from the rest of the Manchester United business. As Edwards put it to me:

> He is not the old-fashioned type of manager. His role is quite sharply defined. Alex would report directly to me as chief executive. Ken Merrett, the secretary of the football club, did a typical job arranging reserve games, dealing with team travel and the rulebook. The way we ran things at Manchester United, Alex's role would be no different to the coaches at Inter Milan, AC Milan, Barcelona or Real Madrid. I think more and more clubs in this country run the same way we do. We could not have had a George Graham situation in our club because I did all the buying and all the selling. I did all the contracts.

This system was in force long before Ferguson arrived. "I had done that since Dave Sexton and Ron Atkinson. Alex is probably a lot different from Sexton and Atkinson, but my policies had not changed."

Unlike many other Premier League managers, Arsene Wenger for instance, Ferguson has no office at Old Trafford. His office is at Manchester United's Carrington training ground and when I mentioned to Edwards that Ferguson gets to work at 7.30 in the morning, he said: "It could well be. I don't know. He comes occasionally to the office [at Old Trafford]." Edwards himself rarely ventured to the training ground.

Edwards was well aware that in this battle between himself and Ferguson, only Ferguson could win. Many years ago he told Scholar: "One thing you should never do is get into an argument with the manager on the back pages. If you do you will lose." Scholar forgot the advice in 1991, took on Terry Venables and ended up losing Tottenham. Edwards never made that mistake.

Ferguson, of course, has always been the master of the back page and his handling of a reporter from *The Mail on Sunday* illustrates this. Bob Cass, who knows Ferguson well, had run a story saying Bryan Robson, who was often injured, was making a comeback in a televised Sunday match. It was the back-page lead but as the television cameras rolled there was no Robson, not even on the bench. Roger Kelly, then sports editor of *The Mail on Sunday*, was not best pleased and told Cass so. Kelly then went off to play golf and as he returned home the telephone rang. The caller said he was Alex Ferguson. Kelly thought it was a joke but it was the man himself and he told Kelly that Cass had the right story but Ferguson had made a late change and Cass was not to blame. It showed how Ferguson can control the back-page agenda.

To a great extent the Ferguson-Edwards relationship was also shaped by the lessons Edwards drew from his father's relationship with managers. Louis Edwards had got very close to Tommy Docherty. "My father got too friendly with Tommy Docherty. He used to go to races and things like that with him." Then when he got the sack over his affair with Mary Brown, the wife of United physio Laurie Brown, Docherty was quite bitter about it. "I think I had a very good working relationship with Alex Ferguson," said Edwards. "But if you say did we go out socially together, no we didn't."

Ferguson felt that he was hamstrung by United's inflexible wages structure, which determined that the top players were paid roughly the same amount, which in the early '90s was about £23,000 a week. "My hands were tied, he wrote in his autobiography. "I think the restrictions applied to wages prevented us from being the power in European football that we could have been in the '90s." This was a factor that prevented Alan Shearer moving to Old Trafford from Southampton. He went to Blackburn instead. As Freedman told me: "I think the money became excessive in Martin's valuation. Shearer was going to totally break the wage structure of Manchester United, which I don't think Martin wanted to do at the time, or could afford to. The other thing was I don't think Shearer really made his commitment to United, which I think Alex wanted. Alex didn't want a mercenary saying, 'I can get X amount more from you guys.' Alex wanted someone to say, 'I am committed to United and I'll come for United.' I don't think Shearer ever did that."

Ferguson would later conclude it was not such a loss to miss out on Shearer. "Had we secured Shearer, it is highly improbable that we would have gone for Eric Cantona," he wrote. "Could Shearer have illuminated Old Trafford as the great Frenchman did? I think not."

For Ferguson the problem he had with Edwards was about money not only in the transfer market but, "about my own wages. I feel I should have received a better salary for my period at United than was forthcoming from Martin, who is extremely guarded with money... I appreciate that life at United has changed drastically since the advent of the plc and that Martin Edwards had a difficult job. The new set-up had sadly reduced communication between us. Gone are the days when we maintained a constant, healthy dialogue."

These arguments over money between Ferguson and Edwards turned into something of a boardroom saga, each episode more acrimonious than the last. The seeds of this were sown in the first year of the Premier League in 1992, when there had been ructions over share options — Ferguson was less than happy that Edwards had given Robin Launders, the accountant, four times as much as he had given his manager. In 1993 Ferguson, having won his first title, found he earned a lot less than his fellow Scot, George Graham. Arsenal had rewarded Graham, who had won two championships, two League Cups and one FA Cup, by making him the country's highest paid manager. Ferguson mentioned Graham's figures to Edwards, only to be told that Edwards had checked with David Dein and the figure was not right. Ferguson did, however, get a new contract.

But this was only round one. Round two came at the end of the 1994–95 season, when United, having promised a repeat of their Double season but missing Cantona, won nothing. The season also saw Paul Ince, Andrei Kanchelskis and Mark Hughes depart. Ferguson had instigated Ince's departure. As he would describe the England midfielder a few years later: "He's a bully, a f***ing big-time Charlie." But not everyone at Old Trafford was happy Ince had gone. Ferguson was most upset when Edwards interrupted his holiday to tell him his assistant Brian Kidd was suggesting it was not such a good move. Or to learn that Hughes had signed for Chelsea due to pension problems.

Ferguson returned from holiday to find the *Manchester Evening News* holding a poll asking whether he should be sacked. It was at this point that he went back to Edwards and asked for a pay rise: "My timing may have been ill-conceived but I still felt seriously aggrieved over having been lumbered with a pay deal that left me trailing so far behind George Graham."

Edwards advised Ferguson to see Professor Roland Smith, chairman of the plc at his Isle of Man home. Ferguson, having learnt from his 1993 experience, went armed with Graham's contract and demanding a six-year deal that would see him through to 60. He also wanted a role in the club after retirement.

Smith, who had Watkins with him, was ready to counter-attack, saying, "Some people at Old Trafford think you are not as focused as you have been." A six-year contract was out, no United manager ever had such a contract, and there could be no guaranteed role for him after retirement. But the whole thing would have to wait until June 1996, when the remuneration committee would meet.

Ferguson says he came back from the Isle of Man flattened, confused and worried, although this probably drove him on to achieve the second Double in 1995–96, with United moving to a higher gear from October 1995 when Cantona returned from suspension.

But the night before United achieved their second Double, Ferguson had a tremendous row with Watkins about his contract and seriously considered resigning. Ned Kelly, United's former head of security, recalls the reaction of Edwards, looking nervous standing outside the stadium dressing rooms on the day of the final: "I asked him if he was all right. 'You won't believe this, Ned, but Ferguson telephoned Maurice Watkins at his hotel and told him that unless he got his bonus and pay rise he wouldn't be leading the team out today. He was serious. He told Maurice that he could lead the team out.'"

But if Ferguson was fed up, Edwards had also begun to consider replacements, one of them being Terry Venables. His job as England manager was ending in June after the European Championship and, after a board meeting, Edwards approached Freedman and said they were thinking of Venables. Freedman could barely contain himself: "What, Terry Venables? You must be mad." Ferguson, at the same time, was approached by Jimmy Armfield for advice on who should be the next England manager and expressed some interest in taking over from Venables. According to former FA chief executive Graham Kelly: "It soon became clear that [Ferguson] was interested in succeeding Terry Venables as England coach."

In the end a deal was struck and although Ferguson was not happy he consoled himself by thinking he had made "huge strides in relation to my existing agreement". Nevertheless just before the 1998–99 season began, which would see United achieve the unique treble of Champions League, Premier League and the FA Cup, he came close to resigning.

Ferguson was on holiday in France during the 1998 World Cup when he learnt that Brian Kidd had been approached by Everton and United were giving him a new contract to keep him. It seemed to him that Kidd always got money whenever an approach came. Then he learnt Kidd was suggesting that instead of Dwight Yorke, United should buy John Hartson. Enraged, he flew back from holiday to confront Edwards and Roland Smith at Smith's HSBC offices in the city. When Edwards, after a long speech of praise, wondered whether Ferguson had allowed his celebrity status to go to his head and, worried about his new-found interest in racing, questioned his focus on his job, Ferguson asked: "Do you want me to call it a day?" "No, no," both directors replied and Ferguson was pacified.

But though Ferguson stayed, Kidd was soon on his way out and it showed the interesting relationship Ferguson had with his No. 2. Kidd was a coach much in demand. He had secured a new four-year deal in March 1998 when Manchester City had been sniffing round. Before the season began Everton came calling, offering Kidd more than three times what he was paid by United. Kidd asked for permission to speak to Everton and this had nearly led Ferguson to threaten to quit. Kidd got a new contract that made him the best-paid coach in the country.

On November 21, Blackburn slumped to the bottom of the league. They sacked Roy Hodgson, who was so upset by this that he decided to abandon England and seek work abroad, a decision the future England manager came to regret. The club were desperate to get Kidd. Ferguson's view was he did not think Kidd really wanted to go to Everton or even to be a manager. He felt Kidd was too insecure, too full of doubts about his own ability to become a manager. But Blackburn, desperate to avoid relegation, offered him vast riches, believed to be around £1 million. While United were prepared to up his contract and deal with certain of the issues, the main problem, as Peter Kenyon, then the deputy chief executive, told me, was that: "Brian was offered such an amount of money he could not afford to turn it down. He had a burning desire to be a manager, to be No. 1, and there was no guarantee of that at Old Trafford. He did not ask for it because he knew he would not get it, but he implied that. He definitely wanted to prove that he could be No. 1."

On the afternoon of December 2, as Tottenham met Manchester United in the League Cup quarter-final, Kenyon, Edwards and Smith held a meeting at HSBC with Kidd and his adviser. Edwards, in his previous public statements, had said that Kidd would leave Old Trafford over his dead body. But at that meeting it was clear that even such a dramatic gesture would not stop Kidd from going to Blackburn. On the way to the game that night, the traffic was heavy and Kidd was becoming anxious about getting to White Hart Lane in time. When the driver said it was still a mile away, Kidd jumped out and decided to run to the ground. But it turned out to be three miles and it was a more than a little breathless and less than composed Kidd who arrived at White Hart Lane. Ferguson came to the post-match press conference, having spoken to Edwards and Kidd, but angrily brushed aside any reference to Kidd going and the criticism on the back pages was reserved for Edwards and the plc for not doing more to keep Kidd and preserve the Kidd-Ferguson partnership.

Ferguson's true attitude towards Kidd only emerged nine months later in his autobiography. Then he wrote: "I saw Brian Kidd as a complex person, often quite insecure," he said. "Deep down I would have had serious reservations about Brian ever taking charge of United. I suspect that the constant demand for hard, often unpopular, decisions would have put an intolerable stress on his temperament."

By then the Sky bid for Manchester United had made more people aware of the wretched relationship between Edwards and Ferguson. For Lord Tim Bell it was to come as a considerable shock. Bell, the great public relations guru and adviser to Sky, was present at a meeting at the HSBC offices with Edwards, Smith, Kenyon and David Gill, the finance director. Bell was there to hold the hand of Mark Booth, the American head of Sky. He wanted an English person who might know something about football. Bell recalled to me:

> I had gone there with only one objective, which was to get Alex Ferguson to endorse the Sky bid. We knew that no matter what the resistance to Rupert Murdoch was, if Alex Ferguson said or even half-said that this was vaguely a good idea, this would completely wrong-foot all the opposition. Before I went into the meeting with Manchester United I had had a meeting with Mark to try and find out how much he would spend on getting Ferguson on side. I said, "As a matter of interest, how much... nearly two million, what do you want to offer?" He said, "I don't know, two million would probably do it, maybe more or whatever it takes to get him on side." I really just wanted to walk in and say, "What do you think it would cost Ferguson to say yes?" But, with the board there, we couldn't be quite that crude. So Booth said, "Would it be a good idea if we met with Alex Ferguson?" We suggested that Mark might have dinner with Alex Ferguson and just ask what he thought about it, have a chat and introduce himself.

The reaction of Edwards completely surprised Bell. As Bell recounted to me later, Edwards said: "Christ, no! You don't want to see him. He's a troublemaker. If you tell him, he'll leak everything. He's totally hostile." Bell recalls:

> It was a nightmare. When Sky inquired if there was any way we could involve Ferguson in the transaction and make him benefit from it, Edwards said, "Don't give him the money for Christ's sake. The man's useless." Unbelievable! It is like when you find a journalist on the paper that seems to be the top writer. Then you meet the proprietor and he says, "I hate the bastard. He never co-operates and so on." Clearly Ferguson was not friendly with Edwards and Edwards was not friendly with Ferguson. They'd had a bad time during the summer. They'd obviously had a huge disagreement about Dwight Yorke and they'd obviously had disagreements about other things as well. I think it was to do with money. I'm not so sure it wasn't also that Edwards wanted him to buy other players and he had failed to do so.
>
> I said we could explore what it would take to inspire Alex into saying, "What a good idea." And Edwards looked at me and said, "What sum are you talking about?" I said, rather crudely, "You know, £1 million, £2 million, something like that. Special one-off payment, golden handshake, whatever." He said, "But I've just given him his first warning letter for misbehaviour." I said, "What?" He said, "It's not right, it's unacceptable, I mean, he's a pain in the arse, he never does what you tell him. I've just given him his first warning, you know. When he comes to the second one, then we'll sack him."
>
> I said to him, "You can't be serious. He's the greatest football manager the world has ever seen. The most popular man the world's ever seen." He said, "Christ". I said, "Well, maybe you should withdraw the warning, maybe that'll get him on side. Tell him, Sky's insisted that you withdraw the warning letter."
>
> The conversation deteriorated from there. Edwards said, "No, you can't discuss money with him and you can't trust him with money. I mean, he's no idea what money's worth. He's just out for himself. He doesn't understand that he's an employee of the club and must abide by the club's rules. You know, he's just a bit too big for his boots — that's why I have given him a warning letter." The other board members just stared as Edwards ranted on. I got the feeling that they had actually agreed to this and it was only when they heard it said out loud that it dawned on them what an utterly stupid idea it was.

The impression Bell received was:

> The players were all very well and you need to have players, otherwise you couldn't put a team out, and that the manager was OK, he had his job to do, but it was the board who had actually created this great institution and who, frankly, were doing the fans a favour by letting them in and doing the players a favour by allowing them to play for Manchester United. And the manager had better toe the line; otherwise he wouldn't be the manager any more. It was my last experience of what I call "the deference society", where the manager was a catering person, the players were van delivery boys, and the board were the decision-makers.
>
> I was absolutely amazed. I thought that they would have a very acute idea of what their assets were worth and how valuable they were and how they should be treated — with some care and caution — and I got the impression they thought that anybody who worked or played for Manchester United was being done a great favour, and that should be reflected in low wages and no demands of any kind whatsoever: just do as you're told.

This conversation would have repercussions which cast an interesting light on the Edwards-Ferguson relationship. When in December 1999 I revealed these facts, Ferguson understandably reacted furiously. There was, I believe, some talk of legal action against Edwards, which came to nothing.

When Ferguson came to write the paperback edition of his book, published in 2000, the final chapter referred to my revelations and said as follows:

> Somewhere in the middle of the protracted commotion over our absence from the FA Cup, the newspapers found another justification for working Manchester United into a few provocative headlines. They were based on criticisms of me attributed to Martin Edwards but this particular story was so lacking in credibility that it was petering out almost as soon as it was launched. It had originated in a book written by Mihir Bose, which contained claims that Martin described me as being useless with money. Bose is usually defined as an investigative journalist but I would have to question the quality of his investigation. Martin wrote to me categorically denying that he had ever spoken to the man about me. The remarks quoted amounted to such blatant nonsense that I had never for one moment believed the chairman could find himself capable of uttering them. For a start, Martin has no knowledge whatsoever of my personal finances so in that area there could be no foundation for comments of any

kind. Suggestions that my record with United had shown me to be useless with money would be rather difficult to sustain, considering that Martin's fortunes have swollen by upwards of £120 million over the past 10 years as a result of his shareholdings in the club. There was no substance to the story and I can only assume that Bose had been listening to a lot of tittle-tattle which, as I have observed earlier, is always plentiful around a big organisation like ours.

It was just the sort of robust defence one would expect from Ferguson, including questioning my ability to research, but what was interesting was that Edwards had denied making the remarks about Ferguson to me when, as I had made clear, he had made them, not to me, but at a meeting at HSBC in the days leading up to the leak of Sky's bid for United. So he was denying something I had never claimed.

I had never claimed Edwards was my source and so this was the classic non-denial denial. Edwards was helped by the way I originally had to write my story. At that time, with the Sky bid having recently been rejected and memories still fresh, Bell, while telling me the story and allowing me to use it, would not be identified as the source. Later Bell allowed me to identify him as the source and given a much fuller version of what happened.

With Sky failing to co-opt Ferguson, and with a section of the fans always bitterly opposed to Edwards, the Sky bid for the club saw an even greater divide between concerned fans and the club. But as if all this did not matter, that was the season that Ferguson marked his moment in the sun by winning the treble of the League, FA Cup and Champions League.

To compete on three fronts, United had to rely on the rotation of their squad. The key to the treble season was undoubtedly the squad's strength in depth, especially in attack where Dwight Yorke, Andy Cole, Teddy Sheringham and Ole Gunnar Solskjaer, four outstanding players in their own right, bought into the philosophy and all contributed goals (particularly the last two, who both scored in the Champions League final after being introduced as second-half substitutes). Another key inclusion was that of Jaap Stam at centre-back.

But one very important element contributing to the victory in Europe was the effect of the Bosman ruling, which meant UEFA no longer dictated to Ferguson what sort of team he could field. This, as he often complained, had played a big part in the fact, that for all his dominance in the domestic competitions, his Manchester United teams had struggled in the Champions League. Soon after establishing domestic supremacy in the mid-1990s, Ferguson had worked out that he needed to reduce the workload of the first team, more so as he sought European glory. So he had decided not to field his best team in the League Cup, a hugely controversial move when it was first announced.

"I think Alex would mention it," recalled Edwards, "and say, 'Look, I'm going to struggle in this cup or that cup. We'll struggle to win all four. Something's got to give a little bit. It's a chance for us to play some of our squad players.' The board never criticised Alex for his policy in the League Cup."

In the 1995–96 season United were embarrassed by York City in the League Cup but it also meant that the kids, Butt, Scholes and the Neville brothers, got a chance to show what they could do. However, in Europe Ferguson had to change his teams due to UEFA's three-plus-two rule which limited clubs to fielding three foreign players plus two 'assimilated' foreigners — those who have been playing in the country for five years or played there since youth-team level such as Ryan Giggs. Ferguson complained about that and his early forays into Europe's premier cup competition were a struggle.

In the 1993–94 season United were held to a goalless draw by Galatasaray at the intimidating Ali Sami Yen ground, a match overshadowed by Cantona and Bryan Robson clashing with Turkish police in the players' tunnel — the Frenchman was sent off as United went out of the competition. The travelling supporters complained of their treatment at the hands of local police and fans. Upon their arrival in Turkey, United were greeted with placards reading "Welcome to Hell" and "No Way Out".

The following season came what Ferguson acknowledged as his nadir. His team were trounced 4–0 by Barcelona in the Nou Camp — their heaviest defeat in European competition for 17 years (Porto had beaten United 4–0 in a European Cup-Winners' Cup tie in October 1977). Two goals from the Bulgarian Hristo Stoichkov — his first was his 100th for Barcelona — one from Brazil striker Romario and a fourth late in the game from Spanish right-back Albert Ferrer destroyed the then Premier League champions. United were missing Cantona to suspension and Lee Sharpe to injury. Ferguson had replaced Peter Schmeichel with reserve keeper Gary Walsh, who had never played a European match overseas, to ensure the three-plus-two rule was observed. After the loss, Ferguson lamented: "We were well and truly slaughtered. At the end of the night it was a pretty humiliating experience. It was the most emphatic defeat I've experienced."

By the 1998–99 season Bosman had made three-plus-two history. United had beaten Milan in the quarter-finals with Ferguson saying before the match: "When an Italian tells me it's pasta on the plate, I check under the sauce to make sure. They are the inventors of the smokescreen. They come out with, 'The

English are so strong, we're terrible in the air, we can't do this, we can't do that.' Then they beat you 3–0." United won 3–1 on aggregate. Their resolution had emerged in the semi-final where, losing at home to Juventus in the first leg, Giggs scored in injury time to make it 1–1 and United went on to win 3–2 in Turin.

This set up a final staged in Barcelona against Bayern Munich that nobody could have predicted. United had finished second to Bayern in the group stages and until the first minute of time added on in the Nou Camp were trailing to a sixth-minute Bayern goal. The Germans were already gathering along the touchline to celebrate. Lennart Johansson, the UEFA president, was on his way down thinking he was going to present the trophy to the Germans when first Sheringham and then Solskjaer scored. When he got to the pitch level and looked up to see Manchester United – 2 Bayern – 1, he thought the scoreboard had suffered an electrical failure.

Until then Ferguson, who was without Roy Keane and whose tactics had been severely questioned, had seen United outplayed by Bayern. Now, as the German players lay prostrate on the grass unable to believe what had happened, Manchester United celebrated as the first English club to win the Champions League/European Cup since Liverpool in 1984. It was sweeter still on the 90th anniversary of the birth of Sir Matt Busby, who had made success in this competition such a goal for the club. The victory cemented the reputation of Ferguson's sides for their unwillingness to concede defeat. As he put it: "We don't give in, we play right to the end. It's not an accident: it's part of the make-up of the team." It was after this match that Ferguson uttered the words that have since been endlessly recycled: "I can't believe it, I can't believe it. Football, eh? Bloody hell."

The Scot deserved his celebration, but it should be remembered that United had only qualified for that Champions League campaign as the second placed side in English football, Arsenal having won the title in 1998. And though he had seen off all his managerial rivals so far, the threat posed by the foreigner who ran Arsenal and another foreigner who would later arrive at Chelsea would prove a much stronger test.

THE FERGUSON RECORD

Sir Alex Ferguson (Manchester United 1986–present)
12 league titles in 23 seasons: 1993, 1994, 1996, 1997, 1999, 2000, 2001,
    2003, 2007, 2008, 2009, 2011
5 FA Cups: 1990, 1994, 1996, 1999, 2004
2 Champions Leagues: 1999, 2008
1 Cup-Winners' Cup: 1991
4 League Cups: 1992, 2006, 2009, 2010
1 Super Cup: 1991
1 Intercontinental Cup: 1999
1 FIFA Club World Cup: 2008
10 FA Charity/Community Shield: 1990 (shared), 1993, 1994, 1996, 1997,
    2003, 2007, 2008, 2010, 2011

Sir Matt Busby (Manchester United 1945–1969 and 1970–71*)
5 League titles in 25 seasons: 1952, 1956, 1957, 1965, 1967
2 FA Cups: 1948, 1963
1 European Cup: 1968
5 FA Charity Shield: 1952, 1956, 1957, 1965, 1967
*Returned for 21 games during the 1970–71 season before retiring completely

Bob Paisley (Liverpool 1974–1983)
6 league titles in 9 seasons: 1976, 1977, 1979, 1980, 1982, 1983
3 European Cups: 1977, 1978, 1981
1 UEFA Cup: 1976
3 League Cups: 1981, 1982, 1983
1 European Super Cup: 1977
6 FA Charity Shield: 1974, 1976, 1977 (shared), 1979, 1980, 1982

Notes: Ferguson, Busby and Paisley are the only managers in post-war English
football to win more than three titles. Three managers have won three titles:
Stan Cullis (Wolves 1948–64), Bill Shankly (Liverpool 1959–74) and Arsene
Wenger (Arsenal 1996–present)

SIR ALEX FERGUSON'S MANAGERIAL CAREER

Manager since: November 6, 1986
Current: 26 Seasons
Date of Birth: December 31, 1941
Previous Clubs: Aberdeen, St Mirren, East Stirlingshire

1976–1977   Promotion to Scottish Premier League
                 East Stirlingshire Manager June 1, 1974 to October 1, 1976;
                 0 Seasons

1979–1980   Scottish Premier League champions
                 St Mirren Manager November 1, 1974 to May 31, 1978;
                 4 Seasons

1981–1982   Scottish Cup winners

1982–1983   European Cup-Winners Cup winners
                 Scottish Cup winners
                 Awarded OBE

1983–1984   UEFA Super Cup winners
                 Scottish Premier League champions
                 Scottish Cup winners

1984–1985   Scottish Premier League champions

1985–1986   Scottish Cup winners
                 Scottish League Cup winners

1989–1990   FA Cup winners
                 Aberdeen
                 Manager August 1, 1978 to November 5, 1986
                 8 Seasons

1990–1991   European Cup-Winners Cup winners
                 Charity Shield winners

1991–1992   League Cup winners
               UEFA Super Cup winners

1992–1993   FA Premiership champions

1993–1994   FA Carling Premiership champions
               FA Cup winners
               Charity Shield winners
               Manager of the Year (FA Carling Premiership)

1994–1995   Charity Shield winners
               Awarded CBE

1995–1996   FA Carling Premiership champions
               FA Cup winners
               Manager of the Year (FA Carling Premiership)

1996–1997   FA Carling Premiership champions
               Charity Shield winners
               Manager of the Year (FA Carling Premiership)

1997–1998   Charity Shield winners

1998–1999   UEFA Champions League winners
               Intercontinental Cup winners
               FA Carling Premiership champions
               FA Cup winners
               Manager of the Year (FA Carling Premiership)
               LMA Manager of the Year
               LMA Manager of the Decade
               Knighted

1999–2000   FA Carling Premiership champions
               Manager of the Year (FA Carling Premiership)

2000–2001   FA Carling Premiership champions
               BBC Sports Personality of the Year
               (Lifetime Achievement Award)

2002–2003   FA Barclaycard Premiership champions
Manager of the Year (Barclaycard Premiership)

2003–2004   FA Cup winners
Community Shield winners

2005–2006   League Cup winners

2006–2007   Barclays Premier League champions
Manager of the Year (Barclays Premiership)

2007–2008   UEFA Champions League winners
FIFA Club World Cup winners
Barclays Premier League champions
Community Shield winners
Manager of the Year (Barclays Premier League)
LMA Manager of the Year

2008–2009   UEFA Champions League runners-up
Barclays Premier League champions
League Cup winners
Community Shield winners
Manager of the Year (Barclays Premier League)

2009–2010   League Cup winners

2010–2011   Barclays Premier League champions
Community Shield winners
UEFA Champions League runners-up
Manager of the Year (The Barclays Premier League)
LMA Manager of the Year

2011–2012   Community Shield winners

Chapter 7
SOME FOREIGN LESSONS

Sir Alex Ferguson has always said that, as a Scot, he could never manage the England team. If his sense of alienation from the English nation and his outsider's focus have possibly given him an extra edge, then it is not surprising that the only two other managers to offer him a sustained challenge since the Premier League began are both genuine outsiders. And of the two, Arsene Wenger is by far the more important and arguably the most influential foreigner to manage a football team in these islands.

Wenger was not the first foreign manager in English football but he was the first to win the title. No Arsenal manager has presided over more matches than Wenger. No manager in north London has enjoyed the same level of success. What is more, no manager, born outside the UK and Ireland, has had a greater impact on the game, both at Arsenal and in English football in general, than the 62-year-old from Alsace.

Before Wenger, few foreign managers had succeeded in England, even though some clubs had looked outside British and Irish football for managerial inspiration around the time the Premier League was launched. Dr Jozef Venglos, born in Czechoslovakia in 1936, managed Aston Villa in the 1990–91 season, following Graham Taylor's appointment as the England manager. Venglos did not quite lead Villa into the Premier League as the club only just avoided relegation before he was sacked. Argentina's World Cup winner Ossie Ardiles took control of Tottenham in June 1993 following the Sugar-Venables bust-up, becoming the first foreign manager of the Premier League era. As a Tottenham hero for a decade he was considered almost home-grown, but this did not save him from the sack in October 1994 after an undistinguished period in charge. The accepted wisdom was that foreign managers just did not work in England.

Arsene Wenger changed all that. Since he arrived at Highbury in 1996, his Arsenal teams have won three Premier League titles and four FA Cups (two League and Cup Doubles — in 1998 and 2002). Arsenal have qualified for the Champions League every season, reaching the final in 2006, and were also losing finalists in the UEFA Cup in 2000. Perhaps his most remarkable achievement came in the 2003–04 season, when his "Invincibles" went unbeaten throughout the entire league season.

A cerebral and studious coach, Wenger suffers, comically at times, from myopia when it comes to spotting his players' indiscretions on the field. And in his first seven seasons in charge, his team's disciplinary record — 52 red cards — was one of the worst in England. Yet the conveyor belt of talented teams that Wenger has produced, season after season, for the past 16 years, have played some of the most entertaining and stylish football in Europe.

His fellow managers have no hesitation in acknowledging his greatness. Yet, Arsenal have not won a trophy since 2005 and their fans have been growing increasingly restive over his unwillingness to splash out on big-money signings. The nadir was reached in the 2011–12 season when for the first time in the Wenger era shouts were heard at the Emirates of "You don't know what you're doing." As it happened the match where these shouts were loudest was to see the Arsenal season turn round. Turfed out of the Champions League and losing 2–0 at home to Tottenham, they hit back to win 5–2 and then went on a charge up the table to secure another Champions League qualification.

This vindicated the view of Wenger's qualities that had been expressed earlier by Roy Hodgson. When I had put the Arsenal fans' criticisms of Wenger to the England manager, he responded:

> Arsene Wenger wins in two ways. He wins because his team is always in the Champions League and he wins because every year he puts out an Arsenal team who play very good football. Sixty thousand pay good money to watch them play and every year the club make a profit. If that is not success I don't know what success is.

In some ways almost everything about Wenger has been unusual, almost from the moment he arrived in England. Arsenal sacked Bruce Rioch shortly before the 1996 season after just 61 weeks in charge — the briefest managerial reign at Highbury. Wenger, then at Japanese club Nagoya Grampus Eight, could not take charge immediately and it was not until September 30 that he arrived.

Very little was known of this austere-looking figure and only football aficionados could have listed his string of French clubs, which included Nancy and AS Monaco, where he had won the French league title in 1988 and was voted French manager of the year. Even less was known of his Japanese club, where the year before he came to London he had been voted Japan's manager of the year.

So it was no surprise that on the day he appeared at Highbury, the London *Evening Standard* ran the headline "Arsene Who?" The Premier League website, celebrating 20 years of the league, has a picture of Wenger being interviewed outside Highbury's marble halls, looking dishevelled and very like the "Professor" players in the dressing room nicknamed him due to his appearance and mannerisms. His clumsy manner also led to him being called "Inspector Clouseau" after Peter Sellers' bungling French cop. As Wenger remarked in May 1997: "One of the biggest bets was how long I would last. Everybody was betting that I would be gone by January 1."

But if the press was hostile, the players were quick to recognise the qualities of the manager and his training methods, to the surprise of the Frenchman. Speaking to *The Independent,* Wenger said of his early days in charge:

> I was surprised by the attitude of the players when I came. I thought they would be more resistant to a foreign manager, but they were positive. When you can convince somebody that he can play better by doing something, he will accept it — or he is an idiot. I think generally players are very intelligent, so it is down to the manager to convince the players. Then you have to win games — if you don't, then nobody believes in you. The players were better technically than I expected. English players do not look as good as they are because of the pace of the game and because they are not encouraged at the back to take risks in the build-up. This cautious attitude prevents defenders from showing their technique.

Nowhere was his influence felt more than with the famous Arsenal back four, who were all in their thirties. He may have looked like a geography teacher but Wenger's training sessions were meticulous in their detail. Sessions were shorter, sharper and timed to the second — unlike the physical tests of endurance that were commonplace under traditional English regimes. Silence was encouraged at half-time so his players could relax and calm themselves down properly rather than rant and scream about the match. The temperature was often turned up on the team bus to keep players' muscles supple. "To work hard the whole week and then spoil it by not preparing properly is silly," he once said.

Paul Merson was a fan. "His ideas are so good," the midfielder said. "Even running is done with the ball. We never used to do that, we'd just run for three hours." Tony Adams was equally effusive: "I'm pushing into areas I only used to visit at dead-ball kicks," said the Arsenal captain. "I love it when the crowd sing, 'Tony Adams on the wing.'"

Indeed, the first Premier League championship that Wenger won in 1997–

98 exemplified his style. Arsenal overhauled an 11-point gap on Manchester United to claim the title by a point and victory in the FA Cup secured the Double, the fifth time this had been achieved in the 20th century.

But it was the way they clinched the league that stood out. In their final game on May 3, Arsenal thrashed Everton 4–0 at Highbury. Tony Adams scored the final goal. But this was not one of his trademark headers from a set-piece, but a goal any forward would be proud of. Beating the offside trap as he ran on to a through-pass from Steve Bould, another defender, he thumped a sumptuous half-volley into the Everton net. For the Arsenal fans nothing could be sweeter, for under George Graham, Adams and Bould had become experts at deploying the offside trap to stop opposing forwards. Now they were showing they could spring it perfectly as well. As Adams disappeared under a pile of delirious Arsenal team-mates, Wenger exchanged handshakes with all his coaching staff in the dug-out for the success of the play.

By this time players' diets had been analysed and dramatically changed. Vegetables and vitamin supplements were encouraged. Alcohol was not banned but discouraged. According to Wenger, his two-year stint in Japan as manager of Grampus Eight had opened his eyes to the importance of dietary requirements. "It was the best diet I ever had," he said. "The whole way of life there is linked to health. Their diet is basically boiled vegetables, fish and rice. No fat, no sugar. You notice when you live there that there are no fat people. I think in England you eat too much sugar and meat and not enough vegetables."

The combination of pre-match stretching and use of masseurs and osteopaths added years to the careers of his veteran players. Word quickly spread throughout football and such practices are standard now.

Wenger's overseas network of scouts and contacts brought players of the quality of Thierry Henry (at a cost of £10.5 million), Patrick Vieira (£3.5 million), Kolo Toure (£500,000) and Cesc Fabregas (nominal compensation) to Highbury. The most profitable deal was Nicolas Anelka, a £500,000 signing, who left for Real Madrid for £23 million. Not every deal has worked out — for every Anelka, there has been a Francis Jeffers or a Jose Antonio Reyes — and in particular some of the English players Wenger has signed have let him down. Jeffers, Jermaine Pennant, Matthew Upson and Richard Wright were all failures when they wore the red and white of Arsenal.

But for all the foreign talent that Wenger brought, and we shall discuss some of them a little later, he was indebted to the little-remembered Rioch for providing him with, arguably, the most influential foreign player Arsenal or the Premier League has seen: Dennis Bergkamp.

Bergkamp came from Internazionale, with the Italian club in the middle of wholesale changes, as Rioch's first signing in June 1995 for a fee estimated at £7.5 million. This set a new club transfer record, smashing the previous mark of £2.5 million. Bergkamp, an established Dutch international, initially struggled to adapt to the English game, not scoring in his first five league matches, and was mocked in the press and ridiculed by Tottenham chairman Alan Sugar.

Sugar had by then become cynical about foreign players. The previous season he had himself signed Jurgen Klinsmann, the Germany striker, for Tottenham on his boat in Monte Carlo. Ironically, Klinsmann was eager to come to Spurs because he did not like playing at Monaco where Wenger was the coach. When Sugar told his manager Ossie Ardiles that he had secured the German and that he was on his boat, the Argentinian thought at first this was just another of the chairman's typical English jokes.

There was some suggestion that Klinsmann might not go down well at a club noted for their Jewish connections. But, joining immediately after the 1994 World Cup, he charmed everyone at his first press conference by saying he had come to London to look for a diving school, a reference to his reputation as a diver to win free-kicks. He embraced life in England, driving around London in a VW Beetle, scored 29 goals and was voted player of the year by the football writers. Klinsmann was only the third foreign player (Irishmen excluded) to be named by the Football Writers' Association as their Player of the Year. The other two were his compatriot Bert Trautmann (Manchester City) in 1955–56 and Dutchman Frans Thijssen (Ipswich Town) in 1980–81.

But to Sugar's fury Klinsmann exercised a clause in his contract to leave at the end of the season for Bayern Munich, leading Sugar to coin the phrase "Carlos Kickaball", denoting foreign football mercenaries who came to England only for the money. During a television interview Sugar took the signed shirt Klinsmann had given him, threw it at the interviewer and told him he could use it to clean his car. Sugar would later regret this impulsive behaviour and Klinsmann would successfully return to Tottenham in 1997 but it coloured the way Klinsmann was perceived as a player, having used his year in the Premier League to revive a faltering career.

No such charge could be laid against Bergkamp, who left an indelible stamp on the English game. This was to be acknowledged by Sir Dave Richards, the Premier League chairman. At Doha in the spring of 2012, he highlighted it as the moment when the Premier League began to attract the world's best talent. As he told me:

> When Dennis Bergkamp came to Arsenal he changed the total spectrum of our game. Because he was the first real foreigner to be bought. And when

he came he showed his talent, which was fantastic and it was a fantastic thing for me. I watched him and I thought we could have the Bergkamps of the world here. People wanted to watch him and it happened.

It is interesting that Klinsmann did not register with Richards, although his Tottenham debut had been at Sheffield Wednesday, the club Richards chaired before taking over at the Premier League. This was the match where Klinsmann, as part of a pre-arranged routine, performed a "diving" goal celebration. Yet, when I mentioned Klinsmann to Richards, he kept repeating: "No, no, Bergkamp was the first."

However, for all Bergkamp's achievements it is also worth remembering that, in 1999, there would have been no Manchester United treble — and no Ryan Giggs slaloming wonder goal in extra time in the FA Cup semi-final replay against Arsenal — had Bergkamp not failed to score from the penalty spot. Then, in the dying seconds of normal time at Villa Park, Bergkamp was thwarted by a brilliant Peter Schmeichel save. And that miss might also have left a legacy that was to haunt both Wenger and Ferguson.

Henry Winter of *The Daily Telegraph* believes that after the defeat Wenger, still angry over Bergkamp's miss, failed to shake Ferguson's hand at the final whistle. From that moment, Winter says, Wenger lost the Scot's respect. We shall have more to say about their relationship later but it is worth stressing that Bergkamp's miss was a rare blemish in an Arsenal career which blossomed with Wenger's arrival as the Arsenal manager recognised his talent and used him as the fulcrum of the team's forward play.

Wenger added to this foreign inheritance with his own foreign purchases and two of the men he brought to Arsenal illustrated his prowess at spotting raw talents and turning them into truly outstanding players. Thierry Henry arrived in the Premier League in August 1999 as a relative unknown, a slightly erratic winger. Eight years later he departed as one of the greatest players to have graced English football, with widespread plaudits ringing in his ears, numerous honours on the mantelpiece and plenty of individual records broken. Wenger, who knew his French football, was well aware that the young Frenchman was blessed with exquisite technique, sensational pace, tremendous vision and creativity and set about bringing this out. The transformation made Henry not only a supreme striker, a dead-ball expert and penalty taker but as the club captain, the Arsenal dressing room's most talismanic figure.

After surpassing Ian Wright's mark of 185 goals, Henry went on to set a club record of 229 — three goals were scored in the 2011–12 season during his brief return to the Emirates on loan from New York Red Bulls. Yet it was the variety of the goals he scored — the devastating finishing, the poise and balance when he terrorised retreating opponents — that appeal more to the Arsenal faithful than bare statistics.

For Arsenal, during the glory years of 2001–02 and 2003–04, in which he scored a combined total of 71 goals, Henry was indispensable. It is hardly surprising that the football press named him the Football Writer's Association's Footballer of the Year a record three times in four seasons. He finished runner-up twice in the running for the FIFA World Player of the Year award. Two league titles, three FA Cups, four Golden Boots and five player of the year awards form the core of his CV while in England. It was only the Champions League that eluded him, as Arsenal were defeated by Barcelona in the 2006 final in Paris.

Tens of thousands of Arsenal fans voted for their Gunners' Greatest Moments in 2007 — and Henry was involved in five of the top 10. A year later, he eclipsed everyone to top the Gunners' Greatest Player poll. This makes very interesting reading: 1 – Thierry Henry; 2 – Dennis Bergkamp; 3 – Tony Adams; 4 – Ian Wright; 5 – Patrick Vieira; 6 – Robert Pires; 7 – David Seaman; 8 – Liam Brady; 9 – Charlie George; 10 – Pat Jennings.

But while the fans ranked Patrick Vieira fifth, he was perhaps Wenger's greatest signing. Wenger was still a month away from taking control of the club when he persuaded the board in the summer of 1996 to invest £3.5 million in a little known French footballer of Senegalese descent who had been devoid of first-team action at AC Milan. It was a tremendous leap of faith, especially when the 20-year-old did not speak a single word of English and possessed only raw yet unproven talent. But as he grew in both stature and confidence, adapting tremendously quickly to the Premier League, Patrick Vieira became one of his generation's most effective midfielders.

A dynamic 6ft 4in, with the lungs and stamina of a top-class athlete, the composure and passing distribution to match any other midfielder of his era, Vieira became the axis of Wenger's team as Arsenal claimed two domestic Doubles and went on an historic unbeaten league campaign throughout 2003–04. They were the first team to achieve the feat since Preston North End, the old Invincibles, went 22 league matches unbeaten in 1888–89. A banner at Highbury put it best: "Some you win, some you draw." Arsenal's record was 26 wins, 12 draws and no losses. The Premier League commissioned a special gold version of the championship trophy to commemorate the new Invincibles. Henry scored 30 goals that season, Pires chipped in with 14 but for all the plaudits for that pair's silky skills, the commitment, authority and leadership displayed by Vieira was the key component in the club's success.

There were many occasions when Vieira overstepped the mark: ill-discipline was a major factor of Wenger's early years in charge and nobody typified that more than the Frenchman, who received 10 red cards in his time in north London, including two dismissals in the opening weeks of the 2000–01 season.

The first of his 10 red cards with Arsenal came in the season he arrived and they continued at regular intervals. They are worth recording:

1997–98	Jan 17	vs. Coventry
	Feb 18	vs. Chelsea
1998–99	Dec 28	vs. Charlton
1999–2000	Oct 2	vs. West Ham
2000–01	Aug 19	vs. Sunderland
	Aug 21	vs. Liverpool
2001–02	Aug 25	vs. Leicester
2002–03	Sep 1	vs. Chelsea
2003–04	Sept 21	vs. Man Utd
2004°05	Nov 24	vs. PSV Eindhoven

In the dim and distant past an Arsenal player who was sent off would never have played again. Perhaps it was in this long-lost Corinthian spirit that Wenger was accused of being too steadfast in his support for Vieira. But the midfielder's athleticism and force of character were essential to Arsenal's success and perhaps the not-so-occasional lapses were deemed a price worth paying, even by an Arsenal manager who showed an appreciation for the beautiful side of the game.

Not that Vieira was necessarily nasty and vindictive — just very combative and enthusiastically competitive. In September 1998, Vieira was fined £20,000 by the FA after police filed a report on an incident in the tunnel at the end of Sheffield Wednesday's 1–0 home win over Arsenal. Vieira had left the field flicking V-signs at Wednesday supporters. A year later, he was banned for six matches and fined a record £45,000 when he was sent off, accused of spitting at West Ham's Neil Ruddock and involved in another incident with a police officer in the tunnel.

It is worth comparing Vieira's poor behaviour with what was happening around him. That match at Hillsborough also saw Paolo di Canio sent off as the Italian reacted in a petulant manner to a decision by referee Paul Alcock by pushing the official over (Alcock's theatrical fall sparked great hilarity in the media). The 30-year-old was banned for 11 matches (an eight-game ban on top of his automatic three-match suspension for the red card he received) and fined £10,000 by an FA disciplinary committee. Di Canio said: "I am very, very sorry for what happened. I had a fair hearing, for which I am grateful."

Di Canio was not the only bad boy that season. Robbie Fowler had his fair share of negative headlines. The Liverpool striker's "snorting" of the white goal-line after scoring a spot-kick in Liverpool's 3–2 win over Everton led to condemnation, a fine and a four-match ban. He also received a further two-match suspension for a "homophobic" gesture made towards Graeme Le Saux at Stamford Bridge earlier in the season.

Perhaps Vieira's fiercest rivalry was with Roy Keane, and his clashes with the Manchester United captain were often at the heart of the most combustible moments in matches between the two clubs, notably at Highbury in 2005, in the tunnel before the game.

Vieira confronted United's Gary Neville and Keane intervened, telling referee Graham Poll: "Tell him to shut his f***ing mouth" — an encounter broadcast to the nation on Sky TV.

Admittedly, goal-scoring was not his forte — 33 goals scored in 406 appearances — although he will be remembered for netting the decisive goal to conclude the "Invincibles" story, the winner against Leicester at Highbury on the final day of that record-breaking season.

For years there was constant transfer speculation — reports linked Vieira to Real Madrid and Inter Milan — while Sir Alex Ferguson even claimed in 2004 that Vieira had wanted to move to Old Trafford a year earlier but "had not been allowed to". He finally went to Juventus at the age of 29 for £13.7 million at the end of the 2005 season. It is fair to say that even though he was joining the slow-paced environment of Serie A, Arsenal enjoyed the best of Vieira's career — as well as a £10.2 million profit on what they had paid AC Milan nine years previously.

His last contribution for Arsenal was scoring the winning penalty in the 2005 FA Cup final. Arsenal beat Manchester United 5–4 on penalties after a 0–0 draw. It was Vieira's last moment in an Arsenal shirt and as the 20th season of the Premier League came to an end it remains the last trophy Arsenal have lifted. No Vieira since 2005, no trophy since then. Coincidence or not?

Certainly, in the years since 2005, Arsenal's style has often seemed over-elaborate and their results less impressive. Wenger might have allowed himself wistful thoughts of the galvanising effect Vieira had on his most successful teams. Wenger has failed to bring in players with the leadership qualities embodied first by Tony Adams, and then matched by Vieira. Cesc Fabregas tried his best, particularly when handed the captaincy, but he could not go where Vieira had gone. The only consolation for the young Spaniard was that he did get the better of his predecessor in March 2006 when he faced a fading Vieira, still with Juventus, in a Champions League tie at Highbury.

Vieira's partnership with his World Cup-winning partner Emmanuel Petit was also crucial. And the signing of Petit was particularly pleasurable for Arsenal's fans. Tottenham had shown interest in the pony-tailed French midfielder. Indeed he went to White Hart Lane and met chairman Alan Sugar, manager Gerry Francis and managing director Claude Littner. Littner even offered to organise dance classes for Petit's girlfriend in an attempt to persuade him to sign. Petit listened and then asked Sugar to organise a taxi. Sugar thought he was going back to his hotel and paid the taxi up front. But Petit headed straight to the home of David Dein where Wenger was waiting, and he promptly signed for the Gunners.

By the time this story emerged to delight Arsenal's fans they recognised that Wenger was carrying through a revolution in the playing style of their club. Though Arsenal had for decades been the more successful north London club, their style of play did not attract neutrals. Millions recalled Spurs' Double team of 1960–61 and their expansive, enthralling football. Few outside the faithful celebrated Arsenal's Double side of 1970–71; the only consolation for the Arsenal fans was that they had clinched the league that year at White Hart Lane — as a banner at the Emirates always reminds the visiting fans. Indeed, Arsenal fans had self-deprecatingly celebrated their dour style with the song "1–0 to the Arsenal", testimony to many a victory clawed out through tenacious defending and very few attacking forays.

Wenger was to change all that as he built his reputation — indeed his legacy — with a sumptuous style of passing football. So wedded were the team to a passing game that in a match against Manchester City, when Arsenal won a penalty Pires even tried to pass the ball to Henry from the penalty spot. He actually fluffed his pass and no goal was scored it was clearly a ploy that originated on Arsenal training ground. In recent years, their failure to deliver trophies has invited criticism that Wenger's teams have too often sacrificed efficiency in search of an extra pass and the "perfect goal", but Wenger has stayed true to his beliefs.

In this he has presented a stark contrast with Ferguson. Ferguson's quarter-century at Old Trafford has seen him build four teams, from the Cantona-inspired one that started him off on the road to glory, via the Beckham and Scholes "kids" team of the mid-1990s and the 2008 European Cup-winning team to the present one. During all this time he, like Wenger, has had problems filling various positions and, interestingly, both managers have had problems with goalkeepers. Ferguson has struggled to find a replacement for Peter Schmeichel, while the same goes for Wenger and David Seaman. Yet Wenger's goalkeeping problems pale in comparison with Ferguson's when he bought Massimo Taibi from Venezia for £4.5 million as his No. 1 goalkeeper in 1999. The Italian's errors, which included letting a weak shot by Southampton's Matthew Le Tissier dribble through his legs, were of such an order that he was dubbed the "Blind Venetian" and he had to be written off after only four matches.

And like Wenger, Ferguson has had his share of duff buys. Not even the greatest Ferguson fan can say his purchases of Kleberson, Eric Djemba-Djemba or Juan Sebastian Veron were shrewd. Veron, who was then United's most expensive signing at £28 million, had forced Ferguson to change his team formation to accommodate him and it was to lead to one of those public moments which did not please the Scot. Ferguson often addressed fans' forums but did not usually attend Manchester United AGMs, which he saw as plc stock exchange business that had nothing to do with the football team. But in 2003 he was persuaded to do so by the new chairman Roy Gardner, who had taken over from Roland Smith. Ferguson was soon to regret this.

One fan at the meeting described Veron as a carthorse whom he needed to clear out of the United stables. Ferguson, visibly reddening, said: "I am not even responding to that." But in the end Veron went and Ferguson has continued his policy of constantly renewing both the squad and his back-room staff. And in this last point the contrast could not be greater with his French adversary.

Ferguson arrived at Old Trafford with Archie Knox as his No. 2. Then he brought in Brian Kidd and seemed reluctant to let him go to manage Blackburn in 1998, saying he would not succeed as a manager on his own — Ferguson was proved right, as Blackburn were relegated and Kidd was quickly sacked. Then came Jimmy Ryan, Steve McClaren, Carlos Queiroz — not for one but two tours of duty in Fergie's kingdom — Walter Smith and Mike Phelan.

This sort of turnover in No. 2s does not happen often in football. The insecurity of the manager's position makes them want to protect their own backs, so they gather round them a group of people they can trust. This team, incorporating a variety of other coaches besides the No. 2, forms a happy band that follows the manager wherever he goes.

But Ferguson has felt secure enough in himself to keep changing his coaching team. His thinking is that he needs fresh faces, the players need fresh voices and such constant renewal prevents a team from going stale.

Wenger, for all the revolutionary changes he has introduced at Arsenal, has stuck largely to the same backroom team. Pat Rice, whom he inherited as No. 2 in 1996, finally retired this summer while first-team coach Boro Primorac came to Highbury a few months after Wenger. Looking at the characters of the two men, you might expect Ferguson to be the traditionalist and Wenger the revolutionary, not just in the selection of players but also the rotation of his backroom staff. But the self-taught man from the Gorbals has proved the real revolutionary. Unlike Wenger, he has understood that if you want renewal in a football club you must start with your own coaching team.

The writer Jim White, who is a fan and has written the biography of Manchester United, sums up Ferguson like this:

> He is a great pragmatist. He is not committed to any one philosophy or any one principle. He is committed to getting success and willing to try anything that works. So he has taken to sports medicine and sports science and modern means of communications. Ferguson's quest for knowledge has changed how managers in the Premier League now think. You see managers like Roberto Martinez and Andre Villas-Boas and you feel to be a manager you need a PhD. Ferguson never went to university but he has set new standards that managers have to follow. Their intellectual capacity has increased. He is a self-taught man but sees himself as an intellectual. That is why he has always got upset by constant references in the media to "Wenger the professor" as he feels he is just as great an intellectual as Wenger.

Not surprisingly, the public spats between the Scot and the Frenchman have been some of the most riveting in Premier League history. Wenger, the only man to rival Ferguson's longevity in the league, has also never been afraid to stand up to his rival, particularly when it came to mind games. When the Manchester United manager claimed his team played the best football in England, Wenger responded elliptically: "Everyone thinks they have the prettiest wife at home," a comment Ferguson appeared to take as a personal slight.

The antipathy between the two clubs pre-dated Wenger's arrival. After a brawl at Old Trafford in October 1990 involving 21 players, Arsenal were docked two points and United one. But at that stage both teams were managed by Scots. Ferguson had a good relationship with George Graham and the two men, as we have seen, even shared such secrets as the details of their contracts. This would never happen between Wenger and Ferguson.

There has always been an edge to their relationship, with Ferguson complaining that Wenger "has come here from Japan and now he is telling us how to run our football". And in 2002, six years after Wenger arrived, Ferguson felt it necessary to lecture him on English football etiquette. As Arsenal beat United to the title by seven points, Ferguson complained: "He never comes for a drink with the opposing manager after matches. He's the only manager in the Premier League not to do so. It is a tradition here. It would be good for him to accept the tradition." Three years later in 2005, Wenger said: "Ferguson's out of order. He has lost all sense of reality."

With their two teams competing for the top prizes these series of digs in the media were accompanied by some remarkable incidents. This included the infamous "pizza-gate" affair of October 2004. That day United ended Arsenal's 49-game unbeaten Premier League run with a 2–0 victory which included a controversial penalty. If events were combustible on the pitch, they were explosive off it.

Wenger called United striker Ruud van Nistelrooy "a cheat" in a post-match television interview. Ferguson attempted to confront the Frenchman in the tunnel about his comment and ended up with a slice of pizza in his face, allegedly thrown by an Arsenal player. No member of the Gunners' playing staff was formally identified but the hand that threw it was believed to be that of Cesc Fabregas. Ferguson, who had to change his shirt before he appeared on television for his post-match comments, said: "Their behaviour was the worst thing I have seen in this sport. They got off scot-free." Wenger refused to apologise, repeating his criticism of van Nistelrooy.

However, in recent seasons both managers have made obvious attempts to improve relations. Relations thawed to such an extent that when United thrashed Arsenal 8–2 in 2011, Ferguson defended Wenger's record, saying: "I think it is unfair to criticise him. The job he's done for Arsenal and the philosophy he has — he has given Arsenal some very entertaining players. He's also sold well and looked after the Arsenal coffers. People forget these things." Ferguson went on to express his disgust at those who questioned and criticised Wenger. The current cordial relationship between the two has seen the pair share the stage at various League Managers' Association events. Of course, this may also reflect the fact that Arsenal are no longer major contenders for the title.

Chelsea's transformation into title contenders was largely brought about by another foreigner whose relationship with Ferguson began, as with Wenger, with a missed handshake but developed very differently.

Whereas Wenger led the influx of foreign players at Arsenal, Chelsea had been regularly importing foreign stars in the decade before Jose Mourinho arrived from Porto. Between the start of the Premier League in 1992–93 and the summer of 2003 when Roman Abramovich bought the club from Ken Bates, Chelsea signed 63 players, some of whom were among the world's top footballers. But the buying policy, certainly in the mid-90s, seemed to be for high-profile players over the age of 30: Ruud Gullit, a former European Footballer of the Year, arrived at the age of 32, Mark Hughes came to Stamford Bridge at 31, while the likes of Gianluca Vialli (31), Gianfranco Zola (30),

Didier Deschamps (30) and Emmanuel Petit (30) signed when they were in their fourth decade. Although Chelsea also brought in many young players, only five of them — John Spencer, Celestine Babayaro, Mario Melchiot, Eidur Gudjohnsen and Frank Lampard — really made a lasting impression.

Many of the foreign names, particularly the older ones such as Gullit, Vialli, Gustavo Poyet, Frode Grodas, Brian Laudrup, Winston Bogarde, came on free transfers. Chelsea were hardly a big club then, had not won a trophy since the FA Cup in 1970, and had yo-yoed back and forth between the top two divisions. But one attraction for these players coming to England was the tax situation. As non-domiciled earners they were only taxed on their earnings in England, not on their global income and this could be very advantageous. The list of players reads:

Date of birth	Age	Name	Club	Fee	Date signed
1992–93 season					
19 Sep 1973	18	Nick Colgan	Drogheda	Undisc.	1 Aug 1992
11 Sep 1970	21	John Spencer	Rangers	£450,000	1 Aug 1992
11 Aug 1965	27	Robert Fleck	Norwich	£2.1 mil	13 Aug 1992
12 Feb 1959	33	Mick Harford	Luton	£300,000	13 Aug 1992
25 Mar 1973	19	Anthony Barness	Charlton	£350,000	8 Sep 1992
2 Dec 1960	31	Nigel Spackman	Rangers	£485,000	8 Sep 1992
21 Aug 1970	22	David Hopkin	Morton	£300,000	25 Sep 1992
16 Aug 1968	24	Dmitri Kharine	CSKA Moscow	£200,000	22 Dec 1992
8 Sep 1969	23	Steve Livingstone	Blackburn	£350,000	23 Mar 1993
7 Feb 1973	20	Andy Dow	Dundee	£250,000	15 Jul 1993
1993–94 season					
21 Oct 1969	23	Jakob Kjeldberg	Silkeborg	£400,000	1 Aug 1993
18 Nov 1967	25	Gavin Peacock	Newcastle	£1,250,000	12 Aug 1993
29 Jan 1966	27	Mark Stein	Stoke	£1.5 mil	28 Oct 1993
1 Oct 1968	25	Paul Furlong	Watford	£2.3 mil	26 May 1994
6 Aug 1971	22	Scott Minto	Charlton	£775,000	28 May 1994
1994–95 season					
2 May 1967	27	David Rocastle	Man City	£1.25 mil	12 Aug 1994
1 Sep 1962	32	Ruud Gullit	Sampdoria	Free	31 May 1995
1 Nov 1963	31	Mark Hughes	Man Utd	£1.5 mil	23 Jun 1995

Date of birth	Age	Name	Club	Fee	Date signed
1995–96 season					
22 Dec 1967	27	Dan Petrescu	Sheff Wed	£2.3 mil	8 Nov 1995
9 Jul 1964	31	Gianluca Vialli	Juventus	Free	24 May 1996
29 May 1970	26	Roberto Di Matteo	Lazio	£4.9 mil	1 Jul 1996
22 Jan 1968	28	Frank Leboeuf	Strasbourg	£2.5 mil	1 Jul 1996
1996–97 season					
24 Oct 1964	32	Frode Grodas	Lillestrom	Free	1 Nov 1996
5 Jul 1966	30	Gianfranco Zola	Parma	£4.5 mil	8 Nov 1996
19 Jan 1975	22	Danny Granville	Cambridge U	£300,000	20 Mar 1997
29 Aug 1978	18	Celestine Babayaro	Anderlecht	£2,250,000	21 Apr 1997
20 Dec 1966	30	Ed de Goey	Feyenoord	£2,250,000	11 Jun 1997
11 May 1971	26	Bernard Lambourde	Bordeaux	£1,500,000	13 Jun 1997
15 Nov 1967	29	Gustavo Poyet	Zaragoza	Free	30 Jun 1997
1997–98 season					
15 Jun 1973	24	Tore Andre Flo	Brann	£300,000	1 Aug 1997
17 Oct 1968	28	Graeme Le Saux	Blackburn	£7 mil	8 Aug 1997
4 Mar 1969	29	Pierluigi Casiraghi	Lazio	£5.4 mil	29 May 1998
22 Feb 1969	29	Brian Laudrup	Rangers	Free	7 Jun 1998
6 Jun 1970	28	Albert Ferrer	Barcelona	£2.2 mil	9 Jun 1998
1998–1999 season					
15 Mar 1981	17	Mikael Forssell	HJK Helsinki	Free	31 Jul 1998
25 Aug 1980	17	Luca Percassi	Atalanta	Undisc.	1 Aug 1998
Feb 6, 1981	17	Samuele Dalla Bona	Atalanta	Undisc.	27 Oct 1998
6 Oct 1968	30	Bjarne Goldbaek	Copenhagen	£330,000	9 Nov 1998
1999–2000 season					
4 Nov 1976	22	Mario Melchiot	Ajax	Free	13 Jun 1999
15 Oct 1968	30	Didier Deschamps	Juventus	£3 mil	21 Jun 1999
10 Mar 1973	26	Chris Sutton	Blackburn	£10 mil	5 Jul 1999
7 May 1966	33	Jes Hogh	Fenerbahce	£300,000	8 Jul 1999
7 Aug 1973	26	Gabriele Ambrosetti	Vicenza	£3.5 mil	14 Aug 1999
21 Feb 1978	21	Stuart Reddington	Lincoln Utd	Undisc.	26 Aug 1999
30 Mar 1972	27	Emerson Thome	Sheff Wed	£2.7 mil	23 Dec 1999
3 Aug 1978	21	Rati Aleksidze	D Tbilisi	Undisc.	1 Jun 2000

Date of birth	Age	Name	Club	Fee	Date signed
27 Mar 1972	28	JF Hasselbaink	Atl Madrid	£15 mil	2 Jun 2000
15 Sep 1978	21	Eidur Gudjohnsen	Bolton	£5 mil	20 Jun 2000
10 Apr 1972	28	Mario Stanic	Parma	£5.6 mil	28 Jun 2000
13 Jan 1983	17	Sebastien Kneissl	E. Frankfurt	Free	1 Jul 2000
2000–2001 season					
6 Sep 1973	26	Carlo Cudicini	Castel Sangro	Undisc.	3 Jul 2000
22 Oct 1970	29	Winston Bogarde	Barcelona	Free	31 Aug 2000
16 Aug 1968	32	Slavisa Jokanovic	Deportivo	£1.7 mil	10 Oct 2000
12 Aug 1977	23	Jesper Gronkjaer	Ajax	£7.8 mil	29 Dec 2000
13 Jan 1972	29	Mark Bosnich	Man Utd	Free	18 Jan 2001
17 Aug 1977	23	William Gallas	Marseille	£6.2 mil	21 May 2001
20 Jun 1978	22	Frank Lampard	West Ham	£11 mil	14 Jun 2001
2001–2002 season					
22 Sep 1970	30	Emmanuel Petit	Barcelona	£7.5 mil	26 Jun 2001
15 Aug 1976	24	Boudewijn Zenden	Barcelona	£7.5 mil	2 Aug 2001
2002–2003 season					
17 Aug 1978	23	Enrique de Lucas	Espanyol	Free	1 Jul 2002
27 May 1984	18	Filipe Oliveira	Porto	£500,000	1 Aug 2002
30 May 1973	30	Marco Ambrosio	Chievo	Free	1 Jun 2003
24 Aug 1977	25	Jurgen Macho	Sunderland	Free	1 Jun 2003

The 1996–97 season had seen Gullit become the first foreign manager to win the FA Cup as the Dutchman guided Chelsea to a 2–0 victory over Middlesbrough at Wembley. It was the first time in 26 years that the club had won the competition. Gullit had already established Premier League landmarks as the youngest manager at 34 and the only black manager.

Gullitt was later to tell me:

> When Glenn Hoddle brought me to Chelsea [from Sampdoria] people thought, "Oh Chelsea, what the hell club was that?" They never thought about it. I have a Chelsea friend who says "I thought it was a joke when I heard you were coming to Chelsea." But I was very happy and my memory of football is the appreciation of the crowd in this country. I did things on the football field they'd never seen. One ball came over, I took it on my chest and played on. They loved it because normally they saw the defender head the ball and bang it back to the opposition. For me, that was an everyday job in Italy. People didn't applaud for that. Here they applauded me and that was such a nice feeling. It gave me an extra boost. I'm very proud that I had the opportunity to play here. When I came to England, all the best football players went to Italy. Now the best players come here, which is a big change.

Under his successor, the Italian Gianluca Vialli, Chelsea became the first English club to field an all-foreign starting XI at Stamford Bridge on Boxing Day in the 1999–2000 season. The line-up against Southampton was: Ed de Goey (Holland), Albert Ferrer (Spain), Emerson Thome (Brazil), Frank Leboeuf (France), Celestine Babayaro (Nigeria), Dan Petrescu (Romania), Didier Deschamps (France), Roberto Di Matteo (Italy), Gabriele Ambrosetti (Italy), Gustavo Poyet (Uruguay) and Tore Andre Flo (Norway). Flo scored both goals in a 2–1 win. Home-grown midfielder Jody Morris played the last three minutes for Petrescu, while Jon Harley came on for Ambrosetti in the 75th minute. Dennis Wise, the team captain, was missing through illness. Graeme Le Saux and Chris Sutton were also unavailable at the time.

Vialli defended his selection by saying:

> I never thought about it. I've got a squad of 22 players and the more I've got available then the better it is. Sometimes a team picks itself because of injuries and suspensions. It makes no difference as long as we talk the same language on the pitch. We had a few players out — and unfortunately a few of them were English — but nationality is not important.

By the time Abramovich bought the club Vialli had gone, to be replaced by his fellow Italian Claudio Ranieri. He had a more than respectable record of 76 wins from 146 matches and played a part in Chelsea easily outstripping Tottenham as London's second club behind Arsenal. Ranieri had more than £250 million to spend on players and led the club to their highest position since 1954–55 and the semi-finals of the Champions League. But it soon became clear that the Tinkerman, as he came to be known for his fondness for chopping and changing his line-up, was not going to last. He just did not offer what the Russian wanted. The European Cup winner Mourinho was the new man for the new Roman era.

The Russian had chosen a singular football manager as if to match what was now being presented as a unique football club: together they were to create the most compelling narrative of the Premier League's second decade.

Mourinho's father, Felix, was good enough to earn one cap for Portugal but his son swiftly realised that his own lack of pace and power would prevent him emulating that achievement. So Jose never played professionally, but moved into coaching and studied it intensely. His attention to detail, particularly in the scouting reports supplied to his players, is the foundation of his success. His man-management skills are legendary — even now, five years on, Chelsea players are still in text conversation with their former manager.

By the age of 29, Mourinho was acting as Bobby Robson's translator at Sporting Lisbon and followed him to Porto and then Barcelona, quickly making himself into more than a mere translator and taking responsibility for the defensive side of the team's play. As manager he took unfashionable Porto to the UEFA Cup and then to the Champions League in successive seasons. Even as Porto celebrated victory in 2004 it was obvious his days in Portugal were numbered, particularly as Mourinho had masterminded a last-minute victory at Old Trafford to dump Manchester United out of the competition. In his typically understated way, Mourinho celebrated with a joyous touchline sprint, punching the air as he went. As he was fond of reminding Sir Alex Ferguson: "You would be sad if your team gets dominated by opponents built on 10 per cent of your budget."

Within weeks he was in London, spending Roman Abramovich's millions as Chelsea manager, showing his liking for attacking power and Portuguese defensive nous by signing the likes of Michael Essien, Didier Drogba, Tiago, Ricardo Carvalho and Paulo Ferreira in a £70 million spree. Not that he would ever accept that the success he secured was built on money alone. In February 2005, with Chelsea leading the title race, he famously said: "We are on top at the moment but not because of the club's financial power. We are in contention for a lot of trophies because of my hard work." He always distinguished what he did from what the owner did, as he made clear in March 2005: "If he helped me out in training we would be bottom of the league and if I had to work in his world of big business, we would be bankrupt!"

By then Mourinho's sayings were collector's items as he had begun to make an indelible mark on the back pages of the newspapers as the new, albeit foreign, Brian Clough. Few managers have had such a magnetic, charismatic effect on the British media. Clough achieved it when he was winning trophies with Derby County and Nottingham Forest in the 1970s and 1980s, providing excellent copy to those reporters based in the Midlands. Even to this day, books are written by journalists about the joys and lessons learnt while in the close company of Old Big 'Ed. Such parallels have been made with the Portuguese. Not only did he fill column inches but he produced effective, trophy-winning teams. Like Clough, Mourinho could walk the walk as well as talk the talk.

Mourinho's magnetic, charismatic presence — although some may argue that he is an egotistical and incredibly divisive character — was evident on his first day in front of the press as Chelsea manager. "I am not worried about pressure. If I wanted to have an easy job, working with the big protection of what I have already done before, I would have stayed at Porto — beautiful blue chair, the Champions League trophy, God, and after God, me. If I stayed there and lost 10 matches and didn't win another Champions League people would still trust me and think I am the best."

Then he delivered the remark that would characterise his dramatic tenure in the Premier League: "Please don't call me arrogant, but I'm European champion and I think I'm a special one."

Statistically speaking, there was little to counter his sentiments. Chelsea won back-to-back league titles in 2004 and 2005 — they had last won the championship in 1955 — as well as two League Cups and the FA Cup, the first at the new Wembley stadium. That first triumph in 2004 saw a Premier League record points total of 95, the record for the most wins (29) and the fewest goals conceded (15) in a season. Goalkeeper Petr Cech kept a record 24 clean sheets. Mourinho also targeted success in the League Cup, which came with a 3–2 win over Liverpool at the Millennium Stadium.

At the start of the 2007–08 season, Chelsea beat Birmingham City 3–2 to set a record of 64 consecutive home league matches without defeat (this surpassed Liverpool's long-standing mark between 1978 and 1981). Wherever he has gone, Mourinho has won trophies — with Inter Milan he completed a historic treble (which included, of course, the Champions League victory in 2010) and with his current club, Real Madrid, he already has the Spanish league on his CV, with more expected to follow.

Off the pitch the charismatic Portuguese was a magnet for the media, his presence in England drawing interest from people who might not normally concern themselves with the goings-on in the Premier League. His attractiveness to women was frequently noted and his stylish attire analysed at length. Even the disappearance of his family's Yorkshire terrier, Leya, took on an element of soap opera and resulted in the Chelsea manager being arrested and cautioned for obstructing police. The dog subsequently turned up in Portugal with Mourinho's wife.

But for all the flamboyance of his gestures beside the pitch, Mourinho took a pragmatic approach to management. His teams switched effortlessly between 4–3–1–2 and a more attacking 4–3–3. The power of his players was too much for the bulk of the Premier League and in three-plus years he never lost a home league game.

By then Mourinho had begun to play mind games as well as Ferguson and as he told the press: "When I face the media, maybe I don't feel it now, here with you, because it's a different sort of interview, but when I face the media before or after the game, I feel it as part of the game."

But even when Mourinho was winning his titles with Chelsea, the relationship with Ferguson was never vicious nor hostile; if anything the Portuguese has always displayed a deferential tone towards the elder statesman. In recent years, the pair have become great friends — so much so that the Special One is strongly tipped to succeed Ferguson when he does indeed retire from management.

The playful relationship did not start so well. When United lost the first leg of a Champions League last-16 tie to Porto 2–1 in 2004, Ferguson refused to shake his opponent's hand at the final whistle because he was so incensed by the "diving" of Porto's players. Then, for the return leg at Old Trafford, Mourinho famously broke managerial protocol by sprinting along the touchline to celebrate a goal with his players. One of the lowest points in the relationship was when Mourinho said that former United winger Cristiano Ronaldo had "no education". Ferguson responded by saying it was "way below the belt" and that Mourinho had "no principles".

But the Portuguese was always willing to concede that the older man knew more and had experienced more. As he said of Ferguson in January 2005: "Maybe when I turn 60 and have been managing in the same league for 20 years and have the respect of everybody I will have the power to speak to people and make them tremble a little bit."

There was never the same respect for Wenger. Relations were not helped when in January 2005, the *News of the World* reported that Mourinho and

Ashley Cole, then an Arsenal player, were involved in a protracted "tapping-up" saga that soured relations between the two London clubs. While the tapping up of players is endemic in football, this case took the practice to a different level by being conducted openly in a London hotel. The paper had discovered a meeting at the Royal Park Hotel in Lancaster Gate, West London, between Cole and Mourinho. The meeting was also attended by Peter Kenyon, Chelsea chief executive, and Pini Zahavi, football's leading deal broker. This meeting had provoked charges of bringing the game into disrepute.

The Chelsea manager and the Arsenal left-back were both found guilty of gross misconduct under Premier League rules — Mourinho's £200,000 fine was reduced to £75,000, as was Cole's £100,000 penalty. This decision resulted in two lines of fine interpretation. The first was that by giving the two men equal financial punishments, the FA Premier League appeals committee were saying that neither was more guilty than the other. However, the second was that by reducing Mourinho's fine by a greater proportion than Cole's, the panel believed the Chelsea manager to be less accountable than first thought because he did not seek the meeting with the player and his agent, Jonathan Barnett.

The Premier League said in a statement: "The committee found favour in part in Jose Mourinho's appeal on his sanctions, deciding that although he had a greater responsibility as a manager and senior club representative, he was less culpable for the arranged meeting."

The FA are responsible for policing the behaviour of all UK-registered agents but they could not take action against Zahavi because he is registered in Israel.

The original inquiry found Cole in breach of Premier League rule K5 that prohibits contracted players from talking to or approaching rival clubs without their employer's permission with the view to negotiating a transfer. The club broke rule K3, which forbids them from approaching Cole by any means while he was under contract. Mourinho, who had initially denied he had been present at the meeting, was found to be in breach of Rule Q, governing managers' conduct. Chelsea were fined £300,000 and were given a suspended three-point deduction.

A Chelsea statement read: "We always regarded the original fine as completely disproportionate to the alleged offence. We are also pleased the appeals committee have publicly recognised that Jose's culpability with respect to the arranged meeting was less than Ashley Cole's. Although we are disappointed the original verdict still stands, we accept the verdict and believe it is time to move on and look forward to the new Premier League season."

Mourinho further damaged his fragile relationship with Wenger in October

2005 when after some comments by the Arsenal manager about Chelsea, Mourinho hit back by saying: "I think he is one of these people who is a voyeur. He likes to watch other people. There are some guys who, when they are at home, have a big telescope to see what happens in other families. He speaks, speaks, speaks about Chelsea."

But in many ways these were minor spats compared to the serious drama and controversy with UEFA, who were seriously unhappy with Mourinho's antics and comments after Chelsea lost to Barcelona on February 23, 2005. This triggered a six-week war between Chelsea and UEFA which would end with the regulators for European football imposing a two-match ban on Mourinho accompanied by a fine of 20,000 Swiss francs (£8,900), with Chelsea fined 75,000 francs (£33,300). Mourinho was banned from the dugout for the Champions League quarter-final ties against Bayern Munich. He had to watch the first leg at Stamford Bridge from the stands and under UEFA rule 70 he was "not allowed in the dressing room, tunnel or technical area before and during the match," nor "allowed to get in touch with his team". To ensure Mourinho did not use a mobile phone, UEFA announced before the match they would "man-mark" him during the two matches.

UEFA's punishments had come after charging Mourinho with bringing the game into disrepute, appearing late for the second half of the last-16 tie against Barcelona at the Nou Camp and failing to appear at the post-match press conference. Mourinho's war with UEFA showed the effect of his personality and the impact he could have both on the media and those who run the game. Indeed it had all the makings of a novella. And like a good novel the flashpoint of the whole affair turned out to be pure fiction, making the saga football's equivalent of the Sherlock Holmes story of the dog that did not bark. This was the claim that after the final whistle following Chelsea's defeat at the Nou Camp, Mourinho was kicked up the backside by Barcelona assistant coach Henk ten Cate. The story led the back pages of the British tabloids and though Chelsea denied the claim, the denial came too late that night for the back pages to be changed.

It was later eventually discredited as something dreamt up by a Spanish journalist, who later admitted doing so. The story then vanished, but the confusion set off the whole sorry mess with subsequent Chelsea assertions being branded as physically impossible by UEFA, while Chelsea's chief executive, Peter Kenyon, complained that UEFA had used deliberately inflammatory language and that "our defence has been dismissed before it has even been considered". The pattern having been set, the war between club and ruling body continued to escalate, with each side unable to comprehend what the other was saying.

After the match, the atmosphere was not improved when Mourinho failed to appear for the press conference, and that Chelsea were a few minutes late coming out for the second half. But what made this issue such a major story was the Mourinho factor. In particular his claim that: "When I saw Frank Rijkaard [Barcelona's coach] entering the referee's dressing room I couldn't believe it. When Didier Drogba was sent off [after half-time] I wasn't surprised."

Mourinho could not have said anything more damaging. In addition, the Chelsea boss made comments questioning the integrity of referee Anders Frisk, which led to death threats being made against the referee by Chelsea fanatics, which in turn led to him announcing his retirement.

Mourinho retracted his statement about seeing Frisk and Rijkaard together a few days later. But Chelsea's assistant coach Steve Clarke and security man Les Miles remained convinced that they had seen Rijkaard enter the referee's room at half-time.

UEFA, using the testimony of their trusted delegate Fritz Ahlstrom, who was in the tunnel at that time, insisted that this was physically impossible. The nature of the Barcelona tunnel and the location of the dressing rooms mean that someone in the visitors' room cannot see the referee's quarters.

But it then turned out that at the end of the tunnel there was a screen, to one side of which is the Barcelona dressing room, and the other the referee's changing area. There was also a desk separating the two doors. Clarke and Miles probably saw Rijkaard behind this screen, talking to Frisk and assumed that he was in the referee's room. In their judgement UEFA appeared to accept that Clarke and Miles made an honest mistake when claiming Rijkaard had entered Frisk's room.

The whole affair seemed to prove to UEFA that Mourinho was a loose cannon and every time UEFA thought they had the situation under control, Mourinho erupted. This explained the ferocity with which they reacted. Chelsea, while publicly defending Mourinho, were shaken by this and this did not help relations between Mourinho and Abramovich. It almost certainly paved the ground for their sensational parting in September 2007. Chelsea never disclosed what exactly happened and there were clearly other factors as well.

There was the case of Andrei Shevchenko, who arrived in 2006 for a club record £31 million. It was clear Abramovich was a greater fan of the Ukrainian than Mourinho and the fading striker's return of four League goals justified the latter's scepticism. The manager left him out of many key games at the business end of the season. And despite the fact that in three seasons Mourinho won six trophies, the one that his owner wanted above all, the Champions League, eluded him. Agonisingly, Chelsea were twice knocked out by Liverpool, a team they comfortably bested in the Premier League.

In September 2007, Mourinho left "by mutual consent" and Avram Grant, a dour Israeli, who had been brought in as director of football and given a seat on the board, was chosen as his successor. Under the terms of his departure he could not join another club, which proved to be Inter Milan, until the following season and when he did Mourinho delivered the Champions League for Inter Milan in his second season. Such was his impact in Italy that his return — to Manchester United, Manchester City, or even back to Stamford Bridge — has been forecast at regular intervals, even though he holds one of the most prestigious jobs in the world at Real Madrid.

In all the talk of Mourinho perhaps replacing Ferguson in the future, one club had been completely eclipsed: Liverpool. The 2010–11 season saw Manchester United win their 12th Premier League title and, more significantly, their 19th English title overall, surpassing Liverpool's record of 18 which had stood since 1990. This had been one of Ferguson's biggest ambitions when he took over at Old Trafford. As he once famously said: "My greatest challenge is not what's happening at the moment, my greatest challenge was knocking Liverpool right off their f***ing perch."

During this time managers had come and gone at Anfield, many of them foreign, and there had been changes of ownership but it had done little to dent United.

Liverpool too had gone foreign in search of that elusive title. Liverpool's quest had started in Paris in 1997 with a dinner between Peter Robinson, then Liverpool chief executive, and Gerald Houllier, then the technical director of the French team. As Houllier recalled to me: "We had a meal in a restaurant. But it was not possible for me to leave the French FA one year before the World Cup." So just after the 1998 World Cup Houllier came to Anfield, ending as he well realised a great club institution: "Before I arrived Liverpool had a Boot Room tradition: Bill Shankly was followed by his assistant Bob Paisley, then Joe Fagan, then Kenny Dalglish, then Graeme Souness, then Roy Evans. My arrival was greeted with, 'Gerard who?'"

But with foreign managers now in vogue, Liverpool had to beat off Celtic, with whom Houllier had a draft contract. Indeed, even before he went to Liverpool, White Hart Lane was on the horizon. "There was talk of me going to Tottenham. But they chose Christian Gross."

Houllier's move to Liverpool was helped in that he had been a French teacher at the city's Alsop Comprehensive School. "I was teaching in the city when Bill Shankly was manager. That's very funny! I had to do one year abroad and everybody was choosing London. I chose Liverpool because they had two football clubs. So I thought maybe I could see many games."

It also meant that when he came to Anfield, "I could speak in English with the players. That's an important factor. So I could hear when some of the players said we'll do the Frenchie in."

To the outside world it seemed elements of the Boot Room tradition remained as, initially, Houllier was in joint charge with Roy Evans. But Houllier told me: "I insisted on joint management with Roy. I was coming from outside and thought that it was good to work together. It didn't work for many reasons. Roy was too soft, nice but weak and, when there was a decision to take he would, well, Peter Robinson will tell you, leave me with a hot potato. Roy would have been a fantastic No. 2, not a No. 1."

Although Houllier would not be drawn on this, one of the problems was the freedom Paul Ince, the captain, was given by Evans as to when he could train. It is an interesting reflection on the relationship between Houllier and Ferguson that when after a year Houllier got rid of Ince, the first call he got was from Alex Ferguson. The Scot had had his own problems with Ince. In 1998 he had publicly ripped into Ince, saying: "He's a bully, a f***ing big-time Charlie." Now he was quick to congratulate Houllier.

Houllier won six trophies at Anfield between 1998 and 2004 with a historic season in 2000–2001 when he won the two domestic cups, both at the Millennium Stadium in Cardiff, as well as the UEFA Cup. Liverpool beat Birmingham City to claim the League Cup — the 5–4 penalty shootout win was the first time the competition had been decided on penalties. Then, Liverpool beat Arsenal 2–1 in the FA Cup final. The icing on the cake was a 5–4 extra-time win over Spanish club Alaves at the Westfalenstadion in Germany, the club's first European trophy since the 1984 European Cup.

Yet for all this the season was dominated by what was happening at Old Trafford. That season saw Manchester United's historic achievement of a third successive Premier League title which matched the feats of Huddersfield Town (1924–26), Arsenal (1933–35) and Liverpool (1982–84). The big difference was that Alex Ferguson was the only manager to have been in place for all three title-winning seasons because the previous clubs had all had managerial changes. United secured their seventh title in nine seasons with a 4–2 victory over Coventry City at Old Trafford in front of a post-war record crowd of 67,637, because second-placed Arsenal lost 3–0 to Middlesbrough later that afternoon. "It's a great feeling," said Ferguson. "It's the hardest league in the world to win so I'm very pleased. It's been a fantastic season and I'm very proud of the players."

Ferguson added:

The achievement of winning three in a row is fantastic. The players have shown phenomenal consistency over the season and we showed today that we always try to win our games. When you win the championship, it is a fantastic feeling because it is the true test of the best team in the country and we have proved that over the years. The attitude of the players throughout the season has been brilliant, absolutely phenomenal.

Houllier could not match that and in the end it was his failure to win the Premier League that saw him depart in 2004. His best finish was second in 2002, but he admits that after he fell ill earlier in that season — suffering heart problems in the middle of a match against Leeds — some of his signings were not good. "The recruitment of El Hadji Diouf and Salif Diao the year I was ill was not up to the standard in terms of attitude for the club. I regret that."

But after returning to France he hungered to re-cross the Channel and over the years he hoped several clubs would appoint him, including Tottenham, Newcastle and Blackburn. The 2010–11 season did see him return as Aston Villa manager but a recurrence of his heart problems meant he had to retire.

Not that his successor Rafa Benitez fared any better as far as the title was concerned. Benitez, a Spaniard, had won two league titles as well as the UEFA Cup with Valencia, and his first season at Liverpool, 2004–05, would prove sensational. This produced the incomparable drama of Istanbul where in the 2005 Champions League final Liverpool came from three goals down at half-time to beat AC Milan on penalties. At half-time Liverpool fans were in tears and a couple even left to drive back to England and did not know the result until days later. The Istanbul miracle meant Liverpool had won the biggest European trophy five times, at that stage three more than Manchester United.

Liverpool's triumph caused a great headache for UEFA. Liverpool had finished fifth in the Premier League, three points behind Everton in fourth, who had qualified for the Champions League. The idea of not allowing the holders to defend the trophy seemed counter to all the traditions of sport and Europe's governing body was forced, against their own rules, to let the club defend their title the following season. For Everton it was their first Champions League campaign; they would have been eligible to play in the European Cup by winning the league in 1985 but UEFA had banned all English clubs from its competitions for five years after the Heysel disaster. As it transpired, Everton failed to make the group stages after failing to beat Villarreal in the third qualifying round.

Even the British government got involved in the row, with the Minister for Sport Richard Caborn contacting UEFA to argue that it would be "a travesty" if

Liverpool were excluded because England were only allowed four places in the Champions League. "It seems only right that the winners should have automatic re-entry rather than having to qualify through the domestic system. It is only common sense," said Caborn. In the end, UEFA relented and allowed the special exception. UEFA spokesman William Gaillard said: "In the upcoming season, England will be the only national association ever, and for the last time, that will be allowed to have five clubs." Gaillard indicated that revenue from the competition would be split five ways, not four ways, between the English clubs.

To avoid such an awkward situation from happening again, UEFA changed its rules so that the tournament's reigning champions would automatically have the right to defend their crown, potentially at the expense of the fourth-placed team. Tottenham fell foul of this rule in May 2012 when Chelsea's Champions League triumph against Bayern Munich secured them entry to the following season's competition at Spurs' expense, even though Harry Redknapp's team finished fourth in the league. A precedent had been set in the 2000–01 season when Real Madrid were able to defend their Champions League title after finishing fifth in La Liga — but only because the Spanish football federation had decided to hand them a place at the expense of Real Zaragoza.

Liverpool had to begin the defence of their trophy in the first qualifying round against Welsh champions TNS in mid-July. But Istanbul was to prove Rafael Benitez's great moment in the sun. He not only failed to win the title for Liverpool but, frustrated by his failure to match Manchester United, he was soon at loggerheads with Ferguson. This all came into sharp focus in the 2008–09 season. "In the second half of the season they will get nervous," chirped Ferguson at the first sign of a serious Liverpool title challenge under Benitez that season. In response, the Spaniard stunned football by launching into his notorious, as well as uncharacteristic, "fact-based" pre-planned tirade at the Scot.

On January 9, 2009, Benitez said:

> The Respect campaign started with the sending-off of Javier Mascherano at Old Trafford by Steve Bennett. That was the referee when they played against Wigan and he couldn't see the handball by Rio Ferdinand. He didn't give a penalty, they won the game and the title. During the Respect campaign Ferguson was charged by the FA with improper conduct following remarks made against Martin Atkinson and Keith Hackett. He was not punished. He is the only manager in the English league who cannot be punished for these things. We had a meeting in Manchester with managers and the FA about that Respect campaign, and I was very

clear... forget the campaign because Mr Ferguson was killing the referees, killing Mr Atkinson, killing Mr Hackett.

Benitez then added:

Only Mr Ferguson can talk about fixtures, referees and other things and nothing happens. Two seasons ago we played a lot of games away on Saturday morning when United played on Sunday and nobody said anything. Now he is claiming everyone is against them. But in the second half of the league they will be at home against all the teams at the top of the table so I think it will be a fantastic advantage. And at Christmas I don't know why United played on the 29th at home when all the other teams played on the 28th. We played at Newcastle at lunchtime, 40 hours after our previous game, so he was not complaining then.

It illustrated how Ferguson had not lost the knack of getting under his opponents' skin. Although the next time the pair met competitively, Liverpool crushed Manchester United 4–1 at Old Trafford, Benítez lost the title because his team could not close out tight games. In the league, they only won three games 1–0; United won an astonishing nine by that score. United expected the winning goal to come — Liverpool did not. In the end Benitez's decision had backfired and proved to be the one of the defining moments of the season.

While in general Anfield fans liked Benitez more than Houllier, the Frenchman, speaking to me after Benitez had been replaced by Roy Hodgson, took great relish in telling the story of the aftermath of Benitez's greatest moment of glory in Istanbul: "When I came into the changing room in Istanbul some of the players said, 'Boss, it's your team'. Twelve out of 14 in Istanbul were players that I had signed or developed. I left Liverpool with a team in the Champions League."

This was a barbed pointer to the fact that when Benitez left Anfield, Liverpool had failed to qualify for the Champions League, finishing seventh despite the presence of Torres and Gerrard in the team. As Houllier summed it up: "When I was at Anfield we won six trophies and, after Rafa Benitez left, one of the players sent me a message. He said, 'Boss, he hasn't beaten you.'"

This may sound like special pleading by Houllier and was made when he still hoped to return as Premier League manager. What it could not disguise was the deep Anfield angst as Ferguson brought home title after title to Old Trafford in a way that no Liverpool manager in the Premier League era has been able to emulate.

The Ferguson era very nearly ended in 2002 but the drama that took place demonstrated once again what a remarkable manager Sir Alex Ferguson is and his hold on the English game.

The 2000–01 season had certainly begun as if it was a valedictory one for the Scot. It had barely begun when on August 28, United sold Jaap Stam to Lazio for £15.3 million. The club claimed that this was a fairly routine transfer. There had been an offer for the player in the summer, the offer was not pursued, there were doubts about the defender's fitness and he had made a poor start to the season. So when an offer from Lazio came in again he was sold. However, as it later emerged the club had been looking to sell Stam for some time, and there was also the involvement of Ferguson's son Jason as an agent in the deal, reverberations of which would haunt the club for years to come. There was also the fact that the sale came a week after Stam's book *Head to Head* was serialised in the *Daily Mirror*. In the book Stam described how Ferguson had tapped him up when he was at PSV and also advised players to dive for penalties. The club vehemently denied that the book had anything to do with Stam's transfer but the public perception was otherwise.

United's poor start had also seen Roy Keane renew his criticisms of United. In November 2000, Keane had described United's supporters as heartless prawn sandwich eaters: "Some people come here and I don't think they can spell football, let alone understand it. They have a few drinks and probably their prawn sandwiches and don't realise what is going on out on the pitch." Now, in the autumn of 2001, he accused his fellow players, in particular the older established players, of not pulling their weight, which had caused a slump in form. Indeed, when they came to Tottenham on September 29, having lost to Deportivo La Coruna in Europe four days earlier, Fleet Street's finest gathered at White Hart Lane to write their obituaries of Ferguson. They seemed to have all the material they needed when Tottenham went 3–0 up at half-time. But in statistically the greatest comeback in United history they scored five without reply in the second half, winning 5–3, and it could have been more. Ferguson called it the best away win of his entire reign.

But even this remarkable victory did little to dispel the feeling that the players were aware they were playing for a manager who was not only going but seemed to have lost his touch. In November, following the defeat at Liverpool, *The Times* headlined their report "The day Ferguson's empire began to crumble" and wondered if it was "a season too far, a fight too many for the ageing heavyweight". After United were beaten at home by West Ham on December 8, they stood ninth in the table and 11 points behind Liverpool.

On New Year's Eve in 2001, Ferguson told Glenn Gibbons of *The Scotsman*:

"I'm going all right. That's been settled for some time now." Just before that he had also hinted to Bob Cass of *The Mail on Sunday* that things might change. Yes, he would retire but then added: "The club are looking for my successor but when the thing comes, nearer the time, who knows what will happen?" The real meaning of these words would only become clear when, with all the world preparing to bid Ferguson goodbye, there was a dramatic volte-face.

United knew that they had to avoid the post-Busby disaster when the retirement of the then United talisman in 1969 proved so traumatic that the club were relegated five years later. United's chief executive Peter Kenyon publicly pledged to avoid a repetition. In my book *Manchester Disunited* I investigated at length what happened and it is worth re-examining a remarkable chain of events that would ultimately lead to a dramatic turnaround. As Kenyon told me:

> We got together and he came in and told Roland [Smith] and me about why he wanted to retire. We had a lengthy discussion in which we asked did he desire this? Had he made the right decisions for the right reasons? This would have been in 2001 and I think, genuinely at that point, it was a lifestyle issue. He had been at the top of the game for many years. I think he recognised that he hadn't done anything else other than football; and that he was now starting to get heavily involved in racing, which he saw as his life after football. He owned Rock of Gibraltar. He mentioned that. Racing was clearly becoming a bigger part of his life and something that he consciously felt would offer him that alternative. And it was something he was interested in, he could get more involved in. Let's us face it, you can't read Alex's mind. But from what we could gather he also felt that there was the security that perhaps would come from his other venture. Once we'd satisfied ourselves he was going, then clearly we had to address the issue. I drew up a shortlist.

The list included Marcello Lippi, Fabio Capello, Martin O'Neill, Sven-Goran Eriksson and Steve McClaren, then assistant manager at Old Trafford. The Italians' lack of English did not help and there was already a foreigner working in England who could speak English well, who after a spell as England manager wanted to return to club football and was also close to Beckham. Soon the shortlist had just one name. Kenyon would not tell me the name but it is clear it was Eriksson. He seemed to have all the qualities: not very confrontational, a man who had done it all levels, a very nice guy with a pleasant manner who would have fitted in well at Manchester United.

There was a certain irony in Manchester United choosing Eriksson as Ferguson had played a big part in nudging the FA to appoint him as their first foreign manager. Back in October 2000, with England looking for a new manager to replace Kevin Keegan, who had suddenly resigned in the toilets of the old Wembley following the defeat at the hands of Germany, Adam Crozier, then the chief executive of the Football Association, had travelled to Old Trafford to meet Ferguson. The Old Trafford board thought the FA wanted to poach Ferguson but Crozier, who got on well with his fellow Scot, knew Ferguson would never want to do that. He had gone to pick his brains about getting the right man and his agreement to let McClaren become part of the new coaching team. In the course of the conversation, Ferguson pointed Crozier in the direction of Eriksson for the top job.

Now United wanted the Swede and with Kenyon having identified him the job was now for Watkins, the man of law and many secrets. Watkins knew how to avoid the sort of indiscreet publicity that two years later would attend Eriksson's contacts with Chelsea, who also tried to poach him. Watkins, a past master at conducting negotiations that required both tact and discretion, met Eriksson at a secret location in London, an obscure hotel. While nothing was signed by the last week of January 2002, it was left with Eriksson agreeing to talk to his employers, the FA, and telling them he wanted to leave. The plan was for Eriksson to see England through the finals of the 2002 World Cup and then take over at Manchester United. Watkins, a lawyer with great knowledge of contract law, knew that it was first and foremost an employee-employer question, with the employee duty bound to inform his employer.

Manchester United also decided to make a formal approach to the FA. But in arranging the meeting they did not tell the FA what the purpose of the meeting was. They planned to tell the FA that they intended to approach Eriksson. This is the sort of thing that goes on in football all the time and the whole thing was conducted in such a fashion that both United and Eriksson could maintain deniability, which they have done to this day. Manchester United were determined to avoid the sort of public embarrassment that Chelsea suffered when Roman Abramovich's courting of Eriksson saw the then England manager emerge from the Russian's London flat. Watkins was altogether more discreet.

Within the FA, the matter was not entirely a secret. Crozier, at that time busy promoting Team England, had got quite close to Watkins during the season and would jokingly tell him: "Keep your hands off our man." Crozier told me:

They never approached the FA with a view to talking to us about Sven. [This is technically true since they had not told them what the meeting was about, just that they wanted to meet about something.] Do I think behind the scenes that they talked to Sven? Yes, I think they did. As I now understand it I think there were a few conversations between Sven and them about what would happen after the World Cup. I don't think there was ever any question of not leading England to the World Cup.

Kenyon says:

It got to the point where we were going to approach the intended candidate [meaning the FA] on the Monday morning. Maurice and I were travelling down on the Sunday in order to sort the matter out. The whole thing was planned with a view to making an official approach before we got into negotiations. We were ready to travel down to London when Maurice got a call. The caller was Ferguson on Watkins' mobile phone. He said: "Can you come to Carrington to see me, I have to see you urgently."

The call could not have come at a more inconvenient time. It was a busy day for the lawyer but Ferguson was insistent. Watkins, who had no idea what was on Ferguson's mind, rushed over to be told that Ferguson had been thinking about his retirement. He had spoken to the family, he was fit, had a recent medical, his wife Cathy did not like the idea of having him hanging about the house and he had decided to change his mind. He now wanted a new contract to take him beyond 2002. Ferguson's about-turn completely threw Watkins.

Watkins, like the rest of the board, had spoken often to Ferguson: do you really want to do this? Yes, he had said, he did. Now, with Watkins and Kenyon virtually on their way to London to make a formal approach about Eriksson, Ferguson, as he had done so often before, pulled the rug from under their feet. Watkins rang Kenyon to tell him that Ferguson had changed his mind. Kenyon then got hold of Roland Smith and brought him into the loop and decided to postpone their meeting with the FA. Soon, other board members were involved.

One board insider at Manchester United says:

There was a big debate on the board. David Gill was very much part of this debate and his view was mixed. He was not the most vociferous for Ferguson staying. Kenyon and Watkins on balance were more for making sure Ferguson stayed. Edwards was not part of the debate but took part unofficially. He was critical of Ferguson and probably would have had him hung, drawn and quartered. To him he remained an employee, no more.

But the voices on the board who were inclined to say "Thanks, Alex, but no thanks" were quickly silenced and the decision was, of course, that he was going to stay and, what a relief, Britain's most successful manager would be carrying on. However, despite this public endorsement it was not easy to sort out a contract. The debate about the contract was much lengthier and grew quite acrimonious.

The insider says: "This was another huge debate. He wanted a longer contract and he wanted more money, something in the region of around £4 million." Some hard work was involved in sorting the contract and eventually he got a two-year contract with a one-year option. Ferguson had started off asking for four years. It took time to work out the details. Ferguson's lawyer at Paull & Williamsons in Aberdeen got involved. The negotiations got very acrimonious at one point with tense meetings between United and Ferguson's lawyer. His sons Jason and Mark, who worked at Goldman Sachs, also got involved in the talks. Jason Ferguson came to see Kenyon and then finally there was his other son Mark who intervened, which led to further meetings before it was all sorted out.

Ferguson's salary had gone up from £60,000 to £70,000 a week, just over £3.6 million a year. This was still less than the £100,000 a week that Roy Keane agreed to a few weeks later after he had made noises suggesting he might move abroad and what Beckham, following protracted negotiations, also agreed to, including a special deal for image rights. At the end of it all, Ferguson declared that once his contract expired in 2005 he had "no intention of staying at the club in any capacity whatsoever."

David Bick, then Manchester United's external financial PR adviser, was following events closely, and recalls:

> As far as Eriksson is concerned they almost signed an agreement with him. I definitely got the impression about Ferguson's retirement that he'd got himself angry about something and it sounded like toys being thrown out the pram but nobody said really whether it was a genuine retirement or whether it was a fit of pique or anger or whatever. When he changed his mind, such was his influence that they just went along with it. They fell into line with that. It was clear Ferguson had a massive grip over them rather than the other way around.

The Manchester United board knew this could be presented to the fans as a great victory and it was said Ferguson had changed his mind because of family reasons.

The first revelation about Eriksson came in Michael Crick's biography of Ferguson in the summer of 2002 but was denied by United and the FA. The paperback edition had a quote from Edwards saying: "It was very, very close indeed. Terms had actually been agreed." The hardback had not identified Edwards, calling him a "senior United official" and did not give the whole quote, omitting the bit about terms being agreed.

The following year more details emerged including Ferguson's real feelings about Eriksson. In February 2003, in an interview with *The Times,* Ferguson for the first time admitted that he knew Eriksson was coming: "I think they'd done the deal all right. I am sure it was Eriksson... I think they'd shaken hands. They couldn't put anything on paper because he was still England manager."

He then went on to give his views about the man:

I think Eriksson would have been a nice, easy choice for them. He doesn't change anything. He sails along and nobody falls out with him. He comes out and he says, 'In the first half we were very good, second half we were not so good. I am very pleased with the result.' I think he'd have been all right for United — the acceptable face. Carlos Queiroz [then Ferguson's No. 2], who knows him because he [Eriksson] was at Benfica and Carlos was from Lisbon. Carlos says what he did well was that he never fell out with anyone. He was best pals with the president and the press liked him. I think he does that. The press makes a suggestion and he seems to follow it.

For a time after the Ferguson volte-face both the board and even some of the fans must have wondered if they had done the right thing in keeping him. The 2001–02 season saw United finish without a trophy, for the first time since 1998. United also lost the semi-final of the Champions League having squandered their home advantage against Bayer Leverkusen by only drawing 2–2 at Old Trafford. This was a bitter pill for Ferguson to swallow. Not only did it mean that United had again failed in Europe but because for much of the season the Champions League final had been held up as the ultimate farewell by Ferguson. It would be staged at the rebuilt Hampden Park, where back in 1960 one of the most magical of European Cup finals had taken place, Real Madrid beating Eintracht Frankfurt 7–3. Unlike most Scotsmen of Ferguson's generation who claim to have been in the crowd that day, Ferguson actually was there.

The season finished so badly that Ferguson gave the impression he would rather be anywhere but on a football field. Towards the end of the season he abused journalists at a press conference, using the word "fucking" many times and ended up calling them "fucking idiots". The journalists decided to print most of the exchanges verbatim, using asterisks to denote his use of the word "fucking".

But in the decade since then Ferguson turned things around to such an extent that Manchester United won four more Premier League titles, an FA Cup, three League Cups, the FIFA Club World Cup and another Champions League title. It is quite clear retirement in 2002 would have been far too early. Now not only Old Trafford but the world of football has given up speculating when Ferguson might leave. Never in the history of the game has there been a manager like him. And this at a time when the game was undergoing radical change both on the field and, particularly, in the boardroom. There Ferguson would face other problems but none of them seems to affect his ability to go on bringing home silverware.

One man who might have been the long-term foreign manager to challenge Ferguson was Carlo Ancelotti. The Italian arrived at Stamford Bridge for the 2009 season having been heavily courted by Abramovich. In his autobiography published in May of that year, *Preferisco La Copa* (I prefer the Cup), Ancelotti had described how he had a James Bond-style secret meeting with Abramovich at the George V hotel in Paris. This was just after Chelsea had lost the Champions League Final to Manchester United in Moscow in May 2008 and Abramovich moaned: "Chelsea don't have personality... this is a team I don't recognise." Ancelotti's response was: "President, your team is very physical, you have to put more quality in the middle." He suggested buying Franck Ribery and Xabi Alonso.

That November when I went to Chelsea's sylvan training ground in Cobham the club were sunk in gloom. Not only had Ribery and Alonso not arrived but although the club led the Premier League they had been dumped out of the Carling Cup and had only one win in six in all competitions. Ancelotti had even been quoted as saying he feared the sack. But when I uttered the word sack Ancelotti looked quizzically at the interpreter, clearly puzzled by the word. After it had been translated the Italian laughed and said: "I never said if I don't win Roman will send me out. My aim is to do the best in this club as I have done in other clubs." And that best was what he achieved at Milan, where he twice won the Champions League — the great prize that Abramovich had set his heart on.

And just to show that any sacking threat was far from his mind, Ancelotti, after telling me he was religious, even discussed whether there might be a football pitch in heaven. "*Paradiso*?" he asked, turning to his interpreter who had been translating from time to time. Then the 50-year-old, who was sitting in an armchair in his office, raised his arms high above his head to indicate heaven, lowered them below his waist for hell and then put his fingertips together near his lips to indicate the middle destination.

"I hope," he told me in English, "I can go to *paradiso*, if I am unlucky, middle. Hell, I don't think I will go to," and he laughed. The laughter seemed to suggest that the Italian had the measure of his Russian owner. In a club where Abramovich said he wanted to win every match and coaches like the Dutchman Piet de Visser acted like his private football adviser, Ancelotti, the fourth manager since September 2007, was ebullient. "He can speak with anybody. I don't have a problem, for I have confidence in myself."

This confidence appeared to derive from the fact that working for rich powerful men, who have made their money elsewhere and see the game as a toy, was not a new football journey for Ancelotti. For two years, at the turn of the millennium, he coached Juventus, owned by Gianni Agnelli, one of Italy's most famous businessmen. And in Milan he had worked for Silvio Berlusconi for eight years.

Comparing this football trinity, he told me:

> I was not close to Agnelli but he had fantastic irony. He liked to joke with the players and the trainer. I had a very close relationship with Berlusconi. He was my president when I played and when I coached. Abramovich is closer to Berlusconi. He has a passion for his club, he likes to speak about football, as does Berlusconi. Both of them like to watch football on television. After a game he comes to the dressing room.

Did this not signify danger, since his predecessor Luiz Felipe Scolari had been sacked following a show of Chelsea player power by John Terry, Frank Lampard, Didier Drogba and Michael Ballack? "No. Down the years I trained lot of players with power." In Milan they included Paolo Maldini, Rui Costa, Andrea Pirlo, Filippo Inzaghi and Andriy Shevchenko. While the player must know who is in charge, Ancelotti has always made sure that there is not a gulf between the coach and the player: "I want to have us at the same level, a man-to-man relationship."

The only flaw for Ancelotti in this English football paradise was the music in the dressing room before a game. "If it is rap I want to change to Elton John, even Pavarotti," but then with a laugh added, "It is impossible!" His love affair with England was helped by the fact that he could live a normal life here. "I can live like a normal person. I could not do that in Italy. I can walk in London without a problem."

Not that this son of a farmer brought up in Reggiolo had much time for London except for work. "I cannot live in London. I am not used to staying in a big city." As in Milan, he lived close to the training ground — in Oxshott. Although rural Oxshott is hardly Reggiolo, there was little danger that this stockbroker belt village would make Ancelotti forget the trials and tribulations of farming life, which are in his bones. "My father made parmesan cheese. It matured and then you sell. After one year you receive the money, you had to wait all that time to receive the money, you had to have patience."

Ancelotti, having signed a three-year contract, was sure he had the patience and while he saw his future destiny managing Roma he was determined to stay and improve his English. Yet despite doing the Double that season, failure the next meant he ended as yet another manager sacked by Abramovich. It showed how the Premier League had changed the English game. Once a Double-winning manager would have had a job for life. Now it did not guarantee him a job even for a season, certainly not with an owner like Abramovich.

The success of Roberto Mancini in the Premier League's 20th season provides a very difference challenge to Ferguson. For though Manchester City, like Chelsea, are backed by vast wealth they have a much more stable management style. While their long-term challenge is difficult to assess the challenge posed by the foreign managers in the English game over the last 20 years is clear. What is less clear is how the English are responding to this unprecedented foreign invasion.

Chapter 8
TACKLING HOME FAILINGS

The 20th season of the Premier League confirmed what had long been established as a feature of England's top division, that it now provides the best stage for the players and managers from around the world to parade their skills. The English may provide most of the cast but many of them often seem to have merely a walk-on part. So while Roberto Mancini became the fourth foreign manager to win the Premier League, and the second Italian after Carlo Ancelotti, an Englishman is yet to win the competition. And at the end of the season, as the Premier League highlighted the five top-ranked players, the only Englishman in that select group was Wayne Rooney. The others were Robin van Persie (Holland), David Silva (Spain), Emmanuel Adebayor (Togo) and Sergio Aguero (Argentina).

Yet an Englishman, Alan Pardew, did achieve a rare double, winning both the Manager of the Year award given by Barclays, and the League Managers Association's top honour. This was his reward for a season which saw Newcastle, who had expected no more than a top ten finish, ending up fifth ahead of Chelsea and entertaining hopes of a Champions League place until the final week of the season. It has to be said that there has long been a parochial side to the LMA awards. Since 1994, only one foreign manager, Arsene Wenger, has won it. As if to compensate, he has been given the prize twice: his second award in 2004 came in Arsenal's epic season of the Invincibles.

Otherwise, British and largely English names, many of whom now seem eminently forgettable, dominate the award — Joe Kinnear won it for Wimbledon in 1994. Yet Pardew's award was more than just fellow managers, aware how much the Premier League is dominated by foreigners, voting for another Englishman to counter the dominance of foreigners. In many ways, in the 20th year of the Premier League, he represents both the pre-Premier League past of English football and provides a guide as to where the Premier League future may be headed.

Pardew, despite his success, is candid enough to admit that there are three teams that stand above all others in the league. "We at Newcastle are not one of the great sides, we haven't got an abundance of talent. Manchester City's second team could give my first team a good run for their money and probably so could Manchester United and Chelsea; no one else is that good. Everton's second team couldn't give my first team a run for their money. Arsenal, perhaps, not so much the season just gone but in previous years could have done that. But those three clubs can because they've got Champions League strength in there."

Pardew readily confesses that he is "an old-fashioned man". This is underlined when he says: "I am a tea person really. I always have tea in the afternoon and I'm a bit fussy with my tea. You ask anyone who has worked for me, it has to be in a teapot! I won't accept my PA or any of my staff to do it any other way. That was instilled in me by my dad probably. Tea has to be in a pot, a china pot."

Unlike many in modern football, Pardew had an occupation before he earned money from the game, having started his working life as a glazier for his father's company. And the night Pardew received his LMA trophy, his brother was working on the Shard, the new City of London landmark, overlooking the hall where Pardew collected his award.

But what makes Pardew truly unusual is that he is that rare modern manager who started his playing career in non-League football. This has made him very aware of what he calls the "snobbery" of professional football:

> Snobbery in the fact that, "We're professionals and these non-League players, they're this and that. Why are we signing a non-League player? What's this club doing?" When you come into a professional background with academy players the feeling is, "Oh no, we've got the best". But what about little Johnny, who plays for that Sunday morning team, the Old Brompton XI? Is he no good? He's not been through the system, but that doesn't mean he's no good. So you have that kind of snobbery about professional football. I've always been anti that. We do a lot of things very, very well in this country on the football pitch, a lot of things better than most other countries, but there are still some old values that stick with us a little bit.

All this puts Pardew in a good position to judge how the Premier League and the advent of the foreign managers have changed things since he was a player.

> The influence of the foreign manager, the foreign player, on coaching and playing in this country cannot be under-estimated. I genuinely think that foreign managers have been the biggest influence in the last 20 years of the Premier League, in terms of getting into football clubs and changing the

culture and the thinking; Wenger and Mourinho, for sure. Wenger's has been revolutionary! But Mourinho was just as revolutionary, in a shorter time, trust me. He changed the thinking of how the game was played and we learnt so much off those guys and still do.

Pardew may not have worked for Mourinho, as Brendan Rodgers did and who, in the summer of 2012, was appointed manager of Liverpool and has acknowledged his debt to the Real Madrid coach. But Pardew has also learnt a great deal from the Porrtuguese.

I watched a lot of Chelsea when Mourinho was there. I used to go and study his team and study him when I was a manager. When I was out of work I went to see him at the training ground. I was a great admirer of his. He's a brilliant guy. After I won my award he sent me a nice message actually, saying that I deserved the Manager of the Year. That, probably, pleased me more than any other message I got.

The foreign influence, says Pardew, means that:

The English game has changed, the game's more fluid, we're more continental now. We pass the ball more. I wouldn't say the technical gap between the game in this country and abroad has been bridged. What I would say is, we've actually got a format to show our game, whereas before we didn't because of the system of coaching, the Charles Hughes era.

At the start of the Premier League, Hughes was in charge of coaching at the FA. Indeed, he was much in favour of the Premier League being formed, keen as he was to break up the old Football League. His most famous doctrine, evolved after studying many matches, was that to score a goal you only required five passes. That was the guiding coaching philosophy when the Premier League started. Pardew is convinced that:

Charles Hughes put coaching back in this country by 10 years and thank god we're seeing the end of it now. There's still parts of his philosophy that exist and I know it very well because I was brought up through that coaching system. I was not told to hoof the ball, but to understand the percentages. They were saying, 'If you don't play it this way, you won't win'. There was no coaching about keeping possession and trying to alter the opposing team's psychology. You do that by keeping the ball and make them believe they're never going to see the ball. That means you are telling the opposition that they're never going to win. This is what Barcelona do.

There was nothing like that on the coaching programme that I went through, none whatsoever. It was all about set-pieces. So, basically you had two big strikers. You can't play with two strikers any more. You have to have two mobile strikers. You can play with two strikers only if one is a link player, a Rooney, who can link the midfield and attack. Otherwise you're just going to get dominated in midfield. The game is faster and the players are technically better than they've ever been.

Pardew believes the foreign influence on the English game is not the only factor why the Premier League years have changed the English game:

The football boots are lighter, the ball is softer. Older players forget about that. If you put Johnny Haynes, my dad's favourite player, in today's boots, on today's surfaces, with today's ball, he'd probably be England's best player. But it was slower then because the ball was heavier, the pitches were like bogs. I've not played on one pitch this year where my players have come off with muddy boots. Not one! Now, you go back to 1975, some of those clips you see of FA Cup games, it's like a mud bath! Billy Bonds rampaging through the middle! You just don't get that any more! It's a shame, I miss that, if I'm honest.

Such Pardew sentiments are shared by many. As Denis Law, who played for both Manchester United and City, told me as he gazed across the immaculate Old Trafford turf:

When we got to November, it was mud for the next five and a half months. Can you imagine George Best playing on pitches like this every game? You just wonder how good he would've been. The facilities have given the modern players the opportunity to be fitter. But some of the players in the old days would have been just as great today no matter how fit they were. Stanley Matthews and Tom Finney would be great players in any era.

But what makes Pardew's journey fascinating is that he has also experienced the changes in ownership and the revolution in fan expectations that the Premier League has brought to the English game. As with his first club, Crystal Palace, Pardew now works for an English owner, but the world of Ron Noades, who signed him for Palace, and Mike Ashley, his current owner at Newcastle, could not be more different. When Pardew came to Palace from non-League Yeovil, not only did the manager, Steve Coppell, travel down to Yeovil to assess him but so did Noades, who was always confident of his football knowledge.

Noades is the sort of owner who is almost extinct in the English game. A house builder obsessed with football from the age of 11, he refereed until lung illness stopped him. Then in the 1970s he began to buy football clubs in distress, starting with Southall — a non-League club. Wimbledon followed and then, in 1981, Crystal Palace. Noades never expected to spend money on football clubs or make a fortune. He did take a salary starting at £25,000 in 1981 and reached £100,000 a year at its peak. But having paid £600,000 for Palace, he could walk away with £30 million because by then, five years in, Premier League football had become sexy and Mark Goldberg, a Palace fan, was prepared to pay that fancy price. Noades recalls:

> I'm quite proud of the fact that of all the directors I've had in football in the four clubs I owned I've never asked any director to put any money into the club. What I used to do is ask them for a £50,000 loan as a qualification for being a director and none of them lost any of that money. But then Goldberg came along and started making promises to all the supporters. The whole of the back page of the *Croydon Advertiser* had interviews with about 20 or 30 supporters all saying that I should step aside, I'd taken Palace as far as I could and we should let Goldberg come in. The talk was with all the money he's going to spend on players — he would move Palace along a lot further. In the end I thought, sod it, they all want me to go, I've been there 17 years.

But the danger of football becoming sexy was that it also heightened fan expectations and paved the way for the disaster Noades had feared. Goldberg, trying to make Palace a superpower, went bankrupt and in the next decade and a half, Palace themselves went into administration twice and had two changes of owners. For Noades, the Premier League years mark a fundamental shift in the attitude of fans towards football club owners. "Fans now expect somebody to come in, pour millions in and then when they're skint, to bugger off. That was not the case with the traditional football fan."

Mike Ashley as owner could not be more different to Noades. Although a Londoner taking over Newcastle, he broadcast his allegiance and, as if to prove this, poured vast wealth into the club: £272 million in interest-free loans. That, as Pardew points out, is 25 per cent of Ashley's wealth. But until the 2012 season, far from earning praise, Newcastle's on-field performances created so much pain for Ashley that three years ago he came close to selling the club. But, unable to find a buyer who could match his price and make sure he got his money back, he did not sell. All this time the fans made it clear they could not wait for this Londoner to quit the North East. But Pardew's successes in the 2011–21 season have marked a significant change:

> I like to think that we have given Mike some pleasure this season. The fans have understood that his actions are for the benefit of the club. There's no return on his investment as yet. But the chanting against him and berating of him has stopped in the stands and that's been a massive battle in itself, in my opinion.

Pardew confesses that he did not expect to achieve this turnaround when, just before Christmas 2010, he was appointed manager in place of Chris Hughton. A poll showed only 5.5 per cent of the fans wanted him. Looking back now, Pardew can smile and say: "Maybe even less." Hughton had brought Newcastle, relegated in 2009, back up to the Premier League with 102 points, comfortably winning the Championship, judged by many as the toughest league in the country.

In that first week in December, Newcastle were mid-table having won the match that mattered most to the fans: they beat Sunderland 5–1 at St James' Park. Hughton did hear whispers that he was going to get sacked. His contract ran until the end of the 2011–2012 season and at the beginning of the season talks about a new contract had broken down. Nevertheless, with the club doing well, he was confident the rumours were untrue. Then, after a defeat at West Bromwich, the 53-year-old former Irish national was called in by the Newcastle managing director Derek Llambias.

As Hughton recalls: "What he said was that the club wanted to go in a different direction and that was it. He did not explain what the different direction was and I didn't ask. The conversation didn't even last two minutes. Did it come as a shock? Yes, it did. Our target before the season was to stay in the division. We were mid-table. There were some disappointing results, we had lost at home to Blackpool and to Stoke but we beat Sunderland 5–1, Aston Villa 6–0 and we won at Arsenal, at Everton, at West Ham. That's what we expected, an up-and-down season. We had just come up. But, if your bosses don't want you or they don't rate you, they want to bring somebody else in, then it's only a matter of time. Only they know the reasons why they sacked me."

Newcastle never explained. Before Hughton they had tried to tempt Harry Redknapp and failed and now Pardew's appointment led to fantastic stories that the choice was made, not on football grounds, but because both Ashley and Pardew liked to gamble and had met in a London casino. But as Pardew told me:

I don't gamble. Even at the races, I bet a tenner probably. I'm too tight to bet. It came about because Derek Llambias was at West Ham. He knew what I'd done at West Ham and knew I'd had a rough deal there [sacked by the Icelandic owners after a poor run of results]. He put me in front of Mike and said, "Look, I think this guy could do it". Once I met Mike he liked the way I tackled his vision of the club. That is a vision most managers would shy away from. The budget's going to be tight despite the fact that Newcastle are a big club. You've got 54,000 people coming in, you should compete with the top clubs. The truth is we can't because financially they get deals that we don't get. Liverpool's shirt deal is way beyond anything that we can get. [Liverpool's four-year deal with Standard Chartered in 2010, reportedly worth £20 million a season, represented a £12.5 million increase on what Carlsberg had paid. It was done because of Liverpool's global reach and made their commercial income second to Manchester United.] Liverpool are our competitors really and they've got so much more money than us. So I said, "I will bring success and I can make sure that we bring players through. I proved that at West Ham with my strategy in terms of market value of signing players".

But even after this he confesses:

I did steel myself knowing that the first few weeks and months were going to be difficult. I think if you're going to walk into a job, you've got to take away the fan element of it and just say, "Are you going to be able to win the dressing room?" It is all about gaining the confidence of the players and I had confidence in doing that. Chris [Hughton] is a great guy, he had coached me [when Pardew was at Tottenham] but different to me [sic]. I'm probably more aggressive than Chris as an individual and I had the confidence that I could get the dressing room. And if I got the players on side, then you've got a chance of getting the fans because ultimately one leads to the other. I had to gain the trust of Kevin Nolan. Kevin was the captain and a powerful captain and I needed to make sure of his loyalty. I went round his house before I even met him at the training ground to speak to him. I said, "Look, I know there's probably a lot of disappointment that I'm the manager but I am. I want to work with you and I need your help." And being the great guy that he is, he offered me that.

Even then Pardew felt the fates might be against him. He started his job in the snow, the team could not train outside for the first three weeks and he had to gain the confidence of the players in an indoor arena with no undersoil heating. "Luckily the results were good. We got a great win against Liverpool in the first game. I changed a couple of things in that first game which resulted in one of our goals and that bought me confidence in the dressing room almost immediately."

Pardew has developed his own understanding of football's psychology, a development helped by a career which has seen him manage clubs as diverse as Reading, West Ham, Charlton and Southampton. Those experiences have convinced him that that success in football only comes when the "group" is right.

Such belief in group psychology is not unusual in the game. A few weeks before I met Pardew, I had met Brian McDermott just after his Reading team won the Championship and promotion to the Premier League. McDermott also spoke of getting the group right, but was very reluctant to highlight any one player as crucial to Reading's success. Ian Harte was the only Reading player to make the PFA's Championship team of the year, but McDermott said: "If you asked me who was going to be player of the year, I wouldn't be able to tell you. To me it's an absolute group thing. This season players have come in and out, it's been quite seamless. We all know what we are trying to achieve."

McDermott himself is fond of highly individual stars such as Paolo di Canio and Eric Cantona and would have loved to manage them. But for the Reading manager, Cantona is not the eccentric individual the world knows but a man who on a football field only thinks of the team. As McDermott told me:

> Any manager would do all right with Eric! I've watched lots of documentaries and he's always talking about the team. Very rarely he talks about himself. Nothing is more important than the team. That is what I love when you see the big players: Lionel Messi, Steven Gerrard, Wayne Rooney. The way they work for the team is fantastic.

Pardew, on the other hand, stresses the group, but is not afraid to highlight the individuals who are crucial to the group. So he spent some time trying to convince Ashley why Leon Best was an important member of the squad.

> He's only played about 10 games but he's important because he's our funny guy. He makes everyone laugh, breaks the ice when things are a bit tense. He gets his lip tattooed and goes around showing everybody. Or he will walk around with no shirt making sure everybody knows he's been in the gym.

For Pardew, a football team is like "a pride of lions" and the most valuable hunter in his pack is the Argentinian Fabricio Coloccini, who took over as captain after Nolan left for West Ham.

> He brings a calmness, a winning mentality to the pitch and a sense of order to all proceedings. So if I said to him, "We're going to have Tuesday and Wednesday off," he might ask me, "Why are we having Wednesday off?" He wants to know. It is nice to have a captain like that questioning your decision, "Why are we playing like this?" There is a big difference between a football captain and a cricket captain. I will put in a tactical plan in front of the players and then I will ask them for their input to that tactical plan, "This is what I think we should do." I will tweak it if I don't think they're completely buying into it. That applies to all my players, not just the captain. But he'll have a senior voice in that. So he has got a role tactically as well as in normal general day-to-day stuff.
>
> Coloccini is a classy player. You hear people say, "Oh, he reads the game well." That's difficult to explain to somebody who hasn't played or managed football. You can't coach it. So, for example, he might see that my left-back is in big trouble with a wide player and he'll move himself closer to that area. He'll look to read situations before they evolve. Bobby Moore was probably the greatest at it — but Coloccini does that for us brilliantly; before things even happen he's extinguished it.

It is perhaps Pardew's attitude to Joey Barton that is most revealing. Barton was given a 12-match ban for his violent conduct on the last day of the season when, playing for QPR at Manchester City, he elbowed Carlos Tevez, kicked Sergio Aguero and tried to headbutt Vincent Kompany. Pardew, who inherited him at St James' Park, tried hard to stop him moving to QPR:

> I offered Joey two contracts, one of which he agreed to initially so he was very close to staying at the back end of last year. But, when we sold Andy Carroll [to Liverpool], he thought we were lacking ambition. You can't assume anything in football. I'm not defending his actions at Manchester City in any shape or form but he is a target for a lot of abuse. The trouble with Joey is that he gets upset about anything. Someone not clearing up the dog poo eats into Joey. His behaviour with me was impeccable with one exception. When we played Leeds in a pre-season friendly and I didn't make him captain he got angry and didn't want to play. If he thinks he's got justice then he'll give you justice, though he has a warped sense of justice

sometimes. Joey should serve his time and carry on playing for QPR. It won't be the end of his career. He'll fight to the bitter end because he truly loves football. He's a great student of the game and he's delved into its psychology.

However, while Pardew has no doubt he can improve a player, he does not like to dwell on problems caused by particular players:

> Your coaches say to you, "We've got a problem, this player's not playing, he's sulking around the training ground, he's not adding to the group, he's draining the group." I'll try to address that player, of course. I can try to spend some time with him, sort him out and get him energised again. But I've still got 22 other players and somebody else will adopt that role. The group will never change, there'll always be that player who's upset, who's not in the group. I've got one now, just at the end of the season, he's not in the group, I can't get him in the group. So you can't focus too much on an individual player.

Nothing caused as much debate in the season as Roberto Mancini's handling of Mario Balotelli, his wayward Italian. Balotelli was sent off in the key game against Arsenal; the defeat at the Emirates in the run-up to the season's climax left City eight points behind United and the title seemed lost. Mancini even said this publicly, although as it later emerged privately he was telling his players something very different. Almost every commentator was sure Mancini had mishandled Balotelli. Pardew sees such criticism as standard fare for manager.

> That is what managers have to go through. We were told we were never good enough to compete with the top four or five, we were never going to stay there and we stayed there right until the last game! And the same for Mancini. You're going to get questioned when you're at the top club and you've spent the most money. You have to accept that. He never lost his composure, he stayed in there and in the end he got his reward.

But much as he praises Mancini, Pardew would not have handled Balotelli as the Italian did and his reasoning is all based on how he sees a football group work:

> I wouldn't have played him much. He would have been a player that I would have kept a really tight rein on and only brought him into the group when he performed and he did perform on some occasions. But once he showed a few flashes, you have to make sure that you're strong

with people like him. I've got one very similar myself, in Hatem Ben Arfa, who I had to coax into the group. Actually, the most important thing is not my opinion, it's the other players' opinion. Now, there's no doubt that Balotelli lost the respect of the players in that Manchester City dressing room. The manager then has got a massive problem because if they are not with him, the manager knows that that team is not going to function. That's the same with me. When a player who is not fitting in asks me if he feels he should play in the team, I say to him, "When I believe that the team think you should play in the team, you'll play in the team."

It is interesting to contrast Pardew's views with those of McDermott. The Reading manager, like Pardew, has great self-belief that he can manage any player, a faith that stems from his experience going back to his days managing Slough. Then the wife of a player rang him to complain: "She told me that I wasn't managing her husband very well and how miserable he was. She was right. I wasn't managing him well. I was confrontational and I learned a lot from that. If a player is not happy and I haven't picked it up, I'm annoyed with myself."

He went out of his way to praise Balotelli: "I don't think he's a bad guy, he looks a real good guy. My daughter loves him for all the stuff he does for charity." But he added: "He is not a player that would work in the structure we've got but he is a fantastic player. If we had a different structure, yeah, possibly he could fit in." For the Reading manager, signing a player is about more than just looking at his ball skills. "We go to the nth degree to find out they are the right person to come to the club. If they aren't, it doesn't happen. Doesn't matter about the name, it's just the character."

However, whichever player he signs, McDermott goes through a director of football, a concept the Premier League has brought to England. It has not always worked. Tottenham made great play of using it, but later discarded it and now seem to be returning to it with the departure of Harry Redknapp and the appointment of Andre Villas-Boas as his successor. Redknapp, as manager of Tottenham, used the classical informal system which has been prevalent almost since the game began. As he put it to me: "If I were looking for a player from Chelsea, I would speak to young Frank [Lampard] or Joe Cole. If I were looking for somebody from Liverpool, Jamie would speak to Carragher or Gerrard for me."

Pardew has tweaked a traditional system, which pre-Premier League managers or his first boss at Palace, Coppell, would have recognised. So, no director of football, but he as manager deciding from the choices presented to him by his scout.

We have a great scout in Graham Carr. He was here before me. I knew Graham. He is an ex-manager and he understands what I need. There are not a lot of chief scouts who understand that. Chief scouts may think that they've got a good player, but can he fit into what I want him to do? So we have a very simple policy at Newcastle. If I say I want a right-back, I want three options that fit our budget, fit our age group. Graham basically puts three rough diamonds in front of me. I choose the diamond I want to polish — it's a fantastic system!

Pardew is old-fashioned enough to go and watch players and likes the idea of selling the club to a player he seeks. He had to do that when he recruited Yohan Cabaye from Lille for £4.8 million, one of a handful of signings last season from France.

Cabaye won the double with Lille but there was no mystery that he had a clause in his contract, so we got him for a good price. I went over to see him. I took an iPad, sat down with him for a while and showed him a presentation of our fans, what it's like at Newcastle. I explained to him what a difference there is between Lille and Newcastle and with all due respect to Lille I think he understood that.

Pardew, a Londoner, born in Wimbledon, has himself appreciated that the famous passion for football in the North East of England is not hype:

When you are manager of Newcastle you understand the value of playing for Newcastle. I was at Crystal Palace but up there the passion for the place is just phenomenal. I've got a boy who actually was released. But he doesn't want to go, I can tell. He keeps hanging around. I'm not going to say his name, he's about 18, he's from the area, he doesn't want to give it up. I love that and I'm not forcing him out either. He keeps coming back.

As we have seen, the growth of wages in the Premier League years has caused huge problems and raised the question of how a manager can cope with a player who may earn much more than him. For Pardew that is not an issue:

That doesn't bother me, that doesn't affect me one iota. I've never seen it as difficult because we have defined roles at the football club. For example, do you go to your editor and call him "gaffer"? — probably not, you probably call him by his first name. So you have a different set of principles in football, no matter what you earn. When I was at Crystal Palace, I'm sure Ian Wright and Mark Wright probably earned more than Stevie Coppell, even back then. Steve would probably disagree with that but he probably did. They certainly earned four times what I was earning but you understand that. It's no problem, that's what they do for the team, they are the strikers, they get the most money and we all accept our roles. Money doesn't come into it. When people talk to me about salaries, I always say, "If you cannot motivate a kid who has got nothing to play football you should not be in the game." What's the difference between a kid who had nothing when he was a kid and is now worth £20 million? He's still got that same hunger and desire in him. If you can't reach it and get it out of him for a game then you shouldn't be a manager. So forget about the money. Most of those kids are not from rich backgrounds, they haven't come from some, I don't know, privately educated, handed-down money and studied at Eton. They've had to come from the deprived areas, maybe slums.

Pardew's view of the world may reflect his age. Redknapp, 15 years older, is much more pessimistic about the game and how both football and society has changed. When I spoke to him the year Tottenham made it to the Champions League for the first time he worried that in 20 years' time there may be no English owners left: "They won't have the money." And that the English game was not doing enough to educate players.

The issue had come about as we discussed players drinking and misbehaving, which led Redknapp to say: "There's nothing worse than seeing a picture of your player falling out of a nightclub." So before Tottenham's 2009 Carling Cup final, Redknapp made it clear to his players they could not go on the post-match bender they had indulged in when they won in 2008:

I would not allow what Juande Ramos had after the Carling Cup win, no chance. We got beat but the players knew they were staying the night at the hotel, not going out. Everybody was in bed by 11, win or lose. There has been a massive failure in this country to educate football players at an early age. When they come to a club at 11 they should be taught what to eat. If they come to academies, we should talk to the mums and dads: how to prepare for a game and everything that goes with being a professional. Society has broken down. We used to leave our front door open when I grew up in Poplar. Dad would take me to Highbury on the number 86 bus and share his flask of tea with the opposition supporters. There was no segregation. Footballers used to be part of the same community the fans came from. That has been lost. Modern footballers are part of show business.

But for all the changes in society Pardew is confident that the basic needs that prompt a boy to become a football player have not changed, a conviction he holds to despite the much publicised Tevez affair. This suggested to many that highly paid players were more like prima donnas, an argument that gained weight given how the Tevez-Mancini quarrel erupted. As City played a Champions League match at Bayern Munich, Mancini alleged that Tevez had refused to come on as a substitute in the second half with City losing 2–0. Tevez disputed this. Mancini then declared he wanted him out and Tevez would later say he was treated like a dog by the manager. The end result was that Tevez did not play for several months, at one stage went back home to Argentina, and was heavily fined. He only came back when City were losing momentum in the title race. But Pardew remains convinced that Tevez is just as much the child of the slums as he always was. "You can't tell me that that hunger to win isn't there, of course it's there. The money isn't going to dilute that, I don't believe it. Before he came to West Ham [when Pardew was manager there in 2006] he had been on strike at Corinthians for nine months. It wasn't an unusual thing that he did."

Pardew would one day like to manage England but feels his current CV is not good enough but could not be more pleased that Roy Hodgson was appointed the England manager:

I'm just glad it's an Englishman. I think it is a cultural decision that he needs to be English, I really do. It just got all out of hand and maybe the initial move to Sven was because they just thought another English manager was going to get pilloried by the press. They've changed nothing. The England team have not improved, not won any trophies. These foreign managers have actually done no better than the English managers who went before. The Premier League is different, club football is different. There foreign managers can change the culture of a club, like Arsene Wenger's done. You can do that at club level. I don't think you can do it at England team level.

You've got a group of players who are coming in for two days' recovery and one day's training. You are not going to change them culturally. The only thing you're going to be able to do is inspire them, bring them together, tactically be very, very sharp and make sure your substitutions work, otherwise you're in trouble. As for this overseeing of a cultural development we've got Burton now. But it's not like we're going to have 100 players who are going to be at Burton and coming through a system.

If I were manager of England, I couldn't say, "That's what I want in place, that's what I want them to learn, when they come to the Under 21s, that's how we're going to play." It doesn't happen like that. You've literally got a tournament, every two years, and you've got to get the best players. They are all in different cultures all around the country. A foreign manager isn't going to bring a cultural change to that. What you can do is take from those cultures and bring it to England, that's different.

But if change on the field of play at the national level is difficult, Pardew can see major change at some stage in the question of who manages England. He is convinced that Chris Powell, who ensured Charlton's promotion from League One during the season, could become the first black manager of England. Pardew, who has known Powell since he was a kid at Crystal Palace, wanted him at Newcastle and holds him in high regard. We spoke just after Roy Hodgson had taken on Gary Neville as an assistant coach and Pardew said:

He is the sort of person who I think should be in the England system now, forget about Gary Neville, Chris Powell should be in there now. I think Chris Powell could be the first black England manager and it would be a great thing for this country to have a black manager, especially somebody who has represented the PFA so honourably and so well. He ticks a lot of boxes for the FA, that boy. He brings a good pedigree as a player and he has always been a fit and proper person — he passed the FA Premier League test for sure! He has played for England, played at big clubs, understands players, head of the PFA and now gets 101 points in his second year as a manager —this is a guy who has got massive potential.

To an extent the choice is ironic, for while Pardew may not feel foreign managers have done anything for the England team, Powell himself regards England's first foreign coach, the Swede Sven-Goran Eriksson, as his mentor. Powell had had experience of working with traditional English managers such as Jim Smith, who managed him at Derby and regretted selling him to Charlton. Powell recalled: "Jim was a cup thrower. With Jim it was sink or swim. If you couldn't take the harsh words from him, then you would sink. Not many managers have that style now."

The contrast with Eriksson, who called Powell up for five friendlies leading up to the 2012 tournament but did not take him to Japan, could not be greater:

His style was totally different to what I had been accustomed to. He was organised and very studious. Everyone thinks managers should be loud, very prominent on the touchline, having a go at the fourth official and the referee at all times. He wasn't like that.

Powell was first struck by the Swede's style when he called him up to play Spain in a friendly at Villa Park in 2001, the first Charlton player in 30 years to wear England colours. "Normally you're used to the dressing room being very loud, the music playing. At Villa Park it was so quiet. It was Sven's way of saying to everyone, 'You just take care of yourself. I will leave you with your own thoughts until you go out and warm up.' He made everyone feel at ease. It was a great experience."

And it was Eriksson whom Powell turned to when the new Charlton owners came calling. Powell had gone to Leicester to work for Nigel Pearson and was happy to continue when Leicester's new owners, Asian Football Investments, brought in Eriksson. After a brief spell as caretaker manager between the two regimes, Powell was the Swede's first and reserve-team coach. And it was on Eriksson's advice that he decided not to join Pardew at Newcastle.

Sven didn't want me to go. Then, when I got a phone call saying that Charlton would like to speak to me, Sven said, "If it is as manager, go and speak to them. I know it's a club that's close to your heart and, if you can start at a place like that, fine. As a coach, no. You're doing that here. And I want you here."

What makes Pardew's comments on Powell fascinating is that it came in the season when racism re-emerged in English football, catching most people by surprise. English football had been confident it had seen the back of this scourge and even held itself up as a model for other countries. But then Liverpool's Luis Suarez was banned for eight games and fined £40,000 for repeatedly calling Patrice Evra a *negrito*. The Uruguayan argued the term was not racist, a common term in his country, but the authorities concluded the words were "insulting" and a reference to Evra's colour. This led to an incredible reaction orchestrated by the then Liverpool manager Kenny Dalglish, who effectively organised player protests against Suarez's punishment.

Dalglish's handling of the Suarez affair reflected little credit on the Anfield club and ultimately led to intervention by the American owners and was a catalyst for changes to the club's management structure. However, even as English football was digesting this, there was an incident in a match between QPR and Chelsea that was to prove explosive. In the match played on October

23, 2011, which QPR won 1–0, Chelsea were down to nine men when Anton Ferdinand of QPR and John Terry of Chelsea, then the England captain, exchanged swear words in the penalty box after a penalty claim by Terry.

As Ferdinand revealed in a hearing in Westminster Magistrates Court nearly nine months later: "He called me a cunt, and I called him a cunt back and he gave me a gesture as if to say my breath smelled. I said to him, 'How can you call me a cunt? You shagged your team-mate's missus.'"

This was a reference to Terry's alleged affair with Wayne Bridge's ex-girlfriend Vanessa Perroncel. Ferdinand then jogged away but as he did so he made a gesture of a clenched fist, a cocked elbow and quick to and fro movement which was described in court as a "slow fist pump" to denote sex.

It was then that Terry shouted, "Fuck off, fuck off, fucking black cunt, fucking knobhead."

At the trial, Terry did not deny saying those words. However, his defence was he that was responding to Ferdinand accusing him of racist abuse and the words were not used as an insult but as a sarcastic inquiry.

Ferdinand, however, claimed he had not heard Terry use racist language. Indeed he confirmed this after the players met at the end of the match in the Chelsea dressing room. He only became aware of what Terry had said at around 7pm that day when his girlfriend showed him the footage on her Blackberry. The court also heard that Ferdinand was reluctant to give evidence. It took the police half a dozen attempts to contact him and he only agreed to testify after his older brother Rio's publicity agent, Justin Rigby, got involved. According to police records, Rigby warned the police of "ramifications" if they did not charge Terry. A refusal to charge Terry would, he told them, "appear to black players that it's a case of a white man's word against a black man's word".

Ashley Cole, Chelsea's most prominent black player, gave evidence in support of Terry, saying: "It was handbags. We should not be sitting here." Terry also had testimony from other team-mates saying they had never heard Terry use racist language.

Chief Magistrate Howard Riddle made it very clear the question was not whether Terry was a racist. As he put it in his judgement, "the issue for this court to decide is not whether Mr Terry is a racist, in the broadest sense of the word. I have received a substantial volume of unchallenged evidence from witnesses, both in person and in writing, to confirm that he is not. I understand why Mr Terry wants to make this point. His reputation is at stake. Although I am grateful to all those witnesses who have taken the trouble to provide information on this point, it does not help me in reaching a verdict. It is not relevant to the issue I must decide."

The question, said Riddle, was "whether Mr Terry uttered the words 'f****** black c***' by way of insult. If he did then the offence is made out, regardless of what may have motivated him."

Riddle went on to say:

> There is no doubt the words 'f****** black c***' were directed at Mr Ferdinand. Overall I found Anton Ferdinand to be a believable witness on the central issue. It is inherently unlikely that he should firstly accuse John Terry of calling him a black c***, then shortly after the match completely deny that he had made such a comment, and then maintain that false account throughout the police investigation and throughout this trial. There is no history of animosity between the two men. The supposed motivation is slight. Mr Terry's explanation is, certainly under the cold light of forensic examination, unlikely. It is not the most obvious response. It is sandwiched between other undoubted insults.

Then he concluded:

> Weighing all the evidence together, I think it is highly unlikely that Mr Ferdinand accused Mr Terry on the pitch of calling him a black c***. However, I accept that it is possible that Mr Terry believed at the time, and believes now, that such an accusation was made. The prosecution evidence as to what was said by Mr Ferdinand at this point is not strong. Mr Cole gives corroborating [although far from compelling corroborating] evidence on this point. It is therefore possible that what he said was not intended as an insult, but rather as a challenge to what he believed had been said to him. In those circumstances, there being a doubt, the only verdict the court can record is one of not guilty.

To find Terry guilty, Riddle had to be satisfied beyond reasonable doubt and that was not the case.

The affair refused to go away. As this book went to press the FA resumed its own inquiry into the Terry affair, having set it aside once the police began their investigations. Thirteen days after his acquittal, the FA charged him with "abusive and/or insulting words and/or behaviour", including a reference to Ferdinand's ethnic origin and/or colour and/or race. The FA also charged Rio Ferdinand for endorsing a tweet which had called Ashley Cole "choc ice", meaning black on the outside, white on the inside and widely seen as an insulting slur directed at blacks suggesting that they act as if they are whites.

Many in the game had not understood why the FA had stepped aside in the first place and their confusion was deepened by the FA's action to strip Terry of the England captaincy after a date had been set for his judicial hearing. This sudden FA intervention led to the resignation of the England manager Fabio Capello. In the middle of this I went to see Chris Powell, manager of Charlton, and one of only three black managers in the four leagues. Powell had just won manager of the month and was on course to bring his League One club back to the Championship, a feat he duly achieved at the end of the season. Powell was not only bemused by the FA decision to halt its own investigations at police request, he went further, puncturing the common myth that racism had been eradicated only to suddenly resurface this season:

> That's the mistake, that we thought we'd finished with it. You can't ever think that. It's not strictly just football's problem. We do know it has been part of football in the bad old days but it's a problem that emanates from society. I look at football as a game, it should be available to anyone regardless of where they're from. You should be free to go and sit in a stadium and watch the game, support your team regardless of people thinking you shouldn't be here because of the colour of your skin. I'm loath to talk about it. I shouldn't be talking about it in 2012, I should be talking about football.

When I suggested to him that, surely back in his playing days (Powell made his debut with Palace in 1987, when Pardew was there) it was a more a case of fans' abuse of black players rather than players' abuse of each other, he sighed:

> Oh, there was, don't be fooled by that, without a doubt there was. We all knew it was happening, both from the terraces and between the players. Nothing was done. So don't kid yourself it didn't happen. What I'm saying is back in the '70s, '80s and '90s, nothing was reported because nothing was happening with the authorities. So player-to-player abuse was almost, sadly, accepted in those days. You got on with it but the players fought their corner.

And when I asked him whether he had been racially abused by other players, he looked at me almost pityingly:

> Come on, what do you think? I don't want to talk about then. I want to talk about now. I want players to feel comfortable playing and feel free to report it if things happen. That's what we're seeing. People won't accept it

these days. It's being dealt with now regardless of how long it's taken. In days gone by we wouldn't even be talking about it.

Like Powell, Pardew felt that the football authorities should have dealt with the Terry issue straight away and not waited for the judicial authorities. But unlike Powell, Pardew shares the common view that racism's re-emergence as an issue is a surprise:

I'm not sure where it's come from. I wouldn't say we had eradicated it, but we were pretty close. I don't think some of the foreign players help, if I'm honest. They come from backgrounds where I think racism is still rife. Look at Suarez [who had gone to Liverpool from Holland]. I'm not so sure the Dutch league has not a little bit of that going on with black players. The South Americans, the words they use don't sound right in English. There's no bad meaning in it, it's just a word, but they don't understand the consequences of it, especially in our world. Whether that's slipped back in through the influx of the foreign players, I don't know.

Pardew is also very aware that for all the progress English football may claim to have made on race there are still not enough black or Asian supporters

Generally I still don't see enough black, and particularly Asian, faces at football grounds. Arsenal, I would say, has the biggest cross-section of the community compared to any other club, without a shadow of a doubt. At Arsenal, you see a lot of Asian faces, a lot of blacks. My old club, West Ham, is surrounded by Asians and most of them don't go to the game.

And Pardew has also been concerned that the good Asian players have not emerged.

"There's not a good Asian player," I hear that from my scouts, they just can't find one. I say, "Well, go and find one, there must be one, there can't be none." You are obviously from an Asian background, and if you think of the percentage of Asians we've got in this country; it's ridiculous!

Even before the Terry affair reached the court, the fact that race was once again being discussed as a possible problem in English football had caused much anguish. It led to a Downing Street conference between the Prime Minister, the minister for sport and representatives of football. As this is being written, the FA is preparing a report on what steps should be taken. The re-emergence of race as an issue made it interesting to examine how it was affecting the game at grassroots level. On a November Saturday afternoon I went to a non-League club just up the road from Pardew's old club West Ham to investigate.

At first glance, the match between London APSA and Basildon suggested that things at the non-League level, the game's coalface, could not be better. Spectators get to the ground through a car workshop owned by local Muslims. The match programme had a full-page advertisement: "Let's kick racism out of football." The two teams appeared to be doing just that. London APSA, a largely Asian team, had a white goalkeeper. The visiting Basildon team had several black players and the referee was black.

The match itself, a classic game of two halves, saw London APSA take a comfortable 2–0 half-time lead but in the end were lucky to preserve a 2–2 draw. The game was full of that combination of skill, physical rigour and never-say-die spirit that makes English football so compelling.

Yet even prior to kick-off, it had become clear these surface impressions were very misleading. As the players warmed up, Vince McBean, chief executive of Clapton, whose ground London APSA use for their home games, had said bluntly: "It's not correct that English football has dealt with racism. There are major problems at the grassroots. From a strategic point of view, we have problems as black clubs and black players on, and off, the pitch."

He agreed that racism had changed. "The days of nigger-bashing have gone. Whereas before somebody came up to you and said, 'You black bastard', they don't have to say that no more. It's subtly done now in terms of how the referee deals with us and how the league deals with us."

The tall, imposing 55-year-old, who came to England as a teenager from the Caribbean, served in the Green Jackets with tours of duty in Ireland, Germany and Canada. "In the Army you can deal with racism by taking them round the back. The British Army has changed. Football hasn't, not really."

Clapton itself has changed dramatically since McBean took over in 1999, leading almost to a reverse apartheid. "When I first arrived, the committee was all-white, none of them from the local area, and they had no black players. When I asked why, the committee said, 'Vince, you know, they're thugs, they have no discipline.' Remember we're in the London Borough of Newham where over 70 per cent are from ethnic minorities."

Now, more than a decade later, nearly all the committee and the players, barring three, are black. "It's not a matter of policy. As I started to bring on more black people, the committee of Clapton reduced. The white people left the club." The white chairman recently left pleading too much work.

Of the 50 match officials in Essex League, only three are black and McBean is convinced Clapton cannot expect fair decisions. "In our game here, we're frightened to tackle in the box because it's so simple to give away penalties. Some of the calls that we've had against us are not what I call reasonable."

Insisting race plays a part in referees' decisions, McBean said: "We do not expect a white person to stand up for us against another white person. There's a certain relationship between the referees and white players. Our black players don't move in the same circles. We regard ourselves as the underclass."

Zulfi Ali, president of London APSA, had warmer memories of both the Essex FA, and the league chairman, Robert Errington, both of whom were very supportive when he moved the club from the Asian League to the Essex Senior League in 2003. But the 38-year-old spoke sorrowfully of the racism his players had encountered.

> In our second season we were playing Barking, and Imran Khan, our goalkeeper, had his beard pulled by a white forward inside the box who shouted, "Shave it off you cunt, Paki bastard." Imran chased the player to the halfway line and was red carded. When I complained to the referee he said, "It is nothing, he did not hurt him, punch or slap him."

His most painful memories are of a match 10 years ago in the Essex Business Houses league. "One of our players, Shabhas Khan, only 18, had his face smashed by an opposing player, and his tooth popped out. There was lots of racist abuse of the 'You fucking Paki bastard' type. Fights broke out and I rang the police. The game was abandoned. It is not as bad now. But if any of our players has a beard, he will be called Bin Laden or a terrorist. To them now, it's water off a duck's back."

Khalid Pervaiz, the 27-year-old assistant manager, who adores Ryan Giggs, certainly treats such remarks as jokes. "I have a beard and I hear people say, 'Go back to the mosque', or 'Why aren't you cooking curry?'"

A trialist with Aston Villa in his nearly eight years in the league, he has heard other Asian players complain they have been called Bin Laden. "You get them particularly when you are winning or going into a tackle. When we are playing five-a-side there is a lot of tugging beards and our players get kicked left, right and centre. Then the same team would play other white teams and there would be no kicking."

But, unlike Pervaiz, not all players want to talk about their experiences of racism.

Sham Darr, a 26-year-old who works in the public sector, only agreed to talk, and have his picture taken, if we did not mention his day job. The son of Pakistani immigrants from Kashmir, he had a trial for Leicester City. "I think I did not make it due to racism. I was 19, a winger and people who came to the trial felt I played an immaculate game. It was seen as a publicity stunt. Asian footballer from the East End being given a chance, rather than looking to sign me."

While he agrees that the situation has improved since he first started playing, he insists: "There is still a problem, not so much on the field, but behind closed doors. People in charge of the game in the academies, coaches, managers are all white."

Yet the white players and officials could not have had a more different view. For Laurie Mallyon, the 50-year-old van driver, who was a linesman at the match, these stories of racism might have been from another planet.

> I have been officiating for 15 years in the Essex Senior League and I have seen no racism. In one game I was refereeing 10 years ago, a person called a black guy "You black bugger". I called him over and said, "You cannot do that. You will be in serious trouble if you do". He said, "I am sorry ref, I should have known better, I am half-caste". That was his word. We had no more problems from that point on. If you approach the person who had said these things in the proper manner, then you can nip it in the bud. There is racism on both sides from the white community and the black community. The John Terry incident should not have got into the media. If you keep it in house you can iron it out yourself.

Lee Stevens, club secretary of Bowers and Pitsea, half of whose team are half black, is not only convinced there isn't a problem, but pointed out how his club help ethnic minorities. "A lot of the APSA players are Muslims. They pray to Mecca before a match. We set aside a piece of our ground for them to pray on their mats."

Robert Errington, the president, was outraged to be asked about the numbers of black and Asian officials in the league. "I do not see the point of your question. I find it offensive." When I put to him McBean's allegations that black players could not get fair treatment from white officials, he exploded: "It is a disgraceful thing for him to say."

London APSA's own white player, 34-year-old goalkeeper Ian Stanley, was surprised to hear there was any racism. "If it goes on, I do not know. Being in goal, what happens in the middle or at the other end I would not know."

Stanley, who had been recently recruited to the team, does not mix with his team-mates after the game: "They socialise among themselves." This may not be helped by the fact that many of the team, being Muslims, do not drink.

Zulfi Ali admits this is a problem, and is also not helping his dream for the club to have its own home ground. "To be financially safe, we need to sell alcohol. We cannot do that ethically."

Nor do Asians turn up to support London APSA. Although this was a home game, the 20 or so spectators were almost all from the visiting Basildon team. Anjum Khan, the team manager, admitted: "Asian parents do not want to use their weekend to watch." And with tickets costing £5, "they don't wish to pay."

Worse still, they do not encourage their children to play football. "Religion is more important to them. Kids need to go to the mosque every day. Asian parents do not see football as a career. They want to talk about their son as a doctor or a lawyer, not a football player."

However, Zulfi can see changes in some of the younger generation of parents. At a recent Under 9 match, he says: "The kids had been brought by their mums, many of them in hijabs. As the white parents started shouting and screaming, these mothers in hijabs shouted back. It was funny and wonderful to watch. As long as it is not racist, it is good for these kids to experience a certain amount of argy-bargy, it will make them kids stronger. It is a great way, especially for Muslims, to integrate. You won't party, you won't drink. How else do you integrate?"

But on the evidence of this east London encounter, integration looked a long way off.

Despite this English football has come a long way since the first days of the Premier League. Its success on and off the field cannot be questioned but some old problems remain. And commercial success has also come at a price, not all of it quantifiable in financial terms.

PART 4

MONEY AND THE BRAND

Chapter 9
THE PEOPLE'S GAME,
A RICH MAN'S TOY

In 1991, just as the last Football League First Division season was due to start, I went to north London to interview a businessman who had just taken over a football club. The club was Tottenham Hotspur and the businessman was Alan Sugar. Sugar was not only a successful businessman but at that stage he was an unusual businessman. Having made his money in the booming 1980s, Sugar had survived the recession and become one of the great successes of the Thatcher era at its apex. In Britain businessmen with such a track record rarely moved into football. Indeed, Irving Scholar, who sold Tottenham to Sugar, had lamented this fact to me, comparing Britain with countries such as Italy, where Juventus was owned by the Agnelli family, who also owned Fiat, and media magnate Silvio Berlusconi owned AC Milan. Spain and Portugal also had rich high-profile backers for their football clubs but in the Britain of 1991 Sugar was an exception.

In the interview, he revealed just how exceptional he was. Tottenham had won the FA Cup the previous season and were about to play in the Charity Shield. As every Tottenham fan knows, the club's greatest moment came in the 1960–61 season when they became the first English club to do the Double of League and FA Cup in the 20th century. In 1961 this was considered an almost impossible feat — the last club to do it had been Aston Villa in 1897 — but since then Liverpool, Manchester United, Arsenal and Chelsea have all achieved it. But Billy Nicholson's Tottenham did it in such style that they are still seen as one of the greatest teams to grace the top flight of English football.

So when I met Sugar one of the questions I asked him was: had he fallen in love with the club the year they won the Double? He responded with a counter-question that was very revealing: "Double, is that something from the 1950s?" I wish I had copyrighted that quote, so often has it been used to condemn Sugar as a man who knew nothing about football.

Sugar is an impulsive man. His impulses have served him well in his chosen business field of electronics. He has since become a major television figure with *The Apprentice*. His willingness to dive in head first where a cautious man might tread warily has paid him handsome dividends. His venture into Tottenham was similar. He liked the feel of it, was taken by media reports of Terry Venables trying to rescue the club, if necessary with his own money, and felt there were opportunities for him there. The other incentive for getting on board was that if it he did not then Robert Maxwell, who was again sniffing around the club, might well beat him to it.

On the night of the takeover, Sugar and Maxwell would have a heated discussion over the phone with Sugar employing liberal use of the word "fuck". However, when Sugar came to write his autobiography *What You See Is What You Get* In 2010, this particular four-letter word did not feature, though the word "piss" did, as Sugar asked Maxwell's "lackeys to piss off and let [him] get on with this deal". It was clear this was not a friendly call. Indeed, Maxwell put the phone down on his fellow tycoon, much to Sugar's annoyance.

Sugar had discussed buying Tottenham with Rupert Murdoch. Murdoch had no love for Maxwell. He even told Sugar he didn't want "that fat cunt to get it". Some writers have suggested that Sugar's decision to buy Tottenham was part of an elaborate pre-arranged plan for Sky to get the Premier League deal. Sugar has always denied this and there is no evidence of such a plan. Sugar insists it was so much an impulse buy that it shocked his family, particularly his wife Ann, when she learnt about it.

But to say he had no connection with Tottenham, or awareness of the club, would be absurd. A Hackney boy, he had often accompanied his father and uncle to matches at White Hart Lane, where they stood in the East Stand. However, he had never developed the passion for the club that his brother Derek did. In the last 61 years, Derek has missed only two seasons, although they happen to be 1950–51 and 1960–61, the two seasons Tottenham won the First Division title.

Sugar's relationship with Tottenham was real enough, if not as intense as Irving Scholar's or David Dein's with Arsenal. But after 20 years of the Premier League, clubs are increasingly owned by those who not only have no connection with either the club or city where it is based, but even with Britain. From Sugar to Roman Abramovich and the Abu Dhabi owners of Manchester City, via the disgraced Thai Prime Minister Thaksin Shinawatra, the Premier League story is of a game once proud of its community base becoming a global brand and attracting the rich from around the world. For the Russian Abramovich, the brand was so alluring that it had become almost a rich child's train set.

Yet in another sense the game has barely moved on at all since the Sugar-

Venables takeover of Tottenham in the year before the Premier League was formed. As this is being written, the sorry saga of Portsmouth continues, with the south coast club in administration for the second time and now relegated to League One. The club have had a host of owners, one of whom never even appeared at Fratton Park and some of whom have had the most unsavoury associates. Portsmouth's problems have once again raised the question of who is a "fit and proper person" to own a football club, a question the English football authorities have so often shied away from answering.

No takeover in English football history has been as relentlessly scrutinised as the Sugar-Venables takeover of Spurs. The scrutiny came from the media, with two *Panorama* programmes raking over it in minute detail, and from a Department of Trade and Industry (DTI) inquiry. The inquiry resulted in one of the men who bought Tottenham admitting to lying during the takeover. That man was Terry Venables, whose intense desire to move from the dug-out to the boardroom had first attracted Sugar to the club. As the affidavit of Graham Richard Horne, deputy inspector of companies at the DTI in 1995, declared in the case the DTI brought against Venables, the former England manager had indulged in a "charade" and "a piece of window dressing designed to deceive". The Horne affidavit would go on to accuse Venables of giving false information in the offer document and perpetrating "an undisclosed and sham loan".

As has now been well documented, including in my book *The False Messiah, the Life and Times of Terry Venables,* on the night the deal to buy Tottenham was done Venables could not produce his share of the purchase money. He had to rely on money from Sugar to complete the deal. Sugar was repeatedly reassured by Venables' adviser Eddie Ashby that the money would turn up. Sugar, having forked out on the night, had to wait 10 days for Venables' money to emerge. It was many years before the truth about how Venables raised his share of the funds was revealed.

Ashby had his own secret. He had been declared a bankrupt at Brighton County Court on June 6, 1991, two weeks before the takeover. And on the night the deal went through he made sure he did not come face to face with Midland Bank, the club's bankers. Despite his bankruptcy Ashby continued to work with Venables at Tottenham and his secret also did not emerge for a long time.

The full story of how Venables got the money emerged only in January 1998, five years after Venables had been forced out of Tottenham. By then he was chairman of Portsmouth. The DTI, following a three-year investigation into how Venables acquired Tottenham and managed his other businesses, produced a 48-page document which Venables did not contest. The charges included bribery, lying, deception, manipulation of accounts, giving himself money that should have gone to creditors, failing to keep proper accounts and allowing a bankrupt to manage his companies. Venables accepted the DTI's 19 charges of serious misconduct and accepted a seven-year ban on acting as a company director. He was also fined £500,000.

The charges related to mismanagement of four companies: Tottenham Hotspur plc and Tottenham Hotspur Football and Athletic Company Ltd, the London drinking club Scribes West Ltd and Edennote plc, the company used by Venables to buy his share of Tottenham. The DTI investigation revealed that in his offer document to buy Tottenham, Venables had given false information and perpetrated "an undisclosed and sham loan".

Venables was not present in the courtroom as Elizabeth Gloster, QC for the DTI, told Mr Justice Evans-Lombe that Venables' conduct in relation to the four companies "has been such as to make him unfit to be concerned in any way with the management of a company". Gloster went on to clarify that the agreed seven-year ban was in the "middle bracket" of disqualification periods, applying to serious misconduct which did not merit the top bracket of 10 to 15 years.

Venables in his statement of mitigation, which accompanied his acceptance of the DTI's version of events, pleaded that he had suffered from "extraordinary bad luck". He also blamed Ashby, saying he had trusted him not to overstep the mark. "This trust sadly turned out to be misplaced." Ashby's help in acquiring Tottenham may have been crucial and the two men had been bosom friends, but by the time the DTI brought its case to court the two had clearly fallen out. Venables went on to blame Ashby for the loan of £1 million that Edennote took from the failed company Landhurst Leasing to help finance Venables' purchase of Tottenham. Technically, Edennote was contracting Venables' services to Tottenham. In order to get the loan Venables had to lie, invent a pub called Miners, a road called Claremont Road in Cardiff, claim ownership of three other pubs and pay a bribe of £10,000 to an official of Landhurst in order to change the terms of the lease. Venables signed a personal guarantee, although he would later deny signing it.

Ashby would later rebut the Venables allegations. Ashby, himself, had been on trial at Knightsbridge Crown Court a few months earlier, in September 1997. The previous year he had been disqualified as a company director for nine years after the DTI brought an action against him in relation to a group of clothing companies he partly owned, which had gone into receivership with debts of more than £3 million. But now he faced possible jail for breaking bankruptcy laws. Venables had given evidence for Ashby, who was working as his assistant at Portsmouth. From the witness box Venables took the opportunity to castigate Sugar, saying it was Sugar's greed that had led to their falling out: "He got big eyes, he got greedy and wanted the lot." Richard Latham, prosecuting Ashby, would describe Venables' testimony as a "soapbox" performance, while the judge observed: "In only a minority of cases did he give a simple, direct answer to a simple direct question." Ashby's defence did not convince the jury and he was convicted and jailed for four months. He emerged from jail just before the Venables DTI verdict.

It is, of course, worth stressing that the real story behind the Tottenham takeover would never have emerged but for a very public row between Sugar and Venables for control of the club. This row had come in the early days of the Premier League, when it was by no means certain that the league would prosper, let alone become a great worldwide brand. Much has changed since then, most dramatically the sums of money involved.

When Sugar teamed up with Venables to buy the club, Tottenham owed the Midland Bank £11 million, an eighth of the price Real Madrid paid Manchester United for Cristiano Ronaldo in 2009. The money Venables had such a struggle to raise was £3 million, a third of what it cost Carlos Tevez in lost wages and fines during the 2011–12 season, following his falling out with Manchester City manager Roberto Mancini. However, for all the many changes that 20 years of the Premier League have brought about, the one story that has not changed is that football still cannot police who comes in as owners, as the problems at Portsmouth and Rangers in Glasgow vividly demonstrate.

Also unchanged is the fans' faith in football people and their right to manage football clubs. When Sugar and Venables took over Tottenham, the Spurs fans and the footballing public and media hailed Venables as a man of football who had rightly come to claim his prize. Tottenham's financial crisis which led to the sale had seen the creation of the Tottenham Independent Supporters' Association (TISA), a vocal and effective champion of Venables. TISA's overwhelming support for Venables played a role in the takeover. Indeed, as Sugar was to find out two years later when he fell out with Venables and ousted him, he was so loathed by the fans that he felt like the man who had shot Bambi's mother.

Venables had argued that, having managed football teams, he was now ready to manage a club, to move from the dug-out to the boardroom. He was widely seen as the man of football who could do more than just manage players. Kate Muir had described him in *The Times* just after the takeover as "football's renaissance man, the Leonardo da Vinci of the league". And even as Sugar moved against him, Venables continued to present himself as the man of football. So the day after his row with Sugar went public, and with the two men involved in a bruising court case for control of the club, Venables went on television to declare: "I just believe the club is the people. I have always believed that. The club is not the building, or the grass, it is supporters, the people, the players, and you are dealing with people... it is not something that he [Sugar] does. He deals with a different business and he goes back to that every Monday. I do that every day. That's where I put my life and my experience into it and I have got to this stage hoping it doesn't slip away easily."

Not many people could match Venables' background in football but what is significant is that as the Premier League was being launched the need for football owners to advertise their links with their club was considered just as important as their riches. Nobody did this better than David Murray. Murray, a successful businessman who had made his money in steel, had bought Rangers in the 1980s, just before the Premier League was formed. He quickly realised that fans could be tapped for money by clubs in ways never before seen in Britain. This went far beyond match days. In the old days clubs and fans had a simple commercial relationship: clubs sold fans match tickets, with the sale of season tickets bringing important income to the clubs in the close season.

Season ticket sales were vital to fund the purchase of players for the forthcoming season. In a successful club there was always a waiting list for season tickets. But other than buying season or matchday tickets, fans were not seen as providing other sources of revenue. After all, football grounds were decrepit, with extremely limited facilities; supporters were just meant to turn up, not complain too much about the dreadful conditions, and go home.

David Murray changed all that at Rangers. I have a vivid memory of this when in 1989, as the formation of the Premier League was being plotted, I attended my first Old Firm match. Ibrox had already been transformed by Murray and looked a treat. Inside the ground there were designated dining rooms which could be hired out to supporters for parties, birthdays, even weddings. And fans could buy Rangers products such as whisky. When I asked how a club could become a retailer, as if it was a Sainsbury's or a Tesco, I was told that fans who drank whisky would much prefer to buy the Rangers brand than that of any other retailer. They had a bond with the club and would prefer to pay the money they would normally give to a retailer to the club instead. For good measure Rangers beat Celtic that day, as if to indicate that commercial success went hand in hand with playing success. Soon the rest of football woke up to Murray's innovations and his ideas found eager followers across the border in England.

David Dein, then running Arsenal, took up the bond scheme Murray had used to renovate Ibrox to do the same at Highbury. It was also copied less successfully by West Ham to upgrade Upton Park. As Keith Wyness, the former chief executive of Aberdeen and Everton, puts it: "Murray was at the forefront of increasing commercial revenue, the forefront of a number of initiatives, one of the pioneers." This was several years before the Bosman ruling and the rise of the Champions League resulted in smaller countries and their clubs, like those in Scotland, becoming marginalised. However, in the early years of the Premier League, Rangers was not the only model for clubs seeking ways to increase their income. They also turned to a model closer to home. It had appeared discredited but as the Premier League established itself it had once again gained favour. This was Tottenham's example of floating on the stock market.

Tottenham's then chairman Irving Scholar had justified the flotation in 1983 on the grounds that it would help the club raise money and clear their debts. Scholar had come to power in response to the financial problems caused by the development of the club's new stand. This was the age of privatisation, epitomised by the massive advertising campaign "telling Sid" about the gas shares he could subscribe to and make a profit. In this climate Scholar thought offering shares in a football club would do the double: fans would get a stake in the club and the money this would raise would take care of the club's debt.

By 1991, despite the fact that Tottenham's flotation was not considered a success, Manchester United had followed the Spurs example. Tottenham's failure was put down to bad management by the Tottenham board rather than exposing any fundamental divide between football and the stock market. Martin Edwards, who alone among the United directors had experience of being involved in a public company through his father's firm, Louis Edwards & Co, took some convincing. As he told me: "I was warned, if you float this will no longer be a private company; you won't be able to do everything you want. You will have to look after shareholders' interest and pay dividends. And although it will give us what we want in building the Stretford End, there will be restraints on us in the future. Everybody was aware of that."

However, Edwards was also well aware that by floating he could finally clear his debts:

Don't forget in 1991 I had heavy debts. I had to pay those off. They were certainly in seven figures. I'd carried the debt since 1978. Indeed my house was in debt to the bank. I was not prepared to carry on for the rest of my life being in debt to the bank. We had a situation where I was the majority shareholder, holding 50 per cent, but how could I liquidate my position? The choice was instead of selling to an individual, go public. Plus the fact that we also wanted to raise money to build the Stretford End.

The directors now had a ready outlet for the shares. For Edwards this was very sweet. Finally, after many fruitless years and one humiliating experience of trying to sell the club to Michael Knighton, he had found the ideal route. The flotation was going to raise the £7 million necessary to rebuild the Stretford End and he could sell some of his shares, pay off his bank manager, and cash in on a scale no previous director of a football club could have imagined. In October 1999, seven years after the Premier League began, Edwards sold another chunk of shares, 7.5 per cent, for a cool £41 million. By then, through his various share sales, he had realised £79 million. At that stage he still owned 6.5 per cent, which at the price United was valued by the stock market in 1999 was worth another £30 million. Given that his original investment had been £600,000, that was a fabulous return. His father Louis had paid between £31,000 and £41,000 to acquire a 54 per cent controlling interest in the 1950s, so the Edwards family could be said to have done extremely well out of their investment in Manchester United.

What is more, as a result of the flotation, Edwards had squared the circle no previous football club chairman had quite managed: have his cake and eat it too. He would sell some of his shares, make money and still retain control.

The Tottenham experience had made the City cautious and when United floated they were keen to give the impression that the club would behave in a responsible way. In order to do so Manchester United created what was called a transfer fee reserve account. The United prospectus said: "At the discretion of the directors this reserve may be increased both from profits after taxation arising from cup success and from transfer fee receipts, and may be used to the extent available, to offset the effect of transfer fee payments on reported profits in any particular year."

The idea behind the account was to reassure the City that Manchester United would not use all the money they made to splash out on players and that the dividend policy would be maintained. In fact, over the years, the reserve was never used but its existence would feed any number of stories of how much Ferguson had in the kitty to spend on players. But this was pure accounting fiction. The figure in the reserve was a pure accounting entry, it never represented hard cash and never determined United's ability to deal in the transfer market.

The creation of the Premier League also made the stock market feel it understood football better. Majid Ishaq of merchant bankers Rothschild, who has advised many football clubs including the Glazers during their takeover of Manchester United, says:

> What happened with the advent of the Premier League is that you had a visible structure whereby the financial community, the analysts and the investors and fund managers could say, "I now understand the profit and loss of a football club. They have this three-year contract from these people called Sky who are going to pay £600 million over three years and our guys get this proportion of it." The profit and loss account became more transparent, so investors could work out and predict the cash flows and predict the pluses and minuses. Historically you couldn't do that. Also a consequence of being on Sky meant that the media and commercial opportunity for the clubs themselves was greater. So if I were an investor and all of a sudden somebody says, "Would you like to buy shares in Aston Villa, it is about to list?" or "Manchester United is about to list", you have got enough brokers to say, "We could sell these shares in the market". You always had fans who will buy shares, but really it is about getting institutions to buy shares. To make money they would need an analyst report, people to cover the shares. So in the early 1990s when they all went public, you had enough analysts writing on it.

But despite this new-found interest in football shares, for the City they were never like other shares, indeed the market soon called them "orphan" shares. As Ishaq explains:

> The problem is if a team had a bad result at the weekend, the share price went down, which is completely wrong and it's false. It is not about one game. It is long-term performance which determines where financially you are. The result was you couldn't get enough proper institutions to buy shares. So fans ended up buying some of these shares and some of them framed the share certificates in their bathrooms. You didn't get institutional shareholders buying shares, you didn't get analysts then continuing to write research. An analyst was not going to write research on Aston Villa or Millwall or Southampton. These were all publicly quoted and they were all too small. So they became orphan assets in terms of shares. We called them orphan shares in the market. The wider stock market was ignoring them because it wasn't a class and category people were investing in. A lot of them were too small and were not going and raising money from the markets. They would probably have struggled

because actually they weren't making that much profit. The reason why they weren't making that much profit from most of those teams was they were paying too much out to players.

In that sense, as so often, Manchester United were to prove the exception. Edwards had always insisted that the club would never spend more than 50 per cent of their income on players' wages. In stark contrast, during Blackburn's championship-winning season, their wage bill was 95 per cent of income. United also kept a tight rein on transfer spending. Other clubs struggled to do that and the Premier League was still to reach its 10th birthday before many clubs realised that football and the stock market did not mix. They were both casinos, but the football casino had emotion attached to it in a way other companies on the stock market did not. You watch your favourite team in the hope they will win and in the process you forge bonds which go far beyond the immediate match. A club becomes more like family. When they do well you share your joy with this family and when they do badly you grieve. I may not exchange Christmas cards with my football family but I have a bond with them which goes back into history and hopefully will carry on into the future.

That is not the case with the general run of companies. You may hold shares in companies and hope they will prosper, provide good dividends and the share price will go up. But if this is not forthcoming and change is necessary you want the board to be ruthless. There is no emotion involved. It is a practical financial decision to protect your investment. In football change is emotional. Removing a manager or transferring players is not just a question of discarding people who are not working. You are in the business of trading on the loyalties of your fans whose attachments to these individuals they have come to value.

When Keith Wyness took control of Aberdeen he quickly delisted the club from the stock exchange and by the time he moved to Everton in 2004, football's love affair with the market was long over. Wyness explains: "People realised football was not suited for that type of regulation. It was burdensome and there was really no market in football shares."

It is fascinating to see the clubs that were listed on the stock market on April 1, 1998, six years after the launch of the Premier League. Their stock market values show Manchester United, Chelsea and Newcastle at the top with Queens Park Rangers rooted in bottom place. But this was the high tide of the game's fascination with the stock market. The clubs listed next have all since gone private and the names of the current owners indicate the extent of overseas ownership, with seven of the 19 clubs owned by overseas interests.

1. Manchester United (£347 mil) – Malcolm Glazer
2. Chelsea Village (£143 mil) – Roman Abramovich
3. Newcastle United (£134 mil) – Mike Ashley
4. Aston Villa (£70 mil) – Randy Lerner
5. Tottenham Hotspur (£68 mil) – Joe Lewis, Levy family
6. Leeds Sporting (£54 mil) – Ken Bates
7. Sunderland (£41 mil) – Ellis Short
8. Nottingham Forest (£27 mil) – Estate of Nigel Doughty
9. Bolton / Burnden Leisure (£23 mil) – Eddie Davies
10=. Birmingham City (£19 mil) – Carsen Yeung
10=. Leicester City (£19 mil) – Raksriaksorn family
10=. Sheffield United (£19 mil) – Kevin McCabe
10=. Southampton Leisure (£19 mil) – Estate of Markus Liebherr
14. Charlton Athletic (£13 mil) – Michael Slater & Tony Jimenez
15. Millwall (£12 mil) – John G Berylson
16. West Bromwich Albion (£11 mil) – Jeremy Peace
17. Preston North End (£9 mil) – Trevor Hemmings
18. Swansea (£4 mil) – Morgan family, Brian Katzen, Supporters' Trust
19. Queens Park Rangers (£1 mil) – Tony Fernandes

Two other clubs, Liverpool and Arsenal, did not have full listing at this point in 1998 but their shares were available on the market. Both clubs have since been taken private and are now foreign-owned.

The final word on this hopeless marriage between the stock market and football came, appropriately, from Tottenham, when just before Christmas 2011, the first club to be floated delisted.

The Spurs announcement came after some very good figures which for a normal company would have been cause for celebration, indeed even an increased dividend: Record revenues of £163.5 million, up £43.7 million on 2010, operating profit before football trading and amortisation up by 42 per cent to £32.3 million and overall profit of £402,000 for the year up to June 30. This was a huge turnaround from the previous year's loss of £6.5 million, helped by the club's first ever Champions League campaign.

In explaining why the club were going back to becoming a private company, chairman Daniel Levy said: "It is clear to us that increasing the capacity of the club's stadium is a key factor in the continued development and success of the club and will involve the company in considerable additional capital expenditure. Given this requirement, we believe that the AIM listing restricts our ability to secure funding for its future development."

Tottenham, having come to the market to clear debts incurred while trying to build a new stand, now could not see the market helping to raise money to build a new larger stadium. To achieve this, being listed on the stock market was a hindrance rather than a help. The club's finance director said as much when he pointed out that by being listed the club had a certain valuation, and when the money men came to look at what they can lend they immediately marked their sums down.

So there was a realisation that while a football club may be a limited company they could never be like other companies, and to get money they required rich benefactors. Wyness, on his first day as chief executive at Goodison Park, had told Bill Kenwright, the Everton chairman: "We will end up with 20 of the richest people from all over the world owning the 20 clubs in the Premier League. We are well on the way to half the league being owned by foreigners. Bill believed that and that is why he has since then been trying to sell the club and find one of those rich foreigners."

This permanent sale sign that Kenwright has put on Everton, hawking the club round the world, may not have produced any buyers but it has had curious results. Wyness recalls:

> In 2005, Christopher Samuelson approached Kenwright right at the time I joined. He represented Boris Zingarevich [a Russian businessman]. It was all going ahead. Then an article appeared in *The Sunday Times*. Zingarevich got frightened by the media attention and quit the deal. Samuelson came back with the Brunei-based Fortress Sports Fund but no money appeared, no transaction fee was agreed. He said he was let down by the investor.

Seven years later, in the summer of 2012, Samuelson brokered a deal which saw Zingarevich's son Anton take over Reading just as the Berkshire club gained promotion to the Premier League.

Everton's search for an investor goes on and as Wyness recalls: "Keith Harris [who now runs the City investment firm Seymour Pierce] got involved and there were close to 20 different deals. Bill has gone public that he has been duped by certain people and almost sold to a group [masquerading as] a Far East billionaire who turned out to be living in a one-room flat in Manchester."

Some of the other buyers have also proved to be all talk and no money. As Harris told me with a sigh of one deal: "Ah, the would-be buyers, both of them British, turned out to be very flaky. When they had to show up with the money, they disappeared. They led everybody a merry dance."

Yet the Premier League has seen, as Wyness predicted, an influx of foreign buyers who certainly have the money to buy clubs. This foreign invasion has been striking, almost matching the foreign invasion on the field of play. But long before the Premier League was planned, there was one English club owned by a very interesting foreigner. His club were one of the founder members of the Premier League, played a crucial role in making sure Sky secured the initial television deal and just before the Premier League celebrated its 10th birthday he would walk away with close to £35 million, having originally bought the club for a mere £40,000. That man was Sam Hammam and his ownership of Wimbledon is a fascinating story of the changes wrought by the Premier League years.

Hammam, a Lebanese civil engineer who owned a construction company, had come to this country so his wife could give birth in a safe environment since Beirut was then in the midst of a savage civil war. In later years when he was involved with Cardiff, Hammam's Lebanese passport often meant he could not travel with the team on pre-season trips outside the UK. But this was far from his thoughts in the late 1970s. Then he teamed up with Ron Noades at Wimbledon, investing £30,000 to take a third share in the club.

Noades recalls:

> When I bought Wimbledon in 1976 it was a non-League club. In July 1977 we had just got into the Football League. In early 1978 Hammam, who was just about to leave the country, first contacted Chelsea. The call was made via his chauffeur. Sam wanted to invest in Chelsea and was keen to meet the club's officials before he left the country. Chelsea told him to write a letter. The chauffeur, I don't know how, maybe through the Wimbledon switchboard, got hold of me and I said, "Come over straight away."

The result was that Hammam invested in Wimbledon. He knew little about how the game in England worked, as Noades realised when they had their first chat. "When we sat down for the first time I said we could break even without opening the turnstiles. He said, 'What is a turnstile?'"

But Hammam proved a quick learner.

In 1981 Noades, his partner Bernie Coleman and Hammam decided to buy Crystal Palace. However, at the last minute Hammam preferred to stay at Wimbledon and paid Noades £40,000 for complete ownership of the club. By then he had got back the £30,000 which he had paid Wimbledon earlier. All the while Wimbledon had been swiftly rising through the divisions. By then Hammam not only knew about turnstiles but had worked out how he could put on a football performance.

Hammam's ownership was to see its greatest reward when the club won promotion to the old First Division in 1986 and two years later won the FA Cup, defeating Liverpool 1–0 with a goal from Lawrie Sanchez in the final. In the process the team gained notoriety as the Crazy Gang. Wimbledon players loved to upset the opposition by playing loud music on their ghetto blasters before the match. In 1994 Hammam even daubed graffiti on the walls of the West Ham dressing room when Wimbledon played at Upton Park. And while much was made of all the money Hammam was said to have ploughed in, the club were run on a shoestring budget and thrived on their status as underdogs.

As Vinnie Jones, one of the most iconic of Wimbledon players, told me:

> When I scored the winner against Manchester United in 1986 I was on £150 a week. Dave Bassett [Wimbledon manager] gave me a £50 bonus out of his own pocket. I was on £300 a week when we won the FA Cup in 1988 against Liverpool and on three grand for playing and winning. Barnesie [John Barnes] told me each Liverpool player was on 10 grand just for appearing, whether they won or not.

However the rules of football, or rather the absence of rules, meant that Hammam as owner was in a position to make a lot of money through his ownership of Wimbledon. Long before Hammam had emerged, back in 1959, the freehold of Wimbledon's ground at Plough Lane had been sold back to the club. But Merton council had inserted a pre-emption clause which allowed it to reacquire the land for £8,000 if the club went bust and stopped playing football. In 1984, the Wimbledon board agreed that a company controlled by Hammam could buy the site as repayment of the debt the club owed him. He is believed to have got rid of the covenant for £300,000. Another Hammam company, Rudgwick, then acquired the land for £3 million. Hammam applied for a change of use and sold it to Safeway plc in 1994 for £8.5 million, with all the money going to himself. By then Wimbledon themselves had stopped playing at Plough Lane and moved to Selhurst Park, home to Crystal Palace, in a ground-sharing agreement.

There were then no rules or regulations which stopped the outright sale or transfer of freehold ownership of a club's ground to another entity. The Football Association commission of inquiry which looked into the Wimbledon situation recommended that "the football authorities should take a close look at whether they should monitor the ownership of land on which stadia are built and perhaps this land should be held in trust for the clubs so that it cannot be used as an asset by owners/investors to dispose of at will". A decade after this recommendation the football authorities have still to act on it.

In 1997, with the Premier League now well established, Hammam had the extraordinary idea of moving Wimbledon to Dublin. Peter Leaver, then chief executive of the Premier League, wrote to Hammam saying that "the clubs resolved that there was no objection by them to Wimbledon's application to play its home matches in Dublin". As far as the Premier League was concerned, this was a matter for the national associations of England and Ireland. The Football Association of Ireland was not best pleased to hear of Wimbledon's plan to relocate to Dublin. Hammam approached the English FA to intercede with FIFA but Graham Kelly, then chief executive of the FA, felt it could not take any action until the Irish removed their objections. The tone of Kelly's letter makes it clear that the FA would have assisted Wimbledon's move had the Irish been won over.

1997 also saw Hammam sell 80 per cent of Wimbledon to a Norwegian company, Aker RGI, for £25 million. The move to Dublin clearly played a part in this sale for, as the FA commission of inquiry noted: "The Norwegians who invested in the club at that time were led to believe [rightly or wrongly] that the English football authorities would not pose a problem." Two years later Hammam sold his remaining interest for £1.5 million to another company. So, for an investment of £40,000 he walked away with nearly £35 million. How much he invested in the club during his ownership has never been disclosed but, even allowing that these sums were substantial, on any reckoning his investment in Wimbledon proved a very good one. It may not have been in the Martin Edwards league but, given the status of Wimbledon, it was still considerable.

By then, of course, the glory days of the Crazy Gang were a fading memory. At the end of the 1999–2000 season Wimbledon were relegated. But with a Premier League cost base, the new owners decided the only answer was to move to Milton Keynes, a plan bitterly opposed by many fans and the Football League.

A move of this nature meant English football was copying the American franchise style of sport. In May 2002, an FA commission of inquiry reported on all this. It paid due homage to the English pyramid structure of promotion and relegation, the community basis of football clubs and firmly rejected the franchise model, declaring: "Nor do we wish any more than the football authorities or the supporters for franchise football to arrive on these shores." But having said all that, it concluded that Wimbledon had to be allowed to move because it was a very special case.

The commissioners felt the club had precious few community links, having spent half their Football League existence outside their original borough of

Merton. Wimbledon's owners had said that if they could not move they would wind up the club, with Brentford taking their place. But what ultimately drove the commission to its decision was the overall financial position of football caused by the success of the Premier League:

> The current financial outlook for many clubs in Divisions One, Two and Three of the Football League is distinctly bleak. They're caught in a player wages spiral that seems to be out of control. Changes to the transfer system are such that they can no longer sell star players to survive. As we decide this case, Football League clubs are going into administration. There is a chasm which has developed between even Division One clubs and the FA Premier League clubs as a result of the BSkyB deal. The collapse of ITV Digital and the drying up of the transfer market have contributed to the crisis. Many clubs, especially in the Football League, rely on wealthy benefactors who are prepared to sustain them financially. In the current financial climate professional clubs need to encourage investors.

This was as clear an invitation as any and although the details of the judgement were meant to be secret it seemed all the world heard it. Since then investors have flocked to Britain in search of football clubs ripe for takeover. Indeed, just over a year after this momentous decision, a Russian arrived who was to have a dramatic impact on the game in this country. That man was Roman Abramovich. In the summer of 2003, after benefiting from the collapse of communism which had enabled him to make a fortune in Boris Yeltsin's Russia, he bought Chelsea for £140 million.

Abramovich has never explained why he bought the club. Before he bought Chelsea he met Daniel Levy, the Tottenham chairman. There have been persistent stories he really wanted to buy the North London club. Levy has always denied this was the case or that he received any offer. Among the rumours is one that Abramovich flew over the Chelsea ground and decided that was the club. Unlike Hammam three decades earlier, he was not given the brush-off by the owners of Chelsea but eagerly welcomed. Whatever his motives, he had no plans to turn Chelsea into another Crazy Gang. And before long, the Premier League was awash with what many felt was crazy money. These Russian riches unleashed changes that were to prove dramatic and continue to be felt to this day.

In his very first season Abramovich spent £111.3 million on transfers. Not only was this more than anyone had ever spent before in English football, but the Russian dramatically changed the terms of trade. He paid the full transfer fee at the timing of signing the player. This broke with the usual convention of fees being spread over a period of time. Cash on the nail proved a lifeline for clubs facing cash-flow problems. Indeed, it was immensely beneficial to clubs such as West Ham who were then under financial strain, as the then club chairman, Terry Brown, acknowledged. Chelsea's purchase of Glen Johnson and Joe Cole, at a time when the club were under pressure from their bankers was, says Brown, of great help.

Rick Parry, then chief executive of Liverpool, describes Abramovich's spending on transfers as having "a trickle-down effect, so a lot of clubs would say that Chelsea coming in and spending money has actually been beneficial for them. From a Liverpool perspective it wasn't terribly beneficial because it was a lot harder to get players. The net effect was it put prices up, made it a lot harder to compete. We went through a period where you recognised there were two markets. There was one for Chelsea and one for the rest but you consoled yourself on the basis they couldn't get every player and not every player would want to sign for them. So you made the best of the situation."

This was certainly the case in January 2011 when Abramovich paid Liverpool a record £50 million for Fernando Torres. This enabled the Anfield club to go out and buy Andy Carroll for £35 million and enrich Newcastle in the process. Abramovich's intervention in the transfer market has not always been quite that dramatic, nor has his spending matched his first year (see details on page 260). But since 2003 in almost every transfer window it is what Chelsea want that sets the market. Even when Abramovich is not successful, his transfer intentions have had a major impact on the English season. Tottenham's 2011–12 season was shaped by the fact that they resisted Luka Modric's highly advertised proposed move to Chelsea.

Since 2008 and the purchase of Manchester City by Abu Dhabi United Group, Chelsea have been challenged and even overtaken in transfer spending. In 2010–11 the club spent £141 million on players, the third successive season they had spent more than £100 million, double that of Manchester United and comfortably ahead of Chelsea at £91 million. The two big spenders showed contrasting styles. While City had bought a clutch of stars, Yaya Toure, David Silva, Edin Dzeko and Mario Balotelli, Chelsea's £50 million on Torres showed their buying policy had an individual whim about it. In the process Abramovich had shown himself to be like a child with a new train set. He knows his shiny new train set is better than anything possessed by the other kids and while he invites 40,000 people to come and watch, he does not want to share this toy with anyone else. Consider Abramovich's behaviour in the eight years since he took over Chelsea: he has employed a total of eight managers in that period. Abramovich chose to snub the footballing tradition that a visiting owner accepts the hospitality of the home club's board when his team are playing away.

You could argue that this convention has a touch of *Downton Abbey* about it, but before Abramovich I had not heard of a single visiting director or owner refusing such hospitality. When Abramovich watches Chelsea play away I am told his security men sweep the area he will sit in before the match and he keeps himself separate from everybody. It was just as revealing that as he went to the dressing room after Chelsea finally won the Champions League he needed an interpreter to talk to his players.

When the Russian first arrived he wanted to build a team in a hurry and that's just what he did. Since their limited Cup glories in the early 1970s, Chelsea had endured a barren spell which had seen them yo-yo between the divisions. True, in the mid-1990s under Ken Bates' chairmanship the club's fortunes had revived but they were still far from the elite of English football. It required Abramovich to convert them into a top club and very quickly.

The Russian took advice from the people he thought he could trust. So in that first season most of his transfer moves were made not by Chelsea officials, let alone the manager, but by the super agent Pini Zahavi. Chairmen of clubs selling players to Chelsea were surprised to find the Israeli at the end of the phone. Zahavi had always claimed that he played a major part in getting Abramovich to the West London club in the first place. He was not the only one to claim credit but Zahavi undoubtedly played a crucial role.

The Russian has not changed his management style since his early days. So as he has chopped and changed managers, his trusted adviser has been the Dutchman Piet de Visser. His role as a virtual second manager considerably upset Jose Mourinho. Mourinho's predecessor Claudio Ranieri had been sacked by Abramovich's right-hand man, the Russian-born, Canadian-qualified chartered accountant, Eugene Tenenbaum, via a phone call to Italy. Tenenbaum later explained it had to be done that way as the very next day Mourinho was due in town and the decks had to be cleared before the Portuguese, who had just won the Champions League, arrived.

The drama that attended the Mourinho departure involved Abramovich himself. Despite the unprecedented success the Portuguese brought, Abramovich was not enjoying his football. According to a widely accepted version, after a dramatic confrontation in a corridor of the club an argument with Abramovich ended with Mourinho saying, "In that case I am going", Abramovich decided that meant Mourinho had resigned. All this had been made worse by the owner's habit of developing his own links with senior players, creating in effect two tiers of management, one controlled by the manager, the other by the older players. Their intervention in the removal of Andre Villas-Boas, who had arrived at the beginning of the 2011 season, with what was described as a four-year plan, was crucial.

After he had taken over at Tottenham, Villas–Boas was the first Abramovich manager to break ranks and publicly criticise the owner. While being unveiled at Tottenham's new training ground, the Portuguese said: "I respect the decision of the owner of Chelsea but I will never accept it. I told him that for me, it was him quitting on me when he had been so much involved at the beginning in bringing me in and he was also [the one] who was not putting up to the things that he promised. What reason did he give to me? I'm not sure if I can make it public but the reasons don't go along or can't be applied to the fact that I was dismissed."

Interestingly, soon after his takeover Abramovich was given some advice as to how as a rich man he could please the fans. The advice from a then Chelsea insider, a respected and shrewd administrator who had both played the game at a high level and been involved in club administration, was that the Russian should cut season-ticket prices by half. This, he argued, would ensure that Chelsea was not seen as a rich man's hobby. Abramovich rejected the advice.

Had he done so he would have endeared himself to the fans. Instead he hired Peter Kenyon, the chief executive at Manchester United, to whom he paid a transfer fee. There then followed much talk of how Chelsea were aiming to break even, indeed to become self-sufficient. All this did was further damage Chelsea's credibility. When it came to hiring or firing managers, Abramovich has behaved as if he wanted to recreate along the Thames what Peter the Great had done beside the Neva River in St Petersburg. Yet his minions kept telling the world that Chelsea's management was like any other club's. Abramovich was presented as a rather special football private equity investor and it was only a matter of time before the whole financial situation became normal. It did not sound plausible and events since have demonstrated that given the way Chelsea was financed this was impossible.

Chelsea's transfer spending under Abramovich:

2003	£111.3 mil
2004	£95.8 mil
2005	£27.9 mil
2006	£36.2 mil
2007	£12 mil

2008	£28.2 mil
2009	£4.7 mil
2010	£15.2 mil
2011	£72 mil

By 2007, Abramovich's influence on the game was such that it had a dramatic impact on London's premier club Arsenal. As we have seen, David Dein had played a significant role in the making of modern Arsenal, not least in the recruitment of Arsene Wenger. Much taken by what Irving Scholar had done at Tottenham in the early 1980s, he had persuaded Peter Hill-Wood, the Arsenal chairman, to sell him a 17 per cent stake for £290,000. Over the years Dein would increase his stake. Scholar's arrival at Tottenham had marked the start of commercialism in English football. Unlike Tottenham, Arsenal never listed on the big board of the stock exchange. Hill-Wood vetoed this Dein idea, but Dein did introduce commercialism to staid Highbury.

The problem for Dein was the collapse of his sugar business in the 1980s, where he was the victim of a massive fraud. This brought Danny Fiszman, a very wealthy businessman, into Arsenal, with Dein selling him some of his shares. Having once been the unchallenged King of Highbury, with a 42 per cent stake, Dein slowly saw his power wither away while Fiszman's share rose.

The two men might always have fallen out. But it did not help that they had sharp differences over Arsenal's future strategy. Should the club build a new stadium to match that of Manchester United or should they share the new Wembley? Dein favoured Wembley, where Arsenal played some Champions League matches. But Fiszman made sure Arsenal went for a new stadium.

In the long view Fiszman was right and Dein was wrong. Building the Emirates has been a success, although it meant huge borrowings. It also soured relations on the board as the man Fiszman brought in to run the stadium project, Keith Edelman, did not get on with Dein. Indeed, when they both represented the club at Premier League meetings, the joke used to be that it was always a score draw with Arsenal, since whatever Dein said Edelman opposed.

By March 2007, Dein was convinced that in order to match Chelsea, and the bottomless coffers of Roman Abramovich, Arsenal needed foreign investors. He lined up American investor Stan Kroenke, the idea being that he would buy the stake ITV held in the club, buy Dein's stake and also that of another director, Lady Nina Bracewell-Smith. It would also allow Dein to continue to run Arsenal. If anything, his position would have been strengthened at a time when Fiszman had, to a large extent, marginalised him.

Fiszman reacted with unprecedented fury at what he felt was unacceptable behaviour. He alleged that Dein had gone behind the board's back. The result: Dein was unceremoniously bundled out of the Emirates and he even had to surrender his mobile phone. Since then, the board have watched like hawks for any sign that Dein might be coming back. This worry grew as other foreign investors circled the club. The fears centred on the Russian Alisher Usmanov as he also bought Arsenal shares. Dein made no secret of his liking for the Russian and he was often a guest of Usmanov in his Emirates box. He eventually sold his Arsenal shares to the Russian, pocketing £80 million. Back in 1983 when Dein had invested his £290,000, Hill-Wood had thought this was dead money, since the old Etonian chairman was aware that several of his City friends had declined to invest in football, considering it a dying sport. Dein's sale to Usmanov showed how the Premier League years had changed the football investment game. However, Dein's deal with Usmanov only intensified Fiszman's fear of a Russian takeover that might end with Dein back in charge at the club.

Indeed, anybody who got close to the Russian bred fear that Dein might return and this was what led to the board's breach with Lady Nina Bracewell-Smith. Worried by how close she was getting to Usmanov, she was dumped from the board in 2008 hours after she had been unanimously re-elected by the annual general meeting of the club.

Then, four years after Dein had first proposed a plan to counter Abramovich, the Arsenal board agreed to it. When Dein had proposed Kroenke, Hill-Wood had been very critical of an American coming in. Now Hill-Wood said: "The board of directors and I consider it a key responsibility to protect the ethos and spirit of the club. Mr Kroenke, although relatively new to Arsenal, has shown himself to be a man who values and respects the history and tradition of this very special club that we cherish. We are confident that he will be a safe custodian of its future." These could have been the words of Mr Bennett in Jane Austen's *Pride and Prejudice* when a suitor came calling for the hand of one of his daughters.

The difference was that this deal was the work of Fiszman, who died within days of the announcement of the Kroenke takeover. Unlike Dein, Fiszman is revered and a bridge leading to the ground now bears his name. Even as he lay dying, Fiszman made sure of a deal that would ensure that his former friend and colleague Dein would never again get his hands on the club. The relief when Fiszman finally persuaded Lady Nina to sell to Kroenke was so evident that Hill-Wood went out of his way to praise the Bracewell-Smith family for the role they had played in the development and success of Arsenal over the last 70 years. He ended with the promise: "We will be considering appropriate ways to mark this long and valued commitment."

Lady Nina received £11,500 a share for her 16 per cent holding in the club, a third higher than the £8,000 Dein had got, giving her a total of £130 million. She had clearly been forgiven now that she had fulfilled Fiszman's wishes, even if it was at the last moment. But there was no such redemption for Dein or even recognition that he had originally brought in Kroenke. For all the talk of a new chapter in the Arsenal story, Dein could not be forgiven.

Kroenke was the fourth American to buy a major stake in a Premier League club. By then American ownership was almost taken for granted and Kroenke's arrival hardly caused a ripple. This was in stark contrast to the first US investor back in 2005. Then the Glazers had to be rescued from the Old Trafford ground they owned in a police van, such was the fury of some Manchester United fans. But that was hardly surprising given the campaign waged against them by some of the fans and the media hostility which had seen their father depicted as having two heads or sprouting horns on either side of his ears.

Yet if Abramovich was the classic case of a rich man buying a trophy asset, the Glazer family's ownership of the most successful Premier League club perfectly illustrated how the growth of the league had changed both ownership in English football and the relationship between managers, owners and fans. The Premier League was now a brand and these were foreigners who thought they could exploit it better than the natives, while also teaching them some skills in sports management.

Chapter 10
THE GLOBAL SEARCH FOR AN ENGLISH BRAND

On June 27, 2005, the London Stock Exchange announced that Manchester United shares had been delisted and the company was now wholly owned by the Glazers. That day, three of Malcolm Glazer's sons, Joel, Avi and Bryan, flew into London. They were driven to the Ritz where they prepared for a series of important meetings the following day.

The way these meetings were arranged suggested a schedule for a visiting head of state. The style and dignity with which the Glazers were welcomed clearly showed how both the English football authorities and the English establishment were keen to get to know them and impress them.

Their first visit was to the Premier League offices, then at Connaught Square. Over lunch with chairman Sir Dave Richards and chief executive Richard Scudamore, the brothers were asked which of them would be chairman. The answer was that they would share the job and be co-chairmen. There was also some talk at this meeting about the league's collective rights sales. The Premier League had read newspaper speculation that the only way the Glazers could raise enough money to pay back what they had borrowed to buy the club was by trying to sell their TV rights individually and break the collective selling agreement which formed the basis of the Premier League's success. The Glazers firmly denied such intentions. Scudamore and Richards were clearly intrigued by the brothers and there was talk of managing sports franchises in America and the very different sporting culture of that country.

The brothers were next driven to the FA's headquarters, then based in Soho Square, for afternoon tea. The FA did not go as far as scones, but there were some nice biscuits, and the FA hierarchy was in attendance: chairman Geoff Thompson, chief executive Brian Barwick and international director David Davies. The FA wanted to know why they had bought Manchester United. This gave the brothers a chance to explain how they had been fans for years, followed Manchester United and felt they could bring something of their experience of managing a sports franchise in America to this country.

The Glazers' first day was rounded off with a visit to the House of Commons, where they were treated to a steak dinner in the Churchill Room by Richard Caborn, then Minister for Sport. Caborn was about to leave for Singapore to help secure the 2012 Olympics bid for London and here they discussed wider questions of sport, health and obesity, with Caborn talking about a DVD for fitness in schools that Sport England had produced.

They might have impressed the English sporting and political establishment, but it was when they went the following day to what was now their property, Old Trafford, that they were suddenly confronted with the fans' reaction to their purchase of Manchester United. The fans, far from offering tea or sympathy, were mostly hostile, shouting "Die Glazer, Die Glazer!" While the early part of the evening had gone according to plan, with the Glazers photographed as they walked on the turf of the Theatre of Dreams, as night fell the mood changed.

An eyewitness told me: "By 10 o'clock the tunnel leading to the Old Trafford ground and the asphalt outside were full of screaming, quite scary, crowds. Hundreds. It was a very angry crowd, very noisy and it was quite frightening." Unknown to the Glazers, and certainly to the club, the rumour mills in Manchester had been churning all day with the news that the Glazers were on their way. As early as 12.30pm an email had been circulated by anti-Glazer fans saying: "Show him what you think. United fans are being urged to get down to Old Trafford to show their opposition to Glazer in person. Meetings are believed to be going on at Old Trafford all day."

But the club had done nothing to warn the police that the Glazers would be at the club and now, as a growing mob threatened the Glazers' physical safety, Manchester United officials could not figure out how to evacuate their new owners from the ground. That is when they rang the police in some panic, as Andy Holte, then divisional commander of the Trafford division of Manchester police, later confirmed to me:

> We were not aware that the Glazers were at Manchester United. There was a Twenty20 cricket match for which we would have had minimal policing. There are always quite a number of people, maybe a hundred, two hundred at the club, visiting the megastore, visiting the museum. So it is always busy. On that day we had officers at the club most of the day, up to about five officers because of the considerable media interest. We then stood them all down apart from one officer. If more press or people came back in the evening that officer was there as a tripwire. We then got a call from the club that they were concerned about getting the Glazers out of

the club. This is the first time we had heard they were there. We were then faced with having to get officers down to the club. The problem is, people can start to gather very, very quickly, everybody has mobile phones.

The police officer who received the call from the club was actually watching the cricket with his family. The Glazers were finally driven out of the ground at around 11pm in a police van. And it was these pictures, of the Glazers under siege, that were flashed right around the world, gaining much more prominence than the ones the PR had planned, of the Glazers walking serenely on the turf of their new English property, exuding wonder and excitement. For owners who had expended so much time and effort in putting together the £800 million to buy the club this was a terrifying experience. But for the fans it was how they had raised the money to buy their club that caused the outrage.

The question of how the Glazers had financed their purchase had come up at both the lunch with the Premier League and tea with the FA. On both occasions they had been asked, could the debt they had incurred in buying Manchester United be managed? The brothers were in no doubt that the debt was manageable. The fans were convinced it was not and remain convinced of this even now. However, the fact that Manchester United found themselves in this situation was in some ways, as Ferguson would admit later, an inevitable result of the flotation back in 1991. Much as the fans protested, their actions in the past had played a part in allowing the Glazers to take over the club. It was a story of many twists and turns that had marked the first decade of the Premier League before reaching this dramatic conclusion on that summer day in 2005.

The roots of the story can be traced back to 1998, when another foreigner, Rupert Murdoch, suddenly decided he wanted to purchase Manchester United. The BSkyB bid was curious. It was made after chief executive Sam Chisholm retired and was replaced by the American Mark Booth. Chisholm has since told me that if he had ever bid for anything in Manchester he would have tried to buy ITV's iconic *Coronation Street*, certainly not the Old Trafford club.

Booth, who had taken over Sky in 1998, felt he faced a serious problem. In the summer of 1998, Sky had tried and failed to persuade the Premier League to agree to pay-per-view matches. A pay-per-view option had been part of the first television contract Sky had negotiated with the Premier League in 1992. Nothing had been done about it but now Sky suggested that in the 1998–99 season they would like to start pay-per-view. Sky intended to launch their own digital channels in the autumn of 1998 and saw pay-per-view as the ideal vehicle to drive the sale of these. Pay-per-view would do for digital what live Premier League football had done for the main Sky channels since 1992.

Sky initially told Peter Leaver, then Premier League chief executive, that they would like all 320 matches which they did not televise (Sky then broadcast 60 of 380 Premier League games every season) on pay-per-view. This request was later modified to just under 120 matches a season on pay-per-view. Leaver was not convinced. At the league's summer meeting in June 1998 at Stapleford Park, a luxurious hotel set in rolling countryside near Melton Mowbray in Leicestershire, the clubs discussed a proposal that from the 1998–99 season four matches be moved from their Saturday slot to Sunday and put on pay-per-view television. If the experiment proved successful then more matches could be put on pay-per-view. Manchester United, supported by Aston Villa, were quite keen to approve the experiment but the other clubs were not so sure and it was clear that there was no majority in favour. Sky had offered £15 million for the Sunday games, which many chairmen felt was nowhere near enough to disrupt the tradition of football on Saturday.

After the decision was taken, both the chairmen and Sky were anxious to rebut the suggestion that there had been a battle, let alone that Sky had been defeated. The chairman publicly advertised their rejection of the pay-per-view deal as a victory for the fans. The fans had always accused the chairmen of being greedy, of grabbing every money-making scheme that was presented to them without heed to the needs of the fans and the game's traditional values. Now the chairmen could claim they were just as fond of the traditions of the game as the fans and had decided not to accept the experiment as it broke with the sanctity of English football on Saturdays.

Sky had a more difficult job in trying to demonstrate they had won. Like any Murdoch organisation, they were not accustomed to being beaten. Now that they had suffered this unexpected rebuff from the Premier League chairmen, they tried to distance themselves from the whole affair and claimed that the proposal the chairmen had turned down was not a Sky plan at all.

Happy as both the League and Sky were to indulge in such obfuscation, the reality was that several clubs were very keen on pay-per-view, seeing it as the new frontier of money. United were one of them and they felt more than a little miffed by the way Leaver had dealt with Sky's proposal. They had other problems with him as well and as Peter Kenyon, then Martin Edwards' deputy chief executive, put it to me: "If you look at the contracts, there is provision for trials of pay-per-view and I think our view initially was, 'Why don't we take this opportunity of trying it in a period of time which is a controlled environment? Let's not go the whole hog, but there is a provision in the contract and there was an understanding we would have a trial during this period. There were wild discrepancies on reports concerning pay-per-view. How do you know unless you try it?"

Even before Sky's defeat on pay-per-view, Booth had been thinking about buying Manchester United. As an American, Booth had grown up with the idea of media companies owning sports clubs, since media ownership of baseball, American football and basketball teams was common. Indeed, Murdoch had just bought the Los Angeles Dodgers baseball team. However, in the UK the companies who got involved with football clubs were usually local, such as the brewery company who controlled Ipswich. And in most cases they were very passive investors.

Booth's head of business development, the Zimbabwean Kevin Kinsella, had drawn up a list of possible clubs and as Booth told me: "Arsenal and Liverpool were considered but top of his recommendation was Manchester United. He did not think the others made much sense."

Around this time the Restrictive Practices Court was considering whether the collective sale of television rights by the League was legal. It was clear that if the practice were ruled illegal, this would clearly benefit top clubs like Manchester United. United would provide Sky with a solid UK base around which a competitive soccer package could be built in almost all conceivable scenarios. With their very large fan base, the club were likely to be a major beneficiary of pay-per-view when that was launched. Kinsella argued that by buying United, Sky would not only get a prime seat at the domestic football table, but they would potentially secure a place in a European Super League. Plans for such a league were always being floated, with Manchester United the de facto major English representative. At that time Sky had no European football rights, with the major ones all owned by ITV. But if Sky bought United, then, just as Murdoch's purchase of 20th Century Fox in the US had helped him influence movie negotiations, Sky could shape the development of a European Super League to its advantage.

As Booth told me:

> The more we looked at it, the more we thought the opportunity to buy United was a very interesting one. That centred on the fact that if you looked round the world the combination of media companies and sports organisations was a growing trend. The value to the sports organisation, be it a football team or a baseball team, was greater if it was part of a larger organisation. It seemed to us that here something was going to happen along these lines. And in that case we wanted to be first in line rather than maybe at the back of the line.

Some time in June 1998, Booth rang Martin Edwards inviting him to come down to Sky's headquarters in Isleworth to discuss pay-per-view. Back in 1992, Manchester United might have voted against Sky and in favour of ITV and Edwards had also been critical of Sky innovations such as Monday night football. But since then United and Sky had formed a particularly close relationship, with Sky even becoming United's partners in MUTV. Ian West, another Sky official and chairman of MUTV, was also at the lunch. Then, as Edwards and United director Maurice Watkins settled down to the three-course lunch, with a smoked salmon starter and a main course of chicken and rice, Booth said: "Look, Martin, I have got you here under false pretences. When I rang you to invite you for this lunch I said I would like to talk about pay-per-view but I have a bigger agenda which I didn't want to say over the phone."

For a moment, as Edwards and Watkins tucked into their smoked salmon, there was silence before Booth continued: "What I really wanted to talk about is Sky buying Manchester United. We have looked at it and we would like to make an offer to buy your company."

Edwards would later joke with friends that he nearly fell of his chair but he was soon all in favour, as was his board with the singular exception of Greg Dyke. Part of the reason was the board's fear of economic storm clouds then gathering in the world, particularly signs of a downturn in Asia. Board members were also aware of the money they would make. But the bid was immediately denounced by the rest of the non-Murdoch media — *The Sunday Telegraph* broke the story of the bid — and by a well-organised group of fans. The fans' protest produced a lot of noise and the received history of the bid's failure is that this was all due to the superb anti-bid campaign run by the fans. In reality the bid was defeated by much more than just fan hostility. Murdoch's bid failed because the British authorities took against it.

In my book *Manchester Disunited,* I revealed that Sir John Bridgeman, director general of the Office of Fair Trading (OFT), had been sure from the moment the bid was made that it ran foul of competition law. The OFT had just emerged from a lengthy investigation into the market power of Sky triggered by concerns over Sky's monopoly of pay-per-view television and encryption technology. "A number of interesting things were happening around us," Bridgeman told me. "The reason Sky were growing was that they were providing a product no one else could provide. I conducted my investigation and I basically said that, in my view, they were treading the very delicate line of being close to abusing their dominant market position. "

It had been indicated very clearly to the United directors, Bridgeman disclosed to me, that the passage of any Sky deal would be far from an easy ride, although this did not mean the bid would be stopped. "It was likely to be an agreed merger between the parties. It was quite likely that the owners of Manchester United would start cashing in too." Bridgeman ultimately came to the conclusion that the Sky deal would have a restrictive effect both for Premier League football and for pay-per-view television. Bridgeman and his staff had discussions with officials from the Department of Trade and Industry, some of whom were not sure if the bid really violated any competition law or even should be referred at all. Bridgeman denies that he was placed under any direct pressure from the DTI not to refer the bid. The Treasury, under Gordon Brown, was keen on a referral. The fans' opposition was interesting but it was not crucial to his decision. It was more the icing on the cake. The OFT would have come to its decision to refer, irrespective of what the fans did.

Bridgeman advised Peter Mandelson, then in charge of the DTI, to refer the bid to the Monopolies and Mergers Commission (MMC). That night Mandelson ran into Murdoch's daughter Elizabeth and said: "I think I have done something to upset your father." "I think he understands," Elizabeth replied. "Don't worry about it."

Initially, neither Sky nor Manchester United directors were worried but to their great shock the MMC blocked the bid. By then Mandelson had resigned and been replaced by Stephen Byers. Some United supporters, such as the writer Jim White, believe that had Mandelson still been a minister the bid would have gone through. We cannot be sure. What is certain is that the bid proved the starting point of another convoluted battle for the ownership of United which was to end in the takeover by the Glazers. In repelling Murdoch, the fans had wrongly assumed they had the power to decide who owned their club, when they did not. This led them to make fatal mistakes when, seven years later, the Glazers came calling and contributed to the arrival of the Americans in the Old Trafford boardroom.

A few months after the MMC vetoed Murdoch's bid, the Irish racehorse owners John Magnier and JP McManus, using a company called Cubic registered in the Virgin Islands, bought shares in United. This move was welcomed by the fans. They were seen as great friends of Sir Alex Ferguson and it was felt to be strengthening the hold Ferguson had over the club and what the fans hoped would be the elimination of their pet hate, Martin Edwards. In many fans' eyes, this was seen as setting right the great wrong done when that great man of football, Matt Busby, had been denied the right to own the club by Martin Edwards' father Louis.

But the Irish investment in Manchester United would turn out to be a nightmare for the club. The Irish would fall out spectacularly with Ferguson over the ownership rights to the horse Rock of Gibraltar with dramatic consequences for United. The dispute would go public, involve lawyers and court actions. And despite the fact that this dispute between the Irish and Ferguson had nothing to do with football and was a private matter, some fans noisily took the side of Ferguson. For them the Irish were targeting their beloved manager. Some would even threaten the Irish and their racing interests and made plans to picket the Cheltenham festival. This forced Ferguson to issue this statement:

> The reputation of Manchester United is paramount to my thinking. The private dispute I have is just that and I don't want to exacerbate the whole thing. Cheltenham is such a great festival and I don't want it marred in any way. There is a lot of concern about what could happen and I would ask supporters to refrain from any form of protest. I am strongly opposed to any violent, unlawful or disruptive behaviour which may reflect badly on the club and its supporters in general.

The board, in turn, would feel so threatened by Magnier and McManus that they courted the Glazers, seeing them as a white knight to rescue them from the truculent Irish.

Early in 2003 the Glazers had begun buying shares in the club, an initiative led by the eldest of Malcolm Glazer's sons, Avram Glazer, who was very interested in soccer. The Glazers felt they could export the style of sports management they had developed with their NFL team the Tampa Bay Buccaneers to Europe. Tampa had won the Super Bowl in January 2003. But even as 2003 drew to a close the Glazers had given no thought to mounting a takeover of United. The idea of the takeover was actually planted in their heads when they first met David Gill, the chief executive of United, in the first week of December 2003. Then they realised how much the Manchester United board felt under siege from the Irish. At the meeting with Joel and Avi Glazer, Gill and the board made it clear they saw the Americans as their saviours. They told them that if they offered £3 a share to the Irish, they would sell. And that such a move would be welcomed by the board with open arms. There was not much doubt that in the eyes of the board the Irish were the bad guys. I was informed that at this meeting Gill gave the Glazers the firm impression that the board would see them as the cavalry come to save them from the Irish. I was given to understand that such a line had been agreed with Sir Roy Gardner, the Manchester United chairman, and the £3 figure had actually been Gardner's idea.

The figure of £3 a share was to prove an important one, for when in May 2005 the Glazers made their move and approached the Irish, this was the figure they offered and it was immediately accepted. So both the idea for a Glazer bid and a figure that would be acceptable was sown by Gill and the Manchester United board at this meeting. None of this, of course, was revealed until my book was published in 2006. The official explanation offered by United was that this was a routine meeting, the kind the chief executive of a well run plc would have with any major investor and was meant to discuss the investor's plans. A week after meeting the Glazers, Gill had said: "We had an excellent meeting with Malcolm and his sons. He sees the shares as a good investment and that was the end of the discussion." When asked if he was worried about the Glazers buying shares, Gill said very confidently: "I'm not worried." And why should he have been if he had invited the Glazers to bid and even suggested the price that could buy out the Irish?

For years, nobody with inside knowledge of United would even talk about the impact on the club of the Ferguson-Irish row. This silence was only broken by Roy Keane six years later in 2011. By then his infamous spat with Ferguson — he had criticised his team-mates, which led to him leaving the club in November 2005 — had become just a footnote in the club's history. Now, in an interview with David Walsh of *The Sunday Times,* he disclosed how he had refused to attend a dinner to celebrate Ferguson's 25th anniversary at Old Trafford and provided a revealing insight into the relationship between owners and managers:

> People say Ferguson always does what's right for Man United. I don't think he does. I think he does what's right for him. The Irish thing, I was speaking to the manager about it. This didn't help the club, the manager going to the law against the leading shareholder. How could it be of benefit to Man United? It wasn't and we know what happened. What was that all about? Power and control. "They've used me, they've treated me badly," Ferguson told me in his office. I said, "You're not going to win," and he said, "I don't care, no one does that to me," and I go, "OK, off you go. I'm not going to change your mind." Amazing what happens.

Keane was right to express amazement. For while the vocal United fans, always happy to support the manager, took up his cause, made his battle their battle and presented it as vital to United they were unintentionally paving the way for the Glazers. When in May 2005 the Glazers offered £3 a share, the Irish, having had such a miserable time at United, were only too happy to sell. And the net result was that the fate of Manchester United was decided very quickly that summer with a couple of phone calls.

The calls were made by Robert Leitao of Rothschild, who had masterminded the Glazer takeover and organised the finance. For days he had kept in touch with John Power, a legal man who advised Magnier and McManus and with whom Leitao had worked on previous deals. The initial calls had been technical ones about United shares, such as in whose name the shares were registered and whether there were paper certificates or the shares were held in Crest, the paperless share trading system. As Leitao told me: "I had rung John Power some time back, just to say hello, I'm working on it. And I'll come back to you when I've got something to say. He understood and I understood we wouldn't have any more discussions until I was ready to discuss."

Once all the finance was in place, Leitao rang Power rang again, this time offering to buy the shares unconditionally. "He said he would have to phone me back. He phoned me back within 10 minutes and said yes," Leitao recalled.

The Irish had fooled everyone. For months the speculation was they would not sell. The fans opposed to Glazer were sure they would not. Some claiming to be in the know said they would not accept anything less than £3.50. The fans had assumed they had the power, but as Jim White, a biographer of the club, told me, they had followed a very flawed strategy:

> Shareholders United in their triumph [over Murdoch] assumed they had greater potential in stopping future takeovers than they did. The problem is, when Glazer came on the scene the assumption was, well we will do the same thing. We will organise the shareholders. Shareholders can stop him. The trouble is there was no other exterior element to Glazer's takeover. There was no competition element, no media involvement. It was a straightforward takeover so adopting a pure Shareholders United approach just was not going to work. He was going to outflank them. All he had to do was buy the Irish and he had bought the company. The Irish were solely interested in money. They were not interested in Manchester United. They had never been interested in Manchester United. The trouble was the Irish had absolutely no sympathy whatsoever with the Manchester United supporters. Because Manchester United supporters had taken Ferguson's side over the racehorse.

And to make matters worse it was soon clear that Ferguson liked the new owners. Indeed he preferred them to Martin Edwards and the entire plc structure. In his programme notes for United's first Premier League match of the Glazer era, against Aston Villa on August 20, 2005, Ferguson wrote:

Joel, Avran and Bryan Glazer were all in the directors' box at the Debreceni game [a qualifying game for the Champions League, which United won 3–0] and were treated with the respect they are entitled to as owners and directors of the club. I am sure all they ask is for our massive support to keep an open mind on their stewardship and give them a chance.

Not long after this, John Cassidy of *The New Yorker* went to Carrington to interview Ferguson and wrote:

Last summer he laughed off suggestions that he should resign in sympathy with the supporters' protests against the Glazers. "Prior to the club going plc, that is when the fans should have complained, but they didn't," he told me. "They maybe thought it was going into the hands of the fans but you know fine well when you put a club into a plc anybody can buy it. I don't understand why there is so much emotion now." I asked Ferguson whether the Glazers had offered advice about how to run the team. "I think they are expecting me to come up with the ideas," he snapped. "I've been here for 19 years, you know." Chelsea now have two players for each of the 11 positions on the team plus a couple of talented back-ups to the back-ups. Ferguson conceded that United couldn't match Abramovich's spending. "I don't think we can afford that, to be honest with you," he said. "We are working with a squad of about 19 or 20 players. In the past it was a bit bigger, but keeping a squad of more than 19 or 20 happy financially is very difficult. They are all on terrific salaries, so you try not to carry surplus players." Ferguson insisted that he had no intentions of resigning. "I'm not going to be here in 10 years, or anything," he told me. "But I'd like to see this side develop to its full potential."

There could not be a better insight into Ferguson's thinking and how his relationship with the Glazers was developing. This became most evident when for two weeks in November 2005, United faced a major crisis over Roy Keane which, as we have seen, led to his departure from the club. The affair dominated the headlines and there were questions raised about Ferguson's management style. During all this the Glazers said nothing. At the time there had been reports that United had been talking to Ottmar Hitzfeld as a replacement for Ferguson. Martin Samuel, in a *News of the World* piece headlined "Is anyone in charge at Old Trafford?", after observing that there was no word from the Glazers, wondered if it was the Glazers who had got in touch with Hitzfeld or Ferguson himself. Samuel was not being entirely serious, although his comments on the Glazers showed how the Glazer style of management was causing a problem for those used to the ways of English football. Samuel wrote:

> The day the Glazers bought United, Joel should have taken up residence in Manchester. He might have needed to do it behind several tons of reinforced concrete but it would at least have sent a message of professional intent, of hands-on management via something more meaningful than conference calls.

But that was not the Glazer way. Their PR insisted the family did not interfere in what Ferguson and Gill did. They were just happy to back their manager's judgement. This has remained their style and, apart from one interview Joel Glazer gave MUTV soon after the takeover, he has never spoken. And Ferguson's bond with them is as strong as ever. As Jim White put it to me:

> The Manchester United fans who oppose the Glazers' control of the club are dispirited that he gets on so well with Ferguson. But then the Glazers are terrified of him both physically and that he will do a runner and leave. That is why the Glazers are prepared to accept everything he does. Ferguson is obsessed with money. But at the end of the day he has always regarded himself as an employee. He wants to be nothing else. Unlike Terry Venables, he has never wanted to control the boardroom. His control of the players, the dressing room and the training ground gives him enough power over the boardroom. He did encourage the myth that he controlled the whole of Manchester United. That was never the case.

The fans opposed to the Glazers continue to hammer away at the cost of servicing the debts the Glazers incurred to buy the club. Shareholders United has transformed itself into Manchester United Supporters' Trust and is quick to react to any development that has any impact on the ownership of the club. They gleefully highlight how much money the Glazers have taken from the club as if this is yet more evidence of the sinful, un-English behaviour of these American foreigners.

Matters reached a finale when in January 2010 the club raised £504 million through a bond issue. This was meant to pay off nearly all the outstanding debts of £509 million the Glazers had incurred when buying the club. In the previous year to June 2009 the debts at the club's parent firm, Red Football Joint Venture, had risen to £716.5 million. The bond was sold in two tranches: £250 million with an interest rate to bond holders of 8.75 per cent, and another tranche of £276 million with an interest rate of 8.375 per cent, with the seven-year bonds maturing on February 1, 2017. The annual interest bill on the bonds was estimated to be £45 million, close to the £41.2 million in interest paid in the last financial year.

The Glazers could feel they had made a smart move. But the bond issue provoked a strong reaction and the hostile fans were afforded a glimmer of hope that the Glazers might be turfed out when soon afterwards the Red Knights, a consortium organised by high-profile City of London figures such as Jim O'Neill of Goldman Sachs and Mark Rawlinson of Freshfields made it known that they were willing to buy out the Glazers. Both are devoted United supporters. O'Neill had been on the board that had opposed the Glazer bid and Rawlinson had been the legal adviser to the board, helping fashion answers to various Glazer moves to take over the club. But the Glazers made it clear they were not interested in selling and as Keith Harris, who was also part of the Red Knights, admitted to me, they never made an offer or even had a meeting with them. The sticking point was the price. "The Glazers would want £1.5 billion," said Harris. "The Red Knights would have been prepared to go up to a billion." The Knights, according to Harris, had 30 eager investors, each prepared to contribute a minimum of £10 million. "They said, 'Yes, we'd like to be a part of this.' The Red Knights' interest in buying remains undiminished, but the Glazers gave very clear and loud signals that the business was not for sale. And for the time being that is the end of it."

Harris' involvement in the Red Knights venture showed how the role of Manchester United fans who are also prominent City figures have changed, as football has become more like a brand. Harris had long been a confidant of Martin Edwards and an even longer Manchester United fan. Brought up in Manchester, his father took him to Stockport County on Friday nights and United on Saturdays and he still recalls his first match just before Munich against Ipswich at home.

The Harris and Edwards families had old ties. Keith's father knew former United chairman Louis Edwards and had done business with him. The sons renewed this business relationship more than 30 years later when, following United's Stock Exchange flotation, Glenn Cooper, the merchant banker who had organised the float, took a group of City investors up to Old Trafford. Although the match, a 0–0 draw with Liverpool, was less than enthralling, what made Harris' day was that he had lunch in the boardroom with Sir Matt Busby. For a United fan this was like meeting the Creator. The friendship with Edwards that was formed as a result of this visit blossomed and Edwards discovered that he had much in common with Harris. Like him, Harris was a man with wide sporting interests — not for him the modern tribal love of only one club. He could appreciate other clubs and also took an interest in other sports, avidly following Lancashire cricket during the summer.

It was Harris who had been the conduit for the approach made by VCI, the video and publishing group, to buy United in the summer of 1996 at £2 a share. But then events intervened. On May 11, 1996, United beat Liverpool 1–0 in the FA Cup final to become the first team to do the double Double — twice. But although United had gone where no club had gone before, the stock market was not impressed and the share price moved hardly a jot. Yet soon after this the second television deal with Sky was agreed. Sky brushed aside, again with some help from Tottenham chairman Alan Sugar, rivals organised by Lord Hollick's United News and Media Group and a consortium led by Kelvin MacKenzie, then managing editor of Mirror Television, and Michael Green's Carlton. Sky, having paid £190 million in 1992 for five years, now agreed to televise 60 live games a season over the next four years for £670 million. These were undreamt of riches and Manchester United's share price, unmoved by Ferguson's achievements on the field, took off. This left VCI's approach for United dead in the water — they did not even bother to make a formal offer.

Nevertheless, such was the bond between Edwards and Harris, who was then chief executive of HSBC Investment Bank, that the latter was soon acting as an adviser to the club, monitoring and advising on potential United buyers. When Sky bid for United, Harris was on the side of the United board as they advised shareholders to accept the offer. Indeed, Edwards' first stop after his lunch with Mark Booth when told about the bid, was HSBC. At that stage Harris was anathema to the fans who opposed the bid.

"The fans," Harris admits, "took against me then. It was in part a lack of understanding of what is required of a financial adviser. It wasn't a question of, 'Oh, you've got to say no to this because you're a fan.' You can't do that. The duty of a financial adviser of a public company is to advise shareholders whether the terms that are offered are fair and reasonable. And the price of £650 million offered by BSkyB was a fair one, a huge offer."

Harris began to work his way back in with the fans when in 2005 he tried to stop the Glazer takeover by organising an alternative fans' buy-out with the help of investment bankers Nomura:

> On paper, something like 15 or 17 per cent of the shares were in the hands of fans, a mighty amount in terms of defending a takeover. But they were in the hands of thousands of supporters and a lot of them, to be blunt, wouldn't really understand the mechanics of the takeover. Although we

tried hard, against a public company takeover timetable, it just proved impossible. Had there been three or four major shareholders representing 10 or 15 per cent of shares, then something could have been done. Maybe.

But while Harris now cannot praise the fan groups organising the anti-Glazer protest enough, his advice to them is that, if they want the Glazers out, their protests must be more than just an emotional one:

> Waving the green and yellow colours of Newton Heath [which is how Manchester United started life in 1878] is very evocative. But do they persuade the owners that they ought to be selling? I would say categorically, no. If you are serious about change then you have to vote with your feet or your credit card. If you are a season-ticket holder and you don't renew, then you are protesting. Then you are hurting them and if you really want change, that's the way to do it.

But even if the Glazers were prepared to sell, was not the Red Knights' concept flawed, as David Gill, United's chief executive, suggested? How can any football club, let alone one the size of United, be run by a committee? Harris, surprisingly, agrees with Gill:

> No one can deny that. You can't have seven or eight people making decisions. What you can have is an agreement on policy issues. But nobody in the Red Knights' group suggested that David Gill should not be running the club after a takeover.

Yet a big problem for the Red Knights, or anybody wanting to take over, is the position of Ferguson and his closeness to the Glazers. When I raised this issue with Harris he grew very quiet, saying:

> Um, what you have to say is that Alex has been hugely successful and part of that success is being a very loyal, senior member of the team and you wouldn't expect anyone in his position to say anything different from what he said.

When I asked Harris if the Red Knights had tried speaking to Sir Alex directly, he responded:

> I don't really want to go down that path. Football clubs don't enjoy success

without a break — it has never happened. Manchester United's success in this era has lasted 17 years, which is longer than most. But clearly there is more competition coming, with Chelsea and Manchester City, and Alex has to contemplate retirement. The protest against the Glazers is about the debt they have put on the club and a fear over what happens tomorrow rather than a condemnation of what has been happening until now.

The Glazers could argue that while they may have incurred debt they have also transformed the business of the club — in other words, developed the brand better than any other club in England. One Englishman, Keith Wyness, the former chief executive of Everton agrees:

> The debt structure had been very dangerous. They had used quite complex financial models, complex derivatives and complex financial instruments, which the average man in the street, not just the average football fan, did not understand. They have been able to justify the debt. Through their own business acumen they have done a superb job in building the commercial revenue. Nobody can question that. The danger would have been had they not been able to build that successful revenue model as well as they have done. Then the debt could have sunk the club very quickly.

While the Glazers do not agree to be interviewed, people who have advised them do and in the words of Majid Ishaq, also a Manchester United season-ticket holder and a fan since 1976:

> The people who didn't want the Glazers in charge say the club is over-burdened with debt. Actually they are not over-burdened with debt. I will give you one very quick example. If Abramovich walks away from Chelsea tomorrow, they are doomed. And if the Glazers walk away from United tomorrow, United is a sustainable business. You haven't got an uneconomic club like Chelsea. Manchester City. If all of a sudden the wells dry up in Abu Dhabi, what is Sheik Mansour going to do? City is an unsustainable club at that point. Genuinely, if you sit back and say objectively, "Have the Glazers done a good job with United?" or "Has Abramovich done a good job with Chelsea?" Look at the statistics. When the Glazers took over United, Chelsea had won the league two years running. United hadn't got a sniff and everyone thought, the fans thought, we are doomed and therefore this debt burden will doom us even more. Since then, for Abramovich, what a bad investment. Look at how much

money he has put into the club and he has got three championships out of more than a billion pounds of investment, if not more actually because of the operating losses he has to fund. The proof is in the pudding here. Under the Glazers the club makes over £100 million and will probably make well over £100 million going into the future. It is leveraged at four and a half times [representing the amount of debt the Glazers have put on the club], including the PIKs [high-risk payment in kind loans]. It was 12 times so they brought the leverage down over time because the profits have gone up. That is a great place to be.

And even some of the Glazers' most trenchant critics agree. Andy Green, a City expert, started his Andersred blog just as the bond issue was announced. Subtitled, "trying to make sense of the Glazers, debt and football finance," it is probably the most trenchant analysis and commentary available on the complicated world of football and money. He has no love for the Glazers and in the 2010-11 season gave up his season ticket. But in his blog posting of February 21, 2012 Green, commenting on United's second-quarter results from September to December 2011, conceded:

Commercial income continues to grow very fast [up 13.4 per cent during the quarter vs. last year and up 17.7 per cent over the six months]. Much of this growth comes from the £10 million per annum DHL training kit deal. The club has also recently signed new deals with Bulgarian and Bangladeshi telecom operators. This strategy of finding a local telecom partner in a myriad of markets will eventually reach a natural end of course, but I must confess to having been too cautious on United's commercial growth. The "brand" has stretched far further than most observers [including this one] felt was possible. In total, revenue growth of 12 per cent in the first six months of the year is very impressive, even if the impact of the early Champions League exit is yet to be felt... Credit has to go to the club for once again boosting revenues in a tough economic climate. United [along with Real, Barcelona and Bayern] are one of the commercial giants of modern football. Much though it pains me to say it, the Glazers have overseen extraordinary commercial growth [this year commercial income will be more than 2.5 times the level the plc achieved in their best year]. The second half will see weaker media income as the CL [Champions League] exit bites, a timely reminder that on pitch success is never guaranteed.

But what Green argues is that the whole basis of the Glazer ownership means that United are no longer a "normal" football club. Writing in January 2012, he examined what United had done with the money they had received since 2009: £80 million for Ronaldo from Real Madrid, Aon's upfront payment of £35.9 million of their four-year sponsorship up front. These meant at the end of June 2011 the club had £151 million in cash. By September this cash pile had been reduced considerably. Some of it had gone on players — £47 million to buy Phil Jones, David de Gea and Ashley Young, although there were also player sales. It had also been used to pay interest and buy bank bonds.

> These bond purchases go to the heart of how the Glazers run Manchester United and how horribly different they are from other 'normal' clubs. At almost every other football club, any profits are reinvested. Real Madrid made a handsome pre-tax profit of €50 million in 2010-11 and spent every penny of it on transfers. That is not the way United are managed. Over the last two years the club chose to spend that £88 million on buying back bonds rather than on strengthening the squad. Just to be clear, there was no obligation to buy these bonds, it was a judgment made by the Glazers and their management team. The financial return on these bond buybacks is pretty good, with cash in the bank earning 1.5 per cent being used to buy bonds that cost the club 8.7 per cent in interest. But good financial sense is not always good sporting sense if money is diverted from the football club.

Then, after alleging that United did not buy players like Wesley Sneijder and Samir Nasri because they refused to meet their massive wage demands, he concludes:

> United are run not only to make a profit, that is just commonsense, but to maximise value for their owners. That means maximising profits and thus operating on a far lower budget than a club of United's scale can actually afford. In 2010–11, United made so much money that the club could have paid three new players the same wages as Rooney [around £140k a week] and still make EBITDA [cash profits] of £89 million. But making £89 million instead of the £111 million reported by the club would inevitably reduce the price that could be achieved in a listing on the Singapore Stock Exchange, or the value of any future sale to a sheik or oligarch. So the Glazers chose to restrict the wage bill to a level they were happy with and thus chose to make Sneijder unaffordable. Older Reds

will no doubt point out that this dance with the financial devil began when Edwards floated the club back in 1991, and there is much truth in that. The difference, however, is in the scale of impact on Manchester United. Across all the plc years, the total dividends paid were only £59 million. The total cost in interest, fees and debt repayment in the six and a half years of the Glazers is £480 million. So it doesn't really matter if we have about £60 million in the bank (we do). It's that unfortunately for us the club is run to make money for a distant family from Florida and they'll do what they want.

Glazer advisers would argue that this view is wrong. Such has been the Glazers' success that flotation is back on the agenda for football clubs, with the Glazers themselves floating the club. Having considered a Far East flotation, they decided to go for New York instead because of the lighter touch of the US regulators. In Hong Kong the Glazers could not get a waiver to have two classes of shares with different voting rights. In Singapore they might have had dual shares but delays in sanctioning it meant it did not work out. This opened the way to float in their homeland, giving the Glazer shares 10 votes apiece. Public investors, in contrast, receive one vote per share. And with United a controlled company it does not need to follow the New York stock exchange rule that requires a public company to have a board composed mainly of independent directors. The United board will remain as two Malcolm Glazer sons and two executives of the company.

As I write these lines, the timing of the floatation is uncertain because of the Eurozone crisis, and Manchester United Supporters' Trust have called for it to be replaced by a full floatation with one class of shares. Fans also criticised the potential benefits to the club's employees, provoking a strong denial from Ferguson that he stood to gain personally.

As to the general issue, Majid Ishaq says:

I can see that flotation circle coming back again for the big clubs, big brands that are doing big things. The bigger clubs are bigger than football. They have a brand which can be commercially exploited. Look at everything that United have been doing with their sponsorship deals. That creates revenue and income streams. Because the consequence of being taken private and being owned by an individual is at some stage that individual will sell. So you either find another big benefactor, or you float the club. You could still have control. Now could I see a potential for flotation? Yeah, because football has now become a global game, global TV audiences, global media and commercial opportunities, and when I say "media" I am not talking about TV. I am talking about mobile, the internet, all of that. It is just very different. You could float the Champions League. The competition of the Champions League, like Formula One, can be a floated entity. The reason why you can float it is if you look at the Champions League they sell the TV package, they have a bunch of sponsors, Heineken, Ford, Sony, who pay multi-million euros for those deals. You could float that as an entity because the TV audiences it gets around the world are absolutely huge. What are the guys at Liverpool ultimately going to do with Liverpool? If you tell me Liverpool have 300 million fans, that's 300 million customers I can target if I am selling this particular beer. Likewise with the 500 million or 600 million United have. It is a different game.

For these Americans, who include Randy Lerner at Aston Villa, brought up in the very regulated American sporting market, English football provided an opportunity they did not have at home. As Ishaq admits:

If you speak to the Americans they say, "We understand how to make money in a very regulated industry in the States in this space. Within our territory, within our geography." But that is very tightly controlled in a way that American society is not tightly controlled. Then all of a sudden you say to them, "You can come over to England and you can sell Liverpool shirts in London, you can sell sponsorship in the Far East." They say, "My goodness. I can make money out of this because if I can do it in the US in a very regulated market and then all of a sudden I have got the rest of the world to go for when I go and buy Liverpool or Tottenham or Arsenal." They love it. The Henrys of Boston who own Liverpool can't sell outside Boston, can they? They are regulated. So those guys, the American sports business owners, bring two things. They bring capital, but not that much of it, and they bring sports business acumen.

Yet the question remains, should the English football authorities and the British government allow such a free-for-all? The Glazers could not have bought an NFL or Major League Baseball (MLB) or NBA franchise in their own country as they acquired Manchester United. The American sporting model is very different to the one in England, and in essence the Americans run what they call sporting socialism. The clubs in the league see themselves as a chain of restaurants where every restaurant in the chain must be given equal rights to prosper. There may be no promotion or relegation but the bottom club in the league gets the first pick of next year's college players. Moreover, the NFL, MLB and other leagues vet any possible buyers and the existing clubs meet and vote to decide whether a new owner can be accepted. Such restrictions would be unthinkable in England. Such restrictions would be unthinkable in England where the Premier League proudly announce that they are owner neutral. In other words, anyone can own a Premiership club.

However, the Americans' arrival in English football, and certainly the way the Glazers funded their purchase, has convinced one Englishman that the authorities in England have got it wrong. For this man, who made money out of the game and played a crucial role in the formation of the Premier League, the Glazer takeover violates every principle of football ownership:

When you consider the Glazers, they did nothing. What they did was in the boom days when you could go and borrow anything, they borrowed £600–700 million for a takeover bid for Manchester United. Merchant banker, financial advisers, lawyers, all got their fees. They all must have made five million quid in fees throughout the whole thing. These Glazers don't care because it's OPM — other people's money. You have a fee for recommending this deal, you climb on board. The advisers get their money. The Glazers don't care, the Glazers will borrow a little bit more. This is just a transaction for them. And if the market would have gone on like this, some other nutter would have come along, convinced another bank to give them a billion pounds and they would just do a transaction where the same advisers, accountants and lawyers would still cop their five million here and there and the Glazers would walk away with a net £100–200 million. That's the Glazers for you, right. And to a certain extent maybe the people who bought Liverpool [Gillett and Hicks] had the same thing in mind. We've seen Manchester United, we've seen Liverpool, we've seen Aston Villa, we've seen Manchester City, being bought by outside institutions, if you like, for the wrong reason. The purpose of buying a football club is not really because of the passion for the game of football in England, for the development of the game of football in England. The sole purpose is, they're buying a franchise which one day they hope to sell on to someone else, it's just a commodity for them. Should that be allowed?

The voice belongs to that of Alan Sugar. There is one man Sugar would exempt from this foreign ownership and it is, interestingly, the Chelsea owner:

Abramovich, with all of his money, I would say is about the only genuine one I would welcome to the market, and you know why? Because it's his money. He had this mad idea of buying a football club and came, put his own money down, bosh, and he bought Chelsea Football Club.

Sugar's praise of Abramovich, and criticism of the Glazers, ignores the Majid Ishaq point that should the Russian walk away it is hard to see Chelsea not face a situation similar to Glasgow Rangers while the Americans have run a very tight and successful business at Old Trafford. And, the businessmen turned television star admits his critics could have a right go at him:

> What's he banging on about, that Sugar? He put £8 million of his own money into Tottenham and in the end he walked away with 50 million quid. But that is not the reason I came into football. I'm an anomaly, I'm an oddball. In the past it was the local butcher, baker, candlestick maker, who helped and supported their local football club and in some cases people came into football because they wanted the glamour and it got them the publicity. But I was already the so-called City blue-eyed boy from Amstrad. I didn't need to go into football to elevate myself. This was a local thing and the first purpose was to rescue the club out of the financial mess, which is what we did. Then, of course, it was really to try and go forward and to win things. That's why I did it, OK, and hand on heart I didn't do it to make money because I had already made millions and millions of pounds, right? When I went in there I couldn't lose my instincts of a businessman. I did sell it for a profit. I left because I got beaten up, I got completely sick and ill over it and my wife and family said to me, get out, get out. Nothing would have delighted me more for the team to be successful and grow and plough all the money back into it. But life was not good for me in football.

His wider question remains:

> In America, the Americans have had the foresight of saying no foreign owners of media. Rupert Murdoch had to change his nationality in order for him to acquire media assets there. The Football Association may in its wisdom many years ago have said no foreign ownership of football clubs.

Sugar is not an isolated voice on this issue. Gordon Taylor, chief executive of the Professional Players Association, told me:

I've always felt that when the foreign owners came to United and Liverpool buying through big debt leverage, it was really important for the Premier League to say "Excuse me, if a club is being bought on such a mountain of debt, isn't that a possible recipe for disaster for the future?" But the policy is, well, if it happens, it happens. In a way, once clubs went public that was the price of capitalism. That suddenly if somebody comes in to take you over and the shareholders want to sell and make a lot of money, that's the price that you pay. It is different to Jack Walker who took Blackburn, and its a local club, on a magic carpet ride and for a time Elton John did it at Watford. Sir Jack Hayward tried to do it at Wolves and it is like a rich uncle looking after things.

But is not Sheikh Mansour at Manchester City a rich modern, albeit Arab, uncle to City fans? Many fans may feel that, although one of its most famous, the author Colin Shindler, does not and has given up on his old club because of the foreign association. And City's success has been enormously helped by a curious by product of the British belief in the free for all.

The day before Manchester City won the 2012 title — becoming only the fifth club to win the Premier League — Francis Lee, the electric City forward who had scored the goal when the club last won the title back in 1968, was in a reflective mood. However, he did not so much talk of his playing days but his contribution to City's success when he was club chairman for five years from 1994, in particular a deal that paved the way to the takeover by Sheikh Mansour and ultimate success.

The club that Lee had returned to had fallen so far behind its great rivals Manchester United that they often could not even dream of competing in the same league. Lee confessed that when he became chairman, "The club were completely bankrupt. They were really dark days." For the supporters, these dark days had stretched back two decades but Lee headed a consortium that held out immense promise: the club controlled by players who had provided glory on the field, flotation off the field following the Tottenham model, the dream of City once again competing with United and for fans the ultimate pleasure of seeing the end of the hated Peter Swales regime.

Peter Swales, who had been in charge of the club at the start of the Premiership, was, if not quite the classical butcher or candlestick maker who owned English clubs, very much a local businessman, his trade being the electrical industry. Through the '60s and '70s, he had presided over both the rise and fall of the club. Having won the title in 1968, it was Manchester's leading club, finishing ahead of United for six of seven years during the 1970s. But after City were relegated in 1982–83, the Swales era ended in misery although this did not come about until two years after the start of the Premiership. By then Swales had been subject to much abuse by the fans, and even his aged mother was not left alone. However in the style that has often characterised modern English football, when in May 1996, the week before City went down to the second tier yet again, Swales died aged 62, a broken man, the fans observed a minute's silence. This was as if to say that even if he had been the devil now that he was dead he was due some respect.

Yet for all the hype that attended the Lee takeover, his era did not mark a return to glory. Indeed, that period for many City fans was most memorable for a match in 1999, which perfectly summed up the position the club then occupied in Manchester. That was the year Manchester United won the treble. For City fans, the joy was winning the promotion play-off against Gillingham. I was made very aware of this when talking to Will Greenwood. He needs no introduction to English rugby fans as an iconic member of the team that won England its only oval ball World Cup in 2003. For many English rugby fans their abiding memory is of Greenwood sinking to his knees minutes after Johnny Wilkinson kicked for glory in Sydney.

Yet when I spoke to him in 2010 he made it very clear to me that that day in Sydney was nothing compared to the Gillingham match. Millions of English rugby fans might have given anything to be in Greenwood's shoes in Sydney. But Greenwood, himself, would give all that he has, including his World Cup medal, for being in a Manchester City shirt in June 1999 playing at Wembley:

> People tell me of watching the 2003 final. You can keep the World Cup final. I have never watched it again. My favourite moment in sport is City vs. Gillingham, 1999 Wembley. 2–0 up, Gillingham took off Asaba, they thought they had the game won. Then Kevin Horlock scores and Dickov nets and we win on penalties. The place was going mental. I was hugging men I had never met before. I went through every single emotion in the course of 130 minutes that day and I would give my right hand to live that day again.

Now this may be dismissed as the sort of whimsy a man who had created sporting glory for millions can afford. It also may illustrate the different emotional experience of a sporting legend compared to a sporting follower. Greenwood's wider experiences of life has also meant he can place sporting pressure in context. As he told me, "Pressure is when the Bundesbank has cut interest rates, you are on the trading floor and are not expecting it. That is proper panic. Phone ringing, orders needed, everybody going mad. Forget about the drop goal [by Johnny Wilkinson that won England the final]. Jesus, that is like a walk in the park. The World Cup Final is easy compared to a trading floor."

But Greenwood's sentiments are shared by many a City fan. And it was this club that Thaksin Shinawatra, the disgraced Thai prime minister convicted of corruption in his homeland and living in self-imposed exile in the Middle East, took over in June 2007. The first of the foreign owners of the club, Thaksin had been looking for an English club for years, having fallen in love with the Premiership when he was owner of television rights in Thailand. He had failed to buy Fulham and Liverpool before being offered Manchester City for around £60 million and snapped it up. It may seem strange that he should buy a club which had achieved nothing for nearly four decades and had finished 15th and 16th in 2006 and 2007. But Manchester City had one big advantage over Liverpool and Fulham. And this is where we come to the contribution that Lee claimed he made off the field for his club's ultimate success. Lee's claims to be the deal maker could be disputed by David Bernstein, now chairman of the Football Association. It saw Manchester City move from Maine Road, its historic ground, to the City of Manchester stadium. The wider question is who paid for this new City stadium.

The stadium had been constructed for the 2002 Commonwealth Games with public money: £78 million from Sport England and £49 million from Manchester Council. But the authorities, anxious not to have a white elephant on their hands after the games, decided the best option was to rent the 48,000 seat stadium to Manchester City. In return for that, Manchester City gave Maine Road to the council. They also paid £15 million to rip off the running track and convert the Commonwealth Games arena for football. But the best part was the outrageously favourable deal on the rent: a small yearly rent which only became substantial if more than 36,000 turned up for a match. This meant that the club paid between £1.4 million and £2.5 million a year in rent for seven years between 2003 and 2010.

For this the club got a state-of-the-art stadium. Arsenal's Emirates stadium cost £440 million and landed the Gunners with debts of £250 million. Manchester is not London, but a new stadium of the standard Manchester City got could well have cost the club a few hundred million, if in the first place they could have managed to borrow the money.

Lee has no doubts what the move to the new stadium did, "The new stadium made it attractive for people to buy into it." It was certainly the carrot as far as Thakshin was concerned. Years later, explaining to American professor Tom Plate why he chose Manchester City, a club and a city with which he had no known connections, Thakshin said, "Manchester City is a team with good fans and good infrastructure. It's not too difficult to improve."

Observe the word "infrastructure". This makes it very clear the City of Manchester stadium was crucial to the deal. He could hardly have said good infrastructure if City was still playing at Maine Road. Thakshin's year at City saw no major changes, unless bringing Sven-Goran Eriksson is considered a master move. Thaksin appears to have seen it as something enjoyable to do while in exile; sitting in the directors box ranked along with playing golf. It was something to take his mind off as he endlessly plotted a return to power in his native land.

A year after he had bought it, he found the Bank of Thailand had frozen his assets. Had they not done so he would probably still be enjoying owning Manchester City. Instead, he sold it to another foreigner, Sheikh Mansour of the royal family of Abu Dhabi for a reported £150 million, making a profit of £90 million. The new owners had money, knew they would not have to build a stadium, unlike rivals such as Liverpool, and the purchase fitted in neatly with their plans to promote their state. This deal for a Premiership club had come in what may be called the third phase of Arab investment in Western assets.

The first phase in the 1970s had seen the Arabs give money to western investment banks to invest on their behalf. The second phase, in late 1980s early 1990s had involved buying financial stakes in institutions. The third phase started in the early part of the new century, with another oil boom, and saw investment in companies like P & O with the Arab investors also putting in their own management teams as part of their investments. Abu Dhabi's investment horizons had also expanded after the death of the conservative and cautious ruler, Sheikh Zayed who ruled both UAE and Abu Dhabi. Younger, more energetic, dynamic men had emerged and they were tired of being outpaced by Dubai, especially since Dubai did not have oil and had to be rescued by Abu Dhabi after the crash of 2008.

Sheikh Mansour has never told the world why he bought City. According to City chairman Khaldoon Al Mubarak, who has given the odd interview, the Sheikh is an astute businessman who believes, "You can create a valuable proposition in football that has not yet been accomplished." Al Mubarak, who also heads the country's Executive Affairs Authority and has a role in making sure Abu Dhabi conveys the right image to the world, sees owning the club as bridge building between the Arab world and the West. There has certainly been no lack of money to build this particular bridge.

City's rise to supremacy in the four stewardship by Abu Dhabi has seen a total spent of £1.5 billion. Apart from the millions to Shinawatra, there has been £398 million on transfers, £589.8 million on wages and £210 million on other expenses such as travel and administration. Yet not a penny has had to be spent on acquiring a new stadium which would have been the case had Manchester City still been at Maine Road. For new owners like the Americans in Liverpool, a new stadium is always the biggest headache. Abu Dhabi did have to pay more in rent when the lease was revised in 2010–2011 and the stadium was renamed after the country's airline Etihad. The naming meant that the unsuspecting public might think this was a stadium owned by the club. In reality, the club continued to rent but started paying a single fixed sum, which goes up in line with inflation with additional payments linked to City's participation in European competition. Estimated rental receipts for the five years from 2011–12 are £20 million. The figure is a substantial increase on the figure Lee and Bernstein negotiated and the council makes much of club's commitment to helping regenerate one of the most deprived in the city. But all this cannot deny a quite remarkable fact about the champions of England ——that it is a club owned by a foreign state yet the stadium in which it plays has been funded by British tax and rate payers and is owned by the local council. In other words, the British have funded a vehicle for a foreign state.

Of course, when the stadium deal was done, Manchester City was not owned by Thaksin or Mansour, but given that public money was involved, why were restrictions not put on any future sale of the club? Why should British public money fund what is meant to promote the goals of a foreign country?

But for those who run the Premiership there is no fault with this. So David Richards, chairman of the Premier League argues that the arrival of such people should be welcomed:

> Roman Abramovich brought another dimension to the game. He brought super, super stars. He has done a fantastic job. He changed the title run. Now you have got Manchester City. It is good, it gives people hope. Sheikh Mansour has taken Manchester City to a totally different dimension to what anybody would have perceived Manchester City to be. It has made the League better.

Richards does distinguishes between, as he puts it, "people like myself, people like David Gill, Phil Garside [chairman of Bolton], these people are custodians of the game. We have to look after the game. As much as it is a job, this has been entrusted to us, to look after it, to make it better, develop the product. We are not like owners of football like Roman Abramovich. He is not a custodian. He is an actual owner. He entrusts people like Bruce Buck to look after it. He is a custodian. He has to look after the football and make it as good and as secure as it can. But at the same time try and make the business as good as it can."

Here, it is fascinating to compare the very different public faces of the owners of Chelsea and Manchester City. Abramovich, like Mansour, may not give interviews but he is seen at every Chelsea game. And as Chelsea won the 2012 Champions League beating Bayern Munich television cameras focussed on him, commenting how he was like any other fan following the game from a seat surrounded by other fans. The pictures also provided worldwide audiences a glimpse of his various moods, just like any other fan: his anguish as Chelsea conceded a penalty in extra time, his joy as it was saved and his elation as Didier Drogba scored from the final penalty to win the match. In contrast, Mansour has only been once at City and was not there on the final Sunday of the 2012 season when City won the title after 44 years. The whole world seemed to be there but not the owner whose money had made it possible. All we know is what Al Mubarak has said that Mansour is a huge football fan who follows the club from his home on television. He has always wanted to own an European club and make it a world beater. Even if we assume this passion is genuine it still leaves unanswered Sugar's wider question for English football. The English may have created a worldwide football brand but should English rules or lack of them allow foreigners to exploit them?

The 20th year of the Premier League did provide a new foreign owner who was different. This was Anton Zingarevich, son of Boris, who had looked at Everton and then decided not to buy it. Anton bought Reading just as the Championship club were heading for the Premier League. The same man, investment manager Christopher Samuelson, who had brought Everton to the attention of his father, also introduced Reading to Zingarevich. Despite the approach being made in December, the sale was only concluded at the end of May, six weeks after Reading won promotion. Then, with the club valued at £30 million, Zingarevich bought 51 per cent from Sir John Majedski with an option to buy the remaining 49 per cent next year.

What makes the younger Zingarevich different is that unlike Abramovich, Sheik Mansour or the Glazers, he has not taken the vow of a Trappist monk. In his first interview with the British media, Zingarevich frankly spelt out to me, in fluent English, the hard-nosed business ideas that prompted him to buy the Royals:

> I love the sport but not just the game, everything to do with the business as well. There is tremendous opportunity in terms of the growth of the business side of it. We see it with a new Premiership TV deal. There are

25 million homes watching the Premier League in England and there are 500 million around the world. So definitely the international TV rights should bring much more than the English domestic rights.

To me, the Premier League is similar to what happened to the NFL. In America the clubs weren't really worth anything. Then suddenly, with the TV rights coming in, basically, the least valued club there is worth $1 billion. It became a business overnight and, in the Premier League with the volume of money involved, it has became a business.

With a degree in finance, Zingarevich has a vision of the Royals as the new West of England giant. "We don't want to consider ourselves as a Reading club. We want to consider ourselves as a Thames Valley club." That name was the one Robert Maxwell chose for his ill-fated plan back in the 1980s to merge Reading with Oxford. However, Zingarevich's vision is very different. It is to make Reading "basically the premier club west of London. If you look west of London, there is not a single Premier League club. We have great potential there in terms of supporter base. The opportunity for me is through Oxfordshire down to Bristol. That is what attracted me to Reading in the first place."

It helped that Zingarevich knew the Reading area, having studied for his A-levels at Bearwood College in Berkshire. This made him aware that "there is a huge amount of companies that are based there. Definitely this should help with the sponsorship and hospitality and bring in a lot of revenue. I see a lot of potential there."

Interestingly, Reading's location close to Heathrow also played a part. "In player negotiations, it tends to provide a bonus once you go against other clubs. For players who are not from England, it's easier for them to get all their relatives or friends. I'm not saying Heathrow was a decider in buying Reading but that was one of the factors for sure."

Not that the Russian ownership means we are going to see players jetting into Heathrow from all over the world to join Reading in the way they have done at Chelsea or Manchester City. Zingarevich candidly admitted: "Because of UEFA's financial fair play rules that are coming in [intended to limit clubs' debts], you can't just go and do another Manchester City any more. Plus that's not what I want to do."

Reading have to survive in the Premier League but this survival strategy is part of a five-year plan for the club. "It is to become a top 10 Premier League club. I think that we can definitely achieve that."

This will involve, he revealed, "linking up with clubs round the world and forming partnerships". But when I asked if this will involve Russian clubs, the man whose first love is his hometown club, Zenit St Petersburg, he quickly interjected: "Not Russia but maybe India, China, Africa and there's a big opportunity in Europe. We will build our academy, not just domestically but internationally as well. The key is to improve the infrastructure of the club."

This could mean a new training ground, an academy that can "accommodate youth coming from other places" and plans to increase the 25,000 capacity of the Madejski stadium to 35,000 or even more. "Look at Man United, where they started and where they ended up with their stadium. I'm not saying we're going to end up the same. But we'll be doing it in a similar way, gradually. We need to make sure that we increase the supporter base so we can enlarge the stadium and that's going to help our bottom line revenue figures."

To conclude the deal, Zingarevich also had to strike an understanding with the Premier League, as part of the fit and proper person test for club owners. The Football League had originally looked at it with the Russians supplying the necessary paperwork. But when Reading got promoted they said the Premier League would have to pass judgement and after the file was passed to them it led to a meeting with Richard Scudamore, the League chief executive and his team. Zingarevich recalled, "He wasn't really open. He was a little bit surprised seeing a young person come in. He didn't know what to expect."

At one stage during the meeting Scudamore looked across at Zingarevich and Christopher Samuelson who had accompanied him and said, "Everything seems in order. We have written to the Home Office to make sure you are able to come to this country and once we get that we can approve the takeover." This quite surprised Zingarevich, who has been coming to this country for over a decade from his base in Moscow and a visa has never been an issue for him.

Then Zingarevich revealed how Blackburn's relegation after a troubled 18 months under the control of Indian company Venky's may have held up his own takeover:

> The impression I got was that Scudamore and the Premier League were concerned about the Blackburn experience. They wanted to know whether an agent had any control over Reading. I was able to explain to Scudamore what I was trying to achieve. Then he felt more comfortable and we got along.

But the intriguing question left unanswered is whether the money for Reading has come from Anton or his father Boris. The Zingarevich family fortune is estimated at £460 million with Boris, who was a trade union leader under communism, becoming a successful paper and pulp businessman after the collapse of the Soviet Union. For the first time, Anton became a little hesitant, "I don't really want to say whose money it is." But he added, "It's money that I myself have put into the club. I have business of my own: infrastructure construction. But we always, of course, operate as a family, working on corporate strategy in terms of our family business."

The answer suggests this is essentially a family investment — through the Gibraltar-based Thames Sports Investment (TSI) — supervised by Anton. His father, he admitted, "is a kind of a football follower but he doesn't really get involved too much." In contrast, Zingarevich notes that "football takes up too much of my time but it does make me relax."

Chapter 11
THE NEW MONEY CASTES

In 1992–93, as the Premier League season ended with Manchester United winning the title and celebrating their first success in the top flight for 26 years, Wigan Athletic finished second from bottom of Division Two of the Football League, what would have been division three in the undivided Football League. They had 41 points and only Chester City kept them from the bottom rung of 24, although Wigan could say a founding member of the old Football League, Preston North End, was not far above them, having got 47 points and finished 21st.

Wigan that season had been watched by an average crowd of 2,598, which meant in terms of attendance they had finished bottom of their league. Their income, excluding transfers, was £598,000, which made them the second lowest earners in that division, second only to Hull, whose income that season was £421,000. With a net player spend of £20,000 they made a loss of £219,000 and had to borrow, which meant interest payments of £49,000.

Manchester United, in contrast, had a turnover of just over £25 million and after a net spent of nearly £4 million on transfers still made a profit of £4.2 million. It had spent nearly £9 million on its stadium and had authorised and contracted more than £2 million of capital expenditure. Wigan's spend on stadium and other capital commitments, contracted or authorised, was nil.

These figures shows that even as the Premier League celebrated its first birthday there were huge gaps in wealth between the top and the bottom, a legacy of the situation developing for many decades in English football. What the wealth brought by television and sponsorship has done is further widen this gap between the have-nots and haves, but the Premier League could argue it always gives the have-nots a chance to get into the haves league.

Indeed it is worth dwelling on the old third division because 11 of the 24 teams then in that division have risen to the Premier League in the last 20 years: Blackpool, Bolton, Bradford, Burnley Fulham, Hull, Reading, Stoke,

Swansea West Bromwich and Wigan with Bolton, Fulham, Stoke, Swansea, West Bromwich and Wigan still there and joined by Reading for the 2012–13 season. Stoke, which finished as champions of the old third division, could claim they attracted better support than many of the clubs in the Premier League. That 1992–93 season, their average attendance of 16,579 was almost double that of Wimbledon and higher than Southampton, Coventry, Norwich, Blackburn, QPR, Oldham and Crystal Palace, all of whom were part of the inaugural Premier League season. Stoke made it to the Premier League in 2008 under the ownership of Peter Coates, who had bought the club from an Icelandic consortium. Since then the club have been sustained in the top flight by this rich benefactor, the club being a subsidiary of Bet365, the online gambling company owned by Coates and his family. This allowed the club in the seasons beginning in 2009 and 2010 to outspend most other clubs in the Premier League, and in the 2009–10 season they could afford to spend as much as 76 per cent of their income on wages.

Wigan, which ensured their survival in the Premier League in the penultimate match of the 2011–12 season by relegating Blackburn, has since 1995 been owned by another rich home-grown businessman, Dave Whelan. A former Blackburn player, he and his family are worth £537 million, according to the 2012 *Sunday Times* rich list and based in a town more noted for rugby than football it has come a long way since that inaugural Premier League season. The end of the 2011 season showed Wigan's income had risen to £50.5 million, their wage bill alone was £39.94 million. This was still far behind Manchester United's income of £331.44 million and wages of £152.915 million but Wigan could argue that the gap was greater when the new league was born. In that first year, United's income was 50 times that of Wigan, but now it was only 6.6 times.

Unlike many other clubs such as Bradford and even Hull who declined alarmingly after their moment of glory, Wigan have more than just survived. Wigan's wage bill is not as tightly controlled as Manchester United. Since the days of Martin Edwards, United have rigorously stuck to 50 per cent or lower. In 2011, while the Glazer-owned club spent 46 per cent of their income on salaries, Wigan spent over 79 per cent of the club's income on salaries. In 2011, Whelan converted loans of £48 million he had given the club into equity in anticipation of the sale he is said to be planning, but what all this also shows is Wigan have learnt how not to be an outcast in a Premier League which has specialised in creating a new system of castes.

In essence, the Premier League has developed several ownership castes. The much talked-about division may be between clubs' home-grown owners and foreigners. But that is too simple a distinction. More interesting is to see foreign owners who have acquired Premier League clubs because they see it as a brand they can exploit, the owners of Manchester United, Liverpool, Aston Villa and Arsenal clearly falling into that category. So does Tottenham owner Joe Lewis, who may be from England but is based in the Bahamas and in the financial sense must be considered foreign. In this caste there is a sub-caste of clubs led by Manchester United, but including Arsenal and Tottenham, who make sure they manage their business from the revenues the generate. As this is being written it is too early to say whether Liverpool will turn out to be a foreign club who are well managed, but the signs from the 2011–12 season were not encouraging.

Then there are two special castes of foreign owners: Abramovich and Sheikh Mansour who are happy to bankroll success whatever it costs. But the Premier League years have also had a caste of rich home-grown benefactors. And here we have a great Premier League contradiction. Despite the vast glut of television money flowing into the Premier League (see table on following page), a whole host of clubs which still have to be bankrolled by their owners, with the singular exception of Everton. Andy Green, a Manchester United supporter and a financial expert, calls this the "squeezed middle" whose reliance on their owners in the last six years makes fascinating reading.

The club that stands out, of course, is Everton. The club has had no owner money in this period, with the chairman Bill Kenwright making no secret of trying to find an owner with deep pockets. That it should still have enjoyed relative success in the Premier League is a testament to the managerial skill of David Moyes, who on this reckoning must be considered the wonder worker of the League.

In that period, owners at Bolton, Fulham, Newcastle and Sunderland have put in considerable sums of money. When the Premier League was formed, both Newcastle and Sunderland could claim they were caught on the wrong side of history. They were clubs with great footballing histories and despite being outside the new league their support meant that they were bigger than many of the clubs who kicked off the first Premier League season. In 1992–93 Newcastle, who finished as champions of the newly created First Division, attracted an average crowd of 29,018, while Sunderland, who finished 21st in a 24-team league, attracted 17,258. Only Liverpool, Manchester United and Aston Villa in the Premier League had bigger crowds that season, with St James' Park easily surpassing Tottenham, Arsenal, Everton, three of the then so-called Big Five, and also Chelsea and Manchester City.

Revenue, Cashflow and Financing
2005–06 to 2010–11 Cumulative Figures in £'000s

	Everton	Bolton	Villa	Fulham	Sunderland	Newcastle	West Ham	Blackburn
Revenue	425,951	353,674	395,414	314,496	338,755	496,483	430,090	309,359
Staff costs	-281,279	-241,674	-326,601	-257,759	-242,265	-326,724	-316,071	-253,141
Other operating costs	-117,752	-129,471	-120,732	-83,191	-82,007	-145,280	-117,280	-56,193
EBITDA	26,920	-17,527	-48,345	20,532	14,483	24,479	-3,261	25
Operating cashflow	**39,317**	**-15,229**	**-12,266**	**19,717**	**18,344**	**-33,621**	**15,129**	**-699**
Cash interest	-21,296	-16,524	-10,365	-11,635	-15,679	-21,227	-15,868	-5,343
Cashflow before investment	18,020	-31,753	-22,631	8,082	2,665	-54,848	-740	-6,042
Net transfer spend	-48,795	-42,134	-108,906	-54,998	-103,221	-35,349	-53,785	-12,001
Cashflow before financing	**-24,770**	**-82,620**	**-171,025**	**-56,911**	**-104,254**	**-96,410**	**-62,366**	**-22,633**
Owner financing	-	99,000	163,781	72,346	107,805	140,000	3,000	5,000
Wages + transfers	-330,074	-283,808	-435,507	-312,757	-345,486	-362,073	-369,856	-265,142

Source: The andersred blog, http://andersred.blogspot.com/

The story of the four other clubs in the table show the promise the Premier League offers and how these clubs have struggled to reach the promised land. Fulham is almost a classic illustration of this. For years this was a club in a London residential area with a certain maverick charm that made them quite unique in English football. Having started life as a Sunday School team in 1879, with worshippers from St Andrew's Church in West Kensington, Fulham can claim to be the oldest football club in London, formed 26 years before their neighbours Chelsea. Few clubs can boast such a charming location as Craven Cottage, originally a Royal Hunting Lodge, with one side of the ground bordering the river Thames. The club's footballing history has further emphasised their charm. So while they have won no honours they have attracted some great players. One of their owners, the comedian Tommy Trinder, made football history by making Johnny Haynes the first £100 a week player when the maximum wage was abolished. Several other great names have played for the club including Jimmy Hill, Bobby Robson, Bobby Moore and George Best.

Like many English football clubs, they were located in the middle of a residential area but one which was going upmarket over the years and Fulham's ground has often been more valuable than the club's playing staff. So in 1984, Fulham chairman Ernie Clay, having failed in his attempt to develop Craven

Cottage, sold off the ground to property developer Marler Estates. The club had paid a peppercorn rent to the previous landlords, the Church Commission, and the new rents paid to Marler had a significant impact on club finances. In early 1987, Fulham nearly went out of business and a proposed merger with QPR to become Fulham Park Rangers was only prevented by widespread protests by fans and the arrival of new chairman Jimmy Hill and his new board of directors in April 1987.

A decade later, Mohamed Al-Fayed, then the owner of Harrods, arrived and with the Premier League now an established reality, painted the club in suitably gaudy colours. The previous year Fulham had dropped down to the basement of the Football League. Indeed, in 1996, many Fulham fans feared the club might not survive. In January that year the club travelled to Torquay United, who were bottom of the entire League. Fulham, second from bottom, lost in what the club website calls "the blackest day in the entire history of the club". A year later, having won promotion to the second division, Fayed spotted Fulham as the club he could develop into the Harrods of football, or as he liked to put it the Manchester United of the south. His initial managerial team was Kevin Keegan and Ray Wilkins and there would be other changes before Fulham under former France midfielder Jean Tigana reached the Premier League in the 2001–02 season.

Al-Fayed submitted a planning application which would have dramatically increased the size and structure of Craven Cottage. The plans would have turned the stadium into the size of Harrods with 30 flats, a conference centre, shops and restaurants. The club cannot expand its grounds as the four sides are flanked by the park, a block of flats, the river and houses. So in order to achieve this major expansion the stadium would have had to be built up to an enormous height, depriving some neighbouring houses of sunlight.

This proved too much for the local community, who felt the proposed new structure would alter the neighbourhood, which by now had been designated a Conservation Area. The result was the Fulham Alliance, formed with the aim of stopping the development. This pressure group was keen to stress that they were not opposed to the club or football — they were merely fighting to retain their unique quiet residential area. Although many of the members of this organisation were Fulham supporters, it inevitably created friction between residents and fans.

It was not just the immediate local residents who would have been affected; there was the whole issue of the river. Not only would it be the first on the Thames development to actually hang out over the river, but in order to have sufficient space at ground level, it would have to encroach and occupy some of the foreshore. Flooding in London is always a concern and to compensate for loss of some of the river, a separate planning application had to be submitted to the Borough of Hounslow to shrink Duke's Meadow — an attractive bit of river frontage upstream. The residents of Hounslow were not amused to find that their green space was to be shrunk to increase the volume of water being taken from the river by Fulham. Suddenly it was not just the residents of Fulham who were getting up in arms but also those of the neighbouring area of Putney on the other side of the river. Would such a large stadium affect the migrating birds visiting the Wetlands Trust at Barnes? This stretch of the river is one of the few sections of the River Thames suitable for competitive sailing. The local sailing clubs found that the new proposed structure would substantially alter the wind force and direction and greatly reduce the sailing potential. Finally, would the High Street in Putney, already overcrowded on match days, cope with an increase in numbers?

Had this been New York not London the club's location could have been easily settled. Hammersmith and Fulham is the only borough in the United Kingdom with three major football clubs — Chelsea, QPR and Fulham. The simple and obvious solution would have been one location with all the clubs sharing the ground. But in a country where traditions matter such an idea was unthinkable. The fans liked the idea of Fulham as the Manchester United of the south and growing bigger than Chelsea but not moving from their historic home. As it happened the club did have to move. Fulham had arrived in the Premier League with the Cottage still having large standing sections, unheard of in top-level football at the time. According to the Taylor Report, a club had three seasons from their promotion to the second tier in which to convert terraces to seating areas. At the end of their first Premier League season, Fulham moved to share Loftus Road while they developed long-term plans for Craven Cottage.

But even this was not much liked by fans and a "Back to the Cottage" campaign was set up. By then Al-Fayed knew his dreams of matching United were unrealistic, the large stadium plan was binned and in 2004 Fulham returned to play at Craven Cottage, which had been modified as an all-seat stadium. It is a little ironical that nearly 10 years on, the club has submitted a new planning application to rebuild the river stand which will increase the club's capacity to 30,000 — the number submitted in the original application so hotly contested. But this new development is of a much more modest nature. And times have moved on. The club now has a much better relationship with their neighbours. Al-Fayed has realised that for all the riches offered by the Premier League, he would have to support the club from his own resources.

In contrast, West Ham's owners were not prepared or able to supply the sort of funds Al-Fayed has provided, and the club went through several changes

of ownership. These began in 2007 with an Icelandic purchase, before David
Sullivan and David Gold bought the club in 2009. In contrast to Al-Fayed, West
Ham had to react to what the Premier League had become, with a further twist
provided by London unexpectedly winning the right to host the 2012 Olympics.

As one West Ham insider told me:

> We'd come up back to the Premier League in the 2005 season and made
> something like £16 million operating profit and a profit after tax. We were
> in a good strong position and then in the first year back in the Premier
> League we finished eighth and got to a Cup final. So we were on the up.
> The question was how did we move West Ham forward. Tony Blair, Blair's
> staff, Richard Caborn [the sports minister] were all in favour of us taking
> over the Olympic Stadium. Robin Wales, the Mayor of Newham, was for
> it. The only problem was how do we make it happen? In that summer
> of 2006, the chances were if we were to secure the Olympic Stadium we
> were going to have to contribute to it. We as a club were debt-averse. How
> could we find that money? And that is when the thought of selling to get
> a rich backer came up.

West Ham now got caught up in the debate about the post-Games use of
the Olympic Stadium.

The West Ham board had met government ministers and other officials on
July 3, 2006. Terry Brown and his managing director Paul Aldridge met Tessa
Jowell, the Olympics minister, Richard Caborn, the minister for sport, Neale
Coleman, the Mayor's representative on the Olympic Board, and Sir Robin
Wales, Mayor of Newham. The meeting had come about largely because of
Caborn's passionate belief that the Olympic Stadium would become a white
elephant unless a football club took over, since athletics would never generate
any money. He was alone in such a view. Just before the meeting, the Olympic
Board had met and there had not been a single vote in favour of football, with
Seb Coe, chairman of London 2012, firm in his support of the athletics legacy.
However, because Caborn was very keen on the football solution and since
he had had some discussions with West Ham, a meeting was arranged at the
Department of Culture, Media and Sport (DCMS).

For West Ham, a move to the Olympic Stadium was immensely attractive.
They would have a 60,000-capacity brand new stadium in the part of London
undergoing its greatest modernisation in a hundred years, just seven minutes
from King's Cross and by 2013 possibly two hours to Paris. Here was an ideal
opportunity to match Arsenal's new stadium. Sir Robin Wales, a passionate

West Ham supporter, is very keen on football and sees it as the best legacy for Newham. For supporters of the football solution there was also the Manchester City formula where, as we have seen, City took over the City of Manchester Stadium built for the Commonwealth Games at very advantageous terms. But Jowell firmly rejected such an idea. A solution like that for West Ham would mean very nearly gifting the 2012 stadium away. Jowell told West Ham that a football solution would be considered if West Ham accepted there would be a running track — there isn't one at Manchester City — and if they put down £100 million on the table. West Ham were given three days to come up with an answer.

At this point Pini Zahavi, the Israel super agent, brought in Kia Joorabchian to the club and the West Ham board felt they had found a buyer they wanted. Joorabchian introduced them to a rich Israeli called Eli Papouchado. For West Ham this seemed the ideal solution. Papouchado may not have been an Abramovich but he was rich enough to fund a £100 million takeover and put down another £100 million or even more for the Olympic Stadium. Joorabchian also brought two high-profile players, the Argentinians Carlos Tevez and Javier Mascherano, to the club. They effectively came as free transfers to West Ham but their economic rights were held by MSI, a company controlled by Joorabchian. This had been a development in the years following the launch of the Premier League in South America. With football there in desperate economic straits but the countries still producing excellent players, outsiders bought the rights for the players and sold them on to European clubs. In this case the arrival of the players was almost a down payment, part of a strategy which would lead to Joorabchain and his allies buying the club.

In the words of the West Ham insider then at the club: "They were all in it together. The buyers probably had some interest in those players. They were top-quality players. We had the option, i.e., someone saying, 'Look when we are in as owners we'll exercise the option that you have and they'll be West Ham players.' This was not unusual, loads of clubs had this."

West Ham allowed Rothschild access to their books and sensitive contracts while they worked closely with Joorabchian. By then, as Richard Caborn confirmed to me back in October 2006, West Ham were in talks with Olympic authorities about moving into the 2012 stadium. "There is a very serious negotiation going on between West Ham and the Olympic authorities about the stadium. Talks are going on about whether they could do a similar thing to Manchester City when they took over the Commonwealth Games stadium in 2002," he said.

Then two things threw the takeover into doubt. West Ham had their worst run for 74 years, eight successive defeats. Rothschild began to fear West Ham might be relegated. In that case they would not be worth £100 million. Sunderland, then in the Championship, had been sold for £50 million. All this resulted in a meeting at the exclusive London club Les Ambassadeurs where Joorabchian and Zahavi met Rothschild with Papouchado on a conference call from Israel. Rothschild had done their due diligence and Papouchado, who did not know much about football, was not happy about the £9 million or so owed in transfers. He wanted to reduce the price. (Clubs always owe each other money on transfers and, depending on how one calculates the figures, and taking into account money owed to West Ham on player sales, the amount due on transfers in some calculations came down to as little as £2 million.)

For the West Ham board this was tricky. If a man quibbled over a few million would he be ready to fork out another £100 million or more for a new stadium? Beset by doubts, West Ham began to look at other bidders and another buyer, a rich Icelandic businessman, Bjorgolfur Gudmundsson, emerged. The West Ham insider told me: "Kia always claimed there was the money but we had to say enough's enough because we would get relegated if we carried on like this."

Initially Brown and his board were not keen even to talk to the Icelandic businessman but were persuaded by Sir Dave Richards to do so. The Icelanders were so keen they hired Mike Lee, a PR man who had worked for the Premier League, to get Richards to intervene. The insider says: "Richard Caborn was also keen on them on the basis that they were worth $7 billion between them, the son and the father, and this was chicken feed for them and it would help to secure the Olympic Stadium. They paid £85 million to buy West Ham."

It was after the sale that the saga of Tevez and Mascherano began to unravel.

For a start the two players had struggled to get into the West Ham team as then manager Alan Pardew did not seem to rate them. "Bizarre really," says the insider, "we didn't think they were good enough." Indeed the most memorable moment involving them that season was when Jermain Defoe tried to bite Mascherano's arm after a tussle between the two in a Tottenham versus West Ham match. Later West Ham's new manager Alan Curbishley decided he did not want Mascherano and Liverpool took him on loan from MSI. Tevez did begin to fit into Curbishley's team and he undoubtedly helped West Ham avoid relegation, sending Sheffield United down instead.

By this time questions were being asked about Tevez's registration. The Premier League charged West Ham under Rule 18, an obscure rule that had been designed for something else entirely. West Ham were confident they could prove their innocence but then suddenly pleaded guilty and in April 2007 the club were fined £5.5 million but not docked points. Sheffield United, which wanted points deducted, took the matter to court and in March 2009 in an out of court settlement, it was agreed West Ham would pay Sheffield United £22 million.

The West Ham insider told me:

> If the club had not been sold and Brown and his board had been in charge, the Premier League would never have found against West Ham. It is likely that Brown would have had a coffee with Richard Scudamore and resolved it, it would never have got into all this mess.

By then, Tevez had long since left West Ham for Manchester United, Iceland's economy had collapsed and there were serious questions being asked about the Icelandic management of the club. It is clear that the Premier League's rise as a world brand prompted Bjorgolfur Gudmundsson's purchase of West Ham. But having acquired it as a trophy asset, Gudmundsson himself did not come to run the club. Instead he had another man to front the sale, a man who had no financial interest in the club at all. This man was Eggert Magnusson, who could claim to be a man of football, being then president of the Icelandic Football Association and a UEFA executive member. While fronting the Icelandic bid he was accompanied by a corporate finance official from the London branch of Landsbanki, one of the country's main banks whose chairman was Gudmundsson. But Gudmundsson was so keen to take a back seat that at one stage his spokesman told me Gudmundsson was not involved in the bid. Indeed, his name was not on the consortium list submitted by Magnusson. Why this subterfuge was indulged in is not clear but it created the impression that Magnusson was buying the club when he was not.

His stewardship involved spending Gudmundsson's money and proved extraordinary. By December 2009 West Ham, whose debt had been £20 million when Brown and his board sold out, had seen debts rise to £110 million. The banks were owed £48 million, £40 million was owed to other clubs, including £22 million to Sheffield United, and there was a further £12 million loan West Ham had taken out in December. That loan was borrowed by pledging 70 per cent of the following year's season-ticket money and 60 per cent of the following season's. Gudmundsson was eventually forced to take over the running of the club from Magnusson, only to find within months that his own country was going bankrupt. Soon he himself was in hock to his creditors and West Ham were effectively owned by the Icelandic banks, their future dependent on the economy of Iceland rather than what the club did on the field of play. All this made a sale inevitable and the club were sold in January 2010 to David Sullivan and his partner David Gold.

Soon after this, Sullivan told me: "They had to borrow this money to stay alive. There is virtually nothing more to sell. The shirt sponsor paid 75 per cent of his fee not just for this season but for two seasons. The club have been robbing Peter to pay Paul, selling the future." In addition West Ham had to provide for the payment due to Alan Curbishley, who had won his case for unfair dismissal, a sum believed to be between £0.75 million and £3.5 million.

Sullivan and Gold had also inherited a huge wage bill. "The average wage of the staff, and this includes footballers, is higher than Goldman Sachs. West Ham have got more people on the administrative and support side earning between £100,000 and £300,000 a year. The place has been run as a charity."

Sullivan was upset that West Ham had pleaded guilty on the Tevez charge, but his anger was really reserved for the Icelanders. "They virtually bust the club." And as far as Sullivan was concerned, the Icelandic wrecker in chief was Magnusson. The fans had loved Magnusson, seeing him as an owner, but as Sullivan put it: "If you keep buying players, fans will love you. Magnusson did not take logical decisions. He did not negotiate well."

Magnusson was later to defend himself, saying he was not the only one involved in making decisions and that his purchases helped West Ham avoid relegation in the 2006–07 season. But Sullivan felt it might have been cheaper to have been relegated.

Sullivan had come to West Ham after getting £20 million from his sale of Birmingham in October 2009, having owned the Midlands club for 16 years. For critics who saw him as yet another person making money from football his response was he could have made that sort of money "buying a few office blocks 20 years ago or a street of houses in Chingford". But wheeling and dealing in property would not have given him the pleasure that owning Birmingham did, nor the sense of achievement.

Nor did Sullivan hide his reasons for coming to West Ham. A Hammers fan since he was 12, after moving to London from his hometown of Cardiff, he saw that "Birmingham are a smaller club than West Ham. Not a single player is on more than £25,000 a year. We have bigger ambitions for West Ham." Yet, so complicated can sales of clubs be that he very nearly bought another London club. Sullivan had approached West Ham in October 2009, within a week of leaving Birmingham. "I wanted to buy a quarter of the club with an option to buy another quarter," he told me. Andrew Bernhardt, the man who had been running the club on behalf of its bank owners, following the collapse of the Icelandic economy, liked the proposal. But the club could not be sold without a proper process. This meant Sullivan and Gold found themselves in a race with three other bidders. With the outcome uncertain, Sullivan was approached by Richard Murray, chairman of Charlton. As Sullivan revealed to me: "Had we not succeeded in buying West Ham we would have bought Charlton. Richard Murray and his consortium have done a wonderful job and he wanted some help. We would have gone in and helped."

But in the end the West Ham deal was done, with Sullivan and Gold getting 50 per cent of the club with an option to buy the remaining 50 per cent in four years. They were believed to have paid £20 million, of which £5 million was to reduce the bank loans, £15 million to the club.

On the night Sullivan became the new owner of West Ham he took the people he had been negotiating with to the first floor bar of the Ritz. As he toasted victory he asked his guests to look across the road at the Walpole, part of his property portfolio. This he told them with pride was once the residence of Robert Walpole, the first man in this country to have the title of prime minister.

Sullivan's ownership was mocked by many, particularly those who still see him as the porn king, who made his fortune selling hardcore magazines and films featuring topless girls. In 1982, he was even convicted of living off immoral earnings, serving 71 days in jail. But for Sullivan his porn past is nothing to be ashamed of. As he told me: "I do not feel embarrassed. I have made a lot of people happy. If I was an arms manufacturer or a cigarette manufacturer, and my products killed million of my clients, I would have a bit of doubt about the whole thing. I was a freedom fighter. I believe in the right of adults to make their own decisions."

The freedom fighter claim may be a bit rich but unlike many an owner of a football club Sullivan is approachable, his wealth is there for all to see and when I visited him at his home there was something very disarming about the way he lived. His home, set in 12 acres in Theydon Bois, Essex, was like all such mansions guarded by electronic gates but he himself opened the door to the house. In the hall, the two butlers holding out trays turn out to be wax models and the small dining room table, next to his kitchen, was decorated more like the bar of a sports club with small wicker baskets containing packets of crisps, dates, biscuits and chocolates. As he finished his lunch of ham and bread he watched Sky Sports News and cheered when a player he had bought when he owned Birmingham scored.

Sullivan in that sense has lived up to a certain image of an English football club owner, not quite the butcher or candlestick maker but one rooted in the land of his birth. Sullivan and Gold's ownership of West Ham neatly rounded off the story of a club whose horizons had been widened by the Premier League years, been sold to a rich foreigner who clearly saw it as a trophy asset only to be sold back to owners who could justifiably claim they had come to buy a club they had always supported.

The story of another foreigner, an American who came to this country in the wake of the Glazers, shows how difficult it can be to acquire and make the best of what may seem like a winning brand.

Aston Villa may not have been part of the Big Five that plotted to set up the Premier League but their status as a big club with a great history is not in doubt. Founder members of the Football League, they have won seven First Division titles and seven FA Cups. Their greatest days were behind them by the time the Premier League kicked off but in the decade before, they had won the European Cup and they remain one of five English clubs to win Europe's top club competition, Manchester United, Liverpool, Nottingham Forest and Chelsea being the others. Indeed in that inaugural Premier League season they came second to Manchester United, 10 points behind the champions, attracted the third highest gates, after Liverpool and Manchester United, and made a profit of £2.9 million. However, by the time Randy Lerner, owner of the National Football League's Cleveland Browns, bought Villa from Doug Ellis in 2006 for £62.6 million, Aston Villa were a struggling club.

For the year ended May 31, 2006, Villa had lost £8.2 million before tax, income fell from £51.6 million to £49 million with attendances at Villa Park down 8.7 per cent. This is less than a third of the income of Manchester United and just a little more than the profit United made in 2005. The club announced they had frozen ticket prices in a bid to boost attendances and hoped the appointment of Martin O'Neill as manager would bring fans back. Lerner, who beat off other bidders, including a consortium organised by Athole Still, agent of former England team coach Sven-Goran Eriksson, clearly thought that for £63 million he was obtaining a club with a great history and now a Premier League brand he could exploit.

Since then, Lerner can only have looked at the Glazers and shaken his head in bemusement for, unlike the Glazers, Lerner has had to constantly resort to his cheque book. By the end of the 2011 season, Villa's debt may only have been a third of Manchester United's £308 million but in every other respect this former giant of English football have declined. Villa's 2011 income of £92 million was not only nearly a fourth that of Manchester United but almost all of it went on wages, £ 83.4 million, a staggering 90 per cent. After other costs this meant an overspend of £73 million in both the 2009–10 and 2010–11 seasons. Changes of managers, which had seen Martin O'Neill and Gerard Houllier leave, meant compensation of £12.4 million being paid out. During this period Lerner has easily topped the list of benefactors of the clubs in the squeezed middle. His £163 million is well ahead of the £140 million Mike Ashley has put into Newcastle.

But if what has happened at Villa is capable of explanation, the events in Portsmouth show how the Premier League may have wowed the world but also set in motion events that it cannot control. So far, neither the football bodies or the authorities show any sign that they even want to control.

While Portsmouth's record of four owners in three years and two administrations — they are currently in one at the moment — is extraordinary, the club's postwar history is one of always seeking the right owner. The fans of this south coast club, famous for its Pompey chimes, love to see themselves as a sleeping giant. They did sleep for a long time after winning the old First Division titles in 1948–49 and 1949–50. In November 1976 they came close to bankruptcy. In those pre-Premier League days, the cash needed was £25,000 and while the club survived they were relegated to the old Fourth Division in 1978, the first time former champions of England had suffered such a fate.

In the summer of 1988, Jim Gregory, the former Queens Park Rangers chairman, who had made his money in the motor trade, bought the club. Ably managed by Jim Smith, who had also managed QPR, Portsmouth might have made it to the first Premier League season but missed out by scoring one fewer goal than West Ham. In 1996, when Portsmouth was owned by Gregory's son Martin, who had little interest in football, the club recruited Terry Venables. Venables, who had guided England to the semi-finals of Euro '96, came initially to manage the club. He was assisted by Eddie Ashby and in February 1997 bought a 51 per cent share for £1.

As Venables took over as chairman, Martin Gregory exulted: "As far as I'm concerned it's the best news I've had in a long time. We stand on the threshold of exciting times and with Terry at the helm I'm convinced that we can fulfil Pompey's potential." Venables also continued to coach Australia and during his reign several Australian players arrived at the club. In 1997, he sold Lee Bradbury to Manchester City for £3 million. He then billed the club £300,000 as a performance fee which he was entitled to under his contract. In December 1997, a month before he pleaded guilty to the charges brought by the Department of Trade and Industry, Venables left Portsmouth. By this time, the club were nearly insolvent, with some players unpaid. Venables, for his £1 investment, had in two years earned £550,000.

Portsmouth's recent story starts in its centenary season, 1998–99. In December 1998 the club went into financial administration. In May the following year, Milan Mandaric bought the club. He also brought in Peter Storrie as chief executive. Harry Redknapp came as director of football, then became manager and with Mandaric willing to fund his purchases Portsmouth thrived. The timing was good as the collapse of ITV Digital had dealt a severe blow to many of the Football league clubs. In 2004 Portsmouth won promotion to the Premier League and seemed to be establishing themselves in the top flight.

Many fans now look back and see this as the best period for the club but the good times did not last. In January 2006, Portsmouth was bought by businessman Alexandre Gaydamak, aged 29 and popularly known as Sacha, for around £30 million. Super agent Pini Zahavi brought Mandaric and Gaydamak together, receiving a commission for this. It is interesting to note the reasons Peter Storrie, the club's chief executive, gives to justify the use of Zahavi. Mandaric wanted to sell but was tired of meeting people who were all talk and no money and so the Israeli Zahavi, famous for doing deals, was the ideal go-between.

There was much speculation that this was not young Gaydamak's money but that of his father, Arkady. Three years after the sale, in October 2009, the father was prosecuted in Israel over money-laundering — a charge which was later dropped when he pleaded guilty to a lesser offence. Gaydamak junior has always insisted it was his money.

The sale provided a glimpse of how the rise of the Premier League had made English football a worldwide target for those seeking property they felt could be developed. Portsmouth were no longer a South Coast club who hoped to rule England again but part of a worldwide brand. This was emphasised by the connections Zahavi had with the club. This included a scouting agreement, a two-year deal worth £400,000 a year. Storrie has justified it on the grounds that Zahavi had contacts in important South American countries such as Argentina, Brazil and Chile. One of the players Zahavi brought was Tal Ben Haim, an Israeli defender. He was signed in August 2009 on a four-year contract for £36,000 a week. Like so many modern players he also had an image rights contract. This payment to a company registered in Guernsey, an offshore tax haven, meant Ben Haim cost £50,000 a week. He is still at the club and over a four-year period that would amount to an outlay of £10 million, a heavy burden on a club who in that period have seen two administrations and been relegated to League One, the old third division. Portsmouth's current administrator Trevor Birch has made 33 people redundant but under the football creditors rule Ben Haim's and the other players' wages have to be met. Otherwise, Portsmouth will not be able to play their matches.

Zahavi also brought Avram Grant to the club. Grant had two spells at Portsmouth. He joined as technical director in June 2006 before leaving for Chelsea. He was back as director of football in October 2009, taking over from Paul Hart as the manager a month later. Zahavi has since claimed he saved the club from bankruptcy by selling players, the most significant being the sale of Sulley Muntari to Internazionale for £12.7 million in July 2008. Zahavi has also claimed that while he was paid some money, when the club went into administration for the first time he was owed £2.074 million. He was just one of 24 agents who were owed a total of nearly £9 million.

The Gaydamak era was when the club went into overdrive on spending under manager Harry Redknapp. They finished the 2006–07 season in the top half of the table for the first time, only one point short of European qualification. The 2007–08 season started with Portsmouth winning the 2007 Barclays Asia Trophy, beating Liverpool 4–2 on penalties after a goalless final. It ended with the club winning the FA Cup for the first time since 1939. Fans joked that the club had held the Cup longer than anyone else as war meant the competition was not played for six years. Nothing seemed sweeter. The FA Cup win earned them a place in the 2008–09 UEFA Cup, the club's first venture into European football.

Soon there were more ownership changes. Gaydamak, unable to finance Portsmouth, or at least that is what he told Storrie, sold the club to the Dubai-based property entrepreneur, Sulaiman al-Fahim in August 2009. This was followed by the most curious sale five weeks later to the Saudi Arabian Ali Al-Faraj, who never appeared once at Fratton Park. A loan was taken out with Portpin, a company owned by the Hong Kong-businessman Balram Chainrai. He became the club's next owner.

During the 2009–10 season, it had become clear to Chainrai that Portsmouth were approximately £135 million in debt and the club were placed into administration on February 26, 2010, the first Premier League club to suffer this fate. His company retained its £17 million secured loan over the club. This meant a nine-point penalty from the Premier League and certain relegation which was confirmed in April 2010.

For a time it seemed the club might die and on October 22, Portsmouth issued a statement saying: "It appears likely that the club will now be closed down and liquidated by the administrators." But then Gaydamak announced the next day that he had reached an agreement which could save it and Portsmouth came out of administration with Balram Chainrai regaining control.

In June 2011, Chainrai sold it to Convers Sports Initiatives, owned by the Russian Vladimir Antonov, with Keith Harris acting as the go-between. Chainrai retained his secured debenture for a debt of £17 million on the club itself. On November 23, 2011, a Europe-wide arrest warrant was issued for Antonov by Lithuanian prosecutors as part of an investigation into alleged asset stripping at Lithuanian bank Bankas Snoras, which is 68 per cent owned by Antonov and had gone into temporary administration the previous week.

Antonov was subsequently arrested at his offices in London and bailed. Antonov has denied the charges.

Within two months, following a winding-up petition by Her Majesty's Revenue and Customs for over £1.6 million in unpaid taxes, Portsmouth went into administration for the second time in two years. This brought another automatic 10-point deduction and relegation to League One. After the 2008 FA Cup win, the club had ranked eighth in the billionaires' Premier League; now they were insolvent.

The Portsmouth saga once again raised questions about the "fit and proper person test". The Premier League made much of how it has changed the rules but as Sir Dave Richards admitted to me: "Portsmouth is an absolute tragedy, an absolute tragedy to lose a club. I don't mind saying we had a wake-up call. We always thought the kind of money the league was supplying to the clubs was quite sufficient. You've got to look back on it and say what went wrong? Now we have changed the rules. Now we have the ability to do things in the club. To withhold payments. To make sure the Revenue is paid, the VAT is paid, the football creditors get paid."

But while Richards says the change of rules mean "the likelihood of that happening seems quite slim", when pressed whether it could happen again in the Premier League he says: "The likelihood of it happening within the Premier League? I can't say it can't happen again because you should never say never. But the regulatory framework that is in the Premier League could help to stop that happening."

Many would doubt that assertion. Ashley Brown, a supporter of Portsmouth for 40 years and now chairman of the club's Supporters Trust, says:

> The recent history of Portsmouth shows why self-regulation in football is not working. The club have been passed from foreign owner to foreign owner, none of whom had any understanding of the club or football. Nor did they share the passion for the club the fans had. The club have been driven to the brink of extinction on several occasions and it is time for the club to be brought back to the ownership of the community for which football was set up to be when the game took off more than a century ago. I am a big fan of the German model of 51 per cent ownership in the country. Foreigners cannot have majority ownership.

But for that to happen there would have to a fundamental change in thinking in English football and among the politicians and there has been little evidence of that.

PART 5

FOOTBALL'S SECRET WORLD

Chapter 12
THE GHOSTLY PRESENCE

The first Premier League season had not even kicked off when the first moves in what would become the great "bungs" story were initiated. At that stage, while the word "bung" was not unknown within the game, the wider public were unaware of it — until a year later, on May 30, 1993, when my colleague Jeff Randall and I ran a front page story in *The Sunday Times*.

Our headline was: "Revealed: Soccer's secret world of cash backhanders" and the story began: "Sensational allegations are about to plunge English soccer into crisis. They will confirm widespread rumours about a secret world of backhanders and under-the-counter cash payments including some of the biggest names in football." Our story was based on a court affidavit of Alan Sugar, then chairman of Tottenham Hotspur, which alleged that Terry Venables, the club's chief executive, while conducting negotiations with Nottingham Forest manager Brian Clough about buying Teddy Sheringham in August 1992, had told Sugar that "Mr Clough likes a bung." He [Venables] explained that Clough wished to receive a payment personally for selling Mr Sheringham. "I told Mr Venables that it was absolutely out of the question and that I have never heard anything like this before and it is certainly not the way Tottenham Hotspur or I do business," Sugar said.

We went on to say: "The allegations come as the Inland Revenue carries out a widespread investigation into alleged irregularities involving transfers and cash payments made to players from many football clubs."

David Kohler, Luton Town's managing director, whose club had been investigated before he took over, said: "I don't know his allegations in detail, but if he's saying there is corruption in football then he is 100 per cent right. Football is bent from top downwards. There is dodgy dealing. A lot of brown paper-bagging [making payments in cash]."

Our story caused a sensation, not least in *The Sun* newspaper which devoted several pages to the story on the Monday. Kelvin McKenzie, then the

Sun editor, had had several reporters working on the Sugar-Venables row and was so grateful to see our report — and also because we gave him a little tidbit that we had not used about the fact that Clough liked to be paid bungs in a motorway cafe — that he sent over a case of champagne.

Venables denied he ever had any contact with Clough on the transfer, let alone that he told Sugar about bungs. "I had no direct contact with Brian Clough since all my negotiations at that time were conducted with Mr Fred Reacher, the chairman of Nottingham Forest... The allegation that I told Mr Sugar that Brian Clough 'liked a bung' is untrue." Clough dismissed the allegations as preposterous and asked Sugar to repeat the allegations outside the privilege of the courtroom.

In making these allegations, Sugar was taking on two of the biggest names in English football. One never became England manager, despite being the people's favourite, the other would get the job following his departure from Tottenham. But, in doing so, Sugar had gone where no club chairman had previously dared to go, by revealing intimate deals of how transfers were conducted. It indicated how English football was changing.

Less than two weeks after our story, the Premier League set up a three-man inquiry, comprising Premier League chief executive Rick Parry, Steve Coppell, who was taking a break from football management, and Robert Reid QC. By the time the investigation reported, nearly four years later, it had examined 10,200 pages of written evidence and questioned 66 witnesses, 42 of them under oath and some of them more than once. The inquiry was also in touch with the Football League, the FA and 12 other FAs round the world, 21 UK clubs and 22 overseas, and took in evidence from no fewer than six different sets of legal proceedings. The whole exercise probably cost more than £1 million. The 1,000-page report covered a whole host of transfers in the modern game, with the biggest section devoted to Sheringham's transfer from Nottingham Forest to Tottenham. No single transfer in British football history — probably in the history of the game — has been more thoroughly analysed.

Talk of the transfer had started just two weeks before the Premier League kicked off its first season in 1992. Venables, then Tottenham chief executive, had been told by Ted Buxton, the club's chief scout, that Sheringham might be available at the right price.

Shortly before the start of the season, Sheringham met Venables and Buxton together with Graham Smith, who ran First Wave Sports Management in partnership with former Arsenal captain Frank McLintock, who in turn had a contract with Tottenham to provide promotional merchandising and marketing services. To all intents and purposes they were agents but they could not use the term as FIFA rules specifically forbade clubs from using agents.

It was not to prove easy to get Sheringham to Tottenham, and when the season started he was still a Forest player. But on Thursday, August 20, during lunch with Tony Berry, a Tottenham director, Venables was called by Buxton. Berry says Venables, on hanging up, told him: "I've got the deal done, but now they want something." Berry asked: "What, Cloughie?" Venables said: "Yes."

Berry told the inquiry that, following another call 15 minutes later, Venables said: "You don't want to know what it is, but he wants —. He's upped the price and he wants something for himself." The timing, the venue, the conversation were all disputed by Venables.

Two days later, on August 27, the deal was finally done. Following a "now or never" phone call between Venables and Fred Reacher, the Forest chairman, personal terms were quickly agreed with McLintock and Sheringham at Tottenham's training ground.

In a normal transfer, that would be it. But this was not a normal transfer. This time £50,000 had to be paid in cash. Who asked for it? What was it for? Venables and McLintock claimed it was money that Tottenham owed First Wave.

Anis Rahman, Tottenham's then credit controller, remembers receiving a call from Eddie Ashby, Venables' assistant, authorising a payment of £50,000, in cash, to McLintock. Rahman rang Colin Sandy, Tottenham's finance director. Sandy stormed into Sugar's office to be told: "Talk to Terry." Sandy said, "I telephoned Mr Venables [who] told me that no other method of payment, not even a bank draft, would do, and if we did not do it this way, the Sheringham deal would fail. I said I would arrange for the cash but that I would not authorise its release unless I received a VAT invoice."

Venables' recollection is very different. "I told Mr Sandy that Frank McLintock had to have the money that night, but I never said that it must be in cash." Sandy rang Rahman, asking him to collect £58,750 in cash, of which £8,750 was the VAT, which was eventually handed over to Ashby and McLintock.

First Wave provided an invoice but since football agents were not allowed it lied about why it was being paid. As it happened Tottenham also received invoices addressed to Ashby for the same amount — £50,000 — and with identical wording from Silver Rose International Ltd (Export). My investigations into this showed that this was a naughty-knickers, Ann Summers-style company based in London's Finchley Road. The wording as in the First Wave invoice said that the £50,000 was "for the assistance in arranging distribution and merchandising network on behalf of THFC in the USA to include travel and all consultancy work involved in the project".

The Premier League inquiry concluded, "The Silver Rose invoices were in our view bogus invoices raised with a view to facilitating the payment of the

£50,000. Although they are addressed to Mr Ashby we are unable to say on the evidence before us that they were procured by him. It is equally possible that they were raised by some third party with a view to their being used in the Sheringham transfer, without reference to Mr Ashby".

McLintock having received his money, put it in a shoebox, and leaving White Hart Lane, put the shoe box on the front seat of his car. He then picked up Sheringham and drove to the Post House Hotel in Luton, where the pair met Ronnie Fenton, Clough's assistant manager at Nottingham Forest. McLintock insisted that, far from giving Fenton anything, he received an envelope containing the transfer forms from Fenton. Why Fenton should drive 90 miles to hand over transfer forms is a mystery — it would have been usual to fax them.

The inquiry concluded that the meeting at the Post House Hotel was attended by Mr Fenton, Mr McLintock and Mr Sheringham, all of whom "deliberately omitted to make any mention of the meeting with the intention of misleading the inquiry. Even when driven to admitting that the meeting took place we are satisfied that all three of these witnesses gave accounts which did not accord with what actually occurred at the meeting.

"We are satisfied that at the meeting on August 27, 1992 Mr Fenton signed the transfer agreement on behalf of Forest and handed it over to Mr McLintock."

But while most of the inquiry's conclusions were unanimous, only two of its members (Parry and Reid) were satisfied that McLintock handed over to Fenton at least a substantial part, if not all, of the £50,000 that he had received earlier that day from Tottenham. According to Parry, Steve Coppell "refused to accept that the fifty thousand had gone [to Clough and Fenton]. We [Parry and Reid] were pretty strong in concluding it had and he said, 'No I don't think we've got enough evidence for that.'"

The inquiry was also critical of how Forest managed their affairs. "In our view... the control over the manner in which business was conducted at Forest was wholly inadequate. Mr Clough and Mr Fenton were allowed to conduct matters without proper supervision or control by the board."

The inquiry had heard evidence that, some time after the Post House meeting, payments had been made to Forest staff. Clough, it seems, was like a Robin Hood, taking money from transfers and distributing them to various people at the club as a gift.

As far as Venables was concerned, the inquiry concluded: "We are satisfied that Mr Venables did not believe that the £50,000 which he authorised on August 27, 1992, to First Wave was simply a payment to First Wave in respect of services by First Wave to Tottenham, whether in relation to Mr Sheringham's transfer or otherwise... Whilst the conduct of Mr Venables cannot be justified, it should be born in mind that, in our view, he regarded the obtaining of Mr Sheringham's services as being essential for the good of the Tottenham team. He did not make or intend to make any personal benefit from the payment of £50,000. In our view he regarded that payment as being an essential prerequisite of obtaining Mr Sheringham's transfer and therefore something which could properly be done on behalf of the club."

For Venables this was vindication that he had been cleared of any wrongdoing and shown to be innocent and his friend the agent Eric Hall declared: "Football is monster, monster clean."

Clough, on the other hand, should have had charges to answer, but he was never asked to do so, nor did any charges arise out of other transfers involving Clough and Fenton, which drew very damning comment from the Premier League report, and included one in which Fenton was said to have collected a bung from a fishing trawler.

In December 1989, Thorvalder Orlygsson joined Forest from the Icelandic club Knattstsprunufelag Akureyrar. Orlygsson needed a work permit and, in their application made to the Department of Employment, Forest stated that a £150,000 fee had been agreed whereas in the event, Forest paid £174,000. So what was the extra £24,000 for?

Fenton told the inquiry that, when he arrived in Iceland to conclude the deal, the club asked for more money, which was agreed. The inquiry concluded that the transfer gave cause for concern, and noted the persistence of stories that Fenton had collected cash from the transfer. Allan Clarke, a Forest employee, said that Fenton had gone to Hull to collect £45,000 in a fish-box from a trawler, a story supported by coach Archie Gemmill and physio Graham Lyas. Fenton denied ever receiving any such money either in Iceland or in England.

The inquiry had no doubts about what happened in the transfers of Anthony Loughlan and Neil Lyne from non-League Leicester United to Nottingham Forest in August 1989. Forest, who were supposed to pay Leicester £15,000, ended up paying £61,000, in three separate instalments. The inquiry concluded: "... there is direct evidence of a fraudulent arrangement by which Mr Clough and/or Mr Fenton acquired a substantial sum of money from the two transfers."

The FA had little appetite to take on a folk hero like Clough. Parry believes that Clough should have been prosecuted. His consolation was that, by then, the inquiry had uncovered another big name, George Graham.

That George Graham was nailed, essentially as a fall-out of the Sugar-Venables row, while Brian Clough never was, remains one of the great ironic Premier League tales.

Arsenal manager Graham was a great friend of Venables and, at the launch of the Premier League, was the most successful current manager in English football, at the height of his powers.

As a player, Graham had been part of the Arsenal Double-winning side of 1970–71. He returned to Highbury as manager in 1986. He won the League Cup in his first year, and then, in 1989 guided them to their first title since the Double triumph.

In eight seasons, Graham won six trophies and was being ranked with the legendary Herbert Chapman. But his transfer spending had provoked derision in the media. As the *Daily Telegraph* put it: "Graham, who should be shopping at Harrods, has had to make do instead with corner shop players like Jimmy Carter, John Jensen, Pal Lydersen, Martin Keown, Eddie McGoldrick and Chris Kiwomya." What nobody knew then was that two of those 'corner shop' purchases had sown the seeds of Graham's downfall, which began a year after Sugar had spilled the beans on the Sheringham transfer. One had taken place a few months before the Premier League was born, the other a few weeks before the League kicked off, and they illustrated how, right at the beginning of the Premier League's existence, the game was changing. And where the Sheringham transfer had been an entirely domestic matter, these involved players from overseas with a Norwegian middle man.

Non-British or Irish players were rare in English football before Tottenham brought Ossie Ardiles and Ricky Villa from Argentina in 1978. But, by the early 1990s, many other clubs, including Graham's Arsenal, were buying abroad, partly because foreign players were often much cheaper than home-grown ones.

The man at the centre of the Graham, and other, transfers was Rune Hauge, an agent for a number of Norwegian players whom he was keen to sell to English clubs. English football had a huge following in the Scandinavian countries long before the Premier League was set up, but Per Omdal, a fellow Norwegian and a long-standing UEFA and FIFA executive member, recalls that: "Interest really began to grow from 1971 when one match every week was shown live on television, first in Norway then in the rest of Scandinavia."

Hauge's enthusiasm for doing business with English clubs was partly inspired by the curious way Scandinavian football was run. As the Premier League inquiry put it:

> In most cases the management of the majority of Scandinavian clubs was part-time and frequently amateur. There is evidence that agents/ intermediaries took advantage of the competitive naivety of the Scandinavian market in a number of respects. There is also evidence that in some cases this led to opportunities for dishonesty.

The inquiry went on to observe:

> Many Scandinavian players had contracts under which they were entitled to be paid part of any transfer paid to the club on their transfer. There is evidence that in some cases the agent/intermediary would negotiate with a player and the selling club terms under which the player would waive his right to receive part of the transfer fee from the selling club and would look to the agent/intermediary for a part of the agent/intermediary's commission instead. In simplistic terms this would be reflected by an agreement between the agent/intermediary and the selling club that the selling club would receive a fixed amount from the transfer and the balance would belong to the agent/intermediary, who would "look after" the player.

Hauge was more than happy to look after the player and take his cut. In the words of the inquiry:

> He was an extremely proactive agent/intermediary. We have seen evidence to show that he created a number of deals in which he participated despite the fact that he acted initially neither for the clubs concerned nor for the player. He was able to insinuate himself into negotiations by identifying a likely player, finding a suitable purchaser, and then persuading the Scandinavian club to sell.

Hauge had met Ronnie Fenton in 1990, and rang him persistently to ask what players his club wanted. Fenton introduced him to English managers, including Alex Ferguson, Graeme Souness, then Liverpool manager, and Mick Walker of Notts County and would also pass on information and opinions on different players and other clubs' requirements.

But, as the inquiry found, there was much more to the arrangement. This was vividly confirmed when Hauge helped Alf-Inge Haaland transfer to Forest from Norwegian club Bryne. The deal was initially agreed in October 1992 but, with Norway outside the European Union, it was December 1993 before Haaland obtained a work permit, so it was not until January 20, 1994 that Bryne invoiced Forest for the sum of £350,000. On January 27 the money was transferred to Bryne's account.

However, Bryne had an arrangement with InterClub Rune, Hauge's company, to pay InterClub any money received over and above £150,000. The inquiry concluded some of the extra £200,000 went to Fenton.

What is truly amazing is that these events were going on despite the fact that, by then, the Premier League inquiry team had been investigating "bungs" for several months. As far as Fenton and Hauge were concerned, the inquiry might as well have been looking at transfers on the moon.

Fenton was not the only English club official Hauge cultivated. He had also developed very good relations with Steve Burtenshaw, then the chief scout at Arsenal. The pair had first met in August 1987 when Burtenshaw became impressed with Hauge's football knowledge. Two years later Burtenshaw had an agreement with Proman A/S, one of Hauge's companies, under which he would receive a fee whenever a continental player moved to a British club on Burtenshaw's recommendation. The agreement included a very interesting clause: "The fee will be smaller according to the number of 'paybacks' which are involved."

Burtenshaw's lawyers had difficulty explaining what the word "paybacks" meant. Asked by the Norwegian investigation: "Does 'paybacks' mean 'palm-greasers'?" Burtenshaw replied, "You could say that. Yes. Introductions, perhaps."

Payments made to Burtenshaw by Proman A/S either side of the July 1990 transfer of Anders Limpar to Arsenal from Italian club Cremonese for a fee of DM4,150,000 (about £1.4 million) were also questioned. However, two other transfers that Burtenshaw was involved in — Pal Lydersen from Norwegian club IK Start in November 1991 and John Jensen from Danish club Brondby IF in July 1992 — were to have a dramatic effect on his boss Graham's career.

Burtenshaw says he played no part in Lydersen's transfer other than, at Hauge's instigation, to watch him play and enquire as to his value, although Arsenal maintained that he, along with Graham and (Arsenal secretary) Ken Friar, was a prime mover in the transfer negotiations.

As for Jensen, according to Burtenshaw, Arsenal were alerted by a fax from Hauge, whereafter negotiations were handled by Graham. He and Graham disagree over who fixed the transfer fee but, on September 19, 1992, Burtenshaw received a third payment, £35,000, from Hauge.

The Premier League inquiry had no doubt what the £35,000 was for: "In the case of the payment of £35,000, we are satisfied that the payment... derived directly from the transfer fee paid by Arsenal FC to Brondby IF in connection with the transfer of John Jensen."

While Graham and Burtenshaw had very different recollections of who did what in the transfers, Graham found his version of events in the Lydersen transfer challenged by three directors of IK Start, who claimed that the original fee agreed with Graham was £215,000. Arsenal eventually paid £500,000 after Graham flew to Oslo to conclude the deal but not, he says, to increase the transfer fee for his own personal benefit.

Arsenal chairman Peter Hill-Wood later told me:

> Graham had told us he was going to Oslo merely to rubber-stamp the
> deal. It did seem odd because he normally did not do that. He told us: "It
> was a done deal. I didn't negotiate. I wasn't even in the same room." Three
> Start directors all said he spent three hours haggling with them. You don't
> take three hours if you are just discussing where you are going for dinner.

Of the £500,000 received from Arsenal, IK Start kept the £215,000 and
the rest of the Lydersen transfer money went various ways, with Graham
receiving £140,500, which he collected from Hauge at London's Park Lane
Hotel on December 23, 1991. According to Graham, Hauge gave several plastic
envelopes to Graham, expressing his "appreciation for all that you have done to
help me open up doors here in England". The envelopes were full of £50 notes.

As far as Graham was concerned this was not money from the Lydersen deal
and he always described it as an "unsolicited gift". The use of the phrase was
significant, not only de-linking it from the transfer but helping him respond to
Inland Revenue questioning as to why he had not paid tax on it.

Another part of the "unsolicited gift" from Hauge — £285,000 — was
linked to the Jensen transfer. Of the £1.5 million Arsenal had paid Brondby,
£749,433.48 went to Hauge's company, InterClub. An entry in InterClub's
books on August 12, 1992 — five days later — under an account entitled "J
Jensen Management 924", reads: "Bank Draft to George Graham JJ" .

Graham never denied receiving the money, but insisted he had not asked
for, or expected, it, and that it was not related to the Jensen transfer. "It no
doubt sounds like a bung, and looks like a bung, but it was a gift," he claimed.

By this time the Inland Revenue had also begun investigating Graham and
Burtenshaw. Like many clubs, Arsenal had been subject to an investigation going
back six years into undeclared payments. Burtenshaw eventually admitted that
he had received money from Hauge. Graham initially remained silent but, in
August 1994, was told by his financial advisers that he must declare the money
he had received, and bring the matter to the attention of Arsenal. He told Hill-
Wood but continued to insist that the payments were unsolicited gifts.

However, when, two months later, Brondby played at Highbury in the
Cup-Winners' Cup, David Dein, the Arsenal vice-chairman, was surprised to
learn that Brondby had kept just £900,000 from the Jensen transfer.

By the autumn of 1994 the Inland Revenue were considering whether
Graham should face charges relating to undeclared payments. Arsenal remained
supportive enough to allow him to spend £4 million on two new players,

John Hartson and Chris Kiwomya, and, in December 1994, he repaid the money he had received, with interest. But on February 10, 1995 the picture changed. At the start of the day, Arsenal were still committed to Graham; indeed, he was given permission to buy Glen Helder for £2 million. Hours later, though, the Arsenal directors were shown the Premier League report on Graham, which concluded that the two payments Graham had received arose from the transfers of Lydersen and Jensen and "would not have been made but for the transfers taking place". On Tuesday, February 21, 1995 Graham was summoned to Highbury and sacked.

Graham was also charged with bringing the game into disrepute under the FA's much-used Rule 26. But a three-man FA commission was not convinced "beyond reasonable doubt" that Graham had conspired with Hauge to siphon away Arsenal's transfer money, although it did suggest he should be disciplined, concluding: "Mr Graham gave evidence about the payments being unsolicited. However, even if this is right, as a respected manager... we find that he must have known how serious a matter it was for him to be receiving this amount from an agent."

Graham was banned for a year and required to pay a share of the FA's legal costs, a ban that, together with the five-month wait for the hearing, he believes cost him £2 million.

Burtenshaw's hearing did not take place until September 1998, after the full Premier League inquiry report was published. He admitted that the £35,000 he had received was an illegal payment, apologised and was fined £7,500 with costs. His position in football was not affected and he continued as the chief scout at Queens Park Rangers. He went on to work for Kevin Keegan at Manchester City before retiring from football in 2001.

Graham, meanwhile, had worked his way back into the game with Leeds in September 1996 before, ironically, being hired by Sugar in October 1998 to manage Tottenham. Sugar was aware of Graham's past but writes in his autobiography: "Everybody was singing his praises as being in the same league as Sir Alex Ferguson and Arsene Wenger." Tottenham were struggling and Tony Berry and Martin Peters convinced him Graham was the man. Sugar, however, believes Graham achieved little despite spending large amounts of money, although he did win the only piece of silverware under Sugar's chairmanship, the League Cup in 1999. In 2001, Sugar sold the club to Enic and, within days, Enic had sacked Graham.

How Graham must have wished that he had been as wise as his fellow Scot Alex Ferguson when the transfer of Andrei Kanchelskis from the Ukrainian club Shakhtar Donetsk to Manchester United in March 1991 presented him with an unsolicited gift. Club lawyer Maurice Watkins, along with Martin Edwards and Ferguson, negotiated a deal, which also involved the Norwegian agent Rune Hauge. The contract provided for a fee of £650,000 plus further payments totalling £550,000 depending on how many matches Kanchelskis played and other events. United also paid £35,000 for Hauge's services.

At that time under football rules the use of Hauge as an agent was illegal. But it was a common practice in English football and, when the Premier League "bungs" inquiry looked into the transfer, it cleared United of any illegal payments, while acknowledging that it had, like many other football clubs, broken football rules.

However, the Kanchelskis story did not end there. On the night of August 22, 1994, United returned late to Old Trafford after a 1–1 draw at Nottingham Forest, and, as Ferguson was about to leave the car park, he was stopped by Grigory Essaoulenko, a Russian agent who was part of the Kanchelskis advisory team, who gave him a handsomely wrapped box. Ferguson threw it in the back of the car and drove home.

The box turned out to be stuffed with £40,000 in cash. The next morning he took it to Old Trafford, emptying it in front of Ken Merrett, the secretary. The money was lodged in the Old Trafford safe and the events documented with the lawyers.

The money stayed in the safe for a year, until Kanchelskis wanted a move to Everton and Essaoulenko returned to Old Trafford to iron out complications in Kanchelskis' contract. This gave United and Ferguson the opportunity to return the money in the safe, which Essaoulenko claimed had been a "thank you" to Ferguson. Ferguson said he was bemused as he had done nothing he would not ordinarily have done.

The story of the £40,000 stashed in the United safe was first revealed by Ferguson in his autobiography published in 1999. Graham Bean, the bung buster appointed by the FA after the Reid inquiry, wanted Manchester United charged but the FA were not about to take on Watkins, the best football lawyer in the business.

By then the Premier League, having entered its second decade, was growing more confident that its bungs nightmare was over. Parry had no doubts that his inquiry had served its purpose and, as he put it to me, far from proving that self-regulation did not work, "we actually introduced a whole new raft of rules within the Premier League governing agents and managers; to make it specifically a breach of Premier League rules if a manager took a bung. It was explicit and it was to be part of managers' contracts, part of their code of conduct which would give us the power then to self-regulate."

In a section called "The Way Ahead", the inquiry had demonstrated how English football was changing: "Football in England has become an example of how a traditional, essentially cottage, industry can be transformed into a streamlined and efficient business capable of competing with any in the world."

But suspicions about transfers remained and, in 2004, a High Court in London heard allegations from Fulham owner Mohammed Al-Fayed that his own manager, Jean Tigana, had misled the club during transfers.

Appointed in 2000, Tigana had been subjected to a number of internal investigations by the club before Al-Fayed directly confronted him with his suspicions, soon after which, in April 2003, he left the club. A month later Fulham lodged a criminal complaint against Tigana in France, accusing him of financial impropriety and "of having dishonestly benefited financially from the Steve Marlet transfer".

Tigana was accused by Fulham of spending roughly £7 million more than was necessary on the £11.5 million signing of Steve Marlet and the £7 million transfer of goalkeeper Edwin van der Sar. In November 2004, Tigana was cleared by the High Court in London of any dishonest or improper dealings, but investigations continued for more than three years. In July 2005, Fulham lost an appeal against the decision and in October 2006 the French tax authorities concluded that Tigana did not owe one penny, in the UK, France or Africa.

As Al-Fayed continued to insist he was right, the bungs story was reappearing — despite Parry's changes — although this time in a form even more dramatic than at the time of Sugar's original court affidavit.

In 2006, Sven-Goran Eriksson, then the England manager, told a *News of the World* undercover reporter, Mazher Mahmood, who was posing as a rich Arab sheikh, that bungs were common in the English game. The story was powerfully reinforced by Mike Newell, then manager of Luton Town:

> You're not telling me the only person guilty of taking a bung is George Graham. I don't believe it. What it needed was someone high-profile to stand up and shout about it, but what you find is a lot of people involved with the agent in doing the deal taking back-handers. That is without question.

Richard Scudamore, Parry's successor as Premier League chief executive, was clearly stung by Eriksson's comments, and a new inquiry was set up, headed by Lord Stevens. Parry feels hiring Stevens was a knee-jerk reaction and that the eventual Stevens report was nowhere near as exhaustive as his own inquiry a decade earlier. But it did lead to a court case where the word "bung" was often used although, as we shall see, that was not what the jury was asked to consider.

The full Stevens report was never made public but it essentially exonerated every Premier League manager and club official from having been involved in bungs, even though a total of 17 transfers, involving players signed by Newcastle, Bolton, Chelsea, Portsmouth and Middlesbrough, were questioned. Stevens told me: "To be frank if we had been asked to audit the Vatican we would have found a similar level of malpractice and mal-bureaucracy. Some was negligence, some was failure to follow proper procedures, some indicated the system was being abused."

However, Stevens was also required to tell the authorities anything that required further investigation and this is where the world had changed since Alan Sugar first spoke out. Back in 1995, when Arsenal wanted to bring criminal charges against Graham, they were advised by counsel: "The police have a lot on their plate." A decade later, the authorities no longer felt they could trust football to manage its own affairs and the victim of this change in attitude was to be Harry Redknapp who, in telling the Stevens inquiry that he had opened a Monaco bank account, had effectively tied a millstone round his own neck.

Operation Apprentice, a City of London police investigation into money laundering, rather than bungs, had begun launching well-publicised dawn raids on the homes of people in football, including Redknapp. Most came to nothing and the cases that did come to court related not to money-laundering but tax evasion. First, Milan Mandaric, the former owner of Portsmouth, and Peter Storrie, the club's chief executive, were cleared of tax evasion charges in connection with a fee paid to a Portsmouth player, Eyal Berkovic. Then, early in 2012, in a higher profile case, Redknapp and Mandaric were charged with tax evasion relating to payments totalling £187,000, which, the prosecution claimed, was undeclared commission on the transfer of Peter Crouch from Portsmouth in 2002. The decision to press charges on something other than illegal payments showed how the relationship between sport and the judiciary had altered.

Under his contract, Redknapp had been entitled to a five per cent commission on the deal. However, the jury was told he believed he was due an additional five per cent, money which he had received. Mandaric denied the payments were linked to the Crouch transfer and related to an personal investment he had made on Redknapp's behalf.

Redknapp was found not guilty in February 2012 and was promptly installed as favourite to succeed Fabio Capello who, by a strange twist of fate, had resigned as England manager on the very same day. For Redknapp it was, as he put it, the end of a nightmare and "a case that should never have come to court".

Notwithstanding the not guilty verdict, the evidence presented at Southwark

Crown Court suggested that, contrary to Parry's claims, and despite the vast influx of money, the game was still run like a cottage industry, with practices most other businesses would find unacceptable.

The Redknapp hearing provided striking evidence that the game can reward managers in a way that would make bankers' eyes water. Portsmouth paid Redknapp more than £4 million per year — four times the bonus that Royal Bank of Scotland chief executive Stephen Hester felt compelled to refuse after a public outcry. Consider that Redknapp was managing a club not sure of their Premier League status; Hester has been trying to rescue one of our major banks whose collapse was felt to be so unthinkable that the taxpayer now owns 83 per cent of it.

Furthermore, on top of the high wages, a manager can also legitimately receive a commission from the sale of a player, a practice introduced to supplement a manager's meagre wages when clubs had little money. Today, most businesses would see such payments as potential conflicts of interest.

Today, 20 years after Sugar brought bungs into the open, English football is still shrouded in secrecy, and we remain in the dark about much of what goes on in the game unless and until events escalate out of control.

The first Premier League inquiry into bungs spoke of transparency as one of the guiding principles for transforming the English game from a cottage industry to a properly run business.

But transparency has been limited. When I asked Stevens why all transfer details, including payments made to agents, should not be disclosed, his response was that such transparency would be bad for the football business. "The problem is football clubs are businesses. There is a commercial sensitivity which has got to be sufficient to allow trading to go on. I have sympathy with any commercial business which is trying to protect its position in the market place."

Stevens also sought to justify his position by saying that for all the media attention about alleged financial wrongdoing, the average fan had bigger concerns: "I would guess the average football fan is much more concerned about somebody diving than he is about what percentage an agent gets paid as a fee. He wants his team to win. When I go to the theatre I don't look at the accounts to see if it is a properly run theatre. I go to watch the show."

Following the Redknapp case there were more calls for greater transparency. Barry Hearn, owner of Leyton Orient, believes English football should follow the American model. "In a boxing match in Vegas you have to declare the gross receipts and in America all the transfer details are disclosed. That is what we should be doing. Not just the total transfer fee but how much was paid to an agent or anyone else, including a manager."

Parry insists: "I do not see why transfer payments should be in the public domain. It is disclosed to the authorities, the FA and the Premier League. It is confidential, commercial information. If I were still in the position of chief executive of a club I would not want to disclose the smart deals I had made on transfers, deals that gave me a competitive edge over other clubs."

"Nonsense," says Hearn. "Within the industry, details of such payments are well known. The agents talk about how much money they got on a deal."

On the practice of managers getting a cut from a transfer, Parry argues: "If the basic aim of the manager is aligned with that of the club, so be it. And just because the manager gets such a commission on a transfer there is no need to disclose it. Disclosure by itself would not make the game straighter or cleaner."

But the authorities are no longer confident that sports bodies can be trusted to carry out their own investigations, reflected in the successful 2011 criminal prosecution of three Pakistan cricketers for spot-fixing and the decision to charge John Terry for alleged racial abuse of Anton Ferdinand (for which he was acquitted). Football needs to understand that it must be transparent and accountable.

If the Redknapp case led to such reform, then it would have done much good. Unless it does, the game, and the Premier League, which ended its first 20 years as it began them, with tales of underhand payments, are not really equipped for the 21st century.

Chapter 13
GLOBAL FOOTBALL AND THE FIXERS

At 6am on Monday, May 28, 2012, two Italian police cars arrived at Coverciano, the country's football training centre. They had come to question Domenico Criscito, a player preparing for Euro 2012 with the Italian squad. His room was also searched. That day also saw the arrest of Stefano Mauri, captain of Lazio, and Juventus manager Antonio Conte, who had just led his club to the Serie A title. The police action related to investigations into alleged match-fixing orchestrated from Singapore. Chris Eaton, FIFA's former head of security, commented that this was an international investigation into match-fixing which had existed "unchallenged for the last 10 years. The money available is so attractive that the criminals involved and their organisations are taking risks. The threat to the integrity of sport cannot be overstated."

This threat had been underlined just a week earlier when on the morning of May 25, 2012, Ronald Noble, secretary general of Interpol, addressed the FIFA Congress in Budapest. In recent years the organisation has faced high-profile corruption charges which has seen the departure of some of its leading lights. But in this instance the man from Interpol had come as an ally in the common fight against match-fixing and illegal betting. A year earlier the two organisations had entered into a 10-year partnership to more aggressively and more effectively tackle corruption in football, and as Noble put it: "The roads of FIFA and Interpol were thus meant to meet — for the beautiful game to stay beautiful and for citizens in all countries of the world to be safer from the actions of organised crime."

He pointed out why it had become so necessary to rescue the beautiful game:

> What was most concerning, from a law enforcement point of view, were the links between match-fixing, illegal betting and transnational organised crime on a global scale. As a result of the huge profits associated with illegal gambling, of the vulnerability of players, and of the ease with which matches

of all levels are accessible for betting on via the internet, corrupting matches or their outcomes has become an activity of interest to transnational organised crime groups. On the one hand, we were seeing more and more cases of match-fixing and suspicious results, which was eroding confidence in the fairness of the game. On the other hand, the problem of corruption in sport has worrisome consequences that go well beyond the world of sport. Match-fixing and illegal betting have been linked to murders, violent assaults and threats of harm by organised crime to collect money from football debtors and family members of debtors. The list of negative consequences goes on and on. No region of the world is immune to the risk that one of its countries could fall victim to corruption in football. The Brazilian match-fixing scandal of 2005, the 2009 Hoyzer affair in Germany, the 2011 banning for life of 47 Korean footballers, and the fining of two of Nigeria's Premier League teams just a couple of months ago represent a handful of examples that demonstrate the global nature of the problem.

Nobel said that this had led Interpol to coordinate, he said, "multi-country enforcement actions targeting illegal football betting schemes through a series of operations code-named SOGA for 'soccer' and 'gambling'. So far, three SOGA operations have been conducted in Southeast Asia. They resulted in nearly 7,000 arrests, the seizure of more than $26 million in cash and the closure of organised crime-controlled illegal gambling dens which handled more than two billion dollars' worth of bets."

Interpol had estimated the global market in match-fixing may be worth £60 million and the real target of the Italian police was a Malaysian man called Seet Eng Tan from Singapore, also known as Dan. He was said to be at the centre of a Southeast Asian syndicate that targeted matches from Finland to the Baltic nations and many other countries. By the time this emerged, the idea that match-fixing was a scourge was no longer a surprise to anyone, indeed it was a constant theme of Michel Platini, the UEFA president.

Yet the Premier League was barely two years old when in 1994 the English game was confronted with sensational allegations of match-fixing. Such allegations were not new in football and can be traced back almost to the start of the professional game. But the match-fixing scandal that emerged in the 1994–95 season was of an entirely different dimension and suggested the global reach of the Premier League had changed things.

The story emerged following a sting operation set up by *The Sun* newspaper with Christopher Vincent, a former business partner of Bruce Grobbelaar, the Liverpool goalkeeper. Grobbelaar and Vincent, who both came from

Zimbabwe, had gone into business together after meeting in London. The business failed and in August 1994 Vincent approached *The Sun*.

The paper, having launched its own investigations, set up the sting. This involved Vincent contacting Grobbelaar, suggesting reconciliation. Their hotel room where they met was bugged by the newspaper. Grobbelaar was seen on video accepting £2,000 from Vincent, who claimed he was representing a Far Eastern syndicate which would pay more — as much as £100,000 — if he was prepared to throw games.

The day before *The Sun* published its story on November 9, 1994, it contacted Grobbelaar, who was at Gatwick Airport. He denied the allegations.

The Sun's story, headlined "Grobbelaar Took Bribes to Fix Games", recorded the Zimbabwean making many sensational claims. One of them went as follows: "Do you think I went to Kuala Lumpur on the off chance? Absolutely not. Because the Short Man had said, 'Any time you want to go to the Far East, you and your wife can go — I'll sort it out.' I got an offer to go to Kuala Lumpur to play... the boss man there, if it was the same person, he's fucking big in Malaysia. He'll say that man... pow! That's it. Finished."

The "Short Man" Grobbelaar was taking about was a Malaysian businessman called Heng Suan Lim, who lived in London and was also known as Richard. The police investigation, codenamed Operation Navajo, which began after *The Sun* sent its dossier to the police, saw dawn raids on the homes of Grobbelaar and three others. After an investigation lasting two and a half years, in which statements were taken from 700 witnesses, four were brought to trial at Winchester Crown Court in January 1997. Besides Grobbelaar they were Hans Segers, who had played in goal for Wimbledon, John Fashanu, who had played as a forward for Wimbledon, and Heng Suan Lim. They were charged with conspiring to corruptly give and receive money to influence football matches. Grobbelaar was also charged on his own with corruption — accepting £2,000 from Vincent to influence a football match. All the men denied the charges and Grobbelaar also denied his individual corruption charge.

The Crown prosecutor, David Calvert-Smith QC, told the court that much of the evidence of the case came from Vincent and that the jury would have little sympathy for him as a witness. "His decision to expose Mr Grobbelaar was as a result of a business quarrel and he went to *The Sun* as a result of a desire to enrich himself." Despite this, said Calvert-Smith, Vincent's evidence was backed by other evidence, and some of the admissions made to him by Grobbelaar about matches he had fixed were born out by videos of the games.

There were also files full of documentary evidence, many of which linked the four men. Calvert-Smith told the court that Vincent first learned of the alleged corruption in 1993, when Grobbelaar told him about a scheme to help Far Eastern betting syndicates. Grobbelaar reportedly told Vincent he was unhappy with his low level of pay at Liverpool and was determined to make as much money as possible over the next two years. Later that day Grobbelaar and Vincent went to a hotel at Manchester's City airport, where the player was allegedly given an envelope containing £1,000 by the Short Man — Heng Suan Lim. Grobbelaar then reportedly informed Vincent that the Far Eastern syndicate for which Lim acted as a go-between was now prepared to pay him between £40,000 and £60,000 per game if he would "do business".

Vincent later learned of a code system used by the players in which "Wimbledon" stood for win, "Leeds" for lose and "Dundee" for draw. Mobile telephone records for Heng Suan Lim revealed extensive communication between himself and Grobbelaar, Fashanu and Segers. This key evidence, claimed the prosecution, backed up much of its case, including Chris Vincent's claim that he and Grobbelaar drove to London for a meeting with Lim — calls had been logged on the mobile phones of the men which showed this to be true.

The prosecution case was that Lim was the link between the players and a Far Eastern betting syndicate which allegedly master-minded the scam. Grobbelaar was accused of taking a £40,000 bribe to throw a game in November 1993 when Liverpool, for whom he was keeping goal, lost 3–0 to Newcastle. He could also have collected £125,000 for throwing a game against Manchester United, it was alleged, but this finished 3–3 after Grobbelaar made some instinctive saves.

Segers was accused of taking large sums of money to throw matches involving Wimbledon in deals set up by Fashanu. The prosecution alleged that in the crucial match against Everton on May 7, 1994, when Everton were on the brink of relegation, Segers had deliberately conceded a third goal. The prosecution told the court that Joe Kinnear, the Wimbledon manager, had told Segers that he (Kinnear) did not know Segers had a favourite uncle up there on Merseyside. Segers' response was that he could not remember and his explanation for the goal was: "I had it covered all the way, but it hit a divot, popped up and changed direction."

Fashanu was accused of handing £40,000 to Grobbelaar following the Liverpool-Newcastle match and receiving £20,000 from Indonesian sources. Heng Suan Lim was said to have contacted the three men on numerous occasions via mobile phone calls.

But the crown could not convince the jury the four were guilty. The first trial was declared a mistrial and a second one saw all four acquitted. All four left court free men. The prosecution argued the dice was loaded against them as the juries were so taken by the star quality of the footballers that Grobbelaar had even been asked for his autograph. In July 1999 Grobbelaar went on to win his libel action against *The Sun,* receiving £85,000 and his costs. On hearing the verdict he said: "Today ends the slur on football, the game that I love. It was not the money I was after. I was only wanting to clear my name in football, which I have done today."

But 18 months later, on January 18, 2001, it all changed when the Appeal Court judges overturned the jury's verdict. Lord Justice Brown said: "I come to consider the probabilities of the case and it is at this point that to my mind Grobbelaar's story falls apart. He had, as it seems to me, just too much to explain away — his entire dealings with Mr Lim. It is not credible to suggest he was anxious to discuss with Mr Lim his prospects for playing in the Far East, the evidence being that Mr Lim was merely a football enthusiast with no connection whatever in the professional game."

As for Grobbelaar's assertion that he had invented claims of match-fixing so he could ultimately expose Vincent as a crook, Lord Justice Parker said: "In my judgement Mr Grobbelaar's explanations of those admissions is so utterly implausible that no jury, acting reasonably, could have accepted it as true."

Grobbelaar took the matter to the House of Lords and the case was heard by five Law Lords. The whole legal battle had now taken on an epic quality of some of the old FA Cup replays. In effect this was the fifth time the case was being heard but it proved the final time with a verdict that Grobbelaar could claim as a victory, though it proved a Pyrrhic one. The Law Lords, by a four-to-one majority, upheld the appeal and accepted that Grobbelaar had been libelled but slashed the award to a nominal £1 and ordered him to pay *The Sun's* costs. In essence the Law Lords held that while Grobbelaar had agreed to fix matches they could not say he had actually fixed matches.

As Lord Bingham put it:

> On all the evidence it defies reason to accept that the appellant did not make a corrupt agreement with Mr Vincent and accept a bribe from him. In relation to Mr Lim, the position is possibly less clear. The tapes contain apparently clear admissions of a corrupt agreement and the acceptance of bribes. But the appellant's fixing and attempted fixing of matches was said to have been done in pursuance of that agreement. If the jury concluded that the appellant had not been shown to have fixed or attempted to fix matches, it could perhaps have felt some doubt about the agreement itself.
>
> The question then arises whether on that basis the jury's award of damages can be upheld. The jury will have had in mind the newspaper's banner headline on the front page of its first issue devoted to this topic

and the similar headline on page 2, quoted in paragraph 5 above. The jury may well have held it against the newspaper that this allegation of match-fixing and attempted match-fixing was persisted in and never withdrawn despite the lack of extraneous evidence to support it. The ambush of the appellant at the airport may have been seen as oppressive, the weight of the newspaper's journalistic onslaught as excessive and the newspaper's attempt to involve the appellant's children as offensive. ("How much of what's been happening have you told the children about? Have they been getting a hard time at school as the result of the allegations against you?")

The jury's generosity towards the appellant is perhaps understandable. But it cannot be supported. The tort of defamation protects those whose reputations have been unlawfully injured. It affords little or no protection to those who have, or deserve to have, no reputation deserving of legal protection. Until November 9, 1994 when the newspaper published its first articles about him, the appellant's public reputation was unblemished. But he had in fact acted in a way in which no decent or honest footballer would act and in a way which could, if not exposed and stamped on, undermine the integrity of a game which earns the loyalty and support of millions. Even if the newspaper had published no more than what, on my interpretation of the jury's verdict, it was entitled to have published, the appellant would have been shown to have acted in a way which any right-thinking person would unequivocally condemn. It would be an affront to justice if a court of law were to award substantial damages to a man shown to have acted in such flagrant breach of his legal and moral obligations.

The Grobbelaar trials had not seen the British police go to the Far East to seek evidence. *The Sun* had been there and come back with nothing substantial and the British authorities decided it would be a waste of time to go there. The police might have missed something by not taking a flight out East. That is certainly the view of Declan Hill, an investigative journalist in the area of organised crime. In his pathfinding book *The Fix, Soccer and Organised Crime,* he writes:

> What is truly extraordinary is that while the investigation was going on in England, at exactly the same time senior members of the Royal Malaysian Police and the Singapore anti-corruption agency were cracking down on the networks of match-fixers in their country. If the European and Asian police had joined forces, soccer might have become a great deal safer and this book might never have come to be written.

The Grobbelaar trial made many in England aware that Premier League games aroused intense interest far from home, particularly in the East. The result was that, every now and again, strange things happened in Premier League games for which the only explanation offered was that this was the work of a Far East betting syndicate. This was dramatically revealed on the evening of February 10, 1999, when Metropolitan Police officers from Greenwich near The Valley, Charlton's stadium, arrested Roger Firth, Eng Hwa Lim, Chee Kew Ong and Wai Yuen Liu.

Firth, the security supervisor at the Valley, had access to many parts of the ground including the electrical control room from where the floodlights were controlled. That evening, at around 8pm, Firth had been seen meeting Liu, Lim and Ong outside The Valley and allowing them access to the electrical control room. Firth left a duplicate key inside the room and subsequently left the ground. Lim, Ong and Liu were seen near the room but did not go inside. The three men went back to their car and it was as they drove away that police arrested them. Firth was also arrested nearby on foot.

When officers searched a bag that Lim was seen carrying they found electrical equipment. An electrical device, a remote control unit, a number of mobile telephones and other electrical items were recovered from the car. Lim and Ong's hotel room in Bayswater yielded a number of electrical devices in various stages of assembly.

Firth told the police that some time before Christmas 1998 he met Lim and Ong at The Valley as they had expressed an interest in security arrangements and claimed that they were interested in adopting stewarding methods in China. Over the next few weeks Firth met with them on several occasions and it was during these meetings that they slowly introduced to him the idea of him allowing them access to the electrical control room so that they could tamper with the system to allow them control of the floodlights. They offered him £20,000 and he agreed to co-operate.

During their meetings Ong indicated that they had been responsible for the floodlight failures at Upton Park during a match between West Ham United and Crystal Palace on November 3, 1997. In this match the lights went out in the 65th minute, moments after a Frank Lampard goal had made the score 2–2. The gang had also interfered with lights at Selhurst Park during a match between Wimbledon and Arsenal on December 22, 1997. Then, with the score at 0–0 and just 13 seconds into the second half, the lights went out and the match was abandoned.

Ong had gone on explain to Firth what they were up to. Many Premier League matches are broadcast live to countries all over the world, including

Hong Kong, Singapore and Malaysia and Ong explained to Firth that there were corrupt betting practices in operation in the Far East on Premier League matches, hence the need to be able to control the outcome of a football match.

Firth said that he had given Ong and Lim access to the electrical control room on February 6 and 7 for some hours. It is thought that they were intending to complete the installation of their equipment over those days with a view to having it ready for use at the Charlton vs. Wimbledon match on February 8, which would have been televised live to South-East Asia. However, Firth was concerned about the number of people at the ground that day and Lim and Ong were forced to leave before their work had been completed. It is believed that they then focused their attention on the match between Charlton Athletic and Liverpool, to be played on Saturday, February 13. The plan was to bring the football match to an end by shutting down the floodlights with a remote control switch should the match progress in a way disadvantageous to the betting interests of those in the Far East. To this end, Firth met up with Ong, Lim and Liu (whom he claimed he had never met before) on the evening of February 10 at the ground.

On August 25, 1999, all four were found guilty and sentenced. Eng Hwa Lim and Chee Kew Ong got four years each, Wai Yuen Liu 30 months and Roger Firth 18 months.

Before this, and particularly before *The Sun* published its sensational allegations, English football had been confident that match-fixing was a scourge it had long since exorcised. Any doubters were quickly reminded of what had become known as the Biggest Sports Scandal of the Century. For English football this was an example of how the authorities had dealt with the corruption then in the game.

That match-fixing scandal had broken on a spring Sunday, April 12, 1964, in the *Sunday People*. The paper's allegations, initially dismissed as "a load of nonsense", led to a police investigation where more than 60 players were interviewed. Ten months after the allegations surfaced, 10 professional footballers were brought to trial at Nottingham Assizes in January 1965 and received prison terms of between four months and four years. One of them was Tony Kay, who before the *People* story broke had been looking forward to a glittering career after winning his first England cap. Instead the £100 fine and the jail sentence he received meant that Nobby Stiles replaced him in England's World Cup-winning team of 1966.

The match in question took place at Portman Road in December 1962. Ipswich, who had won the title the previous season, beat Sheffield Wednesday 2–1. Three Sheffield Wednesday players — the centre-half and captain Peter

Swan, centre-forward David Layne and wing-half Tony Kay — were involved in the fix having made sure of the result. Each man won £100 by backing their team to lose.

The man who had engineered the bet was Jimmy Gauld, an inside-forward for Charlton, Everton, Plymouth, Swindon and Mansfield between 1955 and 1960. How the whole thing took place shows how football worked back in the 1960s. Layne had gone to see West Ham play Mansfield in a midweek Cup replay and, unable to get a seat in the stand, was allowed by the stewards to walk down the tunnel to find a place somewhere. Gauld, nursing a broken leg, was also there and after the match the two had a chat. Gauld told Layne two other games, Lincoln vs. Brentford in the Third Division and York vs. Oldham in the Fourth Division, were also being fixed, a treble was wanted and were the Sheffield players up to it? Gauld had also told Layne how players were earning a great deal of money from such bets. This was a time when rumours of match-fixing were rife in the game. Indeed, Everton were alleged to have been involved in match-fixing in their championship-winning season of 1962–63, but there was no evidence and when the Football League investigated other allegations they found no proof.

However, Layne's drink with Gauld was to prove different. Layne spoke to Swan the next day and they agreed that as they always lost at Ipswich they had nothing to lose. Layne, Swan and Kay each agreed to bet £50. Layne made the collection and handed the money to Gauld, who two days before the match bet not in his name but as a Mr Parry. Ipswich took a 2–0 lead, Sheffield Wednesday duly lost and the players collected their winnings. It meant a profit of £100, a handsome reward in 1964. The Sheffield players travelled down to London on the way to Ipswich on the train and with a new journalist travelling with them Swan made him comfortable by introducing him to all the players. Swan and his team spent the night before the match in London watching *Mutiny on the Bounty* in the West End before taking the train to Ipswich for the match.

More than 40 years later, when Swan wrote his book, *Peter Swan Setting the Record Straight*, he insisted that: "... Nothing the three of us did in the game affected the outcome. We just approached the game as normal, played our usual way and got beat. That was illustrated by the fact that Tony Kay won the man of the match award in the *People* and David Layne also got the highest ranking in the forward line. It was later claimed in court that I had bet on numerous lower league games I knew to be 'bent'; that was totally untrue. Admittedly, I would often bet on the fixed odds, as a lot of players did in those days, even though it was against the rules. I never won anything, though. As for betting on Wednesday to lose, the Ipswich game was just a one-off. Whether it would have led to something else, I honestly don't know."

Swan knew he was carrying a secret and would later tell the journalist Frank Clough. He said: "Frank, I could tell you something that's happened which would shatter English football." But while Swan did not talk, Gauld did. He told all to Mike Gabbert and Peter Campling of *People* for £7,000. Armed with this knowledge, they interviewed Layne and when he confessed and signed an affidavit they knew they had the story. When they visited Swan at his home, Gabbert told him: "We've just been to David Layne and he's owned up to fixing a game at Ipswich. He says you had a part in it." Swan, who had been warned by his mother, who took an interest in spiritual matters, that he would soon face trouble, refused to talk. He insisted and has gone on insisting that he did not fix a match, only had a bet against his team. Gauld received the heaviest sentence: four years' imprisonment and costs of £5,000. Kay, Layne and Swan were also jailed and banned from football for life, although the ban was lifted after eight years and Swan and Layne resumed their careers in lower-division clubs.

With the arrival of the Premier League, English football was no longer just a local affair. It was now broadcast live not only at weekends but also on weekdays far and wide. People who lived in the country where the matches were being played saw fewer matches live on their television sets then those living many thousands of miles away. And the matches were immensely popular, particularly in the Far East. In societies where gambling was part of the culture, gambling on football had now became a passion with millions of pounds wagered on matches. Some estimates were that as much as a billion pounds was gambled on English football in Malaysia, Indonesia, Thailand, Singapore and Hong Kong.

But why should lights be interfered with in a match? The explanation was that, unlike Britain, the "result" of a match for betting purposes stands as long as the second half has started. It did not have to be finished. Some of the stories emerging from Malaysia sound fanciful, almost like a movie plot with bundles of notes wrapped up in newspapers being handed to middlemen at bus-stops late at night, destined for international players. The masterminds included one figure known as "the Blind Man", who made a fortune from a sport he had never seen.

In his journeys through Asia trying to investigate these gambling claims, Declan Hill came across many fascinating stories of who gambles and how. A police inspector, who Hill suspects is on the make, told him: "Always take the favourite: Chelsea, Manchester United and Arsenal. They rarely lose; the bookies will try to make you forget it, but don't. I could show you places to gamble."

Hill provided a structure of the illegal Asian bookmaking syndicate. It consists of two levels — a local gambling level of punters placing bets on the Premier League and other European and local leagues. The bets could be in person, over the phone or internet. There are bookies' runners that report to regional bookies in counting centres. Above them are the national level bosses, overlords, a prominent politician or businessman or the triad underworld. And, while the small fry are arrested and charged, the big operators are left to carry on with their activities.

His most fascinating meetings were with Don, operator of a small casino in Indonesia, and Steve, a shipping executive in Georgetown, a northern Malaysian city. Hill describes them as the Asian Laurel and Hardy as he records their conversation on gambling and cooking.

> **Don**: You took Liverpool to ball [Liverpool to win the game by two goals]. Why? You crazy?

> **Steve**: No way la. You don't what you are talking about. Rafa [Benitez, then Liverpool manager], he knows what he is doing. Take the odds, la.

> **Don**: Bullshit! Fowler he is too old, just fucking around. Go under Eat Ball. Hey. I have a great menu for fish satay with deep fried mushroom...

> **Hill**: When I first met them, Don was bemoaning his luck over an English Premier League match the night before. He had bet the total goal line. The higher and more unlikely the score, the more money you stand to win if correct.
>
> Don had bet on Fulham to beat Norwich with a total score in the game of four goals (3–1, 4–0). The actual result was Fulham beat Norwich 6–0. If they had kept the score down Don would have made 23 times the money on his bet. As it were, he had lost it all.

There is no suggestion that any of these matches were fixed. But the way the tentacles of the passion generated by Premier League football can reach back to the UK was to be gruesomely revealed in 2008. Then Kevin Zhen Xing Yang, a Chinese graduate student, and his girlfriend Cici Xi Zhou were found dead in a flat near Newcastle city centre. Everything suggested this was no ordinary killing and that the couple had been tortured. Yang's throat was slashed, Zhou's head had been smashed in three places.

It eventually emerged that the couple were not quite what they claimed to be. Yang worked for the illegal gambling market in the East. He went to matches and used his phone to give live commentary to the punters back home. He was helped in his task by members of the expat Chinese community. But at some stage it seems he betrayed his employers and was made an example of. The Newcastle police found the killer but in sentencing him to 33 years in jail the judge commented that the defendant was clearly too frightened to reveal the real masterminds behind these gruesome murders. The press conference held to announce the sentence aroused such interest in China that it is believed five hundred million people watched it, five times the number who watched the 2008 Super Bowl.

Declan Hill concludes:

> Kevin Yang, Cici Zhou and their murderers are part of an international revolution. A global phenomenon of gambling and match-fixing that is transforming societies and destroying sports around the world. Many of the leagues in Asia, where it started, and eastern Europe have effectively collapsed, because of this corruption. Now, the fixers are coming to Western Europe and North America and they are fixing hundreds of games.

But for all the allegations of match-fixing around the world, no evidence has emerged that any match-fixing is occurring in the Premier League. However, evidence that spot-fixing may have been going on did emerge in July 2012 when Claus Lundekvam, the former Norwegian international who played for Southampton, was quoted telling the Norwegian TV station NRK — followed by interviews with *The Sun* — how players back in the 1996–97 season had bet on things such as the first throw-in. Several players would put money in a pot, the money would be given to a staff member to place a bet. There would be an agreement with the opposing team to make sure the bet was won. "It's not something I'm proud of. For a while we did this almost every week. We made a fair bit of money. We could make deals with the opposing captain about, for example, betting on the first throw, the first corner, who started with the ball, a yellow card or a penalty. Those were the sorts of thing we had influence over. The results were never on the agenda. That is something I would never have done. We were professional competitors. Even though what we did, of course, was illegal, it was just a fun thing."

This was not the first time a player had spoken of spot-fixing or attempted spot-fixing. Matt Le Tissier, then a Southampton player, had confessed in his autobiography how back in 1995 he had been involved in an attempt at fixing the first throw-in during a match against Wimbledon but it had not worked and it was just a bit of fun.

However, with the authorities aware of the worldwide scale of match-fixing, FIFA soon announced it would investigate.

It was a sharp indication of how the world of football had been changed during the Premier League years. What the advent of the Premier League had done was help create an international pool of football. English football before the Premier League was localised. The success of the Premier League made it global. The league can hardly be blamed if sharks enter the pool but the League's success has given the sharks an opportunity that they did not have before.

Conclusion
THE PROBLEMS OF SUCCESS

Just weeks after the 20th season of the Premier League, hailed as the greatest season in the history of the League, figures emerged for the previous season, 2010–11. They showed that the League, once seen as the idea of a deluded few and whose creation was opposed by many fans, was by some distance the biggest football league in the world. With revenues of €2.5 billion in the 2010–11 season it could boast the highest revenue growth of the five big European leagues — the Bundesliga, La Liga, Serie A and Ligue 1 — of 12 per cent at £241 million. The Germans come second with income of €1.746 million, the Spanish third with €1,718 million, the Italians fourth with €1,553 million and the French last in this group with €1,040 million.

The ascendancy of the Premier League has been evident for many years. It is significant that against a period of unprecedented modern austerity, the Premier League continues to put distance between itself and its European rivals. Back in 2005–06 the Premier League, with income of €1,995 million, led the others but not by so much. Then the comparable figures were Italy €1,277 million, Germany €1,195 million, Spain €1,158 million and France €910 million.

The Premier League could also claim to have done something about the much-debated level of debt. The total net debt of the league, at £2.4 billion in the summer of 2011, was almost a billion less since the summer of 2009, although this was largely the result of owner debt being converted to equity with many clubs surviving because their owners were willing to put their hands in their large pockets.

Yet success comes at a price. The Premier League also spends the most on wages in Europe, €1,777 million, €600 million higher than the next league. For many, this has changed football and made it a world of rich fat-cat players with club success dictated by money. Even players' union boss Gordon Taylor, who started playing when the maximum wage existed and can be expected to defend his members' high earnings, accepts that football needs a new balance:

Professional football is neither a total business or a total sport. It's got to get the balance right and the question is how do you try and make sure that your sporting competition is as fair as possible. You almost need a handicap system like you have in horseracing and even with golf to try to make sure that the latest team just promoted into the Premier League have a chance of winning it. You remember in the '70s and the '80s who won the European Cup — Nottingham Forest, Aston Villa, Manchester United, Liverpool — we had a whole host of teams. Gradually, as money started dictating we're getting fewer and fewer clubs monopolising success and while the Premier League has been a very successful commercial concept, it's almost becoming three leagues within a league. A top-tier of clubs, a middle layer and a bottom layer which only hopes to survive in the Premier League. And from that point of view what could we do to try and balance things out?

The Germans have suggested one way of doing this and this has led them to introduce a rule where the majority ownership of a German club must remain in Germany. The Germans also have a rigorous licensing system for clubs. But for the British to introduce a German style system of ownership would mean fundamental change with clubs, possibly, having to change their limited companies structure. Such an outcome is impossible to conceive. The British have talked of government legislation to bring in a regulator. There seemed a real possibility of that in April 2010, just as the country went to the polls. Hugh Robertson, the Conservative shadow minister, told me:

> The national game needs to deal with four issues. The "fit and proper person test" for club owners, transparency so that people looking at football clubs can see exactly what's going on, the whole question of debt as a percentage of turnover, and governance. There are far too few people that sit on football boards, either in clubs or the organisations, that act independently. Most are part of the game's vested interests.

He went on to warn that if by the end of the summer of 2010 the football authorities had not acted then "the government will have to step in. One of the options would be an independent regulator to run the game." But all that has happened is a House of Commons Select Committee report on the governance of football. Although critical of the present regulations and urging more tightening of rules, this did not seek to impose any government regulations.

The only change likely is to the very peculiar system football has developed when it comes to paying its debts. No playing field could be less level and more skewed. This, the now infamous football creditors' rule, states that a club who cannot pay their debts can default on the money they owe their creditors. However, one type of creditors ranks above everyone else, including the taxman, and must be paid. These are payments to players, coaching staff and any transfer fees due to other clubs. Note this applies only to the wages for players and coaching staff, so that wages to a club's administrative staff, the tea lady, or the coach driver are not covered. The football authorities say that, if a club do not pay their football creditors, they cannot play football.

In 2002, the collapse of Bradford City, once of the Premier League, saw the club owe £2.5 million in taxes, and money was also due to the local authority and the St John Ambulance. They all had to go without but their star player Benito Carbone, on a mere £40,000 a week, was entitled to his full salary. Portsmouth, now in their second administration, provide an even more potent example. During their first administration it was estimated that the club's football creditors were owed in the region of £30 million. This had to be paid in full, with other creditors receiving approximately 16 pence in the pound. This was because wages of between £30,000 and £50,000 a week had to be met if the club were to continue playing football. Yet the builder who did work at the ground went unpaid.

The rule goes back to the time when football was not a business but a cottage industry. That it operates when it is a huge industry is an absurdity. It can be argued that football clubs operate in a very specialised world with their own trade rules. So while poaching of staff in all other professions is common, in football it is a violation of the rules of the trade. A club wanting a player, or a manager, of another club cannot approach the player or manager directly but must go through the club. Few in football now defend the creditors rule. Greg Clarke, chairman of the Football League, told me: "It is difficult to morally justify the football creditors rule." The Inland Revenue has tried and failed to have it declared unlawful and this makes it likely the government may follow through on the Select Committee's recommendation that if the Revenue attempt failed there should be legislation to abolish it. It will recognise that football is a business.

But whether that rule change comes or not, what it will not do is deal with a major problem created by the rise of the Premier League. Here we have a story of the child that has long outgrown the father and condemned him to a life of servitude. The 2010–11 season illustrated this vividly. While the 20 Premier League clubs had an income of £2.3 billion, the remaining 72 clubs in professional football in England between them had an income of under £700 million. Two of them, Port Vale and Portsmouth, are in administration and 13 of the clubs in these three divisions are classified by financial experts as in distress, meaning that they have serious court actions against them, including winding-up petitions and high court writs, or have been issued with striking off notices for late filing of accounts or have county court judgments against them. And there are some with serious negative balances on their balance sheet. As the insolvency expert Gerard Krasner put it: "That 19 per cent of clubs in these three divisions are showing signs of ill-health when directly compared with just 1 per cent of all businesses in the wider economy clearly shows the sector is facing a very challenging time commercially."

The Premier League's answer to this is that it looks after the wider football family. So in the 2010–11 season Championship clubs increased their income by 4 per cent to £17 million largely because of what are called solidarity payments from the Premier League (it also helped that a couple of big clubs, Leeds and Norwich, got promoted). In the 20 years of its existence the Premier League's parachute payments to clubs who get relegated have also increased considerably. So in the 2010–11 season, the first year of the increased parachute payments, clubs in receipt of them had an average income of £29 million. This compared with an average income of £15 million for clubs who had never made the leap to the Premier League. And this was equal to a single parachute payment in 2010–11. What all this means is that the Premier League has in effect parked the old Football League in a granny flat, gives it some money and told to get on with it.

Those who run the old Football League realise this well enough. Their leaders openly admit, as Lord Mawhinney, the former chairman, put it: "The business model for professional football in this country is not sustainable." Two months before the start of the 2011–12 season, Mawhinney's successor, Greg Clarke, re-emphasised this, saying: "Our debt is already approaching £500 million for all the Football League clubs. It could easily reach £1 billion in the next three or four years. That is not sustainable." While the Premier League, currently negotiating a new television deal, has no problem attracting bids, the Football League television deal, which starts in the 2012 season, is worse than its previous one. As Clarke put it: "The three-year deal with Sky, worth £195 million, is a 26 per cent drop on the existing contract. It will have an impact on the season." The BBC did not even bid and, noted Clarke: "They decided that they weren't in a position to bid significant amounts of money for Football League sports' rights. They're cutting back on sports' rights across the margin as part of their cutbacks." Observe the word 'margin' which sums up the marginal position of the old Football League.

Perhaps the most vivid illustration of the overall state of the Premier League, the runaway child of the Football League, in comparison with its parent is the location of the League's annual conference. Last season this Football League's annual conference was held at the Coral Beach Hotel, near Paphos in Cyprus. Yet in 2011 Brighton would have been the obvious choice. This is the normal seaside town the British go to for such conferences and the local club had just won promotion to the Championship. But the League went abroad because, as Clarke told me: "It's too expensive in this country. You can't get any sponsorship. We got sponsorship from the Cyprus Tourist Authority, deals on hotels, deals on flights, cash payments from accountants and lawyers who sponsor our conference." In 2010 the League had got similar sponsorship from Malta and went there to discuss what it could do to cope with the success of the Premier League.

This success has forced the oldest league in the world to change. Mawhinney, a former cabinet minister and Conservative Party chairman, persuaded the Football League in 2004 to rebrand itself. This meant changing the names of the divisions into the Championship, League 1 and League 2. It also brought in sporting sanctions: 10-point deductions for clubs who go into administration and a 'fit and proper' test for club directors and majority shareholders. Mawhinney had to fight the FA to bring it in but admits this was not a comprehensive fit and proper person test. That would have cost £1.5 million, money which the Football League could not afford. The League also forced clubs to disclose who their real owners were. This started the process which led to the ownership of clubs like Leeds, which had remained secret to the wider world, being revealed although this came after pressure from the Select Committee. The League also began to publish every six months how much they paid agents. The coming season will also see the League bring in salary caps.

But this still cannot deal with the basic problem of football. In the words of Mawhinney: "One of the problems football has is that the directors may be successful businessmen but in many cases they ran their own business. So whatever they decided happened. Then they come to football and all those fans out there put pressure on them, usually to spend money. They don't like that. Fan pressure is a shock to the system and they don't have any experience of dealing with public opposition."

And the very success of the Premier League means those club owners in all the other divisions are always under pressure. This is where the Premier League, on the back of its astonishing rise, could do more and be innovative with regard to the structure and governance of football; help the wider football family adapt to the new world the Premier League's success has ushered in. It could do more to introduce a comprehensive 'fit and proper' person test for the entire football world, just not the Premier League. It has the resources for it but having enjoyed success it sees no reason to change or innovate. It did go for a major revolution when in 2008 it proposed an additional round of matches, the 39th game, to be played abroad. The plan attracted universal criticism, not least from the FA and FIFA, and was shot down. But that plan was meant to meet the threat from the attempt by the NFL and other American sports to take their sporting franchises abroad and also placate the Premier League clubs who do not enjoy the international appeal of the bigger clubs. It did not address the fundamental problem of the skewed world of English football, skewed by the success of the Premier League.

A month after the dramatic end of its 20th season, the Premier League announced a record £3 billion television deal. It represented a 71 per cent increase and will give at least £14m more per year for each football club. The three-year deal, which will run from the 2013–14 season, means the team finishing bottom will receive more than the £60.6 million champions Manchester City earned for the 2011–12 season. Broadcasters had agreed to pay £6.6 million for each individual televised match.

BSkyB, while retaining most of its rights, had to pay £2.3 billion for 116 matches per season from 2013–14. It also had a new rival in BT, which won the rights to 38 games, including almost half the "first pick" games on offer. For this, BT paid £738 million over three years. BT, which will show Saturday lunchtime and midweek evenings, made it clear they would have a new sports channel. Sky had seen off other rivals, Setanta and ESPN, but Richard Scudamore saw BT getting 18 of the 38 coveted "first pick" matches as a "game changer". Ian Livingstone, BT's chief executive, and his colleagues have hugely ambitious plans. They have not invested in all this fibre optic cable for nothing, they want to establish a direct relationship with consumers.

Despite the worst recession in the western world for 70 years, the Premier League was immensely attractive and even Scudamore confessed he was "surprised" by the huge increase in fees it could command. To measure how huge, let us remind ourselves that the first television deal back in 1992 had seen BSkyB pay £191.5 million over five years for 60 live matches a year, initially £35 million, rising to £39.5 million in the final year. The BBC paid £22.5 million over five years for Match Of The Day. This new deal did not include the BBC figures and the overseas deal, which was being negotiated as this book went to press.

In addition, soon after this deal was announced the Premier League renewed its sponsorship with Barclays. This deal, running for three seasons from 2013, is worth £120 million. The announcement had come just days after Barclays was fined \$453 million by US and British authorities for providing false data to help manipulate Libor, the London interbank rate and a key global interest rate. As we have seen back in 1992, brewers such as Bass were offering £3 million for a five-year sponsorship deal. It all suggested that whatever else happens in the world it seems the Premier League just keeps marching on.

As it ushers in its 21st season, the Premier League would do well to remind itself that the moment of triumph is also the moment of greatest danger, as the Romans were forced to learn. The tale goes of how a great Roman general, returning to Rome having conquered some exotic foreign land, was always acclaimed by the crowd. But there was also a man riding next to him in the chariot who warned him that his moment of triumph was also a moment of peril. He should be careful that amid the celebrations he takes steps to ensure the next moment does not mark his doom.

Doom for the Premier League has often been predicted and in the last 20 years it has shown a remarkable capacity to prove the soothsayers wrong and buck even the worst recession since the 1930s. But success should not make it ignore the problems of ownership and finance that clubs face, problems for which they are no easy solutions. However, these are problems for which solutions must be found. The Premier League has grown because it has seized opportunities and, lacking any fixed ideology, it has always been flexible enough to move swiftly.

However, its success means it now needs to think about a game plan because its success has changed the game. The old pre-Premier League system of English football, which did allow whatever wealth there was then in the game to trickle down and had a sort of democracy of sorts, has gone. But nothing has replaced it. The Premier League does not feel it has a duty to fashion a replacement. The Premier League has shown itself to be a master tactician. Now it needs to develop a strategic plan to deal with the success it has created. If it fails to develop one on issues such as ownership, then like the Roman general, it may find that its moment of triumph carries the seeds of its own doom.

ACKNOWLEDGEMENTS

I am indebted to many people for their help, encouragement and kindness during the writing of this book.

I am grateful to my old friend Paul Nicholson for re-establishing my links with Chris Akers who kindly allowed me access to his unrivalled archives which provides the most telling insights into how the Premier League television deal, central to its success, was created.

I cannot adequately thank Richard Heller and Richard Weekes. Richard Heller brought his customary wide-angled knowledge of events and issues and Richard Weekes both his unrivalled expertise of football but also his great skills as editor. Without their help and guidance, this book could well have been a mountain too far to climb.

Dan Evans, who was a marvellous editor when I worked for the Daily Telegraph, was a tower of strength and wisdom.

Rob Maul, Nick Spenser and Patrick Halling were diligent in their research into the 20-year history of this fascinating league. And Mike Tate proved a wonderful super-sub providing valuable guidance at short notice.

I would also like to thank my colleagues at *The Standard* led by the editor Sarah Sands and including Ian Walker, Doug Wills, Steve Cording, Tim Nichols and Neil Robinson for all their help.

Duncan Mackay and his wonderful website Inside World Football has both been a source of information and a channel to raise and discuss issues pertinent to his narrative.

The story of the Premier League is one I have followed since its start. Over the years, the various sports editors I have worked for have enabled me to track the League's developments and, in particular, it is sad that I cannot thank in person the late David Welch.

Chris Haynes and James Motley could not have been more helpful in securing promptly information I needed. Sir Keith Mills, who played such a crucial role in London winning the Olympics, has been also been wonderfully encouraging. Joanna Manning-Cooper took time off from her Olympic work to provide valuable guidance on her beloved Portsmouth. And, while I could not share Lord Coe's passion for Chelsea, his football insights were very useful. I am also indebted to Hugh Robertson, John Whittingdale, Maurice Watkins, Barry Hearn, Michael Slater and Derek Wyatt for the very many different ways in which they have helped with this project.

Dan Jones and his team at Deloitte readily made available their valuable study of the finances of the Premier League and modern football. The growth of this information, which parallels that of the rise and development of the Premier League, is a fascinating story in itself. It shows how football has changed in the last twenty years.

In producing this book, I have consulted my own research and writing on the Premier League over the years including interviews with many of the key participants and a full list is appended. There is also a vast amount of material on the subject produced by many others. Since mine is not an academic thesis, I have avoided footnotes but the bibliography indicates the material that has been key to this book. It is by no means a comprehensive list of all the material consulted but I hope a very useful guide.

Susanna Majendie overcame her lack of interest in football to provide information which was crucial and about which she had a unique insight.

My daughter Indira pointed me in the direction of a fellow student with an interest in football and Henry Waterhouse proved marvellously willing.

I am blessed with the love of the most wonderful woman in the world, my wife Caroline, and she has as ever both made sure I kept my sanity and provided me all the help of her office led by the wonderful Nicky Kruger. Without them this book would have been impossible.

BIBLIOGRAPHY

Interviews

Gerard Aigner
Carlo Ancelotti
John Barnes
Franz Beckenbauer
Lord Bell
Amit Bhatia
Sepp Blatter
Trevor Brooking
Greg Clarke
Nick Coward
David Davies
Michael Dawson
Michel D'Hooghe
Paul Elliott
Tony Fernandes
Johnny Giles
Heurelho Gomes
Andy Gray
Ruud Gullit
Ross Hair
Keith Harris
Roy Hodgson
Gerard Houllier
Chris Hughton

Lennart Johansson
Cliff Jones
Vinnie Jones
Danny Jordaan
Peter Kenyon
Dennis Law
Lord Mawhinney
Vince McBean
Brian McDermott
Alex McLeish
Andy Melvin
Sir Keith Mills
Ron Noades
Pere Omdal
Alan Pardew
Rick Parry
Chris Powell
Jamie Redknapp
Harry Redknapp
Peter Ridsdale
Hugh Robertson
Uwe Rösler
Michael Slater
Jeff Stelling

Lord Stevens
Lord Sugar
David Sullivan
Adel Taarabt
Ralph Topping
Neil Warnock
Maurice Watkins
John Whittingdale
Keith Wyness
Anton Zingarevich

Newspapers
Daily Express
Daily Mail
Daily Mirror
Daily Star
Daily Telegraph
Financial Times
Guardian
Independent
Independent on Sunday
London Evening Standard
Mail on Sunday
News of the World
Observer
Sun
Sunday Telegraph
Sunday Times
Times

Magazines
Champions
Financial News
Four Four Two
GQ
New Statesman
New Yorker
People
Spectator
Sport Business
SportsPro
World Soccer

Club Programmes and Annuals
Rothmans Football Annuals 1992/93–2002/03
Sky Football Year Book 2003/04–2011/12

Factsheet
Sir Norman Chester Centre for Football Research, *Racism And Football*
    (University of Leicester 2002)

Official Sources
House of Commons Hansard
Thatcher Archive: transcripts of press conferences
Popplewell Inquiry interim report (HMSO 1985)
Taylor Report (HMSO 1990)

Television Programmes
How TV Changed Football For Ever, broadcast Sky1, 26 June 2007
The Nght Football Changed For Ever, broadcast Sky1, 9 Aug 2011

Unpublished Diary
R. Heller, *In Shadowland*, unpublished diaries of working life with Gerald
    Kaufman MP, 1985–1987

Archive Material
Collection by Chris Akers of contemporary papers, including notes by
    Rick Parry, on Premier League television negotiations 1991–1992

Books
Banks, S. *Going Down* (Mainstream 2002)
Belton, B. *Brown Out* (Pennant 2008)
Bower, T. *Broken Dreams* (Simon & Schuster 2003)
Butler, D. & Butler, G. *Twentieth Century British Political Facts* 1900–2000
    (Macmillan 2000)
Campbell, D. & Shields, A. *Soccer City* (Mandarin 1993)
Cooper, C. *Run, Swim, Throw, Cheat* (Oxford University Press 2012)
Cowley, J. *The Last Game* (Simon & Schuster 2009)
Crick, M. *The Boss* (Pocket Books 2003)
Dalglish, K. *My Liverpool Home* (Hodder & Stoughton 2010)
Dyke, G. *Inside Story* (Harper Collins 2004)
Fynn, A. & Guest, L. *Out Of Time* (Simon & Schuster 1994)
Fynn, A. & Guest, L. *The Secret Life Of Football* (Queen Anne 1989)
Glanville, R. *Chelsea FC The Official Biography* (Headline 2005)
Goldblatt, D *The Ball Is Round* (Viking 2006)

Graham, G. *The Glory and the Grief* (Andre Deutsch 1995)

Gullit, R. *Ruud Gullit* (Century 1998)

Harris, H. *Ruud Gullit* (CollinsWillow 1996)

Hill, D. *The Fix* (McClelland & Stewart 2010)

Horrie, C. *Premiership* (Pocket 2002)

Horsman, M. *Sky High* (Orion 1997)

Humphries, N. *Match Fixer* (Marshall Cavendish Editions 2010)

Inglis, S. *League football and the men who made it* (Willow Books 1988)

Jordan, S. *Be careful what you wish for* (Yellow Jersey 2012)

Kelly, G. *Sweet F A* (Collins 1999)

King, A. *The End Of The Terraces* (Continuum 2002)

Korr, C. *West Ham United* (M Press 2005)

Kuper, S. *The Football Men* (Simon & Schuster 2011)

Lovejoy, J. *Glory, Goals & Greed* (Mainstream 2011)

Malam, C. *The Magnificent Obsession* (Bloomsbury 1997)

Marwick, A. *British Society Since 1945* (Penguin 2003)

Moynihan, J. *Kevin Keegan: Black & White* (CollinsWillow 1993)

O'Leary, D. *Leeds United on Trial* (Little, Brown 2002)

Palmer, M. *The Professor* (Virgin, 2001)

Ridley, I. *There's a Golden Sky* (Bloomsbury 2011)

Rivoire, X. *Arséne Wenger The Biography* (Aurum 2007)

Scholar, I. *Behind Closed Doors* (Carlton 1995)

Smith, G. *We need to talk about Kevin Keegan* (Penguin 2008)

Sugar, A. *What You See is What You Get* (Macmillan 2010)

Thomas, D. *Foul Play* (Corgi 2004)

Tomlinson, A., Young, C. & Holt, R. *Sport and the Transformation of Modern Europe* (Routledge 2011)

Vasili, P. *Colouring Over The White Line* (Mainstream 2000)

Venables, F. *Terry Venables* (Weidenfield and Nicholson 1990)

Venables, T. & Hanson, N. *Venables* (Penguin 1995)

Ward, A. & Williams, J. *Football Nation* (Bloomsbury 2009)

White, J. *Manchester United* (Sphere 2008)

Williams, C. & Wagg, S. *British Football And Social Change* (Leicester University 1991)

Woolnough, B. *Venables The England Era* (Mainstream 1996)

Online Sources

The Ibrox Disaster http://iainduff.wordpress.com

Football Hooliganism online reference article in http://m.politics.co.uk

www.realhooligans.com

APPENDIX

Figure 1. Squads pre-Bosman

1992–1993	Number of players qualified to play for England*	National team make-up of foreign players
Arsenal	24	2 Scottish, 1 Irish, 1 Danish, 1 Swedish, 1 Norwegian.
Aston Villa	16	3 Irish, 2 German, 1 Scottish, 1 Welsh, 1 Australian, 1 Trinidad & Tobagan
Blackburn Rovers	21	2 Scottish, 1 Irish, 1 Norwegian, 1 Swedish, 1 Australian, 1 American.
Chelsea	18	5 Scottish, 3 Welsh, 1 Irish, 1 Northern Irish, 1 Jamaican, 1 Norwegian, 1 Russian
Coventry City	21	3 Scottish, 3 Irish, 1 Northern Irish, 1 Zimbabwean, 1 American
Crystal Palace	23	3 Welsh, 1 Northern Irish, 1 Irish, 1 St Kitts and Nevis
Everton	19	2 Welsh, 1 Scottish, 1 Northern Irish, 1 American, 1 Australian, 1 Polish
Ipswich Town	16	2 Canadian, 2 Australian, 1 Scottish, 1 Welsh, 1 Bulgarian
Leeds United	24	3 Scottish, 1 Welsh, 1 Norwegian, 1 French, 1 Canadian
Liverpool	16	2 Danish, 2 Scottish, 2 Irish, 2 Welsh, 1 Hungarian, 1 Norwegian, 1 Zimbabwean, 1 Israeli
Manchester City	15	2 Welsh, 2 Irish, 1 Scottish, 1 Norwegian, 1 Dutch, 1 Jamaican
Manchester United	15	3 Welsh, 2 Scottish, 1 Irish, 1 Northern Irish, 1 Danish, 1 French, 1 Russian
Middlesborough	18	6 Irish, 4 Scottish, 1 Jamaican
Norwich City	15	4 Welsh, 1 Scottish, 1 Irish, 1 Montserrat, 1 Nigerian
Nottingham Forest	17	3 Scottish, 2 Welsh, 1 Northern Irish, 1 Irish, 1 Icelandic

(Cont'd from previous page)

1992–1993	Number of players qualified to play for England*	National team make-up of foreign players
Oldham Athletic	21	3 Scottish, 1 Irish, 1 Dutch, 1 Norwegian
Queens Park Rangers	21	3 Welsh, 1 Northern Irish, 1 Czech
Sheffield United	25	3 Scottish, 1 Irish, 1 Welsh
Sheffield Wednesday	23	2 Northern Irish, 1 Welsh, 1 Swedish, 1 American
Southampton	20	2 Scottish, 1 Irish, 1 Welsh, 1 Northern Irish, 1 Surinamese
Tottenham Hotspur	22	2 Scottish, 2 Irish, 1 Welsh, 1 Norwegian, 1 Spanish, 1 Icelandic
Wimbledon (now MK Dons)	22	2 Northern Irish, 2 Scottish, 1 Irish, 1 Welsh, 1 Dutch, 1 Jamaican

*(All figures reflect squads at beginning of season.)

Former Premier League clubs (as of 2011–12)

Barnsley

Birmingham City

Blackpool

Bradford City

Burnley

Charlton Athletic

Coventry City

Crystal Palace

Derby County

Hull City

Ipswich Town

Leeds United

Leicester City

Middlesbrough

Nottingham Forest

Oldham Athletic

Portsmouth

Reading

Sheffield United

Sheffield Wednesday

Southampton

Swindon Town

Watford

West Ham United

Wimbledon

Figure 2. Squads just after the Bosman ruling

1996–1997	Number of players qualified to play for England*	National team make-up of foreign players
Arsenal	21	3 French, 2 Dutch, 2 Scottish, 1 Welsh, 1 Northern Irish
Aston Villa	14	4 Irish, 2 Yugoslavian, 1 Scottish, 1 Welsh, 1 Australian, 1 Trinidad and Tobagan, 1 Portuguese
Blackburn Rovers	14	3 Norwegian, 3 Scottish, 1 Welsh, 1 Swedish, 1 Greek
Chelsea	15	3 Italian, 3 Scottish, 2 Norwegian, 2 Irish, 1 Welsh, 1 Dutch, 1 Canadian, 1 French, 1 Jamaican, 1 Russian, 1 Romanian
Coventry City	16	6 Irish, 5 Scottish, 1 Northern Irish, 1 Australian, 1 Zimbabwean, 1 Belgian, 1 Ukrainian, 1 Brazilian
Derby County	15	2 Croatian, 2 Costa Rican, 2 Irish, 2 Dutch, 1 Welsh, 1 Scottish, 1 Swedish, 1 Danish, 1 Jamaican, 1 Estonian
Everton	22	2 Welsh, 2 Irish, 1 Swiss, 1 Russian, 1 Scottish, 1 Danish
Leeds United	18	2 South African, 2 Irish, 2 Scottish, 1 Ghanaian, 1 French, 1 Australian, 1 Norwegian, 1 Dutch, 1 Welsh
Leicester City	22	2 Scottish, 1 Swedish, 1 French, 1 Jamaican, 1 American, 1 Northern Irish, 1 Turkish
Liverpool	17	3 Irish, 2 Norwegian, 1 Czech, 1 Welsh, 1 Scottish
Manchester United	15	2 Norwegian, 2 Dutch, 2 Irish, 1 Czech, 1 French, 1 Danish, 1 Welsh, 1 Scottish
Middlesborough	18	3 Brazilian, 3 Irish, 2 Italian, 2 Scottish, 1 Nowegian, 1 Australian, 1 Welsh, 1 Danish, 1 Slovakian
Newcastle United	15	2 Northern Irish, 1 Colombian, 1 Belgian, 1 Trinidad & Tobagan, 1 Czech, 1 Irish, 1 French

(Cont'd from previous page)

1996–1997	Number of players qualified to play for England*	National team make-up of foreign players
Nottingham Forest	20	3 Northern Irish, 3 Welsh, 2 Dutch, 2 Scottish, 1 Italian, 1 Irish, 1 Norwegian, 1 Croatian
Sheffield Wednesday	19	2 Dutch, 1 Serbian, 1 Italian, 1 Welsh, 1 Scottish
Southampton	20	2 Norwegian, 2 Dutch, 2 Welsh, 2 Northern Irish, 1 Irish, 1 Israeli, 1 Senegalese, 1 Australian
Sunderland	21	2 Welsh, 2 Scottish, 2 Irish, 1 French, 1 Swedish, 1 Polish
Tottenham Hotspur	19	2 Norwegian, 2 Northern Irish, 2 Scottish, 2 Irish, 1 Israeli, 1 Montserrat, 1 Swiss, 1 South African, 1 Danish
West Ham United	19	4 Northern Irish, 3 Australian, 2 Portuguese, 2 Romanians, 2 Welsh, 1 Czech, 1 Nigerian, 1 Croatian, 1 Danish
Wimbledon (now MK Dons)	13	3 Jamaicans, 3 Irish, 3 Scottish, 1 Nigerian, 1 Welsh, 1 Norwegian

(*All figures reflect squads at beginning of season.)

Figure 3. Squads today

2011–2012	Number of players qualified to play for England*	National team make-up of foreign players
Arsenal	6	7 French, 3 Spanish, 2 Dutch, 2 Polish, 1 Senagalese, 1 Cameroonian, 1 Belgian, 1 Swiss, 1 Welsh, 1 Czech, 1 Israeli, 1 Russian, 1 South Korean, 1 Moroccan, 1 Japanese, 1 Danish, 1 Cote d'Ivoire, 1 Ghanaian
Aston Villa	13	7 Irish, 2 American, 2 Scottish, 1 Welsh, 1 French, 1 Spanish, 1 Austrian, 1 Australian, 1 Bulgarian, 1 Senegalese, 1 Cameroonian.
Blackburn Rovers	11	3 French, 2 Scottish, 2 Swedish, 2 Spanish, 2 Australian, 1 Welsh, 1 Montenegran, 1 Algerian, 1 Norwegian, 1 Congolese (Republic of Congo), 1 New Zealander, 1 Brazilian, 1 Serbian, 1 Grenadan, 1 Argentinian, 1 Canadian, 1 Nigerian
Bolton Wanderers	17	2 Jamaican, 2 French, 1 Finnish, 1 Hungarian, 1 Icelandic, 1 Scottish, 1 American, 1 Welsh, 1 Spanish, 1 Belgian, 1 Bulgarian, 1 Croatian, 1 Japanese, 1 Turkish
Chelsea	11	4 Portuguese, 4 Brazilian, 3 Spanish, 2 Cote d'Ivoire, 2 French, 1 Czech, 1 Serbian, 1 Israeli, 1 Nigerian, 1 Ghanaian, 1 Begian
Everton	11	3 French, 2 American, 2 Dutch, 1 Slovakian, 1 Northern Irish, 1 Irish, 1 German, 1 Australian, 1 Argentinian, 1 South African, 1 Russian, 1 Belgian, 1 Spanish, 1 Croatian, 1 Nigerian, 1 Greek, 1 Scottish
Fulham	6	3 Norwegian, 3 Swiss, 2 Northern Irish, 2 Irish, 2 Czech, 1 Australian, 1 Philippino, 1 American, 1 Welsh, 1 Nigerian, 1 Swedish, 1 Russian, 1 Italian, 1 Portuguese, 1 Costa Rican
Liverpool	11	3 Brazilian, 2 Uruguayan, 1 Danish, 1 Spanish, 1 Slovakian, 1 Scottish, 1 Argentinian, 1 Portuguese, 1 Welsh, 1 French, 1 Dutch
Manchester City	10	3 Argentinian, 1 Cote d'Ivoire, 2 Dutch, 2 French, 1 Bosnian, 1 Romanian, 1 Montenegran, 1 Belgian, 1 Serbian, 1 Chilean, 1 Italian, 1 Spanish
Manchester United	15	3 Brazilian, 2 French, 1 Danish, 1 Irish, 1 Northern Irish, 1 Polish, 1 Italian, 1 Spanish, 1 Serbian, 1 Ecuadorian, 1 Mexican, 1 Scottish, 1 South Korean, 1 Welsh, 1 Portuguese, 1 Senegalese, 1 Bulgarian

(Cont'd from previous page)

2011–2012	Number of players qualified to play for England*	National team make-up of foreign players
Newcastle United	14	5 French, 2 Argentinian, 2 Senegalese, 1 Swedish, 1 Dutch, 1 Irish, 1 Northern Irish, 1 Italian, 1 Cote d'Ivoire, 1 Slovenian, 1 Danish
Norwich City	18	2 Scottish, 2 Welsh, 1 Canadian, 1 Belgian, 1 Spanish, 1 Irish, 1 American
Queens Park Rangers	20	3 Irish, 2 Latvian, 1 Nigerian, 1 Icelandic, 1 Ghanaian, 1 Colombian, 1 Czech, 1 Senegalese, 1 French, 1 Brazilian, 1 Malian, 1 Welsh, 1 Portuguese, 1 Italian, 1 Norwegian, 1 Hungarian, 1 Argentinian, 1 Moroccan, 1 Scottish
Stoke City	14	4 Irish, 1 Bosnian, 1 Trindad & Tobagan, 1 Malian, 1 Danish, 1 Welsh, 1 German, 1 Jamaican, 1 Honduras, 1 Uruguayan, 1 Senegalese
Sunderland	17	4 Irish, 2 Northern Irish, 1 Belgian, 1 Benin, 1 Scottish, 1 Greek, 1 Ghanaian, 1 South Korean, 1 Welsh, 1 Egyptian, 1 Swedish, 1 Danish
Swansea City	12	6 Welsh, 2 Dutch, 2 Spanish, 1 Portuguese, 1 Greek, 1 Argentinian, 1 Icelandic, 1 Scottish
Tottenham Hotspur	16	3 Croatian, 3 French, 2 South African, 2 Brazilian, 2 Cameroonian, 1 Italian, 1 American, 1 Spanish, 1 Welsh, 1 Dutch, 1 New Zealander, 1 Australian, 1 Mexican, 1 Togolese, 1 Russian
West Bromwich Albion	9	4 Irish, 3 Scottish, 2 Northern Irish, 2 Hungarian, 1 Nigerian, 1 French, 1 DRC (Democratic Republic of Congo), 1 Slovakian, 1 Chilean, 1 Swedish, 1 Cameroonian, 1 Austrian
Wigan Athletic	5	3 Spanish, 3 Scottish, 2 Honduran, 2 Irish, 2 Dutch, 1 Barbadan, 1 Cote d'Ivoire, 1 Paraguayan, 1 Nigerian, 1 Senegalese, 1 Colombian, 1 Argentinian
Wolverhampton Wanderers	9	6 Irish, 3 Welsh, 2 Cameroonian, 2 Scottish, 1 Danish, 1 Guadeloupe, 1 Algerian, 1 Icelandic, 1 Ghanaian, 1 Serbian, 1 Austrian

(*All figures reflect squads at beginning of season.)

Figure 4. Key trends in Premier League clubs' financing since 1992

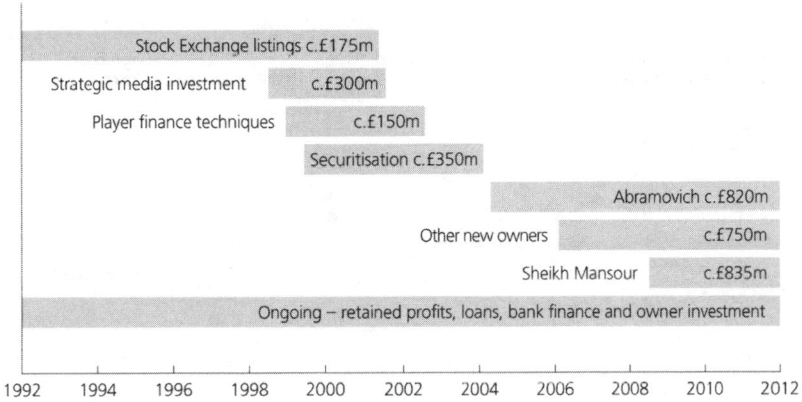

Note: The estimated figures largely relate to the funding of clubs whilst in the Premier League. Capital funding provides monies for clubs and is recognised in the balance sheet of clubs rather than the profit and loss account. The amount from 'other new owners' represents the estimated inflow of funds to the Premier League clubs that have had a change of majority ownership since 2003 (excluding Chelsea and Manchester City).

Source: Deloitte analysis

Figure 5. Premier League clubs — comparison of total wages with league position 2010/11 (£m)

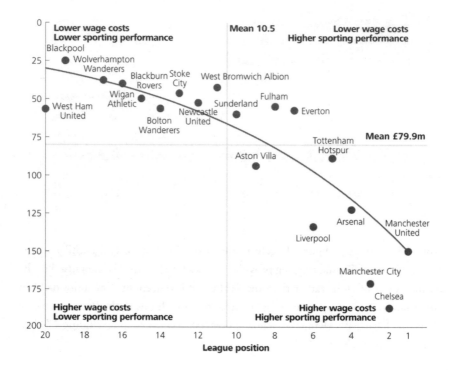

Notes: The figures illustrated in the chart are extracted from the appendices. Hence, all relevant notes in the appendices apply. Relevant financial data for 2010/11 was not available for Birmingham City. The graph is divided into four quadrants depending on total wages levels and sporting performance. Those clubs which are operating below the trend line may be viewed as having underperformed relative to wages levels in 2010/11.

Source: Deloitte analysis

Figure 6. Premier League clubs' revenue streams by category — 1991/92 and 2003/04 to 2010/11 actual and 2011/12 to 2012/13 projected (£m)

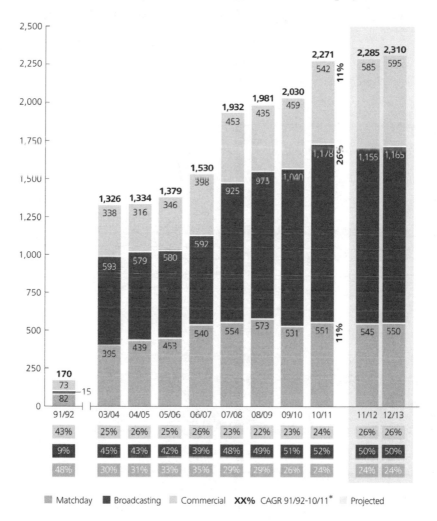

Note: Matchday revenue is largely derived from gate receipts (including season tickets). Broadcast includes revenue from television and radio from both domestic and international competitions. Commercial includes sponsorship, conference and catering, merchandising and other revenues.

Source: Deloitte analysis

*(Percentages reflect Compound Annual Growth Rate from 1991/92 to 2010/11.)

Figure 7. Aggregate operating profit/(loss) for Premier League and Football League 1992/93 to 2010/11 (£m)

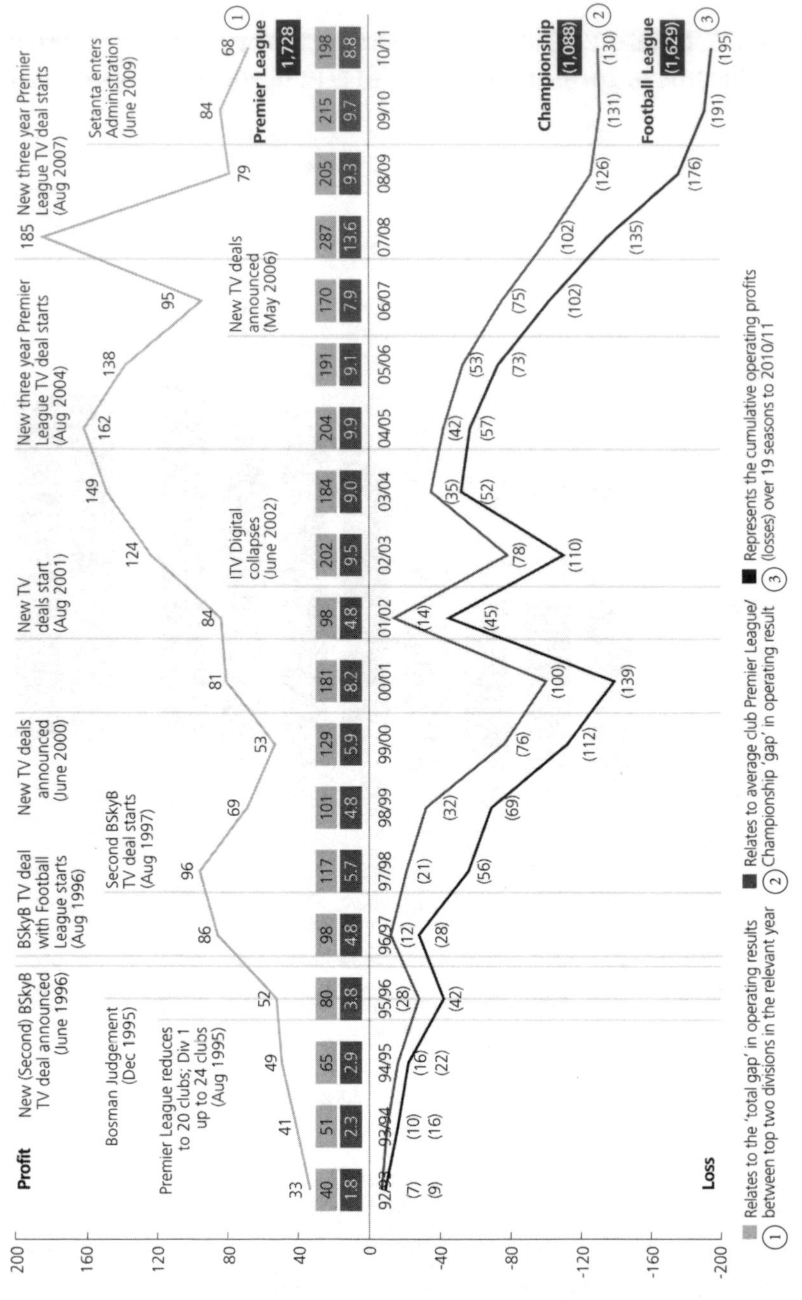

Note: Operating profit/(loss) is defined as operating profit excluding amortisation of player registrations, profit/(loss) on player disposals and certain exceptional items.

Source: Deloitte analysis

Figure 8. Relative growth of Premier League clubs' revenue, total wages and
wages/revenue ratio 1991/92 and 2000/01 to 2010/11 (£m)

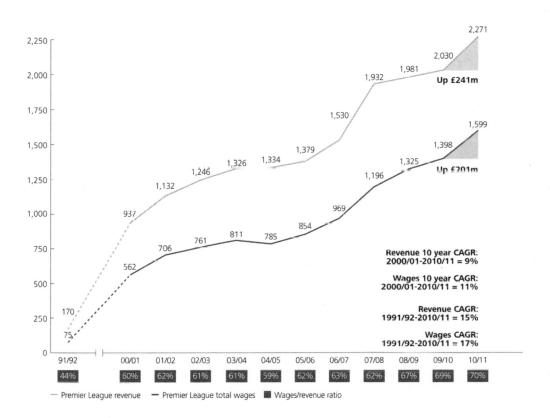

Source: Deloitte analysis

Figure 9. Revenue growth of the 'big five' European leagues — 1996/97 and 2001/02 to 2010/11 (€m)

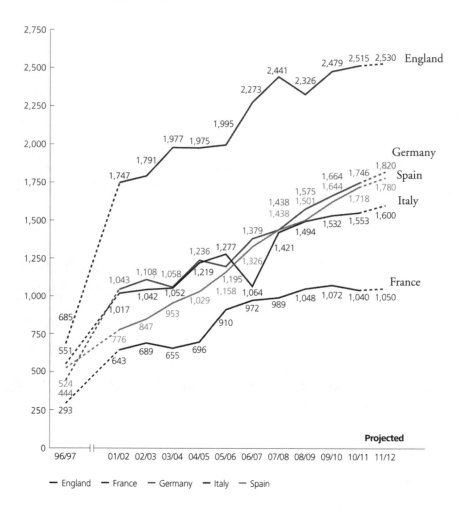

Note: The revenue figures for Serie A clubs between 1999/00 and 2009/10 have been adjusted to aid comparability between leagues. The gross revenue figure for each year in this period has been adjusted to remove the estimated amount of pooled broadcast and matchday revenues, that are received by clubs and recognised as revenue, in addition to the clubs' full recognition of their own broadcast and matchday revenues. No broadcast revenue adjustments have been made in 2010/11 given the return to collective selling. Italian figures for 2010/11 are based on an analysis of clubs' accounts. Certain clubs' reporting period covers a calendar year rather than a conventional football season. Spanish figures are based on a sample of 10 clubs' accounts, with other club revenues estimated.

Source: DFL; Lega Calcio; LFP (France); LFP (Spain); Deloitte analysis

Figure 10. Revenue breakdowns for European leagues 2010/11 (€m)

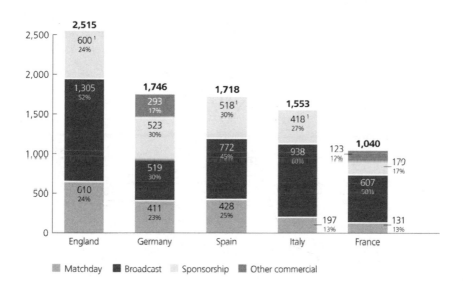

¹ Sponsorship and other commercial revenue combined.

Notes: Matchday revenue is largely derived from gate receipts (including season tickets and memberships). Broadcast revenue includes revenue from television and radio, from both domestic and international competitions. Other commercial revenues include all non-sponsorship commercial revenues, such as conferencing, catering and merchandising. For the Premier League, Serie A and La Liga, commercial revenue is not disaggregated into 'sponsorship' and 'other'.

Italian figures for 2010/11 are based on an analysis of clubs' accounts. Certain clubs' reporting period covers a calendar year rather than a conventional football season.

Spanish revenue breakdowns are based on actual figures for 10 clubs and estimates for the remaining clubs.

Source: DFL; Lega Calcio; LFP (France); Deloitte analysis

Figure 11. Operating profit/loss in four of the 'big five' European leagues
— 1996/97 and 2001/02 to 2010/11 (€m)

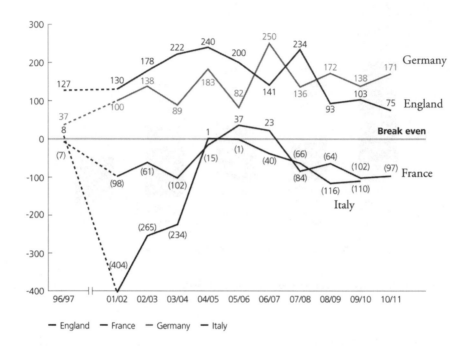

Note: Differences in accounting practices may affect detailed comparisons —
although overall observations are still, in our view, valid. All figures above exclude
player transfer amortisation. It has not been possible to estimate Spanish operating
performance. Insufficient information is available to us to estimate Serie A
operating profitability in 2010/11.

Source: DFL; Lega Calcio; LFP (France); Deloitte analysis

Figure 12. What the Premier League gave the clubs in the 2011/12 season

As at 14 May 2012 (All figures in £)

	Place	Live	BBC	N. Live	Equal Share	Facility Fees	Merit Payment	Overseas TV	Total Payment
Arsenal	3	19	38	19	13,788,093	10,079,652	13,591,116	18,764,644	56,223,505
Aston Villa	16	10	38	28	13,788,093	5,776,562	3,775,310	18,764,644	42,104,709
Blackburn Rovers	19	11	38	27	13,788,093	6,254,272	1,510,124	18,764,644	40,317,633
Bolton Wanderers	13	10	38	28	13,788,093	5,776,562	2,265,186	18,764,644	40,594,585
Chelsea	6	20	38	18	13,788,093	10,557,762	11,325,930	18,764,644	54,436,429
Everton	7	10	38	28	13,788,093	5,776,562	10,570,868	18,764,644	48,900,267
Fulham	9	10	38	28	13,788,093	5,776,562	9,060,744	18,764,644	47,390,143
Liverpool	8	23	38	15	13,788,093	11,992,092	9,815,806	18,764,644	54,360,635
Manchester City	1	25	38	13	13,788,093	12,944,312	15,101,240	18,764,644	60,602,289
Manchester United	2	26	38	12	13,788,093	13,426,422	14,346,178	18,764,644	60,325,337
Newcastle United	5	18	38	20	13,788,093	9,601,542	12,080,992	18,764,644	54,235,271
Norwich City	12	11	38	27	13,788,093	6,254,772	6,795,558	18,764,644	45,603,067
Queens Park Rangers	17	14	38	24	13,788,093	7,689,102	3,020,248	18,764,644	43,262,087
Stoke City	14	10	38	28	13,788,093	5,776,562	5,285,434	18,764,644	43,614,833
Sunderland	13	10	38	28	13,788,093	5,776,562	6,040,496	18,764,644	44,369,895
Swansea City	11	10	38	28	13,788,093	5,776,562	7,550,620	18,764,644	45,880,019
Tottenham Hotspur	4	23	38	15	13,788,093	11,992,092	12,836,054	18,764,644	57,380,883
West Bromwich Albion	10	10	38	28	13,788,093	5,776,562	8,305,682	18,764,644	46,635,081
Wigan Athletic	15	10	38	28	13,788,093	5,776,562	4,530,372	18,764,644	42,859,771
Wolverhampton Wanderers	20	10	38	28	13,788,093	5,776,562	755,062	18,764,644	39,084,461
Sub Total	290	760	470		275,761,860	158,563,140	158,563,020	375,292,880	968,180,900
Birmingham City					7,583,451			7,891,554	15,475,005
Blackpool					7,583,451			7,891,554	15,475,005
Burnley					6,204,642			6,015,090	12,219,732
Hull City					6,204,642			6,015,090	12,219,732
Middlesbrough					2,757,619			1,323,929	4,081,548
Portsmouth					6,204,642			6,015,090	12,219,732
West Ham United					7,583,451			7,891,554	15,475,005
TOTAL					319,883,758	158,563,140	158,563,020	418,336,741	1,055,346,659

Source: Premier League 2011/12 season review

ABOUT THE AUTHOR

Mihir Bose is an award-winning journalist and author. He writes a weekly "Big Sports Interview" for the *London Evening Standard* and also writes and broadcasts on social and historical issues as well as sport for a range of outlets including the BBC, the *Financial Times* and *Sunday Times*.

He was the BBC's first Sports Editor where his job involved investigating and analysing sports stories. His major scoops included revealing the cost of the Olympics, the Premier League plans for the 39th game and Joe Calzaghe's decision to retire. He covered all BBC outlets including the flagship *Ten O'Clock News*, the *Today* programme, *Five Live* and the website.

Before joining the BBC, he was the chief sports news correspondent for the *Daily Telegraph* for 12 years where he created an innovative weekly column, Inside Sport. He also wrote on the editorial pages on such subjects as race, immigration, and other social and cultural issues.

He has written for nearly all the major UK newspapers, editing the "Inside Track" column of the *Sunday Times* and several business publications. He has presented programmes for radio and television, and written 27 books including the first history of Bollywood.

He has won several awards: business columnist of the year, sports news reporter of the year, sports story of the year and Silver Jubilee Literary award for his *History of Indian Cricket*.

Mihir lives in west London with his wife, Caroline Cecil, who runs a financial PR consultancy. He has a daughter, Indira.